AMERICAN EXPANSION IN HAWAII
1842-1898

AMERICAN EXPANSION IN HAWAII
1842-1898

BY

SYLVESTER K. STEVENS

NEW YORK / RUSSELL & RUSSELL

TO
MY MOTHER AND FATHER

CONTENTS

PREFACE

The Hawaiian Islands and their varied relationships with the United States have been the subject of many articles and books, but usually they have dealt with some phase or chronological segment of the subject. This has resulted often in a failure to evaluate and to place in proper perspective all of the varied and complicated factors which have entered into the history of Hawaii and its contacts with the United States. This study, which was begun at Columbia University under the interested direction of Allan Nevins, is an attempt to show the continuity of forces and events in the history of American expansion in Hawaii. It is an attempt also to show that the ultimate annexation of Hawaii in 1898 was the product of typical American frontier expansion, and not a sporadic adventure in imperialism occasioned by the circumstances connected with the Spanish American War. While the events of the years from 1842 to 1898 often were confused and appear unconnected in many instances, there was a thread of continuity. This is true both in terms of the trend of affairs in Hawaii and in the policy of the United States toward the Islands. It is only by viewing the entire period of diplomatic relations with Hawaii as a unit that this continuity is observable in proper perspective.

This does not minimize the importance of the work of the many scholarly historians who have written on so many phases of Hawaiian history and diplomacy. These detailed studies have revealed information of the utmost value and have been drawn upon freely by the author of this book. Without this careful research into the minutae of Hawaii's relations with the United States, a more comprehensive account would have been impossible.

I am indebted especially to Dr. Ralph S. Kuykendall of the University of Hawaii for his assistance in the research and the writing of this book. Not only did he furnish from his own collection indispensable notes on important material in the Archives of Hawaii, but read the entire manuscript in its early stages and in its final form. Many errors of fact which otherwise would have gone unnoticed were thus detected. Doctor Kuykendall's views differed from those of the writer on some points of interpretation, and still do, but his suggestions and assistance were of the utmost importance. Dr. Allan Nevins provided kindly direction and inspiration at every stage of my graduate work at Columbia University and in the writing of this book. I am especially grateful for his aid. The writer wishes to acknowledge also a long-standing debt to Dr. Asa Earl

Martin, head of the Department of History at The Pennsylvania State College, who did so much to encourage me in the early and difficult stages of beginning the quest for the doctorate. Dr. Roy F. Nichols of the University of Pennsylvania is another tried and true friend who did much to aid in the same way.

I am indebted to many other persons, including numerous librarians and associates, too numerous to mention. My wife is deserving of mention for her forbearance during graduate study and for other encouragement and assistance. Mr. Donald H. Kent read the manuscript carefully to check on punctuation and other items. Miss Dolores J. Malloy worked many long hours typing the manuscript in its various stages of completion and exercised great care in checking the manuscript and proof.

SYLVESTER KIRBY STEVENS

State College
Pennsylvania

AMERICAN EXPANSION IN HAWAII
1842-1898

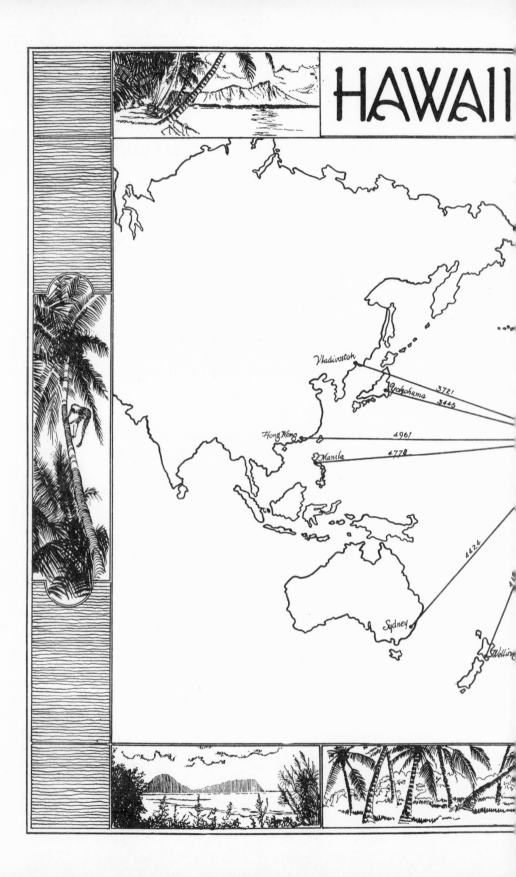

HAWAII

Vladivostok

Yokohama 3721

3445

Hong Kong 4961

Manila 4778

4424

Sydney

Wellin

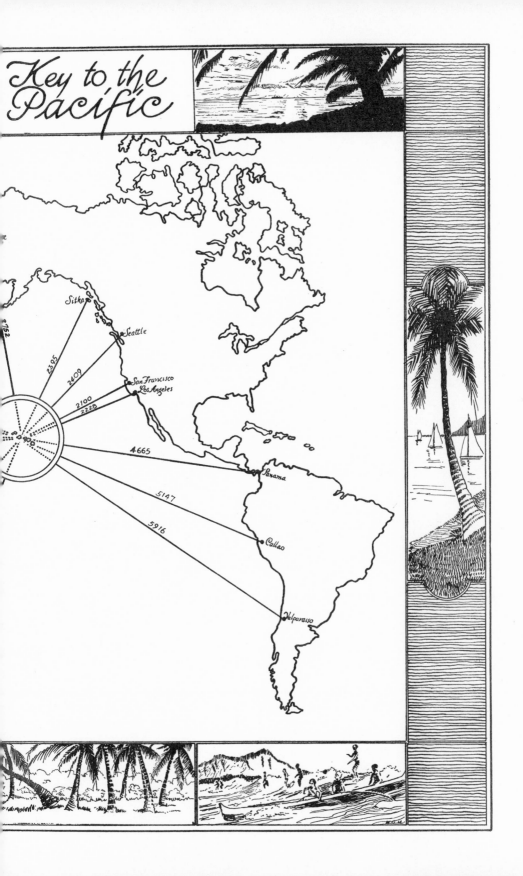

Key to the
Pacific

Sitka

Seattle

2395

2409

San Francisco
Los Angeles

2100
2228

4665

Panama

5147

5916

Callao

Valparaiso

CHAPTER I

FOUNDATIONS OF AN AMERICAN FRONTIER IN HAWAII

On December 15, 1842, two emissaries of that little island kingdom of the mid-Pacific then generally known as the Sandwich Islands were formally presented to Daniel Webster, Secretary of State of the United States. Timoteo Haalilio and William Richards, at the order of King Kamehameha III, delivered to the venerable Secretary and President John Tyler a request for the formal recognition of the independence of the Islands and the full sovereignty of the King. In justification of this plea, which was also to be laid before France, Great Britain, and other major powers, the Hawaiian mission called attention to revolutionary changes taking place within the internal political and social structure of the Islands which marked the emergence of a civilized state, legitimately the subject of recognition by larger nations. In an adroit fashion, the agents of the King called the special attention of the United States to the commercial importance of the Islands, the extent of the rising whale fisheries, and the investment of from five to seven millions of dollars of American capital in the annual business enterprise of Hawaii.[1]

FORMULATING AN AMERICAN POLICY FOR HAWAII

A diary recording the conversations of President Tyler and Secretary Webster as a result of this important communication would be most interesting. Prior to this time the United States had not given serious attention diplomatically to Hawaii. The scattered trading relationships of Americans with the Islands, dating back to days of the China trade and the work of the New England missionaries, had grown during the preceding two decades, but had not as yet justified diplomatic activities beyond those entrusted to the American naval commanders who cruised with watchful and ofttimes ambitious eyes about the Pacific. Indeed,

---

[1] *Foreign Relations of the United States, 1894*, Appendix II, hereafter cited as FR, 1894, contains the correspondence and documents concerning the mission. This volume is made up entirely of selections from American diplomatic correspondence with Hawaii from the earliest exchanges down to 1894. All material has been checked with the State Department Archives and citations will indicate from which source the information utilized has been acquired. See also the account of the mission and its background in Ralph S. Kuykendall, *The Hawaiian Kingdom*, 187-99, hereafter cited as Kuykendall, and Harold W. Bradley, *The American Frontier in Hawaii*, hereafter cited as Bradley. Richards was granted informal interviews with Webster on December 7 and 9 and the Secretary "appeared to know little about the islands. . . ."

1

the Islands had been deemed of so little significance that the appointment of John Coffin Jones in September, 1820, as "Agent of the United
States for Commerce and Seamen," and the famous treaty of December
23, 1826, arranged by Captain Thomas ap Catesby Jones to provide for
amity and friendly commercial relationships, gave no evidence of an
intention by the United States to promote permanent contacts with
Hawaii.

There is no evidence indicating that the Jones treaty, for example,
ever achieved any status as a formal agreement, though both it and the
preceding appointment were pioneer ventures in the diplomatic history
of the Islands.[2] Not only were the relations of the United States with
Hawaii thus in a haphazard state, but the fact must also be emphasized
that prior to the forties the trend of Hawaiian political contacts with the
outer world, since the visits of Vancouver in 1792, 1793, and 1794, had
been British to a decided degree. The Haalilio-Richards Mission represented a definite shift in the diplomacy of the Islands toward gaining a
larger recognition of their existence, and a cessation of dependence upon
any one power for protection and support.

In view of these facts, the Tyler administration had little precedent
upon which to base an Hawaiian policy and was confronted with a delicate task in formulating one. Furthermore, no person in Washington
possessed much information concerning the Islands. Obviously, however, something must be done lest these agents from the distant isles
proceed with their mission and secure from "some of the principal governments" of Europe a recognition denied by the United States. Yet
there existed no decisive pressure in the form of a matured national
interest demanding that the United States assume any new responsibility
in regard to the little kingdom. Moreover, Whig diplomacy as represented by Daniel Webster frowned upon too active commitments in
foreign fields. Continental expansion was foreshadowed in the rise of
the ardent spirit of manifest destiny which ended in war with Mexico
and the acquisition of Oregon. It was clear that this expansion to the
Southwest and Northwest was likely to absorb the attention of Congress and the country. The reply of Mr. Webster, therefore, to the Hawaiian agents, and the President's subsequent message to Congress of
December 31, 1842, together with the appointment of a Commissioner

---

[2] Hunter Miller (ed.), *Treaties and Other International Acts of the United
States of America,* III, Document 54 finds no evidence that the treaty was ever
published or submitted to Congress and lists it as an imperfected treaty, though
both Hawaii and the United States seem to have given it some recognition. The
best account of the mission is Harold W. Bradley, "Thomas ap Catesby Jones and
the Hawaiian Islands, 1826-27," *Annual Report of the Hawaiian Historical Society,*
1930. See also Bradley, 106f.

to represent the United States formally in Hawaii, reveal a cautious response to the issue forced by Kamehameha III and his representatives.[3]

The instructions of the agents of the King expressed the desire of that monarch to secure "by convention, treaty or otherwise" a recognition of the independent sovereignty of Hawaii and the ending of the informal diplomatic relationships characteristic of the past. The President and Webster sidestepped this issue cleverly, minimizing its importance and promising that existing agreements and agencies would be utilized to maintain a close contact with the Islands. "A consul or agent from this Government will continue to reside in the islands," wrote Webster. But the main function of this official, as Webster indicated, would continue to be that of a claims agent adjusting the differences arising between Hawaiians and American traders.

Had the policy of Tyler rested alone upon this statement of intentions, little significance could be attached to the results of the Hawaiian mission. The most significant portion of the Webster note, however, was its assertion of a dominant interest of the United States in Hawaii. Along with this went the equally important declaration that, in the opinion of the President, the existing government of Hawaii was best suited to the conditions of the time and should not be interfered with by any foreign power. Webster vigorously wrote: "The United States . . . are more interested in the fate of the islands, and of their Government, than any other nation can be; and this consideration induces the President to be quite willing to declare, as the sense of the Government of the United States, that the Government of the Sandwich Islands ought to be respected; that no power ought either to take possession of the islands as a conquest, or for the purpose of colonization, and that no power ought to seek for any undue control over the existing Government, or any exclusive privileges or preferences in matters of commerce.[4]

THE TYLER DOCTRINE FOR HAWAII

The President did not pause, however, with this presentation of the American view to the Hawaiian agents. In a message of December 31 to the House of Representatives, largely written by Webster and in-

---

[3] After presenting their plea on December 15, the Hawaiian agents waited eight days without a reply. On December 23 Richards called again on Webster who still appeared noncommittal. Richards then consulted several "persons of influence" in an endeavor to arouse the Secretary. On December 27 Richards and Haalilio were introduced to the President and Cabinet. Richards "hinted" at the possibility of a British protectorate in case of the failure of the United States to recognize the Islands. This produced the desired effect, and on December 30 Mr. Webster's formal reply was received. See Kuykendall, 191f. Bradley, 441f., has further details based on Richards' *Journal*.

[4] Correspondence and other references from FR, 1894, 39-45.

dicating the commercial basis of the whole matter, President Tyler communicated the correspondence involved and further enunciated the policy of his administration. The advance of the Islands in civilization, their growing importance in the commerce of the Pacific, and above all their nearness to the United States and the dominance of her economic interests therein were cited as the justification for an American statement on Hawaii. "Considering, therefore, that the United States possesses so very large a share of the intercourse with those islands," affirmed Tyler, "it is deemed not unfit to make the declaration that their Government seeks nevertheless no peculiar advantages, no exclusive control over the Hawaiian Government, but is content with its independent existence, and anxiously wishes for its security and prosperity." The President then followed with the significant remark, "Its forbearance in this respect, under the circumstances of the very large intercourse of their citizens with the islands, would justify the Government, should events hereafter arise, to require it, in making a decided remonstrance against the adoption of an opposite policy by any other power."

Naturally, the declarations of the President were given wide publicity in the United States. They were received with overwhelming approval and served both to arouse an interest in Hawaiian affairs and to fix in the popular mind the nature of a proper expression of American policy.[5] The transmission to diplomatic representatives in France and Great Britain of the views of the administration emphasized the international significance of Tyler's statement and recorded it as an American doctrine.

Had Hawaii then assumed a greater importance in the sum total of American national interests, President Tyler's views voiced so boldly in December, 1842, might have become as classic as the December, 1823, message of President Monroe. Indeed, from the standpoint of later Hawaiian-American relations, it is no exaggeration to characterize the statements of Tyler as establishing a fundamental line of procedure for Hawaii remarkably similar to the Monroe Doctrine of two decades earlier applied to Latin America. In fact, Tyler extended the fundamental principles of the Monroe Doctrine into the Pacific and applied them to the Hawaiian kingdom, creating there virtually an American "sphere of influence." Its significance in later American foreign policy rests upon the fact that the basic concepts advanced by President Tyler in 1842 with little variation, except under the ardent expansionist di-

---

[5] The files of *Niles' National Register* for the period reveal how largely this resulted from the presidential statements. A brief wave of popular interest in Hawaii followed from this and the later British occupation, where formerly little attention to Hawaii is to be noted.

plomacy of Secretaries of State Marcy and Blaine, were those which governed American relations with Hawaii until its final annexation.

What were the basic elements in the Tyler doctrine relating to Hawaii? They were so simple and matter of fact, and so broadly inclusive of American interests, as to constitute an all-embracing policy from which little variation was necessary. First, the doctrine emphasized the dominant national interest of the United States in Hawaii over that of any other power, a theme constantly reiterated by later presidents and secretaries of state. Secondly, it embodied the pledge to forward the security, prosperity, and independent sovereignty of Hawaii. The assertion of this protective dogma without any formal treaty commitment characterized American policy for decades. Even American supporters of annexation invariably rested their case upon the ground of "protection," though Hawaiian independence might be extinguished.

The capstone of the Tyler doctrine was its emphatic antagonism toward the "adoption of an opposite policy by any other power," to quote the President. Its maintenance involved the twin principles of constant assertion of the American desire for an independent Hawaii free from the exercise of any special political or economic privilege by the United States, and the use of every diplomatic pressure possible to prevent any other power from gaining such advantage. While the first principle was subsequently weakened by the Reciprocity Treaty of 1875, the latter always was vigilantly maintained by the State Department. Hawaii came within the orbit of American national interest under the Tyler doctrine and remained so until the annexation.

BACKGROUNDS OF THE TYLER DOCTRINE

The importance of these basic declarations makes necessary some attention to the influences prompting their promulgation. It is reasonably clear that they were forced by the special circumstances connected with the Hawaiian mission. As a matter of fact, Webster in his first interviews with the Hawaiians appears to have sought to avoid the issue of recognition or even introduction to the President. The intention of Haalilio and Richards to continue their mission in Europe made it necessary for the United States to place its own position in a clear light before the world to forestall embarrassing engagements or guarantees from British or French sources.[6] John Quincy Adams and other Con-

---

[6] The Hawaiian agents later visited both London and Paris where, buffeted by conflicting interests of the two powers, they secured joint recognition of Hawaiian independence on November 28, 1843. Returning to the United States, they began the return to Hawaii in November, 1845. Haalilio died at sea and Richards arrived home in March, 1846. See Kuykendall, 197f., for British and French reactions; also Bradley, 441f.

gressional friends of Hawaii seem to have been more alert to the danger than Webster and were helpful in urging immediate action upon the Tyler administration.

That some statement of American policy toward Hawaii would have been made in any event is probable. For one reason, the Tyler administration was conscious of the future of the United States as a Pacific power. Among its great objectives was the settlement of the American claim to Oregon. Both the President and the public were aware also of the importance of California and its acquisition. From the standpoint of domestic politics, a bold diplomatic stroke would help restore administration prestige, badly shattered as a result of the bitter struggle between Tyler and the Whigs.

The recent opening of China to western powers had aroused the President's ambition to share in the development of that realm. It is significant that the Hawaiian message likewise emphasized the importance of China and the Pacific, and coincided with the Caleb Cushing treaty mission to China. Secretary of the Navy Upshur was urging a program of naval expansion and suggesting Hawaii as a naval way station, while Webster was boasting to Minister Everett in London, "We are no longer a minor commercial power." The recognition of the importance of Hawaii was, therefore, natural once the problem was forced to the front. Hawaii was at the crossroads of the Pacific and possessed of a strategic commercial and naval importance which could not be ignored by any nation concerned with future expansion in that area. The wonder is that Great Britain, France, or Russia already had not fixed it firmly within the orbit of their interest.

Another important factor in influencing a definition of American policy was a growing uneasiness lest international intrigues endanger the independence of the island kingdom. It is significant that Tyler chose to stress the objections of the United States to possible interference with Hawaiian sovereignty by other powers. The United States was already alarmed at the prospect of a threat to Hawaii from British or French sources. It was for this reason that Tyler lost no time in transmitting his views, shortly after their promulgation, to both London and Paris. When the first formal diplomatic agent, George Brown, was appointed as Commissioner to Hawaii in March, 1843, he was specially instructed "to watch the movements of such agents of other Governments as may visit the islands," and to report with care on their activities. Likewise, he was instructed to caution the King against "any just cause-of complaint to the Government of those powers whose policy is to increase their possessions and multiply their colonies abroad."[7] The

---

[7] Instructions in FR, 1894, 60f.

dispatches of Brown to the State Department following his appointment indicate that the prospect of French or British intervention in Hawaii was discussed by him with Webster prior to his departure for Honolulu.[8]

The anxiety of Washington was reflected likewise in the notes to ministers at the French and British capitals. On March 23, 1843, Minister Everett at London was informed of the solemn determination of the United States to preserve the independence of Hawaii. The President would regret exceedingly that any suspicion of American designs would prevent France and Great Britain from pursuing a similar policy.[9] Everett informed Webster five days later that he had discussed the subject with Lord Aberdeen, the Secretary of State for Foreign Affairs, and the latter had told him he had "signified to the French Ambassador that England could not agree to any encroachment on the Sandwich Islands," and had in turn been informed that none was contemplated. England stood ready to guarantee Hawaiian independence, wrote Everett.

The question may still be pressed, however, as to why the United States by the early forties had become interested in Hawaii. America itself was not yet a Pacific power. Why should it be concerned with the destiny of a group of Pacific islands? The full answer requires a brief analysis of the nature and extent of American activity in Hawaii about the time of the arrival of George Brown, Commissioner of the United States, in 1843.

By the early forties there existed two important reasons for a growing American interest in Hawaii—missionary enterprise and economic penetration. At the time of the enunciation of the Tyler doctrine the missionary probably was the principal influence. Even such staid commercial journals as the New York *Journal of Commerce* carried occasional bits of information as to the missionary activities. As noted earlier, the Tyler message relating to Hawaii was directed to the House of Representatives, and was referred to the Committee on Foreign Affairs. John Quincy Adams as chairman cooperated closely with Webster in implementing the President's declarations. It is significant that in reporting them favorably, the religious and moral concern was emphasized above all others.

---

[8] Cf. *Dispatches, Sandwich Islands,* I. Later volumes are listed simply as *Hawaii,* The use of the term Sandwich Islands was common in the first decade of diplomatic relations. All diplomatic correspondence to and from Hawaii is in the National Archives.
[9] FR, 1894, 110f.

In a benevolent spirit the committee affirmed:

It is a subject of cheering contemplation to the friends of human improvement
and virtue, that, by the mild and gentle influence of Christian charity, dispensed
by humble missionaries of the gospel . . . the people of this group of islands have
been converted from the lowest debasement of idolatry to the blessings of the
Christian gospel; united under one balanced government; rallied to the fold of
civilization by a written language and constitution, providing for the rights of
person, property, and mind, and invested with all the elements of right and power
which can entitle them to be acknowledged by their brethren of the human race
as a separate and independent community.

Americans were urged especially to this acknowledgment "by an interest of their own, deeper than that of any other portion of the inhabitants of the earth—by a virtual right of conquest, not over the freedom
of their brother man by brutal right of physical force, but over the
mind and heart by the celestial panoply of the gospel of peace and
love."[10]

THE MISSIONARY FRONTIER

Missionary labors had been a powerful force indeed in pulling Hawaii
from the orbit of British influence into that of the United States. The
arrival of the ship *Thaddeus* at Kailua on April 4, 1820, with its loyal
band of New England missionaries, had marked the beginnings of the
prolonged effort by the American Board of Commissioners for Foreign
Missions of the Congregational Church to establish a Christian civilization in the Sandwich Islands. Before 1840 six companies of workers
had been added to the original group and more than twenty thousand
converts to Protestantism added to church rolls. By 1842 nineteen mission stations had been established, while seventy-nine workers carried
on the missions, two printing establishments, and a half-dozen schools.[11]

---

[10] Cited *Niles' National Register,* February 11, 1843, and checked with official
document as to accuracy. The *Register* through the period provides frequent citations showing the popular interest in the missionary labors. See issue of April 29,
1843, for extracts from the *National Intelligencer.* See also *Memoirs of John
Quincy Adams,* XI, 290. It is significant that Adams, as in the case of the earlier
Monroe Doctrine, was alert to the larger national interests of the United States
and exercised a decisive influence in securing a vigorous and comprehensive statement of American policy in an important general field of foreign relations and with
lasting results.

[11] The Rt. Rev. Henry Bond Restarick, *Hawaii, 1778-1920, from the Viewpoint
of a Bishop;* The Rev. and Mrs. O. H. Gulick, *The Pilgrims of Hawaii,* are general accounts valuable for a history of the missions. The *Annual Report of the
American Board of Commissioners for Foreign Missions,* hereafter cited as *Annual Report,* provides an invaluable record of source information as to the Hawaiian missions. The *Missionary Herald* (Cambridge) is valuable for notes and
accounts. An excellent summary of missionary influence is contained in Kuykendall,
100-16. See also Bradley, chaps. III and IV.

Mere numbers of missions and missionaries, however, fail to indicate the achievement of the American Board in Americanizing Hawaii. Not that the missionaries set out to warp the minds or inclinations of the Hawaiians, for Christian civilization was their goal, but inevitably this civilization was tinged through and through with American ways, customs, and inclinations. The laborers in the vineyard influenced Hawaii in many ways. Certainly one of the most important was through education. The systematizing of the Hawaiian language in written form for use in the Bible and school texts, and the establishment of schools were early achievements. By 1840 it is estimated that nearly fifteen thousand persons had been trained in these schools. In 1847 *The Friend* reported thirty-four native schools in Honolulu alone with more than one thousand pupils.[12]

In 1845 an American missionary, the Rev. William Richards, the diplomatic agent with whom we are already acquainted, accepted the post of Minister of Public Instruction, to be succeeded three years later by the Rev. Richard Armstrong, another missionary. Not long afterward the demand for school instruction in English began to appear.

The influence of the missionary politically has been a matter of considerable controversy. That it was very material and tended in the direction of an increasing pro-American relationship is the opinion of the principal authorities on this period of Hawaiian history.[13] Such seems to have been the opinion also of contemporary European observers of American influence in Hawaii. It was a subject of concern to the British naval officer, Lord Byron, during his visit to the Islands as early as 1825. In conversations with Minister Everett at London in 1843, Lord Aberdeen expressed his distrust of the political influence of the American missionaries and "hoped" they would abstain from it in the future.[14] A similar opinion was entertained by others and the long controversy of the French Government with Hawaii, to be referred to later, was in no small measure the result of the success with which the New Englanders persuaded the King that all Roman Catholics were the agents of Satan, to be excluded rigorously from any position of advantage in Hawaii.

THE MISSIONARIES MODERNIZE HAWAII'S GOVERNMENT

By 1842 Hawaii was in a state of rapid evolution toward responsible and representative institutions, replacing the arbitrary power of kings

---

[12] January 15, 1847.
[13] Cf. article by Kuykendall, "American Interests and American Influence in Hawaii in 1842," *Annual Report of the Hawaiian Historical Society*, 1930.
[14] Everett to Webster, March 28, FR, 1894, 111; Kuykendall, 196f.

and chiefs formerly characteristic of the native monarchy. The political organization of Hawaii had been little more than "a feudal autocracy." Powers of the King were absolute with the exception of meager limitations established by custom and the necessity of consulting a Council of Chiefs. Individual property and civil rights did not exist in any formal sense. Modification of the ancient feudalism of old Hawaii developed rapidly, however, with the Declaration of Rights and Laws in 1839 and the adoption of the Constitution of 1840. New property rights and civil privileges emerged, together with the recognition of the right of the people to select the lower house in a bicameral legislature. The former Council of Chiefs became a House of Nobles and an Appellate Supreme Court was established. Legislative amendment of the Constitution gave a further basis for limiting the King. A legal basis for popular limitation of absolutism had been created which was to figure prominently in later Hawaiian history.

In this process the American missionary played an important role and the basic ideas employed were of American origin. As early as 1826 the native ruler, acting under missionary influence, had sought through the American Board an advisor on governmental problems. Failing, because of the Board's indifference, to obtain the desired assistance, the King turned to the Rev. William Richards, who, until his death in 1847, was one of the strongest influences in shaping the political destiny of the Islands. Richards, severing his connection with the Mission, became the first of a series of American missionaries who served as advisors and directors of governmental policy. The decade witnessed a further evolution toward democratic government in an increasingly modern type of political and legal administration for Hawaii.[15]

THE EARLY COMMERCIAL FRONTIER

American influence was heightened by developing economic interests in a process of rapid growth. By 1843 the Islands were experiencing an economic revolution, which ultimately provided stronger ties with the United States than the more intangible missionary interest. Economic contacts had long antedated the voyage of the *Thaddeus*. The early commercial expansion of the United States following the Revolution gave rise to the famed and romantic China trade. Closely associated with it was the maritime fur trade of the Pacific Northwest. After about 1785 this came to be largely a Yankee monopoly. The Hawaiian

---

[15] See Kuykendall, chap. x, for detailed analysis of constitutional developments of the period. See *Dictionary of American Biography*, XV, 560-61, for sketch of Richards.

Islands were of vital importance as a source for supplies and as a way station in the long voyages from New England to the Pacific Northwest, and then to China and the return to the Eastern United States.[16]

It was then but a step to the rise of the sandalwood trade. This fragrant Hawaiian wood, highly prized in China, became an important article of commerce as early as 1812, and its export was shortly controlled by shrewd Yankee traders. For a brief period it became a great source of wealth to the King, a few native chiefs, and the traders. Within a decade after 1812 the industry had sharply declined as the result of exhaustion of the sandalwood forests. Americans had dominated the export of sandalwood, however, and this became an important factor in developing further economic interests in the Islands.[17]

This peculiar industry had hardly declined before a new and more permanently valuable source of trade had developed. About 1819 New England whalers in the Pacific began to appreciate the importance of the Islands as a supply center and way station. Kuykendall estimates that by 1822 no fewer than sixty whalers touched at Honolulu, and at the end of the decade the number was at least one hundred annually. A new source of wealth was created. Money began to replace barter in the Islands; exchange was being written and mercantile establishments founded to provide supplies for the whaling vessels.[18]

By the early forties the American whalers had created in Hawaii an outpost which operated powerfully to bring the Islands within the orbit of American concern. The Hawaiian diplomatic agents, Haalilio and Richards, used this fact with telling effect in pressing upon Tyler and Webster the need for new diplomatic relationships upon the part of the United States. The Hawaiians declared that some ninety to one hundred whaling vessels and twelve to fifteen merchant ships under the American flag visited their shores annually. The property value represented by the vessels was estimated at five to seven million dollars annually. Three to four millions were more or less permanently invested in the Islands by the whaling industry.[19]

---

[16] H. W. Bradley, "Hawaiian Islands and the Fur Trade, 1785-1813," *Pacific Northwest Quarterly,* XXX, should be consulted. Kuykendall also presents valuable new material on early commercial history; see chap. vi.

[17] Thomas G. Thrum, "The Sandalwood Trade of Early Hawaii," *Hawaiian Almanac and Annual,* compiled and published by Thomas G. Thrum, 1905. Kuykendall, 85f., provides interesting details; also Bradley, chap. ii.

[18] Ralph S. Kuykendall, "Early Hawaiian Commercial Development," *The Pacific Historical Review,* III, provides the most scholarly account of developments to 1830. See also Bradley, chap. v.

[19] Messrs. Richards and Haalilio to the Secretary of State, December 14, 1842, FR, 1894, 41f.

When Commissioner Brown arrived in October, 1843, he was obviously startled by the extent of the American commercial interests. More than 60,000 tons of American shipping had touched the Islands during the preceding nine months, with vessels and cargoes valued at $8,000,000. The great importance of the Islands as a base for provisioning vessels and as a naval center impressed him, and he urged this fact upon the State Department.[20] The business was not static, but increased every month. The *Polynesian* for October 18, 1844, presented government statistics showing that already that year, 373 whalers worth some $18,225,910 had touched at Hawaiian ports. "The great preponderance of American property engaged in this business will strike every one," it affirmed.

The utilization of the Islands as a way station led to the rise of mercantile establishments for the purpose of furnishing supplies. This investment was likewise American. Many of the necessary supplies had to be brought in and the result was an increase in imports. The majority of these prior to 1848 were from the Atlantic ports of the United States. While for the four and one-half years preceding September, 1840, the total imports of Hawaii had been $1,567,000, by 1846 they had reached $598,382.24 for that year alone.[21] A profound revolution in both the internal and external economy of the Islands was then under way. It constituted the birth of Hawaiian capitalism, and was dominantly American in origins and development. Its significant consequences and further progress will be observed later.

That this rising economic interest directly influenced the Tyler administration is not to be doubted. In fact, the language of Webster in his reply to the Hawaiian agents and that of the President in stating his policy to the House left little room for questioning this basis for their statements. "Of the vessels which visit the Islands, it is known that a great majority belong to the United States," wrote Webster on December 19. Tyler accepted the estimates of the Hawaiians as to the extent of American commercial relations, and referred to the strategic commercial location of Hawaii and the preponderance of American interests.

COMMISSIONER BROWN'S DIPLOMACY

The immediate result of the Tyler doctrine was a strengthening of the bonds of diplomatic contact. Congress having appropriated funds

---

[20] Brown to Upshur, November 4, 1843, *Dispatches, Sandwich Islands,* I.
[21] Statistics for 1840 from *Niles' National Register,* June 29, 1844; for 1846 from *Pacific Commercial Advertiser,* January 26, 1859. Both are from official sources.

for a new diplomatic agent with the title of Commissioner, George Brown of Massachusetts was appointed in March, 1843. The meager means of contact with the Islands at this date is illustrated by the tortuous voyage necessary for the new agent. He went out by way of Panama and Tahiti, in vessels under the English flag, arriving in October.

The Commissioner plunged into his duties with vigor and early assumed an attitude characteristic of later appointees to the post—an enthusiasm for the commercial and strategic importance of Hawaii to the United States. At the same time, Brown was quick to report upon the transformation under way in the government, and the growing friction between native and foreign interests which was to determine the course of Hawaiian politics for many decades and ultimately to undermine the monarchy. A commercial treaty with the Islands, fostering closer economic relationships with the United States, was urged upon the State Department as a means of cementing advantages already gained.

While Brown pursued his duties with energy and sincerity, his appointment ultimately proved unfortunate. Tact, most important of virtues in diplomacy, was lacking in his personality. Somewhat irascible and domineering, Brown had little respect for the monarchy. His first presentation to the King ended in a tirade upon the evils of intemperance and an effort to secure a pledge of total abstinence. The Commissioner suffered likewise from an exaggerated sense of the importance of protecting American rights. He early revealed his intention not "to allow the interests or the honor of the U. States, or any of its citizens, to be interfered with, or trampled upon." Brown shortly became entangled in a bitter controversy over the right to trial in the native courts of one John Wiley, an American citizen convicted on a rape charge. Brown's arbitrary procedure led the government to sever diplomatic relations with him and forced his ultimate recall, though his original contentions were supported by the State Department.[22]

INTERNATIONAL COMPLICATIONS IN HAWAII

While Brown's mission proved unsatisfactory and certainly accomplished nothing toward forwarding improved relations, the most im-

---

[22] The Rev. Richard Armstrong of the Mission characterized Brown as "hot headed" and bullying in letters to American friends dated September 18, 1844, and November 5, 1846, Armstrong Chapman Papers, Library of Congress. This collection is a valuable source as to conditions in Hawaii and the missionary point of view.

portant aspects of Hawaiian diplomacy centered in Washington, London, and Paris. Even before Brown received his instructions, the Hawaiian monarchy had become involved in the toils of imperialist diplomacy and international intrigue. Within two months the declaration of Tyler was put to the acid test both as to its sincerity and positiveness.

On February 25, 1843, provisional control over the Hawaiian Islands was forced from the unwilling but frightened King by Lord Paulet, commanding the British warship *Carysfort*. The seizure of control by the British officer in part resulted from the increasing controversy of the native government with foreigners in its territory. In the words of the Rev. Richard Armstrong, the King was desirous of doing right, but he and his chiefs were "not competent to manage the complicated concerns of a commercial community, where national jealousy, cupidity, and conflicting interests combine to entangle them on every hand."[23]

Matters were at a critical stage by 1843. Great Britain, France, the United States, and to a lesser degree Russia, possessed a definite interest in the future of Hawaii because of its strategic relation to general Pacific commerce and naval power. To understand the situation, it must be remembered that prior to about 1830 British interests in Hawaii had been almost completely dominant. The awakening of the Islands after that date had shifted them more and more toward American control. This had become a cause of concern to the British and was reflected in the growing uneasiness of the Foreign Office over the political influence of the American missionaries.[24] Great Britain itself was little inclined to interfere with the independence of the Islands, but determined that no other power should secure exclusive advantages. In 1824 upon the occasion of Kamehameha II's visit to England, Canning, British Foreign Secretary, had cautioned him that both Russia and the United States had their eyes upon Hawaii. The same year Lord Byron, conveying the body of the dead King and his retinue to Hawaii, was instructed that Great Britain could claim the Islands both by right of discovery and cession through Vancouver. Canning emphasized, however, that Great Britain had no desire to enforce its claim. Should any other power attempt to secure control, Lord Byron was informed that "you are to take the Islands under his Majesty's protection, and to deny the rights of any other Power to assume any Sovereignty, or to make any exclusive settlement in any of that group." Lord Aberdeen in 1843 told the Hawaiian emissaries, Richards and Haalilio, that he had received complaints from the British Consul of partiality

---

[23] Letter dated March 3, 1843, Armstrong Chapman Papers.
[24] Cf. Everett to Webster, March 28, 1843, FR, 1894, 111.

to the Americans. He also expressed his suspicion that the United States, while it did not hold colonies, was attempting to exert an influence over the Islands favorable to itself.[25]

French activities in Hawaii were more recent, but extremely menacing because of their aggressive character. As early as 1827 French Catholic missionaries had appeared in Hawaii and four years later had been expelled by the Hawaiian Government, influenced mainly by American missionaries. Continuous controversy ensued and culminated in 1839 in a demonstration by Captain Laplace of the French frigate *Artemise,* demanding recognition of the rights of the Catholics and favorable commercial privileges for France. A guarantee fund as evidence of good faith was extorted from the King along with a commercial treaty giving exceptional commercial and legal privileges to French citizens.[26]

By 1842 the French had assumed definitely the right to protect Roman Catholic missionaries in the Pacific and Foreign Minister M. Guizot had announced a program designed to secure a network of key naval and commercial stations in the same ocean. The same year witnessed the seizure of the Marquesas Islands by Admiral Du Petit-Thouars, while once more a French naval vessel appeared at Honolulu charging the kingdom with bad faith in the treaty of 1839. It was only by assurance that steps were already under way to remedy the difficulty that more drastic action was avoided. In some measure, fear of French aggression had been behind the departure of the Haalilio-Richards mission to enlist American and British guarantees as to independence.

While Lord Paulet ostensibly acted to protect claims by British residents, and especially to adjust the land claim and other grievances of the British Consul, Richard Charlton, actually it appears that he hastened to place Hawaii under British protection in order to forestall possible seizure by the French Pacific fleet. That his fears were justified is indicated by the statement of Americans at the time. The Rev. Richard Armstrong wrote regarding the French ". . . we have been expecting from their movements that they only wanted time and opportunity to take possession here. . . ." While the French diplomats at Paris and London were busily issuing assurances that no designs upon the Sandwich Islands were intended, their naval officers were inclined to follow the prevalent custom of the day—to seize the territory, leaving the home

---

[25] See Kuykendall, 197, and *Report of the Hawaiian Historical Commission,* 1924, 33; and 1926, 19-20. Also Bradley, chap. VIII.
[26] The French and Catholic difficulties are capably summarized in Kuykendall, 137-52.

government to justify the action later. Lord Paulet, regarded as a discreet and able officer, took matters into his own hands and forced the provisional transfer of Hawaii to a British Commission which governed until July, 1843.

AMERICAN REACTIONS TO HAWAII'S DIFFICULTIES

While the increasing gravity of these international rivalries was far from unknown to Washington, it is doubtful whether any such event as this had been believed possible. Whatever the situation, American newspapers had hardly ceased commenting upon the Tyler message on Hawaii and recording the departure of Commissioner Brown for the "interesting" Sandwich Islands when news of the British "outrage" reached Washington. Prior to this time it could hardly be said that the public had definitely recognized the importance of Hawaii to the United States. Comment as to missionary activities and items on trade and Hawaiian internal development were too infrequent in the press of the time to justify an assertion that the nation was interested consistently in the Islands.

News of the Paulet episode, however, touched the springs of national interest. The ground had been prepared for a display of resentment by the mounting suspicion that British imperialism was everywhere intriguing against American expansion. Persistent rumors of British designs upon California and Texas, and the growing tension over Oregon all served to arouse antagonism against that power. As early as 1841, the *Boston Mercantile Journal* had taken the view that the Sandwich Islands were the object of the grasping hands of the Hudson's Bay Company.[27]

Actually, the United States had more to fear from the French, and might well have welcomed the Paulet seizure. The state of public feeling, however, was such as to prevent any such view from prevailing. The American response to the news of the Paulet cession combined a bitter condemnation of British imperialism with a shrewd calculation of the importance of Hawaii to the United States. For the first time it can be said that some portion of the American public temporarily caught a glimpse of the growing Hawaiian interests of the United States.

Typical of the shrill denunciation of Great Britain was the *New Orleans Bulletin's* condemnation of the "outrage" as "one of those

---

[27] Cited in *Niles' National Register*, October 2, 1841. The Company located an agency at Honolulu in 1834 and had extensive trade relations with Hawaii.

sudden, bold and reckless strokes of policy with which that powerful, ambitious, insolent and crafty nation is wont to startle the world; and the very daring and energy of which have hitherto given her almost perfect immunity in her aggression."[28] A more devastating array of adjectives would be hard to find, but the *Democratic Review* of July, 1843, followed suit with caustic comment as to this "abomination of injustice" and "bold and brutal" attack upon a defenseless and weak power.

The significance of the Islands to American policy was not overlooked. The *Democratic Review* followed its condemnation with a careful evaluation of the importance of Hawaii. The editor declared: "To us it is a matter of scarcely less grave concern than to the plundered people themselves. . . . The vital consequence of their independence to the interests of the United States in the Pacific cannot be overestimated." The *Review* pointed out: "Their situation . . . becomes doubly a matter of consequence when our Oregon territory shall be thickly settled, and when the communication across the Isthmus of Panama is opened, an event not much longer to be delayed."

Niles' National Register for June 10, 1843, adopted a similar view, asserting: "They form upon the American Pacific border a point of importance similar to that of Bermuda or Halifax on the Atlantic, or of Jamaica or the Bahamas on the southern, or Quebec and Kingston on the northern frontier." Attention was called likewise to the rise of American settlements in Oregon and "the western spread of the American tide of population," which "will give them soon a further significance."

In New England, where the religious and economic concern was strongest, indignation ran high. A public meeting in Boston adopted resolutions asserting the right of the Islands, in view of the civilized competence of their government, to independence. It further resolved, cannily enough, that "the permanent occupation of them by any foreign power would prove exceedingly injurious to the commercial and mercantile influence of American citizens, most particularly to those engaged in the whale fisheries."[29] While the remainder of the country was inclined to view the future importance of the Islands as most significant, New Englanders feared the immediate loss of a valuable trade, the displacement of missionary agents, and the destruction of twenty years of Congregational labor by an Anglican establishment.

---

[28] Cited in *Niles' National Register,* June 10, 1843.
[29] *Niles' National Register,* June 24, 1843.

When the State Department received news of the British occupation from Acting Commercial Agent William Hooper, with a petition from Kamehameha III begging the interposition of the President to secure an impartial hearing and settlement, it showed no astonishment. The Department had been aware of the danger to Hawaii, and at London Minister Everett had undertaken already to sound out British opinion. As noted earlier, Lord Aberdeen had assured the United States of the British desire to maintain the independence of the Islands. Thus Washington was in a position to take a calm attitude.

Everett sent further assurance in a dispatch dated June 1, 1843, in which he informed the State Department of an interview with Aberdeen regarding the rumored occupation. The Foreign Secretary knew no more about the matter than the American Minister, but emphasized the fact that the action was unauthorized and indeed undreamed of. In view of this, Everett wrote calmly, "Upon the whole, when I reflect how distinctly and how recently this Government is pledged to the United States, to France, and to the Sandwich Islands themselves to recognize their independence, I cannot doubt but that the act of the commander of the *Carysfort* will be readily disavowed."[30]

Two days later he was able to present further assurances, for Aberdeen placed before him all the available information in British hands on the incident. By the fourteenth, Everett reaffirmed the same view and ten days later H. S. Fox of the Foreign Office set forth to Secretary of State Upshur the unauthorized character of the incident and the intention of Great Britain to adhere to its previous declarations in favor of the full independence of Hawaii.[31]

THE TYLER DOCTRINE APPLIED

In the meantime, Washington had applied fully the principles of the Tyler doctrine to the existing situation in a note to Everett dated June 13, 1843, and designed for presentation to the British Foreign Office. The opposition of the United States to any intervention by a foreign power in Hawaiian affairs was set forth in vigorous language. Warned Hugh S. Legaré, temporarily Secretary of State, "Yet there is something so entirely peculiar in the relations between this little commonwealth and ourselves that we might even feel justified, consistently with our own principles, in interfering by force to prevent its falling into the hands of one of the great powers of Europe." The existing Ameri-

---

[30] Everett to Legaré, extract FR, 1894, 111f.
[31] *Op. cit.*, 115f. See also Kuykendall, chap. XIII, and Bradley, chap. VIII, for many details.

can interests as well as the potential importance of the Islands in relation to the opening of China were of "paramount" importance. The
Secretary added: "It seems doubtful whether even the undisputed possession of the Oregon Territory and the use of the Columbia River,
or indeed anything short of the acquisition of California (if that were
possible), would be sufficient indemnity to us for the loss of these
harbors."[32]

If politics makes for strange bed-fellows, diplomacy makes for
stranger ones. This was certainly the case in the Hawaiian crisis. In
the Islands, according to the Rev. Richard Armstrong, many American
residents were anxious to prevail upon the King to seek the protection
of France against Lord Paulet. In Washington the same view seems
to have been given passing consideration. In his note to Everett, Secretary Legaré pointed out, "France is interested in cooperating with us.
. . ." He also emphasized the probable interest of Russia and suggested
that Everett utilize the French and Russian agents at London to re-
enforce his own demands. Everett himself informed Legaré on July 1
that he stood ready to enlist "the representatives of the other maritime
powers" unless the British took early and positive action to disavow
Paulet.[33] Such tactics, however, were rendered unnecessary by the
British assurances.

The disavowal previously referred to was acknowledged appreciatively
by Secretary of State Upshur on July 5, and the British were once
more informed of the deep concern of the United States for the integrity of Hawaii. As the President wrote three days later to former
Secretary of State Webster, the United States had been gratified by
the Fox communication, but it had been deemed important to make a
firm reply "to guard against any ambiguous or hidden intent."[34]

By this time Rear-Admiral Thomas, in charge of the British Pacific
Squadron, had proceeded to the Islands and on July 31 restored the
flag of the King. This course was fully approved by his government
and ended the forced occupation. As a climax to the incident, however, Great Britain, determined to eliminate the danger which had
precipitated the affair, pressed for a joint Anglo-French recognition
of the independence of the Islands. On November 28 Lord Aberdeen
and St. Aulaire, French Ambassador at London, signed an agreement
on Hawaii in which both powers agreed "never to take possession,

[32] FR, 1894, 111f.
[33] *Ibid.*
[34] Lyon G. Tyler, *The Letters and Times of the Tylers*, II, 272. On the scene,
Commodore Lawrence Kearny, commander of the U. S. East Indian naval forces,
had arrived at Honolulu in July and protested the British occupation.

either directly or under the title of protectorate, or under any other form, of any part of the territory of which they are composed." Efforts to include the United States failed.

What might have constituted a severe check to Tyler's Hawaiian policy proved to have strengthened it. The Paulet affair served definitely to arouse a greater American concern, both public and official, over the future Hawaiian interests of the United States. American diplomacy had been influential in securing a final satisfactory settlement of the crisis. Fundamental principles of Tyler's doctrine had been affirmed. It was now supplemented by the bilateral declaration of France and Great Britain binding the two chief possible opponents to a mutual check upon each other. This served to make the unilateral declaration of the United States stronger than before. The foundation of both the Tyler doctrine and of a developing American interest in Hawaii were thus firmly established by 1844.

A DECADE OF FEEBLE DIPLOMACY

From the diplomatic standpoint, the relations of the United States with Hawaii for the next decade were devoid of importance. In October, 1845, Anthony Ten Eyck sailed for Hawaii to replace Brown, complaining the while of his inadequate salary and the general deficiencies of his mission in a manner which augured ill for his success as a diplomat. Arriving in June of the following year, Ten Eyck proved little improvement over his predecessor. Like Brown, he was inclined to assume the position of an overlord in dealing with the little kingdom. Within a month complaints from Ten Eyck as to the unfriendly attitude of the ministers of the King, the arbitrary character of the government, and the generally inadequate protection afforded American rights flowed to Washington.

A conviction that American rights were not properly regarded, and that the English Consul-General was engaged in securing undue advantages for Great Britain, came to possess the new Commissioner. In June, 1846, he informed the State Department that "a number of the most wealthy, respectable & influential American residents" had petitioned him against the conduct of the native government. A month later he characterized the ministers of the King as "reckless and overbearing." ". . . I verily believe," wrote Ten Eyck, "that nothing but brute force can ever induce them to administer the government with honesty or justice toward foreign residents." By December he had reached the point of suggesting a joint agreement with Great Britain and France for the protection of foreign property rights. The creation of a body of foreigners on the Islands with virtual power to dictate the conduct of trade and establish regulations which the native government would be compelled to enforce was further suggested.[35]

These views, and Ten Eyck's lack of respect for the established authority of Hawaii, were bound to lead to difficulty. He shortly became involved in a bitter controversy regarding the land claims of Ladd and Company, an American mercantile firm organized in 1832 and later interested in the leasing and development of Hawaiian lands. The case was full of controverted points, legal tangles, and generally questionable circumstances, but Ten Eyck plunged into a defense of the most extreme American claims and demands. Hawaiian officials were shortly accusing him of advising the agents of the Company and actually appearing before a Court of Arbitrators as its legal agent. He was likewise accused of publicly ridiculing the King and the Hawaiian Government and attempting to secure American naval assistance in enforcing the demands of the firm.[36]

Another difficulty arose from the attempt of the Commissioner to bully Hawaii into signing a treaty with the United States embodying unusual exemptions for American citizens from the operation of Hawaiian law and justice. In 1846 the King had been forced into treaties with Great Britain and France which were highly objectionable to Hawaii. Ten Eyck had been instructed to negotiate a treaty for the United States. The American diplomat was presented with an unusual opportunity to win the confidence and friendship of Hawaii by offering a reasonable treaty, with due regard to the rising spirit of sovereignty and nationalism characteristic of the kingdom.

This chance for a brilliant stroke was ruined completely by Ten Eyck. Late in 1846 he presented the outlines of a proposed treaty embodying his ideas of the rights and privileges to be accorded Americans. It was arbitrary and completely unacceptable to the Hawaiians. His demand for the trial of Americans in both criminal and civil cases by a white jury not subjects of the King, chosen by the representatives of the

---

[35] *Dispatches, Hawaii*, II, contain the Ten Eyck communications for this period. Those of June 22 and July 18, 1846, as well as October 1, November 5, and December 21 of the same year are important. See also May 25, December 24, 1847; November 20, 1848, for further complaints. The correspondence from American commissioners and ministers is cited hereafter simply as *Dispatches* unless from another source than Hawaii.

[36] See note from Foreign Minister R. C. Wyllie to Secretary of State, June 8, 1849, *Notes, Hawaii*, II, for review of complaints against Ten Eyck. The Ladd claims are surveyed by Mrs. Laura F. Judd, *Honolulu, Sketches of Life Social, Political and Religious in the Sandwich Islands from 1828 to 1861.* See also Kuykendall, 251f.

United States, was such as to antagonize both the entire body of advisors of the King and the native legislature, which had just passed
resolutions condemning such provisions in other treaties. Both France
and Great Britain already had promised to modify the treaties by which
they had secured similar privileges.[37]

The Hawaiian authorities, already sorely tried and indignant, rejected
the Ten Eyck treaty draft. Foreign Minister R. C. Wyllie informed Ten
Eyck that Hawaii would never consent to an influx of Americans
into the Islands under such privileges, for that would mean a repetition
in Hawaii of the history of Texas in relation to Mexico. Ten Eyck
thereupon tactlessly replied that Americans in Hawaii would be justified
if they should choose to emulate the Texans of 1836.[38]

News of this blunder produced the most severe rebuke ever administered an American agent in Hawaii. Under date of August 28,
1848, Secretary of State James Buchanan undertook a stinging criticism of his Commissioner for losing a valuable opportunity to promote
American interests, and fully justified the Hawaiian refusal to accept
the treaty draft presented. In no uncertain terms the Secretary reviewed
the principles of the Tyler doctrine and emphasized the regard of the
United States for the fullest possible sovereignty for Hawaii.[39]

The rebuke served only to intensify the bitterness of Ten Eyck, and
early in 1849 he was recalled. The Commissioner continued to sputter
and fume until the end, and a final communication to the State Department bitterly indicted Buchanan for his "sacrifice" of his agent at
Honolulu "in the vain hope of advancing his own political interests. . . ."

All in all, the results of American diplomacy in Hawaii down to
this time had been altogether unfortunate. The Rev. Richard Armstrong
rather aptly characterized the diplomatic appointees of the period when
he wrote, "When they get here, they each wish to have things in his
own way, listen to a thousand petty complaints of traders & adventurers, & soon get all turned about."[40] Both Brown and Ten Eyck had
proved absolute failures. Their lack of success had been due in no

---

[37] Twelve years later Foreign Minister Wyllie reviewed the grievances of Hawaii
against the Ten Eyck proposals to Commissioner Gregg and it is enclosed in a
dispatch to the State Department. Cf. *Dispatches,* VIII.
[38] The Ten Eyck version is contained in Ten Eyck to Buchanan, June 2, 1847,
Dispatches, II. The Commissioner attributed the stand of Wyllie to British influence, a charge thoroughly unjustifiable. Any person reading the correspondence
of Wyllie and following his career in Hawaii must become convinced of his deep
patriotism and loyalty to the tiny kingdom which he chose to serve. His politics
were highly national.
[39] Buchanan to Ten Eyck, *Instructions, Hawaii,* II, hereafter cited simply as
Instructions. A portion of the dispatch is in FR, 1894.
[40] Letter of September 8, 1848, Armstrong Chapman Papers.

small measure to inability to understand the new Hawaii in a process of evolution at this time. Both refused to understand the acute consciousness of nationality developing in this formerly obscure and backward kingdom, and the necessity of bowing to it in any successful diplomacy.

The work of diplomats during these years was of little moment, however, as compared with the influence of the religious and especially the economic forces which were furthering the rapid development of an American interest in Hawaii. Trade relationships shortly overshadowed the labors of the missionary. By 1846 nearly six hundred arrivals of whalers were recorded annually and the fisheries reached the peak of their development in terms of number of vessels engaged. This led to a further expansion of the supply trade and the founding of mercantile houses. In January, 1847, *The Friend* reported fifteen wholesale and thirty-two retail establishments in Honolulu, while the need for further development had created a real estate boom, raising the price of suitable lots as high as $8,000. The expansion continued until by 1850 the number of retail firms in Honolulu had risen to seventy-five. "Mercantile business is almost entirely in the hands of foreigners and they are growing rich rapidly," wrote the Rev. Richard Armstrong on November 5, 1846. He might have added that the foreigners were overwhelmingly American.

CHAPTER II

THE AMERICANIZATION OF HAWAII

To treat the history of Hawaiian-American diplomacy without emphasizing the process of economic and social change in Hawaii would be futile. From the beginning of closer diplomatic relations between the two countries, the pressure behind each major development down to final annexation came invariably from Hawaiian rather than American sources. Just as the Tyler doctrine was brought about by the demand of Hawaii for diplomatic recognition, so other major steps in the evolution of an Hawaiian policy upon the part of the United States were influenced usually by evolutionary forces working within Hawaii. It is necessary, therefore, to direct attention frequently to the internal politics and economy of the Islands.

As emphasized in the preceding chapter, the Hawaiian economy was in a process of expansion during the early forties, and an Americanization gradually took place as a result of the rise of the whaling industry. Equally noteworthy was the influence of the Sandwich Island Mission of the American Board in directing and shaping much of the social and political evolution, and in paving the way for the emergence of a Christian democracy in Hawaii.

Messrs. Haalilio and Richards in 1842 pointed to the emergence of fixed forms of government, courts of justice, and established legal codes and a "regular monarchial Government" of a "limited and representative character" based upon a written constitution, during the preceding twenty-three years. Accompanying this political evolution they cited, as evidence of democratic social progress, the development of a written language, a system of national education, and a new recognition of the rights of private property.[1] Much of this accomplishment must properly be credited to the benevolent American missionary, influencing the decisions of a wise and capable ruler, Kamehameha III.[2]

---

[1] FR, 1894, 41f.

[2] Kamehameha III ascended the throne June 6, 1825, at the age of twelve following the death of his predecessor from an attack of measles while visiting England. He was the first ruler of Hawaii to have been subjected to the influence of a Christian education from youth and proved one of the most able sovereigns in the history of the monarchy. His death December 15, 1854, marked the end of one of the most significant eras in the history of Hawaii.

The period from the acquisition of California by the United States down to 1860 was marked by a continuance of moral and economic forces of American origin moulding Hawaii's destiny into a closer affiliation with the United States. The process was frequently referred to by American Commissioners at Honolulu as "Americanization." It was indeed such, for, as will be demonstrated, the forces of change were predominantly American in origin. As a result, "pressures" were created in the archipelago which determined the course of American diplomacy.

TWO DECADES OF MISSIONARY ENTERPRISE

While it must be recognized that this era witnessed a general decline of the missionary influence in Hawaii, as compared with the new economic forces, it cannot be denied that the missionaries continued important. Their number was never large. From 1820 to 1854 the total number of workers was but one hundred and forty-five, and of these but forty-two had been ordained ministers, the remainder being listed as "lay helpers" and consisting of doctors, teachers, and simply "females." In 1854, according to the American Board, the actual mission force numbered twenty-six ministers, three physicians, eight lay helpers, and forty-one females.[3] Approximately one-third of the workers returned to the United States at the completion of their service, leaving the remainder as a nucleus for permanent American settlement.

The power of the missionaries themselves in terms of political influence over the kings, the chiefs, and on governmental policy, ultimately lessened. During the early years of the Mission it had been considerable, if not paramount. By the middle of the century, however, a number of them were prevailed upon to sever their connection with the Mission and enter directly into government service. The modernization of the governmental structure of the kingdom increasingly necessitated the use of foreign advisors to direct activities and formulate policies. Under Kamehameha III, therefore, naturalized foreigners, a large percentage of whom were Americans and frequently from missionary ranks, became dominant in directing the Hawaiian Government. One of the earliest was the Rev. William Richards. A later figure was the Rev. Richard Armstrong, who became Minister of Public Instruction in 1848, securing his release from the service of the Mission. Dr. Gerrit P. Judd, who came to Hawaii in 1828 as a medical missionary, became in the words of Kuykendall "the most influential advisor of

---

[3] *Annual Report,* 1854, 154f.

the Hawaiian government during most of the time between 1842 and 1854."

The total number of such individuals was not large, but their influence was very great. While they became loyal Hawaiians, possessed especially of a deep sense of fealty to Kamehameha III, they were nevertheless Americans and inclined strongly in periods of crisis to turn to that country as a source of comfort and protection. For the most part their religious background was such as to imbue them with a deep distrust of "Popery" and Anglicanism, which operated against any support of either British or French interests. Quite naturally their ideas as to the conduct of government and the nature of its politics were likewise influenced by this background. Perhaps the best evidence of their influence was the continued protest of the French against American missionaries, which remained a sore point in the relationships of Hawaii and France.[4]

That the missionary element was desirous of subverting the independent existence of Hawaii, however, is a view to be guarded against. One of the cardinal principles of the American Board was that the Hawaiian race should be given an opportunity to work out its destiny. Indeed, the Board persisted in this view in the face of a more realistic theory as to its impracticability which came to permeate the minds of some of those on the ground.[5]

Except under great provocation, the missionaries were inclined to distrust the idea of absorption of the Islands by the United States, though anxious that they should not fall under the control of another power. The Rev. Richard Armstrong wrote December 29, 1848, expressing this view: "These islands are becoming of great importance to Americans, & their independence should be sustained by the United States; else, England or France will find some pretext for seizing the Islands." Still later, on October 8, 1851, he reiterated: "Annexation we do not want, much less a protectorate, both or either would be submitted to as the lesser one of two or more evils. What we do want is protection—& to be let alone." The principal reason for this distrust of foreign domination, whether from American or other sources, was the fear that it would mean an influx of foreign population, extinguish-

---

[4] The letters of the Rev. Richard Armstrong provide an excellent insight into the workings of the mind of one of these men.
[5] See letters of the Rev. Richard Armstrong October 11 and November 5, 1847, expressing doubts as to the ability of the Hawaiian race to maintain itself in the face of the mounting tide of foreign influences. Armstrong Chapman Papers.

ing the native race which the Mission, of course, was devoted to making fully civilized and competent.[6]

In periods of crisis, however, the mind of the missionaries turned automatically to the United States as a protecting angel. The *Annual Report* of the Board and the *Missionary Herald,* which include statements from representatives of the Mission on the Islands, reveal during the late forties and early fifties a marked apprehension of the French, which became the great Hawaiian bugbear. In the face of this threat to independence and Protestantism, the American missionaries at times capitulated to a general approval of the idea of American control.[7]

Another factor leading the missionary element to approve a policy of American control was the growing internal unrest, and the moral and racial decline of the Islands. As early as 1846, the Rev. Richard Armstrong had written friends in the United States: "Now you & the friends of the Hawaiian race in N. E. may as well take it for granted first as last, that the native chiefs can never govern this restless, enterprising, and sometimes factious foreign population." A year later, as he began his service with the government, Armstrong was firmly convinced of the ultimate disintegration of the native monarchy. Granting this view, it was inevitable to look to American control as the eventual destiny of Hawaii.

There developed during the closing years of the reign of Kamehameha III a definite trend toward demoralization of the ruling class. Intemperance and loose morals contributed to the death in 1854 of this once able ruler.[8] This was a state of affairs not to be tolerated by the New England conscience and gave rise to increasing expressions of vexation from missionaries. The view that American rule represented

---

[6] The Rev. William P. Alexander, a member of the Mission, wrote in 1853 to his brother in the United States: "Perhaps *Hawaii* may be the name of the 32nd star in our national ensign. On some accounts I would like to have it so. We would then be out of the reach of the insults from the French. On the other hand, however, the native Hawaiian race would be trampled in the dust. . . . For the sake, therefore, of the aboriginal race, if we can be independent and enjoy peace, I wish not to be annexed and pray it may never be consummated." Cited in Mary C. Alexander, *William Patterson Alexander in Kentucky, The Marquesas, Hawaii,* 306.

[7] The Rev. William Alexander wrote November 15, 1854, in contrast with his views a year earlier, "If therefore God in his providence shall so order events that we become annexed, I will thank Him for it." See Alexander, *op. cit.,* 335f. The change was produced by fear of the French, the Mormons, and California filibusterers.

[8] The dispatches of Commissioner David L. Gregg to the State Department through the period make frequent references to this. Those published, however, softened references to the condition of the King.

the only means by which the moral regeneration of Hawaii might be aided came to prevail in many quarters.[9]

The missionaries exercised some influence over American diplomacy and diplomatic appointments. The resident missionaries always maintained close contact with American naval commanders appearing at Honolulu and transmitted directly to them their views and comments. Since this provided a major means of diplomatic contact, this influence must have been most important. With the appointment of Commissioners and Consuls, these offices and their occupants were matters of concern to the Mission and the Board. Pressure was sometimes exerted for and against individual officials. The recall of both Brown and Ten Eyck was influenced by criticism coming from the missionary element. Following Ten Eyck's recall, the Rev. Richard Armstrong wrote to his brother-in-law, Reuben Chapman, "When a new President comes in can you not stir yourselves & send us either a good consul-general or a good commissioner?" It is significant that Elisha H. Allen of Maine, the next Consul, was a close personal friend of the same Reuben Chapman. R. W. Walworth, prominent representative of the Board, on January 3, 1849, wrote Buchanan in the interests of an appointment favorable to that body.[10] Both Allen and the next Commissioner were in sympathy with the Board.

The activity of the Mission and the American Board was broader, however, than this rather indirect method of affecting policy. Evidence indicates that during the pre-Civil War era members of the Mission as individuals, the American Board, and its individual members used various means to influence American diplomacy.

During the period of the French crisis, lasting from about 1849 to 1854, the Board was active in urging a vigorous defense of Hawaii upon the State Department, and it seems fair to assume that its protestations were of no mean importance in affecting American policy.[11] Secretary Webster was sympathetic to the appeals of New England missionary interests. A letter in the State Department records indicates that sometime in mid-1850 a representative of the Board conferred with both

---

[9] The Rev. William Alexander wrote November 15, 1853, "The King & many high around him are drinking and rendering the nation contemptible. . . . I think we shall not have much quiet, till we are united with the U.S.A." See Alexander, *op. cit.*, 335. Similar views were expressed by Armstrong. The influx of a lawless element from California added to unrest as to the moral future of Hawaii.

[10] Letter in the Buchanan Papers, Historical Society of Pennsylvania.

[11] See the following chapter for the more detailed history of this problem.

President Millard Fillmore and the Cabinet on matters affecting Hawaii, and a special committee was organized to press the administration to defend Hawaii against the French.[12]

From Hawaii, Armstrong bombarded his brother-in-law with letters urging action. October 23, 1850, he wrote regarding Webster, ". . . can you not arouse him to *growl* a little at the French?" The following year, Mrs. Armstrong, while visiting in the United States, conferred personally with the Secretary of State and was assured that the administration would take a hand in the French imbroglio.[13] Earlier in June, Chapman forwarded a letter from Armstrong to Webster and added to it a declaration of his own as to "the need of a decided declaration from our government to France . . . that the *real* independence of the government of the Islands must be preserved. . . . " The same communication refers to conversations of Chapman with Webster as to further matters of Hawaiian policy, showing a close understanding between the two.[14] Later that month it is significant that Webster instructed the American Minister at Paris to proceed along the lines suggested.[15]

THE "NEW ENGLAND CONSCIENCE" IN HAWAII

Another important influence of the Mission was the contribution to the population of the Islands of what might be termed a "New England conscience." The *Annual Report* of the American Board for 1859 declared: "The labors of the missionaries, and the settlement of their children there, will make the people of the Islands, of whatever race, to resemble in some measure what the Pilgrim Fathers made the people of New England." No person conversant with developments in Hawaii can fail to appreciate the significance of this statement. The deep impress made upon the warp and woof of Hawaiian civilization was never to be erased.

This influence was largely exerted through the moulding of the Hawaiian educational system. By 1850, as noted earlier, the demand for instruction in English began to appear and by the following year no fewer than five such schools were operating. The *Annual Report* for the latter year, commenting upon the fact, declared it indicated "the Anglo-Saxon is increasing in numbers, capital and business" and carry-

---

[12] R. W. Walworth to Fillmore, September 12, 1850, *Miscellaneous Letters.*
[13] Letter of Mrs. Armstrong to her husband dated October 8, 1851, in Armstrong Chapman Papers.
[14] *Miscellaneous Letters.*
[15] Webster to Rives, June 19, 1851, FR, 1894, 97f.

ing forward the process of Americanization. The total number of schools and pupils continued to increase year by year.

Equally important, however, was the weaving of missionary morality and personalities into the new economic structure. A respectable number of members of the Mission not only deserted its services for governmental positions, as already indicated, but others entered into business. The Rev. Richard Armstrong, for example, who left a meager Mission pittance for $3,000 a year from the Hawaiian Government, shortly became a landholder and speculator. His letters reveal that by 1849 he was the owner of six hundred acres and declining a friend's offer to invest for him in the United States on the ground that his money was yielding him twelve and one-half per cent in Hawaii. By 1850 his holdings amounted to eighteen hundred acres and he sought funds in the United States for further speculations.

On January 15, 1850, Armstrong wrote, "Many of the missionaries are securing tracts of land, with a view to their support here." Two months later he asserted, "The missionaries are one by one withdrawing from the Board & seeking their support here." Eight or nine had done so up to that time. *The Polynesian* for May 7, 1852, listed ten missionaries who had acquired land under the new land laws, averaging nearly four hundred acres each. The American Board did not frown upon the practice, but seems to have encouraged this mixture of the material and spiritual. In 1850 S. N. Castle, financial agent of the Board since 1836, "at the suggestion and by the wish" of the Board, engaged in a partnership to establish what became one of the oldest and most important mercantile houses of the Islands.

Members of the Mission themselves not only sought material gain, but their descendants became leaders in the economic advance that was to characterize Hawaii for decades to come. One has but to trace the ancestry of outstanding leaders in later Hawaiian history in order to appreciate the extent to which sons of missionaries saw the main chance and took advantage of it as planters and merchants. Hawaii became a Pacific New England. The typical Hawaiian businessman of American origin was of the same stock, dominated by a stern Puritan conscience, that had carved a land of agriculture and trade from the New England wilderness. They were men of learning and culture, with deeply moral instincts.

This Puritanism, the heritage of the Hawaiian Mission, was reflected time and again in the later history of the Islands and profoundly influenced relationships with the United States. It appeared in such actions as a resolution of the Royal Hawaiian Agricultural Society in

1851 voting down a proposal to develop distilleries in connection with the sugar mills. It was reflected in the missionary reaction against the alleged immorality of the court of Kamehameha III.

In later years, it was traditional Yankee thrift which helped promote the rising protest of businessmen against extravagant and corrupt government. The New England conscience revolted time and again against the moral weaknesses of native rulers, and in the final days of travail in Hawaii in 1887 and 1893, these reactions were of importance in determining the future of the Islands in relationship to the United States. The Mission ended in 1863 but its conscience lived on.

NEW AMERICAN ECONOMIC ENTERPRISES

The gradual passing of the missionary was accompanied by the fuller development of the stakes of American economic enterprise. The forties and early fifties witnessed a further development of the whale fisheries as a factor in Island economy. While the largest number of whaling vessels to visit Hawaiian ports was reached in 1846, the later decline in numbers by no means indicated the passing of the industry. Through the remainder of the forties and a large part of the following decade the whale fisheries continued to constitute the backbone of Island economy. From 1851 to 1858, according to statistics in the *Pacific Commercial Advertiser* for January 26, 1859, the gallons of sperm oil transshipped from Hawaii increased from 104,362 to 222,464; of whale oil, from 909,379 to 2,551,382, and whale bone from 901,604 to 1,614,710 pounds. Approximately four hundred vessels a year constituted the whaling fleet for these years.

The revolutionary effects of this industry upon the rise of a new capitalism in Hawaii continued to be felt. Island imports continued to increase, and the bulk remained in the forties from the eastern Atlantic ports of the United States. Total imports expanded considerably until checked by depression in the late fifties, while those directly from the eastern ports of the United States rose from $245,681.40 for 1845 to a peak of $741,981.90 by 1853.[16] Rope, cable, iron, naval stores, and miscellaneous supplies, including food stuffs, obviously supplies for the whaling trade, constituted the principal items.

Exports of "domestic produce" from Hawaii, also increased. The *Advertiser* is the authority for the fact that these increased from $301,625 for 1846 to $536,522.63 by 1850. Total exports rose from $363,750.74 to $783,052.35 during the same period. Much of this

---

[16] Gregg to Cass, October 7, 1857, enclosing official figures, *Dispatches,* VIII.

growth was made possible by a new interest in agricultural improvement, the product of the demands created by whaling.

The whalers, however, were not to continue as a source of wealth. A sharp decline appeared in 1858 and the amount of sperm oil sent out fell to 156,360 gallons; whale oil to 1,668,175 gallons, and bone to 1,147,120 pounds. The following year marked a brief upsurge, the Indian summer of the industry. Over five hundred arrivals were listed, though the quantity of oil and bone shipped remained below former levels. The American Civil War and the new use of petroleum in the United States spelled the doom of this picturesque industry. In 1862 the number of whalers had dropped to a paltry seventy-three. As early as 1860 candid commercial journals were beginning to admit that the "good old days" were over.[17]

While those with a pessimistic outlook were inclined to view the passing of the whalers as the end of all things, such was not the case. The forces which were to create an even greater economic revolution were in operation even before the decline of whaling. Once more the source of the new development was American. The conquest of California and the acquisition of Oregon as a result of the manifest destiny diplomacy of the bold and irascible James K. Polk thrust the boundary of the United States to the shores of the broad Pacific by 1848. Hawaii immediately assumed greater importance.

HAWAII AND CALIFORNIA AND OREGON

The basis of new relationships between Hawaii and these possessions was under way even prior to their conquest. As early as 1845 a Honolulu correspondent of *Niles' National Register* noted that Oregon "already consumes a considerable amount" of Hawaiian produce.[18] The following year the Rev. Richard Armstrong informed his correspondents, "A brisk trade is opening with Oregon and California. . . . The sugar & molasses of the islands will be in demand in these territories & they will bring lumber, flour, salmon, etc. in exchange." Not only had commerce emerged, but some restless pioneers, pausing only briefly at the new frontier, came on to Hawaii, contributing to an expanding American population.[19]

---

[17] Cf. *Advertiser* of October 4 and December 20, 1860, for comment.

[18] October 11, 1845. See Bradley, 221-23, for notes on earliest trade contacts with the Oregon country.

[19] Armstrong wrote October 11, 1847, "A brisk intercourse is beginning to be carried on between this place & California, & this is another source from which foreigners are coming into the islands. What land will not the universal Yankee take possession of?"

The influx of population into California and the Pacific coast resulting from American occupation and the fabulous gold rush days gave
impetus to these trends. A resulting economic "boom" of no mean
proportion appeared in Hawaii by 1850. The demands of the whaling
fleets for the products of Hawaii were nothing as compared with those
of the rapidly expanding population of California. Mad with the lust
for gold and confronted with an undeveloped country, the newcomers
could not possibly produce sufficient food to supply their needs. An
immediate demand for the agricultural produce of Hawaii was the result. From June 10 to October 11, 1848, twenty vessels cleared Honolulu for California, and all "well freighted."[20] Writing on June 19,
1850, Armstrong reported that "every bean, onion, potato, or squash
we have to spare is at once snatched away to California to feed the
hungry multitude there." Irish potatoes were selling for eight dollars
a bushel, and sugar from nine to ten cents a pound, with other prices
in proportion.

The same year the Rev. William P. Alexander informed relatives in
America: "These islands feel more and more the effects of the mighty
State that is springing up so near us at California. . . . The extrava-
gantly high prices paid for vegetables to convey hither have excited
the people to industry at last. . . . Every lot and garden is planted, &
the islands will be able to freight a great number of vegetables during
the coming year."[21] Spectacular increases in exports appear in customs
house records. Exports to the Pacific coast ports of the United States
from Honolulu leaped from a meager $12,788.25 for 1848 to $25,222.46
in 1851.

ECONOMIC REVOLUTION IN HAWAII

The effects upon the internal economy of Hawaii were immediate.
A greatly increased demand for land resulted. By 1850 land formerly
worth one dollar an acre was valued at five. An increasing foreign
population, mainly from California, poured into the Islands. Surplus
lands were taken up rapidly. The King and chiefs already had been
forced under pressure to broaden means for landholding. By act of the
Legislature rights to land ownership previously limited to naturalized
citizens were extended to foreigners and the last remnants of a feudal

---

[20] *Philadelphia Public Ledger,* January 30, 1849.
[21] Alexander, *op. cit.,* 303f. Similar evidence will be found in the *Annual Report*
of the Mission for 1850 and for 1851.

land tenure swept away.[22] In 1847 the Great Division divided all land among the King, the chiefs, the Hawaiian Government, and tenants who were actual cultivators. The purchase of land in fee simple by individuals was provided for through a Land Office created in 1846.

The most important aspect of the agricultural revolution engendered by the California trade was the remarkable rise of the Hawaiian sugar industry. The first crude sugar mill was erected in 1837. By 1839 several thousand pounds were produced and the first export of sugar to the United States was under way. As early as December, 1838, the ever alert Armstrong was writing of the new industry to friends in the United States.[23]

Development was slow, but after 1841 exports averaged over two hundred tons a year and the number of plantations slowly increased. Lack of a profitable market and a scarcity of labor and capital hindered more rapid growth. Freight charges and the competition of nearer West Indian sugars made it virtually impossible to market Hawaiian sugar in the eastern United States. Despite handicaps, an insistent propaganda by those interested in promoting Hawaiian agriculture served to stimulate and promote the infant enterprise.

THE SUGAR TRADE

Almost providentially, the beginning of the decline of the whaling industry was marked by the emergence of a Pacific coast sugar market. The newly organized Royal Hawaiian Agricultural Society at its first meeting in June, 1850, held out a glowing prospect: "The extension of the territory and government of the United States to the borders of the Pacific, the wonderful discoveries in California, and the consequent, almost instantaneous creation of a mighty state on the western front of the American Union has, as it were, with the wand of a magician, drawn this little group into the very focus of civilization and prosperity." Alert to the new industry and an eager speculator in sugar lands, the Rev. Richard Armstrong wrote the same year: "There are sugar farms here now worth $30,000 and $40,000. . . . Our sugar planters are prospering admirably. Most of them began with nothing

---

[22] Sanford B. Dole, "Evolution of Hawaiian Land Tenures," *Papers of the Hawaiian Historical Society,* No. 3, provides an excellent history of land tenure in Hawaii. See Kuykendall, chap. xv, and W. D. Alexander, "A Brief History of Land Titles in the Hawaiian Kingdom," Thrum, 1891.

[23] Lorna H. Jarrett, *Hawaii and Its People;* Josephine Sullivan, *A History of C. Brewer and Company, Limited: One Hundred Years in the Hawaiian Islands, 1826-1926,* and Kuykendall, 171-82; 314-17; 323-33, contain many important facts regarding the early Hawaiian sugar industry.

& now they are rich men." California and Oregon were consuming more sugar at attractive prices than Hawaii could produce.

Boom proportions of this new development resulted in temporary collapse. Overspeculation in lands and overinvestment, coupled with other factors, produced a sharp reversal of fortunes during the period from 1851 to 1854. The rise of the new markets, however, and the new economic contacts developed with the United States were upon too substantial a foundation to be ruined. The Pacific coast trade was established by 1854 on a sound foundation. Sugar and its allied products had become the principal item of export from Hawaii. The *Pacific Commercial Advertiser* for January 26, 1859, furnishes statistics showing an increase in sugar exports from 289,908 pounds in 1855 to 1,826,620 pounds for 1858. Exports of molasses in the same period increased from 38,304 to 87,513 gallons. The value of sugar exports expanded from $536,522.63 to $628,575.21 over the period. The overwhelming percentage of these increases was represented by exports to Oregon and California.

The trade was by no means one-sided. The Pacific coast shortly proved able to provide its own basic agricultural commodities and to export to Hawaii quantities of vegetables, meats, grains, dairy products, as well as lumber and fish from the Pacific Northwest. The *Oregon Spectator* of September 23, 1851, heralded the arrival of a cargo of Hawaiian sugar with visions of the exchange of commodities which might follow. One week later, it editorialized, "With our constantly increasing population, there will be a corresponding increase of supplies needed; for which the products of Oregon can and ought to be exchanged." By November it reported a regular line of sailing vessels to the Islands projected. Within the next few years the files of both California and Oregon newspapers indicate by their advertisements the rapid rise of communication with Hawaii. During the early years, Oregon assumed a preponderant position in the trade due to the heavy exportation of its lumber and salmon. Later, however, the dominance of California and its virtual monopoly of the sugar market was assured.[24]

Perhaps the most significant result of the new economic revolution under way in Hawaii was the rapid rise of the sugar planter. The emergence of this group and its importance in the social and political evolution of the Islands has been attributed frequently to the effects of the later reciprocity treaty with the United States. This is an erroneous impression. By the time of the American Civil War, an era of

---

[24] The *San Francisco Steamer Bulletin* of May 6, 1857, provides an excellent analysis of the trade for that period. See also Kuykendall, 319f.

large-scale sugar planting had begun to emerge. The sugar industry had gone through the early stage of many pioneer enterprises, small scale and more or less individually controlled and operated. The forties and fifties served as this period of incubation in Hawaii. The experience of that period coupled with the severe depression of the early fifties served to convince informed opinion that small-scale sugar planting was impractical.

The depression tended to eliminate the small planter and aid the rise of larger-scale production. On October 4, 1860, the *Advertiser* summed up the opinion of the Honolulu business community in the assertion, "It has been demonstrated that sugar plantations on a *small scale,* and based on a little capital, will not pay." Scarcity of labor and the necessity for use of the most improved and costly types of machinery in order to produce the grade of sugar necessary to compete in a world market had been the principal factors in producing this situation. By 1852 the organization of a joint-stock company for sugar planting was under discussion and within a year the first of this type had appeared. Scarcely more than a score of planters had become by 1860 key figures in controlling sugar production. The whaling era was at an end, and with it a varied commercial economy. In spite of efforts at diversification under the new agricultural regime, sugar became the one staple commodity. With the control of its production went the power to shape the social and political affairs of Hawaii.

An immediate and significant result was stress and strain within the native monarchy. Previously, few serious difficulties had appeared in the relationships of the native population and government with foreigners. Foreigners were few in number and had lived in Hawaii by sufferance of an indulgent and increasingly enlightened government desirous of the benefits of civilization. This was true not only of the missionary but also of the trader and planter. No strong economic or other power created serious problems as to control of these foreigners by the native monarchy.[25]

POPULATION CHANGES IN HAWAII

This situation had changed rapidly. As early as 1844 the Rev. Richard Armstrong reported a great increase in the numbers and influence of naturalized foreigners, whose naturalization meant little or nothing. A

---

[25] The American Commercial Agent, William Hooper, March 7, 1843, reported to the State Department that his own census showed 404 American citizens resident, a "large proportion" of which were interested in land, but a "majority of which" held titles merely by gift. Cf. FR, 1898, 45f.

year later he repeated the same fact, recorded his fears of its results, and noted the increasing restlessness of the native population. Again in October, 1847, he wrote, "The idea that this floating, restless, money-making, go-ahead white population can be governed by natives only is out of the question." Fears were expressed that the history of Hawaii would repeat that of Texas.

The increase in foreign population was rapid during the next decade. From 1840 to 1850 it increased from one thousand to fifteen hundred; by 1854 it had reached the two thousand mark and within the following six years increased another thousand as a result of importation of Chinese laborers. This was accompanied by a marked decline in the native population. From 1836 to 1850 this decline had averaged twenty-two per cent; from 1850 to 1860 it was seventeen per cent. In round figures the number of native Hawaiians decreased from 71,019 in 1853 to 58,765 by 1865. Observers were beginning to predict the end of the native monarchy.

Prior to the era of economic expansion, the principal permanent foreign element was made up of small numbers of American missionaries and a few merchants and traders of diverse nationality. *The Friend,* analyzing the population of Honolulu in 1847, however, presents a picture of a much different type. Three hundred and fifty-three male foreign residents were listed for the city. Seven were missionaries and the remainder ranged from five lawyers and twenty merchants to one hundred and fifty "mechanics." The total Island foreign population was estimated as six hundred, of whom but one hundred and forty-six had become Hawaiians by naturalization.[26]

The evidence also indicates a changing attitude upon the part of the foreign population toward the natives. The missionaries had been motivated by a benevolent desire to mould the future of an independent native monarchy along Christian and civilized lines. Increasing numbers of the new foreign population were merely seeking private fortunes. "There is an innate contempt of natives among foreigners generally, unless actuated by Christian principles, which leads to a disrespect of their rights of soil, person or reputation," wrote Armstrong in 1847. In the opinion of Armstrong and the missionary element generally, the increasing influx of foreigners with this point of view was a matter of concern. Indeed a chief problem of the Mission in Hawaii became the development of a proper spirit of humility and humanity upon the part of this foreign element.

---

[26] January 15, 1847.

The economic power created by the rise of the sugar planter and his close ally, the Honolulu merchant, became equally important as a problem in Hawaiian affairs. Men no longer secured fortune in Hawaii by pleasure of the ruler and chiefs. A new class of enterprising and ambitious men who saw the advantages of new developments and took full advantage of them was created. The increasing emergence of planters and merchants constituting a controlling interest in the economic life of the Islands complicated their political evolution. This new class demanded responsible and economical government based upon constitutional and legal principles which would give the fullest protection to property rights. Furthermore, it desired ability to influence, if not completely control, the government and its policies. The idle whim of King and chief could no longer stand as the basis for the political structure of Hawaii.

THE DECLINE OF ABSOLUTISM IN HAWAII

In answer largely to this new pressure, the Hawaiian Government went through a process of rapid change. As noted earlier, October 8, 1840, witnessed the promulgation of a constitutional regime creating a legislative body of two chambers. The upper was known as a House of Nobles and represented the hereditary power of the ancient nobility of Hawaii; the lower house of seven members was made elective in response to the demand for some popular direction. The organization of a judicial system headed by a Supreme Court; the emergence of a ministry with departments for the administration of foreign affairs, finance, internal affairs, and education; and the codification of the laws were steps taken toward responsible government during the decade.

These reforms, however, did not fully satisfy the desires of the foreign property holders. Unrest over taxation and the control of fiscal policy by a native government continued. A definite breach between the missionary element and the mercantile-planter class appeared for a time as a result of the conflicting views of the two on political policy. The missionaries were accused of influencing the King against further democratization of the government. A rising demand for the further extension of controls over the native monarchy appeared.

In 1850 an attempt was made to meet this by increasing membership in the lower house of the Legislature to twenty-four as contrasted with seven. The elections held under the new arrangement resulted in definite control of the body for the first time by the American property-holding element. This did not satisfy the protesting group, however, and a year later a commission of three was appointed to revise the Constitution of 1840. The result was the Constitution of 1852, approved by the Legislature and Kamehameha III. It became operative in December of that year.

An annual legislative session was made mandatory, a responsible ministry established, and the House of Nobles severely limited in power. The lower house was given expanded powers, and election by universal manhood suffrage provided. Its membership was further enlarged to a limit of forty. Especially significant was lower house control over fiscal legislation. The old absolute monarchy had been irreparably weakened, and the power of the foreign property-holding element again increased.

The advance made toward a responsible constitutional government did not end the conflicts engendered by the differing interests of foreigners and natives. The economic uncertainty characteristic of the early fifties in Hawaii served to produce a spirit of unrest among the planting and mercantile interests which was reflected in further political controversy. The death of Kamehameha III in December, 1854, marked a turning point in Hawaiian history. Forty-one years of age at the time of his death, Kamehameha III had won the affection of his people in the thirty years of his reign. His rule had given Hawaii its greatest period of progress and civilization. During his time a semi-feudal island kingdom had been transformed into a modern constitutional monarchy worthy of respect from the outside world.

The elevation of Prince Alexander to the throne as Kamehameha IV brought into power a youth intensely loyal to the traditions of the Hawaiian race and interested in maintaining powers of the monarchy. In training he was perhaps more foreign than native. He wished to pattern his government after the English form. Possessed of a kingly bearing and a fine educational background, he was well suited to assume the responsibilities of the kingship. His views included a suspicion of the foreign element, so far as it might desire to weaken native rule. The objective of the new ruler until his death in 1863 became the fullest preservation of the independence of his position and of his people.

Mutterings of discontent were evident against the new regime at frequent intervals. The ability of the natives under a universal suffrage system to outvote the foreigners irked the latter. Charges of extravagance and mismanagement were common against the monarchy, while the Puritanism, which so strongly tinged the character of the American propertied class in Hawaii, produced grumblings against the alleged moral decline of the King and the native leaders.[27] The attitude of outsiders was well summarized by Commissioner David Gregg in 1855. ". . . I cannot help being incredulous," he wrote March 12, "as to the ability of the Hawaiians to maintain their separate nationality for any great length of time." He continued, "A decaying population, resources altogether inadequate to the public improvements demanded by the necessities of business and the progress of the age,—the perfect standstill of all that ought to be in motion,—everything indicates the ultimate necessity of external support, or else the utter subversion of security, order and prosperity."

THE FURTHER AMERICANIZATION OF HAWAIIAN ECONOMY

The connection between these internal difficulties and American policy was immediate and important. The interests in Hawaii in conflict with the natives were almost entirely American by the 1850's, and increasingly so thereafter. As early as 1847 at least one half of the naturalized foreigners was American.[28] In 1855 W. Goodale, Collector General of Customs, valued American property interests at five millions in terms of permanent investments. At the peak of the whale fisheries over a twelve year period ending in 1857, 4,402 American vessels visited Hawaiian ports to 405 for all other nationalities. It was estimated that 1,250 out of 2,017 merchant vessels were American owned.[29]

Minister McBride in October, 1863, informed the State Department that "not less than four-fifths of the commerce connected with these islands is American." He went on to affirm, "The merchants, traders, dealers of all kinds, and planters are principally Americans." "All the sugar plantations of any note on these islands, with the exception of two or three, belong to Americans," he reported.[30]

---

[27] By this date, short items in American newspapers as to conditions in Hawaii appear frequently with comment on political affairs. Cf. *New York Tribune,* September 7, 1858, for above. A summary view of Hawaiian political history is provided in Kuykendall, and William D. Alexander, *A Brief History of the Hawaiian People.* Much of the material for the preceding analysis, however, has been drawn from reports to the State Department provided by the Commissioners and comments in the *Annual Report* of the American Board from year to year. Also Ralph S. Kuykendall, "Constitutions of the Hawaiian Kingdom," *Papers of the Hawaiian Historical Society,* No. 21.

[28] *The Friend,* January 15, 1847.

[29] Compilations of W. Goodale, Collector General of Customs, 1857. Enclosure Gregg to Cass, October 7, 1857, *Dispatches,* VIII.

[30] FR, 1894, 134f. Armstrong also pointed out the predominance of American planters. The membership of the Royal Hawaiian Agricultural Society indicates the same fact.

The conflict of interest between these propertied interests and the native government was certain to influence relations with the United States. In much the same fashion that aggrieved Americans in Texas in the 1830's and later turned to the mother land for aid and comfort in the face of conflict with the government of Mexico, so did the Americans in Hawaii. The tendency to assume this point of view in case of either political or economic disturbance in Hawaii increased.

It is important, however, to remember that Americans interested in property in the Islands were not at all times annexationists seeking to subvert the sovereignty of Hawaii. The degree of such extreme sentiment was in ratio to the seriousness of their grievances. Furthermore, there invariably existed strong differences of opinion among the Americans as to the extent of the protection to be desired from the United States.

AN ERA OF POLITICAL CRISIS

The importance of this was well illustrated between 1854 and 1855 during the period of unrest resulting from a combination of depressed business conditions and political disturbances. While the diplomacy of the era will be treated later, it is apropos to touch upon the causes of the crisis at this point. As noted earlier, agitation had forced a new frame of government from the King in 1852, but had not quieted entirely the political unrest of the times. In April, 1853, Commissioner Severance was reporting to Washington that renewed criticism of the monarchy upon the part of foreigners was developing. Some of the more dissatisfied American residents were reported as willing to join with British interests, or possibly secure the aid of California filibusterers in overthrowing the government. The situation had become so disturbed by August that Severance declared the King might "sell out" on easy terms to the United States to preserve peace.[31]

By the end of the year a definite annexationist sentiment had developed among the American residents. In mid-August, a memorial was submitted to the King by "the most respectable merchants and planters" petitioning annexation. The rise of this threat to Hawaiian independence resulted in a merry game of counter intrigue upon the part of British and French interests to checkmate the Americans. This in turn resulted in forcing the pro-American Doctor Judd from the ministry; but, much to the pleasure of the American Commissioner, Judd was replaced by Elisha H. Allen, native of Maine, and former American

---

[31] See especially dispatches dated April 5, August 15 and 25, 1853, *Dispatches,* IV.

consul.[32] In fact, the machinations of the British and French agents appear to have further assisted the drift toward the United States.

At the time of the arrival of a new American Commissioner, David Gregg, late in 1853, the political crisis was at its peak and Gregg was soon visited by members of a Committee of Thirteen, an organization of the more radical American residents, who declared their support of annexation. Unless it were shortly accomplished, "revolution and a republic" were declared to be the only alternative.[33] From that time until the death of Kamehameha III, the agitation for annexation remained a live issue in Hawaii and was not finally subverted until the restoration of some degree of prosperity at the end of the decade.[34]

This was not the only way, however, in which the new developments in the Islands were affecting a change in the American position. As has been noted, the economic changes of the period after 1848 developed a startling shift in commercial contacts with the United States from New England to Oregon and California. By the Civil War, the national interest of the United States in Hawaii was localized mainly on the Pacific coast in general and in California in particular.

FILIBUSTERING AND MANIFEST DESTINY

During the decade following the gold rush, a blatant manifest destiny sentiment developed upon the part of Americans which became so aggressive as to seriously frighten the Hawaiian authorities. The rapidly growing frontier of the United States on the Pacific produced, as has been noticed, an overflow population which reached Hawaii. For several years following 1848 an increasing number of typical American pioneers began to assemble in Hawaii. A fair percentage of these were of a restless and turbulent type, constituting a threat to the normal social and political evolution of the Islands. Many were not hesitant to proclaim their dissatisfaction with the established authority and to threaten revolution and a republican Hawaii.[35]

The combination of this influx of Americans with an increased recognition of the importance of Hawaii economically to the Pacific coast resulted in many expressions of sympathy from that quarter. The reception in Hawaii accorded such declarations as those of the *Oregon States-man* of November 18, 1851, may well be understood. Commenting upon

---

[32] Severance wrote gleefully to Secretary Marcy on September 8, 1853, "You will perceive at once how much has been gained by getting him into the Council."
[33] Gregg to Marcy, January 5, 1854; also February 11, *Dispatches*, V.
[34] Gregg reported as late as February 1, 1856, that the agitation was very active. The reception of these overtures will be treated in the following chapter.
[35] The letters of Armstrong provide many important references to this problem.

the new Hawaiian trade relationships and the increased American population, this organ asserted: "The fact is, where our countrymen migrate they sow seeds of self-government, which naturally find root in the hearts of men and causes a longing for the free institutions of America; nor will they rest satisfied until they become incorporated into the glorious union . . . it is the inevitable destiny of the Sandwich Islands." A year later, November 3, 1852, the same journal continued in the same vein: "Those Islands are the West Indies of the Pacific coast. . . . That those islands will ultimately form a part of the American Union, we regard as inevitable."

As early as 1849, James Jackson Jarves, acting as a special Hawaiian diplomatic agent, represented to the United States the fear arising in Hawaii from "the probability that adventurers of all nations, congregating in California, would be likely to enter into machinations contrary to the peaceful order of this Kingdom." During the early fifties the California and Honolulu press were full of rumors of proposed filibustering expeditions. For the most part such activities met with approval on the Pacific coast. They became such a cause of apprehension to Hawaii as to alarm the King into seriously considering the peaceful disposal of his kingdom to the United States.[36]

These more radical expressions of American opinion tended in time to disappear. However, the press and statesmen of the Pacific coast continued to preach the doctrine of a dominant and manifest interest in the Hawaiian Islands upon the part of the United States. The declarations of Representative McCorkle of California in Congress on August 30, 1852, presented a view approved almost unanimously. In a long address, the Californian reviewed the religious and economic activity of Americans in Hawaii and declared its control by the United States "is not only of the highest importance to California and the Pacific, as a matter of security in time of war, and especially in a war with Great Britain, but their trade is of vast importance and their possession almost necessary to the United States, in a successful prosecution of commercial enterprise with Asia and the Pacific Islands." His demand for the annexation of the Islands as a matter of national policy met with general approval in Oregon and California.[37]

The revolutionary changes under way in Hawaii and their connection with the expansion of the American Pacific frontier did not escape the attention of the nation at large. It is a mistake to assert that Hawaii

---

[36] Cf. *The Polynesian,* April 24, 1852, for Hawaiian apprehensions; also Severance to Webster, February 10, 1853, *Dispatches,* IV.

[37] The address appears in *Cong. Globe,* 32 Cong., 1 sess., Appendix 1081ff. The *Oregon Statesman,* November 13, 1852, presents an especially emphatic endorsement.

assumed a position of recognized and indispensable importance to the United States in the light of general public opinion or national statesmanship after 1848. It is correct, however, to emphasize that a more alert national interest was evident. The rise of the sugar industry, for example, attracted attention generally among the business community. Such journals as De Bow's *Review* and Hunt's *Merchants' Magazine and Commercial Review* by 1854 and 1855 had begun to devote space to the development of the new industry and to emphasize the dominance of American capital and enterprise.[38] The press likewise began to carry more frequent dispatches dealing with the progress of the Islands. While those in San Francisco journals were more detailed, the *New York Tribune* and other eastern papers were not lacking in scattered items.[39]

HAWAII AS A PACIFIC OUTPOST

Washington was not unaware of the changed situation and reflected the general trend of American opinion. Officials concerned were quick to recognize the new importance of Hawaii in the light of the thrusting of American territorial limits into Oregon and California. Instructing Commissioner Eames in February, 1849, Secretary of State Buchanan referred to "the great impulse which the intercourse between the Islands and our territory on the Pacific recently received, and the probability that this intercourse will augment in rapid ratio. . . . "[40]

In his annual message for 1851, President Fillmore pointed out that "they lie in the course of the great trade which must at no distant day be carried on between the western coast of the North American and eastern Asia." The President went on to indicate that the early conditions prompting an American interest in the Islands have been "greatly enhanced by the sudden and vast development which the interests of the United States have attained in California and Oregon. . . ."[41]

This appreciation of the increased importance of Hawaii reflected the growing belief in the destiny of American commercial empire in the Pacific. It was an era of rapidly expanding Yankee commerce, and

---

[38] For the former, see especially the January, 1855, issue. Also Hunt for 1853 and 1854.

[39] A careful examination of *Tribune* files leads to the conclusion that the interest in Hawaii was rather feeble in the eastern section, except under unusual circumstances such as rumors of annexation or some foreign attack upon Island independence. Then a stiffening attitude was observable.

[40] *Instructions*, II.

[41] James D. Richardson, *A Compilation of the Messages and Papers of the Presidents, V*, 120f.

steam navigation was broadening the entire field of trade in the Pacific area. New treaties negotiated with New Granada and Nicaragua pointing the way to new routes across the Isthmus, Cushing's negotiations in China, and those of Perry and Harris with Japan were all evidences of this new spirit of American enterprise in the Pacific theater during the forties and fifties. More than one half the Protestant missionaries in China were Americans, spiritual brothers of those in Hawaii. Tyler and his successors were applying to Hawaii specifically a policy which reflected the sentiment expressed by the Secretary of the Navy in his *Annual Report* for 1853: "A new empire has, as by magic, sprung into existence. San Francisco promises, at no distant day, to become another New York, and our prosperous trade in the Pacific, amid the wonders of commerce, to bear the same relationship to China and Japan which that of the Atlantic coast bears to the continent of Europe and Great Britain." Such developments for the future meant that Hawaii was of the utmost importance as a coaling and supply center both for naval and commercial vessels. The United States was beginning, therefore, to have an eye to the preservation of its independence from possible control by any other power.

It should not be assumed, however, that the American national interest in Hawaii had reached such proportions by the Civil War as to constitute a mandate for possession. The American policy there, as elsewhere, remained one of support of integrity and independence rather than partition or seizure. This was the fundamental principle behind the Tyler doctrine. Also behind it were now marshalled national interests which were increasingly economic, as well as moral, and a strong local interest on the Pacific coast based on commerce and the spirit of frontier expansion. These interests and the principles behind them were subjected to severe testing under conditions which we will describe in the following chapter.

CHAPTER III

Reciprocity Versus Annexation

From the mid-forties until the Civil War brought an abrupt end to any extended concern with Hawaiian affairs, the twin issues of commercial reciprocity and political annexation were pressing constantly for the attention of the State Department. Neither found any considerable support from the general public in the United States. The increasingly acquisitive nature of American diplomacy, however, under the administration of Franklin Pierce came very near to the accomplishment of the political union of Hawaii with the United States. From the Hawaiian standpoint, the growing desire for commercial reciprocity with its eastern neighbor also came close to the realization of its goal.

The discussion of both issues and the diplomacy connected with their attempted consummation tended to bring into ever closer focus the relationships of Hawaii and the United States. Throughout the whole era the basic principles of the Tyler doctrine remained ever present as the most fundamental of American policies relating to the Pacific. Bedeviled by foreign complications, Hawaii was forced to turn to the United States for protection, while the latter power used its diplomacy toward that end. These significant years in Hawaiian-American relations now deserve our attention.

BEGINNINGS OF THE RECIPROCITY MOVEMENT

The movement for reciprocal trade relations between Hawaii and the United States preceded any annexationist ideas of importance in either country. Commissioner George Brown had been one of the earliest to press upon Washington the importance of a treaty of commerce with the Islands in view of their commercial and naval importance. His difficulties with the native government made impossible satisfactory diplomatic overtures and there is no evidence indicating that the suggestions of the Commissioner were considered seriously.

By 1847 this situation had been altered through the growing interest of both governments in some improved commercial relations. From the American standpoint, the new belief in the future of the Pacific as a center of expansion commercially made Hawaii assume a new importance. In Hawaii the general economic evolution of the times had reached a point where a pressure for more satisfactory commercial commitments became stronger upon the part of the foreign interests engaged in trade and planting. At the same time the Scotch-born Robert C. Wyllie had assumed charge of Hawaiian foreign affairs in 1845. From an early date this loyal and able servant of the Hawaiian Government became convinced that the preservation of its independence depended upon the fostering of commercial relations and treaties with the major powers to provide an expanding economic life and satisfy the ambitions of the foreign property-holders for economic gain. Wyllie further believed that the more satisfactory the general commercial relations of the major powers with Hawaii the less the tendency to interfere with its internal affairs or to attempt by force the extortion of special political or other privileges. So long as Hawaii held open the door of economic opportunity to foreigners, both within and without, internal quiet and freedom from external interference might be assured.

Following the development of advantageous, though not completely satisfactory, treaties with France and Great Britain, Wyllie turned to Schuyler Livingston, American Consul General for Hawaii, in August, 1847, with propositions for a similar agreement with the United States mutually "beneficial to their commerce and favorable to the internal interests of these Islands."[1]

Further evidence of the anxiety of Hawaii to perfect its commercial arrangements with the United States was afforded by the dispatch to California in 1848 of Theodore Shillaber as a special agent to secure "a provisional arrangement on the basis of a perfect reciprocity of Flags & Import Duties." The growing trade with that area had aroused a keen interest upon the part of Hawaii.

THE TREATY OF 1849

In the meantime, the fact that the United States was not remiss in recognizing the importance of improved commercial intercourse with the Islands is evident. As noted earlier, Secretary of State Buchanan had instructed Commissioner Ten Eyck to advance this object and berated him vigorously for his mishandling of treaty negotiations. In February, 1849, Buchanan informed the new Commissioner to Hawaii, Charles Eames, of the desire of the President for a "Treaty of Commerce and Navigation" similar to those enjoyed by the United States with leading powers. "The President," he stated, "is willing to conclude with the Hawaiian government a treaty of reciprocity." The new commercial

---

[1] Wyllie to Livingston, *Notes, Hawaii*, I. Livingston was utilized because of the unsatisfactory character of Hawaiian relations with Commissioner Ten Eyck and the attempt of the latter to force a humiliating treaty upon Hawaii.

prospects of the nation as a result of its Pacific coast possessions were cited as demanding such a treaty. The proposed engagement, it was suggested, should be carefully drawn so as to prevent its possible utilization by foreigners using the Hawaiian flag to compete in American trade in the Pacific, and was limited to eight years.[2]

Shortly after this in April, 1849, the appointment of James Jackson Jarves by the King to negotiate a new treaty with the United States was announced by Hawaii. At the same time Dr. Gerrit P. Judd was in the United States acting as a special diplomatic agent. In San Francisco, Commissioner Eames, meeting Judd while on the way to Hawaii, seized upon the opportunity to negotiate hastily a treaty of amity, commerce, and navigation with the Hawaiian statesman.[3] Two treaties with Hawaii were actually negotiated in 1849 due to the fact that Jarves and Secretary of State John Clayton in Washington on December 6 concluded still another treaty draft. A treaty embodying articles from both and deemed more "satisfactory" to the United States by the State Department was formally ratified and went into effect in November, 1850. News of the De Tromelin incident at Honolulu spurred the United States in concluding the treaty.

Briefly summarized, the new treaty provided for "reciprocal liberty of commerce and navigation" between the two countries, establishing the principle of mutual tariff arrangements with no discrimination against the trade of either not applicable to other powers. Special provisions guaranteeing the rights and privileges of American whaling vessels in Hawaiian ports were agreed upon and the rights of American citizens in the Islands were carefully defined. The life of the engagement was placed at ten years, subject to automatic renewal unless prior notice to terminate was served by either party.[4] Other than stabilizing commercial relations and defining the rights of American citizens in Hawaii, the treaty accomplished little more than to embody a recognition of the government of the Islands as a responsible power capable of maintaining a law and polity as applied to foreigners. While the United States had refused to both Judd and Jarves any guarantee of Hawaiian independence, it did establish American relations with the tiny kingdom upon a more satisfactory basis of mutual respect and

---

[2] *Instructions*, II.

[3] Eames to Clayton, October 22, 1849, *Dispatches*, IV. Judd attempted to secure as a part of the treaty a guarantee by the United States "never to take possession of any part" of the Islands as a protection or otherwise. Jarvis had been designated to act for Hawaii while in the United States and his appointment was suggested originally by Buchanan as a result of conversations in October, 1848. Kuykendall's account, 374ff., contains further details.

[4] Copy of treaty in FR, 1894, 79-85.

responsibility than had ever before existed. It governed the commercial relations of the two governments until annexation.

The opening of the new decade marked a general shift toward closer and more satisfactory relations. In part this was due to an improvement in American diplomacy. The return of Daniel Webster to the State Department under Whig auspices signalized an era of calm and the end for a few years of the expansionist diplomacy of Tyler and Polk. The new Commissioner to Hawaii of the Taylor-Fillmore administration became Luther Severance, an able and sympathetic person who did much to rescue American diplomacy at Honolulu from the sad state into which it had fallen under Brown and Ten Eyck.

THE TYLER POLICY REAFFIRMED

At the same time, much was done to advance and maintain upon a firm basis the fundamentals of the Tyler doctrine. It is significant in this connection that the instructions issued to Severance by Webster at the beginning of his mission referred specifically to the declarations of President Tyler as still constituting the basic principles behind American diplomacy at Honolulu. The expanding influence of the United States in Hawaii was called to the attention of the new Commissioner and the strict regard of the United States for the preservation of Hawaiian independence stressed.[5]

Even prior to the departure of Severance, however, President Taylor in his annual message of December 4, 1849, had taken occasion to reaffirm in a positive fashion the dictates of John Tyler made seven years earlier. Defining American policy Taylor declared, "The position of the Sandwich Islands with reference to the territory of the United States on the Pacific, the success of our persevering and benevolent citizens who have repaired to that remote quarter in Christianizing the natives and inducing them to adopt a system of government and laws suited to their capacity and wants, and the use made by our numerous whale ships of the harbors of the islands as places of resort for obtaining refreshments and repairs all combine to render their destiny peculiarly interesting to us." The President voiced his desire "that the islands may maintain their independence and that other nations should concur with us in this sentiment." "We could in no event consent to their passing under the dominion of another power," warned Taylor.[6]

These views were further repeated by President Fillmore in his message of December 2, 1851. Expressing the interest of the United States

---

[5] Webster to Severance, July 20, 1850, *Instructions,* II.
[6] Richardson, *op. cit.,* V, 17.

in the early settlement of Hawaiian difficulties with France, the Whig leader called attention to the American regard for the independence of Hawaii. This sentiment was influenced, he declared, by the "existing and prospective importance of the islands as a place of refuge and refreshment for our vessels engaged in the whale fishery, and by the consideration that they lie in the course of the great trade which must at no distant day be carried on between the western coast of North America and eastern Asia." Reiterating the earlier statements of Taylor, he remarked, "We were also influenced by a desire that those islands should not pass under the control of any other great maritime state, but should remain in an independent condition, and so be accessible and useful to the commerce of all nations."[7]

NEW TROUBLES WITH FRANCE

The occasion for these vigorous assertions of American policy was the renewed difficulties of Hawaii itself with a powerful European nation. The offender was that perennial disturber of Hawaiian peace— France. The early difficulties of the two governments, which had constituted much of the prelude to the Paulet incident, have been cited. While the joint declaration of France and Great Britain in 1843 against any interference with the Islands had seemed to dispose of the difficulty, in reality it had not done so. In 1848 a new French consular representative, M. Dillon, had revived the long-standing controversy with Hawaii over the rights of Catholic missionaries. The Island was charged further with failure to adhere to the terms of its commercial convention with France, especially as respected duties on French spirits.

Rear Admiral de Tromelin, French naval commander for the Pacific, appeared August 13, 1849, at Honolulu with the frigate *La Poursuivante,* followed shortly by *Le Gassendi.* While his disposition appeared at first to be friendly, conferences with the French Consul, M. Dillon, produced a change and on August 22 the two French officials joined in presenting a series of ten demands to the Hawaiian Government. Unable to comply with them, the King was forced to submit three days later to the landing of French forces which occupied the fort and two public buildings for five days. Considerable destruction of property and the seizure of the royal yacht resulted from the occupation.[8]

---

[7] *Ibid.,* V, 720f. The President declared that the United States was first to recognize the independence of the Islands, followed by "several of the leading powers of Europe," a reference to the joint Anglo-French declarations.

[8] The principal facts in the French difficulty are set forth in Kuykendall, 388f. Dispatches of American officials contain much of the correspondence, demands, etc., incident to the controversy. Judd, *op. cit.,* contains much useful information of a contemporary nature.

From the first the Hawaiians sought American and British aid. The American Consul, Joel Turrill, was appealed to for protection of American lives and property and contested the right of the French to intervene. On August 22 Hawaii forwarded to James J. Jarves, already in the United States and designated, as we have noticed, to negotiate a commercial treaty, an appeal for the "friendly mediation" of the United States. In September Doctor Judd sailed from Honolulu, accompanied by the two youthful Hawaiian princes, Alexander Liholiho and Lot Kamehameha, to assist Jarves and particularly to intercede at London and Paris. In Washington the Hawaiians were informed by Secretary Clayton in November, 1849, that the United States would not only mediate "but *remonstrate*," and that while the United States did not want to seize the Islands it would not consent to allow any other nation to take them.[9]

Thus the United States was forced for the second time in a decade to face the issue of foreign interference with the sovereignty of Hawaii. The danger was two-fold. There was the possibility of a permanent violation of Hawaii's independence by France. The British might be thrown into a panic and abrogate the agreement of 1843 by taking a hand directly. Unless the United States demonstrated its ability to protect Hawaii, the incident might mean the permanent loss of the Islands. While it was not known to Washington, Doctor Judd carried secret instructions which permitted the disposal of the Islands in return for protection of the rights of the King.

The whole affair constituted a serious threat to American influence and was so regarded by the American business and missionary interests. From Honolulu the Rev. Richard Armstrong aptly wrote, "American interests are entirely paramount here, so far as numbers & wealth are concerned, & these interests cannot fail to suffer should any serious disaster befall the Islands."

In view of the serious situation, Whig diplomacy seemed torpid and slothful. While the administration, as already indicated, was moved in December, 1849, to reaffirm the Tyler doctrine, it was not until June 3, 1850, that the State Department promised Judd and Jarves that the President would "cheerfully do anything in his power compatible with the cardinal policy of this Government" to aid in settling the French difficulty. In fact, the Hawaiian agent, Doctor Judd, had already secured

---

[9] Correspondence in FR, 1894, 73ff. Clayton's statement is cited in Kuykendall, 379. Judd went on to London and Paris. He secured a promise of British mediation and a new commercial treaty, though the British were involved in adventures in Greece which made it difficult for them to remonstrate with France with good grace at this time.

assurance of the good offices of Great Britain and was now seeking to engage the United States in some tri-partite arrangement to guarantee Hawaiian independence.

Secretary Clayton on July 1, 1850, submitted to Minister Rives at Paris the desires of the Hawaiian Government for the exercise of American influence to settle the French controversy, and expressed the opinion that the latter power had been "unnecessarily harsh" in dealing with the Islands. The importance of Hawaii in respect to "our possessions on the Pacific and the bonds commercial and of other description between them and the United States" was cited, and also the fact that the latter "could never with indifference allow them to pass under the dominion or exclusive control of any other power." Any participation of the United States in an international agreement protecting the Islands was repudiated, however, as "too little in consonance with our usual policy. . . . " Rives was to press France for a settlement of its Hawaiian problems. There is no evidence that the Minister did anything other than to acknowledge receipt of the communication and to present it.[10]

These rather feeble gestures upon the part of the United States did nothing to halt the French aggressions. Controversy over the position of the missionaries of France and the commercial treaty continued under a new Consul, M. Perrin. By March 10, 1851, Commissioner Severance reported to the State Department that the native government fully expected a repetition of the de Tromelin incident, so insistent and provocative were the demands of the French.[11] So serious had the situation become that on March 12, 1851, the Commissioner handed a document fully drawn up and executed constituting a formal transfer of the sovereignty of the Islands to the United States by the King, to be used in case of hostilities with the French.[12] The British Consul General, William Miller had been approached previously with a proposition to raise the British flag, which he had been unable to do.

By the end of the month this particular crisis had passed. The charges of M. Perrin had been waived in part pending a settlement directly with the French Government. The change in front was due directly to the realization that extreme demands were threatening to throw the Islands into the arms of the United States. The power of the weapon

[10] Correspondence in FR, 86-88. Department archives reveal no more than was published and indicate no decisive action by Rives. Clayton informed Judd and Jarves that the United States would use force if necessary to retake the Islands. See Kuykendall, 398f.

[12] FR, 1894, 89-97. Interesting details are in Kuykendall, 400f.

[11] *Dispatches*, IV.

of threatened cession, approved by the King and Council, was further reinforced by the passage June 21, 1851, of a resolution by the Hawaiian Legislature granting emergency powers to the King to conclude such a cession of sovereignty should the French persist in their arbitrary demands.

In the meantime, the State Department at Washington had been prodded by the American Board into more vigorous action. "Our whole safety now lies in hugging close to Uncle Sam, & don't let Mr. Webster commit himself one hair to France or England, unless they will agree to let us alone," the Rev. Richard Armstrong had written from Hawaii. The Board, as has been seen earlier was not slow to assert the desired pressure, and June 19, 1851, Webster undertook to ascertain from Minister Rives at Paris the reasons for his failure to act upon the earlier instructions of the Department. The Secretary enclosed information provided by the Rev. Rufus Anderson of the American Board to the effect that the French were expected to resort shortly to hostile measures against Hawaii. In vigorous language Webster called upon Rives to exert himself in presenting the objections of the United States to the entire French policy.[13]

Thus prodded, Rives replied that he had held several conversations with the French and had reason to suppose their intentions were conciliatory. Recent rapid changes in their department of foreign affairs had rendered progress difficult. Later in July, Rives reported the "painful surprise" of the French at the insinuations in the dispatch of June 19. Paris declared that French policy had been dictated by the fact that it had no "controlling influence" at Honolulu similar to the missionary and economic penetration of Great Britain and the United States. This made necessary at times "a more energetic tone of negotiation than either of those powers to obtain an equal treatment with them. . . ." Rives, who apparently labored under a pro-French view, suggested that the British were using the incident to excite the United States into assisting them in striking at the French.

On October 30 Rives again addressed the State Department and declared that France was extremely annoyed at the American intervention. The policy of the United States had encouraged the resistance of Hawaii to a point where it "refused absolutely to listen to any of the

---

[13] *Ibid.*, 97-105, contains all correspondence not cited otherwise. A committee representing the Board had called attention to "hostile movements" of the French and urged protective measures upon Fillmore and his Cabinet in September, 1850. In June, 1851, Reuben Chapman called Webster's attention to a letter from the Rev. Richard Armstrong and speaks of conversations with Webster concerning French difficulties. Chapman refers to conversations relative to proposing to Russia "a mutual guarantee of the independence of the Islands." See *Miscellaneous Letters.*

demands of the French Government, and made no other reply to the French consul than that if these demands were pressed they would immediately put themselves under the protectorate of the United States." Paris likewise called attention to the American failure to become a party to the Franco-British agreement of 1843 respecting the Islands and suggested the United States could with little grace question France.

ANNEXATION PROFFERED AND REFUSED

In the meantime, Washington had been confronted with the prospect of accepting either a protectorate or complete control over the Islands. A document providing for provisional cession placed in the hands of Severance in March, 1851, had been carried to the United States by Lieutenant R. E. Johnson of the U. S. S. *Vandalia,* and the American Consul, Elisha H. Allen. Allen had two conferences with Webster and also saw President Fillmore and the Secretary of the Navy, as well as presenting a dispatch from Minister Severance. The dispatch explained that the King was desirous of securing a joint protectorate from Great Britain, France, and the United States, but if unable to obtain that, wished to place Hawaii under American control. "The King would prefer," wrote the Commissioner, "that his Kingdom be received as an independent state, under protection merely from foreign aggression." However, if this could not be done and the King should "continue the victim of foreign oppression, the mere shadow of a King, without the power, but with responsibilities measured only by the arbitrary will of the strong, he will resign the Sovereignty of his Islands into the hands of the United States, under the guarantee of his private rights. . . ." The possibility of a secret agreement to this end to be utilized only in case of emergency was further suggested.[14]

For an administration committed to reversing the land grabbing propensities of its predecessor, this was indeed an embarrassing situation. Furthermore, one of the cardinal points of the Tyler policy was the preservation of an independent Hawaii. In two communications, one an official dispatch and the other a private instruction to Severance, under date of July 14, 1851, Webster proceeded to outline fully the reaction of the United States to the proposal. "This Government still desires to see the nationality of the Hawaiian Government maintained, its independent administration of public affairs respected and its prosperity and reputation increased," affirmed the Secretary. "But while thus indisposed to exercise any sinister influence itself over the counsels of Hawaii," he continued, "or to overawe the proceedings of its Govern-

---

[14] Severance to Webster, March 31, 1851, *Dispatches,* IV.

ment by the menace of the actual application of superior military force, it expects to see other powerful nations act in the same spirit." The actions of the French were characterized as "wholly inconsistent" with the independence principle and the United States could not view them with "indifference."

Emphasizing the paramount nature of American interests, Webster declared: "The Hawaiian Islands are ten times nearer to the United States than to any of the powers of Europe. Five-sixths of all their commercial intercourse is with the United States, and these considerations, together with others of a more general character, have fixed the course which the Government of the United States will pursue in regard to them." That the administration did not regard this as idle statement was indicated by information from Webster to the effect that the Navy Department "will receive instructions to place, and to keep, the naval armament of the United States in the Pacific Ocean in such a state of strength and preparation as shall be requisite for the preservation of the honor and dignity of the United States and the safety of the Government of the Hawaiian Islands."

Webster thus placed Hawaii in effect under the protection of the United States without entering into any agreement. Privately, Webster warned Severance against any direction, request, or encouragement of hostile action by any American naval officer against the French. He likewise cautioned against implications to the Hawaiian authorities that the American policy would be any other than one of strict regard for their independence. The Secretary was careful also to point out that Americans in the Islands who had ceased to become citizens could not expect the protection of the United States, nor should they expect favorable reception of annexationist or other political agitation. By these instructions Webster fulfilled the requirements of developed policy and threw a protecting arm about the monarchy without opening any avenues to an American subversion of Hawaiian sovereignty.[15]

The repudiation of the proposed cession was not in accord entirely with general American opinion. The annexation fever, while absent from the hearts of the Whigs, took hold in other quarters and flamed out in criticism of the failure of Washington to act favorably upon the proposal. Rumors of the proposition became general on the Pacific coast during the early spring of 1851 and aroused popular interest. In the eastern United States the news a little later was not greeted unfavorably. The *New York Tribune,* for example, June 28, 1851,

---

[15] Dispatches in FR, 1894, 99f. Copies of the official dispatch were sent to Paris and London.

commented favorably upon Hawaiian annexation. "Its civilization and its commerce are American; its laws and government are already, to a great extent modelled upon ours," the *Tribune* affirmed. The value of established economic interests and the prospect for their increase, in the opinion of this organ, made Hawaii a region of paramount interest to the United States.

Californians were disgruntled at the failure of Fillmore to act upon a project of so great importance to their section. In the Senate on June 12, 1852, Senator Weller of that state introduced and secured the passage of a resolution calling upon the President to submit information as to whether an annexation proposition had been presented. On June 26 the administration denied the public interest in the matter and refused to submit the desired information.

August 6 a similar resolution sponsored by Senator Seward of New York requested the President, if compatible with the public interest, to appoint a Commissioner "who shall be instructed to inquire into the expediency of instituting negotiations for the acquisition of those Islands by the United States." This was dismissed likewise by Fillmore. The refusal of the President either to act or to furnish the annexationists with information led to a bitter attack in Congress in August by Representative McCorkle of California upon the administration for its "English policy" in Hawaii. The Congressman declared that the President had neglected the national interests of the United States in favor of British influence with Hawaii, a point of view widely accepted in his section.

There is no evidence that the President was influenced by this criticism. The definite opposition of the administration to expansionist diplomacy was further manifested in its favorable attention to a proposal for a joint protectorate over the Islands with Great Britain and France. While such a proposition had been advanced by the Jarves-Judd mission in 1850, it had been repudiated and the Hawaiian agents informed that the President was not inclined to consider such a course without "great deliberation." It appears, however, that by 1852 the President and Webster were both willing to consider the possible linking of Hawaii with Cuba in a triple protectorate arrangement with Great Britain and France to guarantee the checking of expansionists in both localities. The approach of the political campaign and the death of Webster checkmated the proposition and led to its definite repudiation.[16]

---

[16] R. W. Van Alstyne, "Great Britain, the United States and Hawaiian Independence," *Pacific Historical Review*, IV, should be consulted. Also A. A. Ettinger, "The Proposed Anglo-French-American Treaty of 1852 to Guarantee Cuba to Spain," *Transactions Royal Historical Society*, 4th series, XIII.

The Fillmore policy succeeded in forestalling annexation and upheld the principles of the Tyler doctrine with success, if with little vigor. The failure of the proposal for a triple protectorate was fortunate indeed from the standpoint of its effect upon future American relations with the Islands. The difficulties of Hawaii with the French, the success of Commissioner Severance in winning the confidence of the Hawaiian authorities, and the forbearance of Washington in not pressing the opportunity for a foothold offered by the cession proposal combined to give a powerful urge toward better relations with the United States.

HAWAIIAN OPINION ON ANNEXATION

It is doubtful that there had been any united support for annexation upon the part of any large part of the American residents of the Islands. Commissioner Severance reported in March, 1851, that annexation was "often hinted at, and sometimes freely discussed in private. . . ." The idea was favorably received by the sugar planters, but Severance was forced to conclude that the mercantile element "may not like to substitute the American tariff for the Hawaiian."

Severance thus touched upon two important conflicting interests which had much to do with determining the possible drift of Hawaii under American control. The prospect of annexation was not desirable from the standpoint of all groups of Americans interested in the economic development of the Islands. While the planter looked with favor upon the idea of an enlarged market, the merchant had little to gain from American control. This division of opinion constituted one of the best guarantees for continued Hawaiian sovereignty and independence.

The missionary interest likewise at this date opposed the idea of annexation. Writing in October, 1851, the Rev. Richard Armstrong voiced the view of this American group when he declared, "What we do want is protection—& to be let alone." "If compelled to seek annexation . . . ," he wrote, "it would be done with deep regret that a necessity existed." Sharp differences of opinion existed further between the American economic and religious influence in the Islands. Severance reported at this time that he found "many Americans" who "hate the missionaries" and were anxious to eliminate entirely their influence. The missionary stood as the champion of the native in his struggle for advancement. This position often brought the missionary influence into sharp conflict with the propertied interests which entertained less regard for the native and wished to control him for the benefit of their own political and economic power.

The absence of any united support for annexation at this date from the body of American residents meant that its failure was not greeted with disappointment. Hawaii itself, reported Commissioner Severance, was "much pleased" at the attitude of the United States and never desirous of annexation as such, but merely as an alternative to French domination. The "emphatic and manly avowal" of Webster in ordering the return of the document of cession, and "the pious and honorable course" of Severance won the commendation of Minister Wyllie. For the first time since 1843 the diplomacy of the United States might be said to have won the full confidence of Hawaii. There was no further need to fear the permanent drift of the Islands toward a reliance upon Great Britain for protection.

RENEWAL OF THE RECIPROCITY AGITATION

Significantly enough, the temporary passing of the annexation excitement witnessed the appearance of a definite drive for reciprocity with the United States. The desire of the planters for the expansion of their Pacific coast market now supplemented the more political objectives behind the schemes of Foreign Minister Wyllie. Early in 1852 the semi-governmental organ, *The Polynesian,* began a campaign to develop public interest. It dwelt at length in its January 17 issue upon the growing trade of Hawaii with Oregon and California. "We want their productions, and they want ours," it affirmed. A convention of planters and merchants to advocate reciprocal trade measures was urged. Fears that the introduction of foreigners dangerous to Island security, or that the rise of imperialistic desires on the Pacific coast might result from such a step were scouted.

The recently organized Royal Hawaiian Agricultural Society was quick to endorse the new campaign and accept the suggestion of *The Polynesian.* On February 28, 1852, it formally petitioned the King to open negotiations with the United States "for the admission of the sugar, syrup of sugar, molasses, and coffee produced on your Islands, in all the ports of the United States, free of duty, and to be pleased to enact that in consideration thereof, the flour, fish, coal, lumber, staves and heading of the United States, shall be admitted free of duty in all ports of your Kingdom, open to foreign trade."[17]

The Hawaiian Government was quick to respond. and, following action by the King and Council with the endorsement of the Legislature, Commissioner Severance forwarded to Washington news of au-

---

[17] Cited, *The Polynesian,* March 5, 1852.

thorization of the ending of duties by Hawaii upon a list of specified commodities, provided the United States would reciprocate by ending its charges upon the importation of sugar and allied products.

This definite bid for a reciprocal trade arrangement was hastened by growing economic distress in Hawaii. The unfortunate consequences of speculation and overexpansion occasioned by the California boom were now at their peak. Explaining the move in a later communication to the State Department, Commissioner Severance emphasized that "the sugar planters were laboring under a great depression, involving to a great extent all the commercial interest, for the planters were in debt to the merchants and could not pay." Rising political unrest, stimulated by these conditions, was a factor in leading the government to give quick ear to the protests. Political and economic factors in Hawaii were now united behind reciprocity. The long drive, which ended with final success more than two decades later, was on.

The ingenious bid for a favored commercial position presented in the Hawaiian proposal was completely ignored in the United States. By January, 1853, Severance was impelled to recall the matter to the attention of the State Department. By dint of improvements in machinery and processes of manufacture, together with normal improvement of economic conditions, the planters were now in a much better position. "They still, however, most anxiously desire to get their sugar admitted into California and Oregon, their natural markets, free of duty, and of course, wish to get their supplies from the American coast in the same way," informed Severance.[18] These proposals were doomed to failure.

---

[18] *Dispatches*, IV.

CHAPTER IV

Shadows of Manifest Destiny

Change of administration had brought new leaders and new policies into control in the United States before the receipt of the reciprocity bid referred to in the preceding chapter. In the Presidency was the handsome and confident Franklin Pierce, who had proclaimed March 4, 1853, "The policy of my administration will not be controlled by any timid forebodings of evil from expansion." The necessity for certain territorial acquisitions as a protection for the expanding interests of the nation became a cardinal point in the foreign policy of Pierce. He was ably supported by his Secretary of State, William L. Marcy.

The new Commissioner to Hawaii became David L. Gregg. His instructions were remarkably similar to those of his predecessor, and indicate again how fundamental were the principles established for Hawaii a decade earlier by Tyler. "While we do not intend to attempt the exercise of any exclusive control over them," wrote the new Secretary of State, "we are resolved that no other power or State shall exact any political or commercial privileges from them which we are not permitted to enjoy—far less to establish any protectorate over them." Gregg was instructed especially to "keep a watchful eye upon all that transpires at Hon., and around it, calculated to endanger the national existence of the Hawaiian group. . . ."

Marcy further emphasized the fact that "after the extension of our laws over Oregon, and the acquisition of California, not only those Islands but also the whole of Polynesia assumed an increased importance to the United States." Developments in China and Japan were further cited. Marcy envisioned a rosy day when intercourse "between our Pacific ports and the ports of the distant East is destined perhaps to be upon as large a scale as that which we now enjoy with all the world, and the vessels engaged in that trade must resort to the ports of the Sandwich Islands for fuel and supplies." Hawaii stood in the same relationship to the United States as Cuba and the Antilles, which the United States would be "pleased" to see "independent of European Powers."[1]

---

[1] *Instructions*, II.

ANOTHER BID FOR ANNEXATION

Before Gregg could get to Hawaii to undertake his duties, important developments were under way which were to raise further problems as to American policy. The troubled political situation noted in the preceding chapter had driven hitherto divergent American interests into a general support of annexation. In August, 1853, a group of nineteen merchants and planters memorialized the King in favor of annexation to the United States to forestall possible revolution and disorder. The movement was so powerful as to produce a united protest to the King upon the part of both the British and French representatives at Honolulu against "any attempt to annex the Sandwich Islands to any power whatever" as in contravention of the Anglo-French agreement of 1843. The troubled Hawaiian Government turned the protest over to Commissioner Severance for a reply. That worthy denied its validity and defended the right of Hawaii to surrender its sovereignty should it desire to do so.[2]

From the arrival of Gregg late in 1853 through January, 1854, the turmoil continued. Increasing demands by American residents of all groups for annexation or a protectorate, and the opposition of other foreign residents produced intrigues and counter intrigues. While the King and his principal advisors appeared favorable, members of the chiefs and Prince Alexander Liholiho expressed a growing native nationalist reaction against the idea. By February 7 Gregg reported to the State Department that the King had instructed Wyllie to open negotiations for annexation, and two days later a dispatch including the formal appeal for such consideration was forwarded. In the meantime, Gregg entertained the proposal favorably, fearing, as he declared, that to do otherwise might throw the government toward British or French influences.

Basically, the change of front from two years earlier was due to growing internal unrest in the Hawaiian kingdom. As has been pointed out in preceding pages, the period around 1854 was one of sharp economic depression following the brief boom produced by the new California and Oregon trade. There had been overspeculation in land and merchandising. As usual in such cases, this condition was conducive to much grumbling and criticism of the King and his policies. Closely allied with this situation was the antagonism of many foreigners active in economic enterprises against the native government and King. The natives, including the King and chiefs, held control of almost all the

---

[2] Cf. Severance to Marcy, August 29 and September 15, 1853, *Dispatches*, IV.

land in Hawaii, levied the taxes, and shaped the policies of the government. The new and more ruthless element in the foreign population was restless under this situation. Honolulu was full of vague rumors of possible revolution against the native monarchy. In the midst of such threats, it was the shrewd conclusion of the King and his aides, both native and foreign, that the best interests of himself and his people would be served by a carefully designed treaty of annexation to the United States.

The thinking of the King's advisors is well revealed in a letter from Foreign Minister Wyllie to William L. Lee in July, 1854. Wyllie wrote: "Before the 6th of February last my idea of saving the King from sudden treason and rebellion was always to hoist the united flags of the United States, Great Britain, and France. But our dangers are internal, and a tripartite treaty would fail to keep the King permanently on his throne unless each of the powers were to consent to keep up a permanent garrison of, say, 100 men, in all 300."[3]

Once having arrived at the conclusion a protectorate was unsatisfactory, Wyllie, Judge Lee, and Elisha Allen in a thoroughly impersonal manner proceeded to weigh the consequences of a complete surrender of sovereignty. Wyllie concluded, and confided to Lee, that "colonial subjection to any European power would not be so favorable to the interests of the islands as their admission as a sovereign State of the United States." "There are no markets in Europe," he observed, "likely to afford such consumption of island produce at high prices as those of California and Oregon." Under necessity Wyllie affirmed he would advise the King to annex himself to Japan "if I thought that it would be best for him, the prince, the chiefs, the Hawaiians generally, and the future interests of the islands as an agricultural and mercantile state."

A further influence affecting the decision to appeal to the United States was the troubled external prospect for the kingdom. The difficult controversy with France was still continuing to plague Hawaii. Relations with the French Consul, M. Perrin, were uniformly unfriendly. Scarcely less serious was the threat to peace and security provided by the menace of California filibustering. From the days of the gold rush this had been a more or less constant fear in Hawaii. Late in 1851 filibustering rumors reached such proportions at Honolulu that Commissioner Severance and Captain Gardner of the U.S.S. *Vandalia*

---

[3] It is obvious, however, that the United States would never have accepted such an arrangement. See Kuykendall, 419f.; also Laura F. Judd, "A Suppressed Chapter of Hawaiian History," *Annual Report of the Hawaiian Historical Society*, 1903.

stationed at Honolulu were called upon to extend assurances of protection to the government. In fact, Captain Gardner had undertaken personally to train and develop a small defense force for the benefit of the kingdom.[4]

Rumors of threatened attack continued to excite the population of Honolulu, however, and the sympathetic tone of the California press toward such projects did little to ease the tension. By 1853 the problem had become so serious that Commisioner Severance had been impelled to call it to the attention of the State Department and warn that the United States should attempt to curb the filibusters. Their efforts, he feared, were forcing Hawaii into dependence upon British and French sources for protection.[5] At the arrival of Minister Gregg the outlook was still threatening, and the undisguised threat of local revolutionists to appeal to California for aid created further danger. By February in 1854, a major menace to the security of the kingdom had appeared.

The realization of these many dangers to the ability of Kamehameha III to maintain his throne was behind the annexation proposal. The order of the King to Wyllie, dated February 6, 1854, to open negotiations was based upon the assumption that "plans are on foot inimical to the peace" of Hawaii and "wholly subversive of our sovereignty" leading to a state of "anarchy." The projected negotiations were approved fully by the Cabinet.

The thoroughly emergency character of the proceedings, however, should be emphasized. As late as August, 1854, Wyllie was writing that should the King be "driven" to the "sacrifice" of his possessions it would be "from an insurrectionary spirit within, combinations to embarrass the administration, and render all good government impracticable. . . ." Hawaii, he asserted, under normal conditions possessed the resources and ability for political evolution justifying its preservation as an independent state. The "cupidity of a few selfish individuals seeking to obtain a speculative value to their lands, contracts &c" aided by California filibustering threats constituted the immediate danger.[6]

Commissioner Gregg was totally unprepared with any formal instructions to cope with the unexpected development. He immediately

---

[4] The *Report* of Foreign Minister Wyllie to the Legislature for 1852 and cited in *The Polynesian*, April 24, 1852, discussed the problem. See also Kuykendall, 408. 418-21.

[5] See dispatches of February 10, *Dispatches,* IV.

[6] Memorandum by Wyllie in Appendix, *Report Committee on Foreign Relations,* 1855, Elisha H. Allen Papers.

forwarded the proposal to the State Department, and accompanied it, significantly enough, with some hastily gathered information as to the sugar industry. He announced himself personally as "willing to enter upon such negotiations at any time," and urged the importance of the whole matter as a check to the possible presentation of a similar request to other powers should the United States delay.

While awaiting further instructions from the United States, Gregg endeavored to keep alive contacts with the Hawaiian Government. Two worries confronted him, anxious as he was to forward the union of Hawaii with his own country. In the first place, the threat of immediate revolt hung over the monarchy. Under date of March 4, 1854, Gregg reported to the State Department continued rumors of revolution, scheduled, according to current gossip, sometime within three weeks. The Committee of Thirteen, originally favorable to annexation as an alternative to revolution, had now reversed its order of preference. It was possible that filibusters might combine with this discontented group to precipitate the overthrow of the government before negotiations could be completed.

Another major difficulty was the undisguised opposition of the English, and especially the French Consul, to American control. Gregg expressed the belief that these individuals had gone so far as to work hand in hand with the revolutionary leaders in stimulating an uprising as a barrier to the schemes of the King. Early in March, M. Perrin approached Commissioner Gregg with a proposal that the three powers, the United States, Great Britain, and France, unite in a guarantee of the integrity of Hawaii. The proposition involved foreign control over the selection of the King, equal representation with the natives in the ministry, exclusion of missionaries from political positions, and the appointment of the native governors of the respective islands by the protectorate. This suggestion was quickly repudiated by Gregg.[7]

THE ANNEXATION DILEMMA

Judging from the instructions ultimately forwarded by Marcy, the possible annexation of the Islands was not a matter of surprise to Washington. Under date of April 4, 1854, following the Gregg communication of February 7 and prior to news of the Wyllie proposition, the State Department had proceeded to outline fully American policy toward possible annexation.[8]

---

[7] Gregg to Marcy, March 4, 1854, *Dispatches*, V. See also those of March 14, 15, and 25 for further information.
[8] Marcy to Gregg, FR, 1894, 121f. Pencil draft in Marcy Papers.

Marcy began his instructions by noting that the President was aware as early as the preceding autumn of the possible transfer of the Islands as a protectorate or property of a foreign power. While the policy of the United States was not to accelerate such a change, should it take place, it must bring the Islands toward the United States. It appeared from the late dispatches of the Commissioner, Marcy noted, that the Hawaiian Government had at last become convinced of its inability to sustain itself as an independent state. The possibility of annexation or a protectorate presented to the United States would find the latter preferring annexation. A protectorate, Marcy informed Gregg, was undesirable, as "this Government would take upon itself heavy and responsible duties for which it could hardly expect compensating advantages."

Should annexation be completed, it must involve the complete end of Hawaiian sovereignty and full control by the United States. A pecuniary allowance amounting to a possible $100,000 annuity "to be distributed in such manner as they would prefer" was suggested as a possible arrangement for the royal family and chiefs. Gregg was authorized to "provide in the amplest manner for the security of individual property . . . but the reservation of political rights or privileges in behalf of individuals would be inconsistent with the political power which it is proposed to vest in the United States."

Once such a treaty was completed, Marcy urged its ratification by Hawaii prior to transmittal to Washington. It was suggested further that one or more individuals accompany the document "clothed with full powers to assent to any modifications of it which may here be made." The importance of concluding the entire transaction as "expeditiously as possible" was emphasized. The need for this was explained by the Secretary in asserting, "I have good reason to believe that some of the leading powers of Europe would be very unwilling to see the Sandwich Islands become a part of the United States, and, if the opportunity occurred, would endeavor to defeat any negotiation for that purpose."

ANGLO-FRENCH OPPOSITION TO ANNEXATION

In calling the attention of Gregg to this fact, Marcy touched upon one of the most significant angles of the Hawaiian problem—the growing entente of France and Great Britain in opposition to further American territorial expansion. The unrest of these powers at the growing imperialism of the United States was not new. The story of the threat-

ened coalition against American designs upon Texas and Cuba during
the manifest destiny upsurge of the forties is well known. The later
diplomacy of the Whig administration had calmed this feeling, but it
was now revived with the emergence of a more ambitious program.

The obvious intent of President Pierce to take whatever steps were
necessary to fulfill the destiny of the United States in Cuba or elsewhere had dashed to the ground the hopes of checking rampant American imperialism by agreement. The rise of the ambitious Louis Napoleon
in France, and the union of that power with Great Britain in the diplomacy of the Near East against Russia, paved the way for a closer
Anglo-French cooperation in proposals for the throttling of American
ambitions. There was objection equally to American attempts to control
either Cuba or Hawaii. Marcy had placed them upon equal footing from
the standpoint of the national interest of the United States.

There is abundant evidence of the practical application of this growing Anglo-French accord. Writing to Lord Clarendon, British Foreign
Secretary, in a private communication dated February 7, 1853, the
British Minister at Washington, John F. T. Crampton, commented
upon the "aggression and domination of the United States in every
part of this Continent" and the necessity of considering ways and means
of checking it. The expansion of California and the expedition of Perry
to Japan were evidence of the growing Pacific power of the United
States on such a scale that the Sandwich Islands "will live more exposed
to a coup de main than even Cuba." The possibility of association with
France, and even Russia, to maintain the neutrality of the Islands was
suggested.[9]

On May 3, 1853, the American Minister to England was reporting
from London unrest as to the growing imperialism of the United
States.[10] The new Minister, James Buchanan, upon his arrival noted
likewise the hostile spirit of the British aristocracy, though he felt that
the masses remained friendly to the United States.

By 1854 the accord between France and Great Britain had grown
closer. On January 31, 1854, Lord Clarendon declared before Parliament the "happy accord and good understanding" between the two
powers, which had been so extended that "there is no portion of the
two hemispheres with regard to which the policy of the two countries,
however heretofore antagonistic, is not now in entire harmony."[11] That

---

[9] Richard W. Van Alstyne (ed.), "Documents on Anglo-American Relations, 1853-57," *American Historical Review*, XXXVIII.

[10] Ingersoll to Marcy, *Dispatches, Great Britain*, LXIV.

[11] Hansard, *Parliamentary Debates*, third series, CXXX, 43.

this unity was becoming more and more in evidence as to American policy is indicated by the declaration of Marcy in March, 1854, regarding the two powers, "They have warned us against forming any other than the ordinary diplomatic convention with the Sandwich Islands."[12]

Buchanan at London was quick to note the united front, and informed Marcy October 3, "United, the two powers believe they can regulate the world." American correspondence from European sources began to indicate the appearance of what might be regarded almost as a coalition against the United States.[13] In London, Aberdeen was expressing his desire to enlist France "on our side" in the Hawaiian affair and another correspondent of Clarendon declared, "We are fast drifting into a War with the U. States."[14] From Washington the British Minister informed his government in September of his belief that it was the "fixed design" of Pierce to annex Hawaii. The situation was indeed ominous.

Marcy, however, was proceeding cautiously. In December, 1853, he had requested that Buchanan in London should sound out just how far the French and British Ministers at Washington reflected the serious intentions of their governments. By January 28, 1854, Buchanan was able to reply that he did not expect the idea of annexation would be well received by Great Britain and still less so by France. The consent of either, he wrote, was "out of the question." Whether the two powers would contest acquisitions to the point of war was impossible to determine. Buchanan himself, however, attempted to throw cold water on the idea of Hawaiian annexation. "These Islands, we can never, at least not for many years, defend against a strong maritime power," he pointed out. "They are too small to contain a sufficient American population for this purpose," he continued, and they "will be the only portion of our territory which we shall not be able to defend against all assailants." The position of Hanover in relation to Great Britain was cited by the Minister as an indication of the possible pitfalls to be encountered.[15]

By March 11 Marcy was again addressing his confidant and advisor on European affairs, Minister Buchanan, pointing out recent develop-

---

[12] Marcy to Spence, March 20, 1854, Marcy Papers. Marcy had written confidentially to Buchanan the preceding December 4 that the French and British representatives at Washington appeared to be a "little uneasy" about the United States and Hawaii. See letter in Buchanan Papers, Historical Society of Pennsylvania.

[13] Cf. *Harper's New Monthly Magazine,* June, 1854, "Editor's Easy Chair," for comment.

[14] Van Alstyne, *op. cit.*

[15] Letter in Marcy Papers. Buchanan pointed out that Cuba did not possess this disadvantage.

ments regarding Hawaii. "The last advices from the Sandwich Islands," he wrote, "render it probable that the Hawaiian rulers with the very general acquiescence of the people will tender the sovereignty of that country to the United States." "Though this Government has done nothing to precipitate such an event," declared the Secretary truthfully, "yet when it perceives that the sovereign power cannot be any longer maintained in the feeble hands of the native rulers, and that the people desire to come under our control, the United States will probably regard it to be their duty to accept the sovereignty of these Islands, though the act should be antagonistic to the schemes of the world-embracing policy of England and France." Even more bluntly, Marcy emphasized that should the recently publicized Anglo-French accord have as an objective, "as I apprehend it is, to prevent our acquisition of these Islands with the consent of the rulers and the people, there is reason to apprehend that a collision before long may arise on the subject between these powers and this country."[16]

An immediate result of the growing American suspicion of Anglo-French policy was an effort to lean strongly toward the support of the Russian cause during the Crimean struggle. Marcy privately expressed his fears to Buchanan that a decisive victory over that power by the Allies would strengthen their anti-American policy and increase confidence in their ability to check American ambitions. Typical of this desire was the vigorous rebuke administered by Marcy to the American Minister to Turkey, Mr. Spence, who had delivered a widely publicized speech critical of Russian imperialism. Spence was informed that "in regard to our international relations no nation on the face of the earth has used us more fairly than the Russian, & with her we have no cause of misunderstanding, and she has never manifested, & I presume she has never felt any jealousy in regard to the present or the future expansion of the U. States." Such was not the case in regard to the allied enemies of Russia, however, and Marcy called attention particularly to their policy relating to American-Hawaiian interests.[17] Definite overtures toward a close understanding with Russia

---

[16] Marcy Papers. Marcy attributed the "insolent" attitude of Spain in regard to Cuba as being influenced by the French and English policy. The rising American antagonism is reflected further in a communication to Marcy from Theodore Sedgwick, March 31. Sedgwick wrote that "it is plain that they [the American people] are beginning to feel that this alliance between the Aristocracy of England & Napoleon *cannot* be in the nature of things an alliance for Liberty or Progress, and that a strong Anglo-French Combination of forces must be hostile to the greatness of this country."

[17] Letter in Marcy Papers. As early as 1851 Webster had offered to Russia the services of the American Commissioner at Honolulu to represent its interests. The assumption as to Russian friendship made by Marcy, however, was not too well

in the Pacific were forthcoming, and in the autumn of 1854 the Russian Minister at Washington was encouraged to provide any suggestions for closer relations between the two powers.[18]

From Great Britain, Buchanan continued to advise against any Hawaiian adventure. On April 18, 1854, he cautioned, "Let us stick to Cuba & not for the present spread ourselves out too far." Shortly before, he had been unable to advise the Department of any satisfactory reply as to British attitude. By October, however, he was able to present the results of an interview with Clarendon. The latter, reported Buchanan, had expressed grave concern over the proposed annexation, and had observed that he "supposed it was perfectly understood among the Commercial Powers chiefly interested, that these Islands were to remain independent. . . ." Buchanan once more expressed personal opposition under "present circumstances" as it "may result in serious consequences."[19]

The British, the Minister pointed out, would hardly go to war with the United States and were anxious to preserve the peace despite much bluster which might indicate the contrary. As to Louis Napoleon he was not so confident. "As a despot, he regards the existence and the rapid advance of the Republic of the United States as a standing censure upon his usurpation and tyranny," wrote Buchanan. "He is bold, wary and unscrupulous, knowing that our naval force is comparatively insignificant . . . , it would be altogether in consistency with his character to attempt to humble us by one of those bold strokes in which he so much delights, and to declare that we shall not have the Sandwich Islands." While Cuba might be worth the risk of war, the Islands were certainly not so important as to justify the chance, was the reiterated opinion of Buchanan.[20]

THE ANNEXATION TREATY

While these international complications were being aired, the negotiations to actually attach the Islands to the United States were making slow progress. Having received full authority from Washington to pro-

---

founded. Minister Crampton informed London in 1853 that "a sort of semi-overture by a recently appointed Russian agent to the Sandwich Islands as to the expediency of their joining us and France in an agreement to maintain their neutrality" had been made to him. See Van Alstyne, *op. cit.*

[18] Frank A. Golder, "Russian-American Relations During the Crimean War," *American Historical Review*, XXXI, discusses the matter.

[19] Buchanan to Marcy, *Dispatches, Great Britain,* LXV.

[20] While Marcy endeavored to secure similar reports from Minister Mason at Paris, the latter suffered from ill health and possessed a pro-French bias. He continued to insist that Louis Napoleon was friendly to the United States. Buchanan became chief foreign advisor to the State Department during the Marcy regime.

ceed, Gregg acquainted Wyllie with the fact, and the latter promised to inform the Cabinet. By May 25, 1854, Gregg was able to notify the State Department that everything was moving with promise. The King was most positive in his support of annexation, and popular opinion seemed increasingly to approve. Efforts of the British and French agents to checkmate the proposition were proving futile.[21]

Though the Commissioner and Wyllie were able quickly to establish the basis for the proposed treaty despite important differences as to whether Hawaii should enter the American union as a state or territory, the final ratification was a matter of genuine difficulty.[22] Despite urging from Gregg, who feared more and more the consequences of delay, it was not until August that the Cabinet was agreed on the project. Then the combined opposition of Prince Liholiho and the indisposition of the King produced a stumbling block to final completion which eventually proved insurmountable.[23]

On August 9 Gregg reported to Washington that the "peculiar condition" of the King was such as to forbid his passing upon provisions of the treaty. The two principal difficulties encountered in the negotiations had been the "inveterate prejudice of the Hawaiian authorities against a territorial form of Gov't, which could not be overcome," and the problem of financial arrangements. Nothing short of $300,000 in annuities, or three times the sum suggested by Marcy, was demanded by the Hawaiians. The government itself was resting on a "volcano" and further delay was dangerous.[24]

By early September the Commissioner was able to inform his superiors that the King had been presented with a draft of the treaty, and it had been translated and explained, but that he had expressed the desire to consult a few of his chiefs in regard to it. Since that time he had been unable to transact any further business. Terms of the tentative treaty had been settled by August 19, and a draft was forwarded to Washington on September 15.

The document involved a complete transfer of the kingdom and its public property to the United States, to be incorporated into the Union as a state with perfect equality as to all other states. The King, his

---

[21] Gregg to Marcy, *Dispatches*, V. Gregg had already negotiated informally with Wyllie.

[22] Protocols and correspondence related to the negotiations may be found in FR, 1894, 616-30.

[23] As early as July, Wyllie had commented to Judge Lee that the Prince was "keeping out of the way" and had failed to return the treaty draft submitted to him.

[24] Gregg to Marcy, *Dispatches*, V. The Hawaiians felt that their rights would be more definitely established under statehood.

chiefs, and subjects were guaranteed "existing personal and private rights—civil, political, and religious—to the utmost extent that is possible under the Federal Constitution" and "all the rights and privileges of citizens of the United States, on terms of perfect equality in all respects, with other American citizens."

Laws and engagements of the existing Hawaiian Government were to be preserved so far as compatible with the Constitution and laws of the United States, while full control of public lands was vested in Congress as part of the public domain. A $300,000 grant in annuities to be distributed by the King at his own wish to the various claimants upon his bounty was provided. An important feature of the arrangement was the inclusion of a secret separate article, against the opposition of Gregg, providing for the provisional declaration of annexation prior to ratification, and establishing an American protectorate pending that action. Should the treaty finally fail of ratification, the original free status of the Islands would be restored.[25]

MANIFEST DESTINY CHECKMATED

News of the progress of the negotiation produced renewed outbursts of activity against it by other foreign interests at Honolulu. Especially vigorous was the action of British Consul General Miller, who appeared before the King and delivered on September 18 an hour long harangue against annexation. While not fully aware of the contents of the treaty, Miller protested the whole movement as the work of "American merchants, landed proprietors, and other citizens of the United States." The attention of Kamehameha was called to the Franco-British agreement of 1843 as an obstacle to any surrender of Hawaiian independence. Playing upon the fears of the natives, Miller called attention to the ruthless treatment of original inhabitants resulting from the American occupation of California. He ended by informing the King that should his independence actually be threatened, the protection of the British flag was authorized. The King was unimpressed by the presentation.[26]

The best efforts of Gregg were not able to speed the final approval of the treaty. The deliberate tardiness of the Prince delayed any further

---

[25] Copy of completed document in FR, 1894, 127f. See also account of negotiations prepared by W. D. Alexander for Commissioner Blount, *ibid.*, 607f.

[26] Comment by Gregg and a newspaper account of the interview are to be found in the State Department materials previously cited. The published dispatch of Gregg under date of October 2, 1854, may be found in FR, 1894, 129f. In early December the King proclaimed an acceptance of aid in support of his sovereignty proferred by representatives of the United States, Great Britain, and France. Gregg objected to this as a ruse and falsification.

consideration through September. Early in October, the Commissioner reported hopes that the matter would soon be disposed of, though they proved unfounded. The policy of delay so assiduously pursued by Alexander since July was successful. On December 15 Kamehameha III died, and with his demise was buried, it shortly appeared, all hope for annexation. The new monarch, Kamehameha IV, immediately ascended the throne. Twenty years of age, he was well educated and possessed of a keen intelligence, combined with a strong conviction of the necessity for preserving so far as possible the personal absolutism of the ancient Hawaiian rulers, and above all Hawaiian independence.

December 29, Gregg was forced regretfully to advise the State Department of his opinion that the new monarch "will be disposed to preserve, if possible, the separate independence of the Hawaiian Islands." A probable return to the earlier program of Wyllie in attempting to secure some joint agreement guaranteeing Hawaiian independence by the major powers was forecast. The fears of Gregg were fully justified, and late in January, 1855, the Commissioner was informed officially that the annexation negotiations were at an end. In their place the new King suggested that the United States, France, and Great Britain would be approached in the order named for guarantees of Island independence. In the event of failure to secure such an arrangement with the United States, Hawaii would proceed to approach the other powers.

By this strategy it is evident that Kamehameha IV hoped to strangle the annexation movement and to place the United States in such a position as to force a guarantee of independence which would forestall its resumption. This effort was checked quickly by Gregg, who replied that the United States would never consent to a joint protectorate, and that any negotiations regarding such a project should be confined to that power.[27]

WHY ANNEXATION FAILED

Informing the State Department of the collapse of annexation, Gregg offered an explanation for the failure of the treaty. The key to the situation he found in the person of Prince Alexander Liholiho, who, "so long as the circumstances held out the hope of a perpetuity of his dynasty," refused to complete the negotiations. A further factor of importance he believed to have been the publicity attendant upon the transaction in the American press, which was calculated "to create alarm and apprehension" upon the part of the natives. They came to dread,

---

[27] Gregg to Marcy, January 24, 1855, *Dispatches*, VI.

declared Gregg, a connection "which even in the United States was regarded as disastrous to their race." A third influence he attributed rather cryptically and without explanation to the opposition of the American consular office "from motives of a pecuniary nature."

It is important to examine briefly the validity of this analysis. Undoubtedly, the Commissioner hit upon the major cause for the failure of annexation in citing the attitude of Prince Alexander and the native population. While a large percentage of the natives were more or less passive in their attitude during the whole crisis, the leaders appear to have been alarmed genuinely at the prospect of annexation. It was not until early August, 1854, that the general public became fully aware of the actual moves of the King toward abrogation of his sovereignty. This had prompted immediate introduction of a resolution in the Legislature by a native member requesting information from the government.

Even prior to this date, however, the native press had been engaged in an attack upon the idea of annexation. The principal argument was racial, stressing the position of the negro in the United States as representative of American contempt for the colored races. Annexation, it affirmed, would mean virtual enslavement for native Hawaiians and the inevitable loss of their lands and social and political liberties. Later mass meetings and addresses of native political leaders continued this argument. The prospective influx of American population from California, and the well-known character of the ruthless pioneer, gave increased weight to such arguments.[28] It seems clear that the fears of the native race for its existence constituted the principal opposition to annexation from within Hawaii, and that Prince Alexander well represented the popular reaction to the proposal.

As to the support for the project and the attitude of the foreign population, the evidence is somewhat confused. For the most part, it can be concluded that the missionary element by 1854 had come to support annexation, mainly because of the belief that the degeneracy of the native monarchy was so complete as to defy efforts at regeneration.[29] Gregg constantly insisted that the American mercantile and planting interests were firmly behind annexation, and this view was endorsed by the British Consul General Miller in his harangue to the King.

---

[28] The correspondence of Gregg through the period contains many translations from native newspapers and other references to the nationalist propaganda. It was asserted by Gregg and others that Prince Alexander personally felt keenly the nature of the color line as drawn in the United States from experiences while travelling.

[29] Letters by the Rev. Richard Armstrong confirm this view. See also earlier discussion of missionary viewpoint.

At the same time, the Commissioner admitted that the Committee of Thirteen, which he referred to as made up largely of Americans, was not consistently in favor of annexation during the period of the treaty negotiations. In fact, it was this group which kept alive the threat of revolution and the establishment of an independent republic. This represented a reversal of opinion from January, 1854, when the Committee had supported annexation. Two explanations for this were offered by Gregg on two different occasions, and they seem logical.

In the first place, many Americans less heavily interested in property and less conservative believed their own opportunities for political place and power would be greater under a republic of their own making and direction than if the Islands were absorbed into the United States. Opportunities for later advantage were apt to be greater than under American control.

Secondly, the feeling of some at least was that the chance for the fuller economic exploitation of Hawaii would be hampered by annexation. American laws and government would not permit, perhaps, the free monopoly of land and resources and the economic advantages to be secured from native rule or a republic, independent and under the control of the exploiting class. That this view was entertained by a fair number of even the commercial and planting class is indicated, despite some broad generalizations to the contrary. In general, there existed much diversity of opinion over the advisability of annexation.[30]

The question arises naturally as to whether annexation could have been consummated in the United States, had the Hawaiian negotiations been completed. While frequently a futile type of analysis, certain aspects of the treaty are brought into focus by brief attention to this problem. The probability is that ratification of the completed treaty by the United States could not have been accomplished. Gregg himself fully appreciated this fact when submitting the text in September, 1854. He had been forced to go beyond his explicit instructions from the State Department on two important points. First, and least important, was the greatly increased financial allowance. Second, and of real moment, were the provisions for admitting Hawaii with full statehood.

This article was the result of insistent demands upon the part of all Hawaiians connected with the negotiation. It has been attributed frequently to a clever ruse of the British interests at Honolulu to defeat the treaty. There is no ground for this belief. Gregg, always quick to

---

[30] Gregg to Marcy, August 8, 1854, *Dispatches,* V, especially analyzes the differing views. During the disturbance of 1851, Commissioner Severance had reported the opposition of the importing community to annexation due to fears of American tariffs.

detect a foreign intrigue operating against him, makes no mention of such an endeavor. The correspondence of Wyllie and Judge Lee, previously cited in other connections, provides the clue to the situation.

Both the American advisors of the King, and those high in native councils, were agreed that statehood was the only means by which Hawaiians could secure that full guarantee of their rights and liberties under American control which they desired. Territorial status would have meant placing Hawaii under the capricious control of Congress with no guarantee as to the future. The demand for full statehood was a natural and almost inevitable product of the conditions producing the entire annexation movement. The surrender of Hawaiian sovereignty under any other conditions was impossible at the time.

In the United States, however, this demand operated as an inevitable barrier to the success of the proposed treaty. The grant of such advanced status to a territorial acquisition would have been contrary to all precedent and, in the midst of the intense political struggle of the times, a threat even to the equilibrium of the Union. Marcy was quick to note this, as was also President Pierce, and January 31, 1855, Gregg was informed that a treaty with such a provision could not be submitted to the Senate. "There are other objections to the draft which you have sent to the Department, though less formidable . . . ," wrote Marcy. The most important of these, he indicated, was the large financial remuneration demanded.

Gregg was instructed to inform the Hawaiian Government that any treaty departing very far from his instructions of April, 1854, would prove unsatisfactory. The general assurance that the United States, should it acquire the Islands, would actively promote their "growth and prosperity" was deemed sufficient consideration. By the time Gregg received these instructions, the negotiations were dead, and the possibility of any further revision to meet the administration objections was out of the question. In view of the general sentiment prevailing upon the part of the native population, increasingly hostile to annexation, and the indicated disposition of the advisors of the King, it is doubtful whether any satisfactory modification of the treaty could have been completed. The time was not yet ripe for the annexation of Hawaii.[31]

---

[31] The question arises as to the effect known Anglo-French opposition and the advice of Buchanan may have had. It is questionable whether it entered into the problem at the time. The treaty was so undesirable as to preclude its consideration, even had no other factors been involved. Marcy was definite in his opinion that the demand for immediate statehood would not have been acceptable. Vigorous protest from England against annexation may have had some influence, but was not fundamental.

One purpose had been served, however, by the agitation—the arousing of further American interest in Hawaii. The increasing economic importance of the Islands had come to be recognized, and now the desirability of their control appeared to nearly all. De Bow in his *Review* for January, 1855, declared: "Whether these islands shall ever be American or not, nature has clearly marked them out as prominent points in the pathway of modern commerce. . . . We believe they will be annexed." Further Americanization of the Islands and an influx of American capital and population were predicted.

While the storm of sectional conflict in the United States was gathering with increasing rapidity, it was impossible to center for long the attention of the general public upon the fortunes of tiny and far distant Hawaii. Upon the Pacific coast the matter was of more immediate moment, and the continuance of remnants of the manifest destiny and filibustering spirit of a few years earlier brought vigorous support for annexation. The vigorous expressions of opinion there were so ill advised indeed as to be regarded by Gregg as militating against better relations by frightening the Hawaiians. Scattered comment elsewhere was brief in nature, but generally sympathetic to a closer American relationship with Hawaii.[32]

ANOTHER RECIPROCITY PROPOSAL

Within Hawaii, the native reaction against annexation and the views of the new King combined to threaten temporarily the growing drift of the Islands toward American sources of support and influence, which had developed so rapidly following the appointment of Commissioner Severance. The very nature of the circumstances connected with the defeat of the treaty negotiation created a strong anti-American reaction. This was reflected temporarily in a tendency to rely more heavily upon British support, as well as that of France. Gregg felt this keenly, and reflected despondently in a report to the State Department January 24, 1855, that there was "too much deference to England and France" upon the part of the new ruler.

This did not persist for long, however, and no more significant tribute to the permanent foundations of American civilization in Hawaii is observable than the manner in which a hostile ruler was swung more and more into channels of policy relying upon the United States. The new King retained the old advisors of Kamehameha III and proved shortly a supporter of "a mild and liberal" governmental policy. He

---

[32] *New York Tribune,* July 20, 1854, contains typical comment mildly favorable.

was keenly conscious likewise of the necessity for national unity and economic progress. None of these objectives could be forwarded by pursuing a policy of deliberate anti-Americanism. The King was led almost inevitably, therefore, into a revival of the old Wyllie scheme for commercial reciprocity with the United States. To the forwarding of such an engagement, Hawaii shortly turned its best energies.

March 12, 1855, Commissioner Gregg informed the State Department that he had been addressed by the Minister of Foreign Affairs calling attention to the act of March, 1852, of the Hawaiian Legislature looking to reciprocal trade relations with the United States. Promising to forward the proposal to Washington, Gregg had expressed himself as favorable to such a measure as "mutually advantageous." To the Department, he pointed out that the Hawaiian Government was moved to the proposal because the sugar planters demanded relief from the American tariff. Could Hawaii obtain it by negotiation, a contribution to political quiet at home would have been made.

Gregg was sincere, undoubtedly, in his expression of sympathy for the proposal. He was, however, skeptical of its ability to preserve the decaying monarchy. American interests would best be preserved, he affirmed, by an independent and "enlightened, wise and impartial Government" for Hawaii. "But," he continued, "I cannot help being incredulous as to the ability of the Hawaiians to maintain their separate nationality for any great length of time." True policy, declared Gregg, dictated that "we should sustain the efforts to maintain Hawaiian nationality." To this end, reciprocal trade relations would make a significant contribution.[33] March 14, 1855, Gregg was able to report the appointment of Chief Justice William L. Lee as Envoy Extraordinary to the United States to conduct reciprocity negotiations. Hawaii, he informed the Department, attached "great importance" to the proposal. Lee arrived at San Francisco April 16 and found strong support for his mission, especially from California's Senator Gwin.

Once in Washington, which he reached July 10, Judge Lee found the situation a complicated one. There is no doubt as to the full support of the proposition by Marcy. The President, however, possessed constitutional scruples. In a dispatch prepared for Gregg, but marked as not sent, under date of May 17, the Secretary had explained that President Pierce pointed out the constitutional requirement that all duties be uniform. Furthermore, the President suggested that under a reciprocal agreement with Hawaii if sugar entered Pacific ports free of duty

---

[33] Gregg to Marcy, *Dispatches,* VI.

from Hawaii it must likewise be permitted to enter Atlantic ports. This would involve existing trade relations with Spanish-American countries and "would probably impart such a stimulus to the production of sugar in those States to glut our market and perhaps ruin the sugar planter of this country." Thus did Pierce single out the objection which for two decades was to stand as the principal barrier to a reciprocity treaty.[34]

Despite the presidential view, the negotiation of a treaty was undertaken, and conversations began on July 12. Ardent support for the proposal appeared from the Pacific coast. Senator Gwin urged it upon Marcy as of the utmost importance economically to his section, minimizing possible dangers to any other region. Louisiana, he pointed out, could not dispose of its sugar at a profit in California regardless of competition, due to transportation costs, and could lose nothing from reciprocity. Another correspondent from the same area extolled the project as worth more than two Pacific Railroads to the development of the coast.[35]

In a communication from the King, it was emphasized that Kamehameha IV sought the "best means of securing the permanent safety of my Kingdom. . . ." Under date of July 13, Lee submitted to Marcy that: "The Government of the Hawaiian Islands propose to admit all flour, fish, coal, lumber, staves and heading, the produce of the United States, into all the ports of the Hawaiian Islands free of duty; provided the Government of the United States will admit sugar, syrup of sugar, molasses and coffee, the produce of the Hawaiian Islands, into the ports of the United States on the same terms."[36] Lee also was desirous of securing American participation in a neutrality convention with Great Britain, France, and Russia.

By July 20 the details of the treaty had been worked out. As finally drafted, it was considerably different from the original proposals of Judge Lee, or the counterproposals of Marcy for a very general treaty to avoid constitutional objections. Under it the free list admitted by the United States included "muscavado, brown, clayed, and all other unrefined sugars," a much narrower and more careful designation than suggested by Lee, syrups of sugar and molasses, coffee, arrowroot, live stock, unmanufactured cotton, seeds and unpreserved vegetables, undried fruits, poultry and eggs, plants, pelts, unmanufactured wool, undressed furs and skins, rags, butter, and tallow. The Hawaiian free

---

[34] Draft in *Instructions*, II.
[35] Correspondence in Marcy Papers, dated April 20 and 30.
[36] *Notes, Hawaii*, II. Before "sugar" was written in pencil "unrefined."

list included flour of wheat, fish, coal, lumber, timber, unmanufactured cotton, and the items enumerated on the above American free list, representing a gain for the United States.[37] At the suggestion of Marcy, the treaty was for a seven year period subject to renewal.

NEW PLEDGES TO PROTECT HAWAII

An important by-product of the treaty negotiation was the establishment of a definite understanding as to American protective policy relating to Hawaii. The United States again sidestepped Hawaii's desire for a joint declaration on independence in favor of a unilateral statement. Lee called the attention of Marcy to the dominance of the American interests in Hawaii and their dependence upon the stability of its government. An American naval force devoted to protection of Hawaii from foreign aggression or filibustering activities was urged. Some definite protective treaty guarantees were desired, an objective Hawaii had long sought. Gregg, however, like his predecessors, avoided this, and presented Hawaii on September 21 with a declaration of American interest in the prosperity and independence of Hawaii, and its concern at "any attempt upon the part of any power, and especially any European maritime power, to disturb the repose or interfere with the Security of the Hawaiian Government." A specific pledge on the part of the United States to use all of its powers to prevent the organization or fitting out of filibustering expeditions, and to defeat any unlawful attacks upon Hawaii was provided in the same communications.[38] This was in answer to repeated Hawaiian fears of California filibustering.

The question arises as to the purpose of negotiating a treaty, when skepticism regarding its constitutional validity was so general. The answer seems to be that those supporting the measure regarded it as of vital importance in contributing to the Americanization of Hawaii. Thus Senator Gwin emphasized its value, not only to his section, but to influences which would "Americanize" the Islands and "smooth the way" for eventual annexation. Indeed, Lee himself seems to have entertained much the same view, and under date of April 30, 1856, praised the treaty's value to the American interests in the Islands which were "fast gaining ground."[39]

---

[37] Full text of treaty in *Senate Documents*, 56 Cong., 2 sess., XXIV. See also Osborne E. Hooley, "Hawaiian Negotiations for Reciprocity, 1855-1857," *Pacific Historical Review*, VII.

[38] *Notes to Hawaii*, I. A major reason for opposition to a protective declaration in combination with other powers was the fear of the Pierce administration that a similar convention might be demanded for Cuba by France and Great Britain.

[39] *Notes, Hawaii*, II.

Commissioner Gregg likewise greeted the treaty with ardent enthusiasm, and declared its effect would be "to secure, beyond question, the
preponderance of American influence in Hawaiian affairs." The idea
of reciprocity was satisfying to two schools of thought. Many favorable
to annexation regarded it as a further step in that direction, though
this view was by no means unanimous. Those opposing annexation
sought through reciprocity to strengthen the economic life of Hawaii
and secure the foundations of prosperity and continued independence
under American protection.

HAWAIIAN REACTIONS TO RECIPROCITY

While the treaty negotiation did not attract any particular attention
in the United States, there is no doubt of the enthusiasm of its reception in Hawaii. The completed text arrived at Honolulu with Judge
Lee September 16, 1855, and was approved the following day by King
and Council. The King himself was reported by Gregg as "highly
pleased." In a rather surprising declaration, he hailed the fact that,
"Under this treaty we may expect to see American citizens raising the
produce which American ships will carry to an American market."[40]

The same jubilation was evident also in the statement of the Minister
of Foreign Affairs, who affirmed, "Its effect is to place our agriculture
in the most advantageous position toward our nearest and best markets
—to enlarge our commerce by increasing our means of paying for what
goods we import—to afford profitable employment for capital and labor
throughout the islands—to encourage the industry of the natives and
the settlement amongst us of industrious foreigners of all nations."[41]

RECIPROCITY AGAIN DEFEATED

The rejoicing, however, was short lived. The prompt acceptance of
the new arrangement by Hawaii was not equalled in the United States.
Submitted to the Senate on December 27, 1855, action on the treaty
was delayed due to the pressure of other matters. By April, 1856, Judge
Lee was impelled to express his concern to Marcy at the failure of the
United States to ratify, while Gregg likewise pointed out the "great
anxiety" occasioned by the delay. In September Lee wrote again of
the "great satisfaction" with which the treaty had been accepted in
Hawaii and on the Pacific coast. He pointed out that it would operate

---

[40] *The Polynesian,* September 22, 1855. See also letters of Elisha Allen in Allen
Papers emphasizing elation of the King and cabinet.
[41] See *Report* for 1856, enclosed Gregg to Marcy, June 30, 1856, *Dispatches,* VII.

more favorably to the United States than to Hawaii, and that unrest was being created by failure of the Senate to act. "Most of the commercial & agricultural interests are in the hands of citizens of the U. S. & as I told you before, any favor extended by the U. S. is simply a bounty to Americans," he wrote.[42] The Hawaiian Government began to express official concern as well. This was increased as grumblings of discontent emerged once more with declining economic fortunes, and threats of revolution became current rumor.

In order to expedite matters, Elisha H. Allen, now Hawaiian Minister of Finance, had been dispatched to the United States in May, 1856, arriving in August, to undertake the explanation of the Hawaiian cause. Allen became a lobbyist for the treaty and attempted to direct a program of propaganda in its favor, working mainly with the Pacific coast press and members of Congress. To Allen, Marcy expressed his own support. Writing August 30 the Secretary declared, "I regard the conclusion of the Treaty as a measure of great importance to both countries, and should be much pleased to have your aid in accomplishing that object." The "considerable opposition" in the Senate was noted by Marcy, and he frankly pointed out that the fate of the treaty "is now doubtful."[43]

Allen was quick to respond to the invitation for aid. October 1 he replied to Marcy, agreeing upon the importance of the treaty and its early ratification. "It is very important for the West Coast of the United States as well as to the Islands," he wrote. Allen emphasized that he believed it to be his "sacred duty" to "render you all the aid in my power" to aid in its passage, and suggested possible changes to meet objections.[44] Marcy did not feel this to be necessary. By this date, however, the prospect for passage at that session of Congress was gone. The treaty had been considered briefly in the Senate on August 16 and 21, 1856, and tabled without opposition, even its strongest proponents fearing to bring the matter to test.[45] Disappointed, Allen left for his old home in Maine with plans to return at the next session and consider possible revisions of the measure in order to advance its chances of passage. Belief that as a revenue measure the treaty should be considered by the House of Representatives, fear in Congress of its effect on the most favored nation clause in other trade treaties, and vigorous opposition of American wool and sugar interests were felt to be the chief obstacles to its success.

[42] Correspondence in *Notes, Hawaii,* II.
[43] *Notes to Hawaii,* I.
[44] *Notes Hawaii,* II. See also several letters in Allen Papers.
[45] *Senate Executive Journal,* X, 147, 155.

Hopes for future favorable consideration were doomed to disappointment. At the next session, the treaty was again considered on February 18 and 20, 1857, and tabled by a vote of 27 to 26. On March 13 it was again considered. Despite the fact that the Senate Committee on Foreign Relations had reported adversely on the measure, a motion to table was voted down by 30 to 14. The hopes of those sponsoring the negotiation were defeated, however, by the rush of activity at the close of the session which deferred consideration until it was lost in the usual scramble to adjourn characteristic of the closing days of Congress.

FACTORS BEHIND THE DEFEAT OF RECIPROCITY

The defeat of the treaty, according to the best evidence available, was due in the main to two factors. Considerable emphasis must be placed upon the opposition of the Louisiana sugar planters. It is significant that Senator Benjamin of that state was the principal leader of the opposition. Hawaiian accounts of the downfall of the treaty generally accepted this view.[46] Press accounts in the United States agree that the proposal possessed excellent prospects for passage until considerations of time forced it from the "must" list of the Senate at the closing sessions through a threat of filibuster from those friendly to the Southern sugar interests.[47]

This is further borne out by the fact that of fourteen votes to table the measure on March 13, four were from Louisiana and North Carolina and five from neighboring states. Knowledge of the fact that the rice industry of Hawaii might be stimulated by reciprocity gave further aid to the sugar planters. The conclusion of Secretary of State Seward ten years later that the treaty was defeated "mostly . . . from an apprehension on the part of Senators from Louisiana that the sugar from those islands would interfere with the demand for sugar, the product of that State," seems accurate.

It is important, however, not to overlook another vital consideration against the success of reciprocity in 1857, which remained a stumbling block for nearly two decades. Writing to Minister of Foreign Affairs Wyllie under date of February 4, 1857, Elisha Allen declared, "In relation to the treaty I can only say that the serious obstacle seems to be the most favored nation clause in other treaties."[48] Coming from

---

[46] Cf. *The Polynesian*, May 9 and June 6, 1857.
[47] Cf. *Washington Star*, March 14, 1857; *San Francisco Evening Bulletin*, April 13, 1857.
[48] Cited, *Report of the Special Committee on Foreign Relations to the Hawaiian Assembly*, 1878. Enclosure Comly to Evarts, August 5, 1878, *Dispatches*, XVIII. See also *Polynesian, op. cit.*

the special agent of Hawaii working to forward the treaty, this statement must be given weight. Bulwarking it, there must be kept in mind the original objection of President Pierce on the same ground. The prospect that other nations with sugar producing colonies would demand equal privileges on the American market was not a pleasing one. Without this, it is quite possible that the minority interest represented by the Southern planters would not have met with so much success in shoving the measure into the background.

Equally important, perhaps, was the general apathy of the American public resulting in an inability to establish any general support behind the treaty. The distance of the Islands from the United States, their lack of economic contacts outside the Pacific coast, and complications of domestic politics were sufficient to account for this. The measure itself attracted no apparent support outside the Pacific coast, and even there its demise in 1857 was regarded as no special disaster.[49] Lacking any marked public interest to support them, the proponents of reciprocity were unable to muster the pressure to overcome the formidable obstacles against the treaty which have been mentioned.

A DECADE OF DRIFT

The end of the reciprocity negotiations marked the close of any further significant diplomatic developments until the post-Civil War period. Within the Islands, it was a severe blow to the hoped for expansion of American economic interests. A period of some tension and political unrest was the result. Some artificial stimulus was provided the economic life of the Islands by the destruction of the sugar industry in the southern United States through war. This acted to expand the market for Hawaiian sugar on the Pacific coast, free from former competition on this market from the South's sugar. Union sentiment was "strong and almost universal" in the Islands during the Civil War, another evidence of the New England influence in Hawaii.

The exigencies of the slavery controversy followed by war between the states prevented any close attention to Hawaii by the United States either in terms of public opinion or official concern during the decade roughly from 1857 to 1867. Fundamental policy and interest had been established so firmly, however, as to permit several years of drift without serious danger. No occasion arose during the period on which any other power challenged American policy or interests in the Islands. In

---

[49] Files of the *San Francisco Evening Bulletin* indicate the general failure to take the proposed treaty too seriously.

1863, in the midst of the Civil War, two events did take place which had some significance and should be noticed. One of these was the official withdrawal of the American Board from support of the Mission in Hawaii. This ended over forty years of continuous subsidy of this missionary enterprise which had done so much to mould the destiny of Hawaii. It had given to the Islands a peculiarly American and Yankee civilization. Now the native population was declining; the entire life of the Islands had advanced from feudalism to a progressive commercial and agricultural economy with modern institutions of government and law. Withdrawal of the Mission symbolized in a way the emergence of Hawaii as a civilized community no longer justifying missionary enterprise to bring to it the light of Christian civilization. The same year the United States elevated its diplomatic representative at Honolulu to the rank of Minister, another significant recognition of the fact that Hawaii had become of age in the community of nations.

CHAPTER V

SUGAR, RECIPROCITY, AND ANNEXATION

The dominant feature of Hawaiian-American relations for more than a decade following the Civil War was the continuous attempt of Hawaii to secure a reciprocity agreement with the United States. Weighty obstacles were encountered in the form of general indifference plus open and active opposition from certain quarters in the United States. The prevailing indifference of American opinion and conditions of internal development were such that the vigorous opposition of a few was sufficient to long delay the issue. On the other hand, an equally strong little group from the Pacific coast, especially in California, became the proponents of the Hawaiian proposal because of the benefits to be derived. Therefore, the reciprocity issue resolved itself into a merry battle of two minorities to sway public opinion and political action.

From the standpoint of Hawaii, reciprocity was a very serious matter. Each year following the Civil War, with its temporary uplift to the Hawaiian economy, demonstrated with increased clarity the fact that the principal hope of the native monarchy for preserving itself from revolution and disintegration rested upon a satisfactory commercial agreement with the United States. The inspiration for the reciprocity drive, as usual, was more Hawaiian than American. It is necessary, therefore, to analyze with some care, if briefly, developments and problems in Hawaii as a basis for its understanding.

The dominance of American interests had been assured beyond reasonable doubt by 1865. Later developments were in the main a continuation of those already under way. The forces behind the transformation of Hawaii from an economy based upon its position as a way station for commerce and whaling to one founded upon an expansion of sugar planting continued to operate with inexorable pressure after 1863. By the seventies the end of the whaling industry was an established fact. By 1872 the number of whalers visiting Hawaiian ports had fallen to a meager forty-two, as contrasted with ninety-two in 1863.[1] In 1876 the American consul was reporting that but four or five American whalers had visited Honolulu during the preceding season

---

[1] Peirce to Fish, May 19, 1873, *Dispatches*, XV. See also *Pacific Commercial Advertiser*, February 8, 1873.

as contrasted with from one to two hundred a few years previously. The entire whaling fleet of the North Pacific had fallen to a dozen vessels.[2] The rising petroleum industry of the United States had spelled the doom of this picturesque activity.

SUGAR BECOMES KING IN HAWAII

The passing of the whaler was accompanied by a definite expansion of the sugar industry. By 1873 a letter to the *Polynesian* on February 8 affirmed regarding sugar, "It is the foundation upon which our material prosperity as a nation rests." Upon its success and further development every other interest in the Islands was dependent. Depress the sugar industry and merchants felt the pinch of poverty, the revenues of government declined, and murmurs of revolution began to fill the air. Sugar had become "King" in Hawaii to a degree hardly less than cotton in the economy of the South prior to 1860. From 1860 to 1864 its export literally had zoomed from 1,444,271 to 10,414,441 pounds, with accompanying growth of the export of its by-products. By 1869, the figure had reached 18,302,110 pounds.[3] Its dominance in Island economy was illustrated by the fact that in 1871 it represented a value of $1,250,000 out of total exports of $1,650,000.[4]

The rise of the sugar industry was subject to American control and influences. The Civil War had acted to produce the first great market for Hawaiian sugar in the United States and much of the expansion of the sixties had resulted from this. The restoration of peace in the United States, with other factors, produced a material decline in the exports of Hawaiian sugar. In 1871 they had amounted to 18,135,500 pounds, slightly less than in 1869, and by 1873 had fallen to 14,828,313 pounds. For a brief time it appeared uncertain whether the Hawaiian planter would continue to enjoy the expansion of the American market for his product.

During this period California importations of sugar were more largely from Manila, Batavia, and China. In 1872, for example, Hawaii furnished but 11,156,335 out of 83,006,378 pounds imported by the California refiners. By 1873, however, the proportion was somewhat larger, amounting to 10,831,211 out of 53,391,098 pounds.[5] Within the next three years the proportion of Hawaiian sugar increased steadily and commanded a price approximately one cent a pound higher than other

---

[2] *Commercial Relations of the United States,* 1876, 46f.
[3] Statistics from *Pacific Commercial Advertiser,* March 12, 1870.
[4] *Ibid.,* February 8, 1873.
[5] *San Francisco Commercial Herald and Market Review,* January 8, 1874.

types because of its finer quality.[6] Despite some early threats to the contrary, the United States continued to be the almost exclusive market for the Hawaiian planter, and the overwhelming percentage of his sugar went to the California refiners.

The growth of the sugar plantations and the expansion of the American market involved a general concentration of trade relationships with the United States. In 1871 the imports of Hawaii from the United States amounted to $776,140.92, while in 1874 they were $806,540.35. Hawaiian total exports to the United States for the former year were $1,332,169.40, and in 1874, $1,158,041.34.[7]

The margin of American dominance was not so comfortable, however, as to negate the possibility of competition. Between 1871 and 1873 the imports of Hawaii from all other sources exceeded those from the United States. Well over one-half the total of Hawaiian exports, however, were received by American ports. The sugar trade was the principal element in this trade. The hold of the United States even here was not unchallenged. By 1873 exports of Hawaiian sugar to New Zealand and Australia had mounted to over seven million pounds, as compared with less than fifteen millions for the United States.[8]

An important aspect of Hawaiian commerce was its concentration in California. This shift had begun with the expansion of the American frontier into that region, and had been steadily accentuated, as has been observed, by the rise of the sugar trade. From 1860 to 1866 trade in American vessels carrying Hawaiian goods to Atlantic coast ports of the United States fell from $112,414 to $48,268. Foreign vessels became the chief carriers of Hawaiian commodities to the eastern United States, their importations rising from nothing to $195,175 from 1860 to 1866. Total Hawaiian exports to Pacific coast ports, on the other hand, increased from $225,445 to $1,345,662 for the six years. On the export side, the value of goods dispatched to Hawaii from America's Atlantic ports fell from $306,648 to $245,593 for the period. Pacific coast exports to Hawaii increased at the same time from $330,841 to $806,046.[9] This trend continued through the succeeding years.

This decline in trade relations with Atlantic ports in the United States was a reflection of the passing of the whaling industry. Chief exports

[6] *Ibid.*, November 30, 1876.
[7] *Commercial Relations*, 1875, 1038-53.
[8] *Hawaiian Gazette*, February 4, 1874.
[9] *Report of the Bureau of Statistics, U. S. Treasury Dept., Senate Docs.*, 39 Cong., 2 sess., II.

from Hawaii to this section at an earlier date had been made up of the product of the fisheries. The New England connections of this industry had created also a considerable business in supplies, accounting for the major portion of Hawaiian imports. By the late sixties, the chief exports of the United States to the Islands had become, in the order of their value, lumber, furniture and wooden wares, hardware, breadstuffs, gold and silver coins, bullion, cotton manufactures, and meat products.[10] Obviously, these were commodities for the most part best supplied by the Pacific coast section. Imports were mainly sugar and its allied products. Since the price for Hawaiian sugar was approximately the same at San Francisco as that for Cuban sugars at New York, the Hawaiian market was automatically limited to the Pacific coast states.

The dominance of sugar produced, therefore, a concentration of Hawaiian commercial interests to a peculiar degree in California, and especially at the port of San Francisco. For example, the domestic exports of the United States to Hawaii for the fiscal year ending June 30, 1875, were $655,174, of which $491,202 originated from San Francisco as contrasted with $60,000 from Oregon and $90,089 from Philadelphia and Boston.[11] As has been pointed out earlier, the major portion of the sugar product of the Islands came to the San Francisco refiners. In 1873 California imported 10,831,211 pounds out of a total exportation to the United States of 14,828,313 pounds of Hawaiian sugar. By 1876 the amount imported had nearly doubled to 17,129,152 pounds for January to November.[12]

This situation resulted ultimately in a close relationship between the San Francisco refining-mercantile interests and the planting-mercantile interests in Hawaii. This was only partially developed, however, prior to the wave of prosperity and speculative development incident to the reciprocity treaty. The refiners and planters were in the early seventies in a process of adjusting some conflicting interests. The Hawaiian planter, because of the small area of good sugar land and high costs of production, was inclined to produce a very high grade of washed sugar suitable for table use without further refining. The price for this grade was naturally much higher than for lower grades. For example, in 1875 the price for the No. 1 grade at San Francisco was slightly over nine cents a pound, while that for No. 2 grade was less than six cents. The incentive for the planter to produce a better grade was obvious.

On the other hand, the California refiners were antagonized by the fact that heavy importation of such a high grade of sugar would make

---

[10] *Ibid.*

[11] Statistics cited in *Cong. Rec.*, 44 Cong., 1 sess., IV, Part III, 2278-79.

[12] *San Francisco Commercial Herald and Market Review*, November 30, 1876.

it actually a competitor with the refined sugar produced by them. There resulted from the conflict of interest a mild battle between planter and refiner which developed increasing enmity during the early seventies and led the California refining interests at one time to oppose reciprocity.[13] The refiners held the whip hand, because the control of the market for all the sugar was in their hands, unless Hawaii should find new markets. The latter prospect became a strong possibility in the seventies and for a time the struggle between California refiners and Hawaiian planters threatened to disrupt the close American economic interest established with the Islands.

THE SUGAR PLANTERS

Within Hawaii the expansion of sugar planting produced a continuance of the trend toward a concentration of control in the hands of a few planters, mainly Americans. In 1872 thirty-two plantations dominated the industry, of which twenty-five were American owned. The total capital investment in all the plantations was then estimated at four million dollars, though their actual worth was hardly over one-half that amount. Probably three-fourths of the investment was by American-born planters, or those of American parentage born on Hawaiian soil.[14]

Several factors combined to force the industry into a monopolistic mold. The scarcity of land and labor, previously noted, tended to place a premium upon large holdings. A further factor was the high quality of sugar production necessitated by this condition, making requisite the use of improved and costly machinery and advanced processes. These could only be utilized on a profitable basis by those with large capital and under a large-scale production system. Thus the rise of a planter aristocracy, observable at an earlier date, continued with unabated force throughout the years prior to 1876. The close association of this group with the mercantile interests, and the predominance of Americans in both, provided an influence of the utmost significance in the development of Hawaii.[15]

HAWAII'S NEED FOR RECIPROCITY

Despite the economic expansion taking place within the Islands along agricultural and commercial lines, the outlook for the future in the

[13] *San Francisco Commercial Herald and Market Review,* January 8, 1874, surveys the controversy. Expressing the refiner viewpoint it declared, "We believe they [the planters] will find it much more to their interest to work hand-in-hand with our refiners instead of running competition to them."

[14] Peirce to Fish, May 19, 1873 (enclosure), *Dispatches,* XV.

[15] *San Francisco Daily Morning Call,* May 14, 1876, contains an excellent analysis of Hawaiian sugar culture for the period.

early seventies was not encouraging. The steady expansion of trade was checked sharply about 1870. In 1869 Hawaiian exports reached a peak of $2,336,358.63, and, for the first time in history, achieved a balance over importations by a slight margin. A year later, a decline to $2,144,942 was noted, and by 1874 a still more serious setback was evident with total exports of $1,840,000. Hawaii was in the grip of another of its periodic depressions.

Various influences contributed to this situation. In part, it was influenced by the decline of the whaling industry. More important, however, were certain conditions confronting the rising sugar industry. Despite the expansion of the sixties, serious problems now confronted this branch of Island economy. In the first place, as has been indicated, the production of sugar in Hawaii was a costly business demanding a large capital investment. High costs of production meant that the most favorable market opportunities must be present, were the planter to succeed. The high American tariffs of the post-Civil War period threatened seriously the advantageous market position of the Hawaiian sugar planter. Declining prices for sugar began to afflict the planter by 1870, and reached a low point in 1872. This seems to have been due in part to overproduction of sugar throughout the world and consequent general depression of the market.[16] Between 1870 and 1875 the price of No. 2 grade of Hawaiian sugar fell from nearly eight cents to less than six cents a pound, while Cuban sugar registered a similar decline, indicating the general condition of the sugar market.

Other more immediate factors influenced the plight of the Hawaiian planter. Competition with sugar from the East Indies, China, and the Philippines had to be faced on the San Francisco market. The conflict with the refiners as to grades of sugar did not improve the situation. The refiners wanted the planter to produce the lower and cheaper grades of sugar, whereas the salvation of the latter always seemed to lie in improving quality. The problem had become so acute by 1873 that many planters faced the prospect of bankruptcy, and property values had fallen at least fifty per cent. Charles Nordhoff reported dolorously to the *New York Tribune* March 11, 1873:

The whaling fleet has almost entirely left them; the sugar planters, many of whom are in debt, are getting in deeper by reason of the price of sugar in San Francisco. . . . The coffee culture has failed. For common or varied agriculture the islands are not fitted. The planters and the people who want to become rich are therefore discouraged.

---

[16] Cf. *Hawaiian Gazette,* January 15, 1873, for Hawaiian difficulties. The *Journal of Commerce of New South Wales* contains important surveys of the general sugar market for the period.

The *Pacific Commercial Advertiser* at Honolulu was no less pessimistic, and declared, "The one great interest of the country—sugar
growing and making,—is languishing, and must continue to languish,
unless we can by some means compete with other sugar-growing countries in cheapness of production." The outlook was indeed dubious.

As usual, economic disturbance was followed by a certain amount of
political unrest within the kingdom. This was reflected in growing criticism of the monarchy, and especially of its fiscal policies. The continuing decline of the native race, coupled with the rising prominence of
foreigners in the life of the Islands, further aggravated the growing
friction between natives and foreigners. From 1866 to 1872 the native
population declined from fifty-eight thousand to fifty-one thousand,
while the foreign population increased from slightly over four to nearly
six thousand. The same trend continued unabated through succeeding
years.[17]

The combination of racial unrest and economic difficulties continued
to threaten the integrity of the native government. In 1861 Commissioner Dryer had reported to Seward, "I am fully satisfied that the
days of this Government under its present ruling dynasty as a Kingdom,
will be of short duration." This echoed opinions expressed earlier, and
was a theory popular with later American diplomats at Honolulu. In
1863 Minister McBride pointed out, "The native population is decreas-
ing so rapidly as to produce the general, if not universal, belief that
within a short period, say from twenty to forty years, there will not
be enough of them remaining to perpetuate this Government."

Not the least among factors creating difficulty was the revival of a
strong native monarchism under Kamehameha V, proclaimed sovereign
in November, 1863. Failing to take an oath to support the Constitution
of 1852, the new ruler called in May, 1864, for elections to a convention
designed to revise the constitutional structure of the country. This body,
following stormy sessions lasting over a month, was dissolved by the
King because of its inability to reach an agreement. Shortly thereafter,
he proclaimed a new fundamental law limiting property qualifications
for suffrage and greatly strengthening his personal power. A period of
political absolutism ensued, with the King pressing for the preservation
of royal prerogative and the maintenance of the fullest possible native
control of the government.

The new sovereign was not long to pursue these policies, however,
for his death occurred in December, 1872, and precipitated a new po-

---

[17] It should be kept in mind that much of this was due to the influx of Chinese.

litical crisis. The passing of Kamehameha V marked the end of the ancient line of Hawaiian sovereigns and no legally designated heir to the throne remained. For the first time since the founding of the government, the natives were called upon to select their own ruler. Under normal conditions this might not have created a problem. However, in view of the welter of conflicting interests and intrigues characteristic of Hawaiian politics, and the definite interest of various foreign elements in the kingship, the election assumed a serious aspect.

ELECTING A NEW KING

The principal candidate for the throne became Prince William Lunalilo. Forty years of age, able and well-educated, if somewhat intemperate, the Prince represented the closest approach to a legal claimant, following the refusal of Princess Bernice Pauahi to assume the throne despite direct request of the King prior to his death. Prince William promised a liberal and "even democratic" administration of the government, and his desire to base his rule upon the will of the people was evidenced by his demand for a popular plebiscite to determine the new ruler. He was regarded as pro-American in leanings, as contrasted with a somewhat pro-English policy pursued by the former King, and was favorable to the restoration of a more liberal constitution.

The leading opponent of the Prince became David Kalakaua, descendant of former powerful Hawaiian chiefs. He conducted a campaign for the kingship based upon a strident appeal to native patriotism and to racial prejudice against the foreigners. He promised to restore, if elected, the native race and monarchy to its ancient glories and position. Kalakaua denounced the democratic Constitution of 1852 and the growing control of political affairs in the interests of foreigners. A demagogic agitator, in the view of the foreign population, this aggressive native nationalist leader aroused much ill feeling and racial antagonism by the nature of his appeals.

The election resulted in the overwhelming endorsement of Prince William, who assumed control of affairs in January, 1873. A pro-American Cabinet and propositions for amendment of the Constitution of 1864 satisfied the American interests on the Islands. According to the American Minister, by early 1873 political affairs had "settled into a calm like that of a summer sea." The new ruler, he felt, would "secure & greatly promote American influence & their interests here over the political and commercial relations of the Kingdom." The new sovereign appeared to have become the most popular King of the past twenty years and preparations were under way for a visit to the United States. New interest in a reciprocity engagement was reported.[18]

Unfortunately, this favorable prospect did not continue. Several factors contributed to the undermining of the new administration. Foremost was the growing economic depression which struck the Islands at the very moment of the elevation of Prince William to the throne. Failure of earlier reciprocity negotiations with the United States, to be discussed later, accentuated the difficulties of Hawaii. A strong trend toward the renewal of agitation among American residents for a republic and possible annexation appeared. This, together with the controversy over a proposed cession of Pearl Harbor to the United States as a bribe for a reciprocity treaty, aroused native unrest. The disgruntled and defeated David Kalakaua cleverly took advantage of this to incite native criticism of the new ruler. The King's growing incapacity as a result of tuberculosis and chronic intemperance did not add to the security of the government.

By late 1873 it was common knowledge that the King could not live long. In September, a mutiny of the troops at the Honolulu barracks called attention to the critical situation. Minister Peirce was so disturbed as to request that the U. S. S. *Portsmouth* be retained at the capital permanently as a safeguard against expected disorders. Similar steps were advocated by the British agent. Fears for a revolutionary outbreak were general, and an open conflict between natives and foreign residents seemed inevitable. The American residents in particular took to arms as a necessary measure of protection.[19] Under the leadership of Kalakaua, a "Young Hawaii" movement assumed menacing proportions, and it was expected that he would be the next ruler unless a prior revolution threw the government into the hands of the foreign population.

KING KALAKAUA

On February 3, 1874, after one year and one month of his reign, the King died without naming a successor to the throne, throwing the

---

[18] The dispatches of Minister Henry Peirce throughout the period, with their enclosures from Hawaiian newspapers, provide an excellent record of Hawaiian politics from which the principal items of this survey have been drawn. See especially those of December 8 and 11, 1872; January 17 and 21, 1873, *Dispatches*, XV. The letters of Charles Nordhoff in the *New York Tribune* in March 1873, are also very valuable. See especially those of March 11 and 19. Kuykendall's "Constitutions of the Hawaiian Kingdom," *op. cit.*, should be consulted for the constitutions in question.

[19] Peirce to Fish, September 16, October 13, December 2 and 18, 1873, *Dispatches*, XV.

politics of the kingdom into another series of convulsions. By February 11, Peirce reported feeling at Honolulu as at a "fever heat," and it appeared that American and possibly British forces might of necessity be called upon to preserve order. Two days later Kalakaua was installed as the new ruler, having been elected the preceding day by the Legislative Assembly, by a vote of thirty-nine to six over Queen Emma, widow of Kamehameha IV. Native opinion was divided, some strong support developing for the Queen, who appeared as the candidate of the British interests. Kalakaua on the other hand, despite his former career, had become the moderate candidate and received the support of most Americans.

The installation of the new ruler was met, according to Peirce, with "jeers and contempt" from the populace, and prompted a riotous demonstration which was only calmed by the landing of American and British marines. By the following month the Minister was able to report the full restoration of order and the emergence of a newly respected government. Kalakaua had thrown aside his anti-foreign views, and expressed interest in the immediate reopening of reciprocity negotiations with the United States. A keen interest in the social and economic progress of Hawaii became characteristic of the new sovereign.

In many respects the elevation of Kalakaua to the throne marked the opening of a new era in Hawaiian history. The old rulers had passed to their fathers; the last of the old missionary element was fast disappearing. The rapidity of the economic and social revolution of the past thirty years had created a new Hawaii. The Islands were assuming a truly modern aspect and the prospect for the future seemed to many to be very bright. The King himself, elated at the prospect for his kingdom, declared optimistically, "This country has now its way opened to flourish like a green bay tree; capital and immigration will be attracted to it; and the rich bounties which God and nature have bestowed upon these beautiful islands will be developed under a good government and able ministry."[20]

A principal basis for this new optimism was the prospect provided by the conclusion of a reciprocity treaty with the United States. To securing this treaty, Hawaii had turned its attention with ever increasing emphasis. The search for reciprocity, it should be emphasized, was a product of the critical economic and political conditions existing through the period just surveyed. The economic difficulties of the planters drove home with renewed pressure the almost absolute necessity of some such arrangement were their interests to continue to flour-

---

[20] Cited, *Hawaiian Gazette*, September 27, 1876.

ish in Hawaii. The unrest of the American property-holding element, and the decline of the native race, likewise made clear to the government as perhaps never before the urgency of such a treaty if the stability of the native monarchy were to be assured. The movement for reciprocity, then, was mainly Hawaiian in origin and stemmed from the peculiar economic, social, and political problems of the Islands. Having surveyed the nature of those problems briefly, it now remains to trace the history of reciprocity.

A BRIEF RESURGENCE OF MANIFEST DESTINY

Naturally enough, the Civil War years were not characterized by an intimate attention to Hawaii. There were, however, revealing flashes of regard emanating from Washington. A significant step already noted was the elevation of the American agent to the rank of Minister. In instructing James McBride, the first appointee to assume this new post, Secretary Seward emphasized in 1863 that the selection was made because of the long familiarity of the new appointee with the "extent of the material interests which bind so closely the Sandwich Islands to the United States."[21]

McBride did not prove to be a worthy candidate for his post. Under his direction, Hawaiian-American diplomacy reverted largely to the type of petty quibbling and quarreling with the native officials so characteristic of the days of Brown and Ten Eyck. In April, 1865, the irascible McBride was succeeded by Edward McCook, a native of Ohio and resident of Colorado territory. The new Minister found himself much more in accord with the government. To Seward he reported in 1866, "The spirit of this whole people is heartily Republican, and thoroughly American."

At this date the reciprocity agitation was beginning to assume importance. While the perplexities of reconstruction were demanding the attention of a majority of Americans, Hawaiian affairs did attract some notice. Under Secretary Seward, the State Department was beginning to toy once more with the idea of a renewal of expansionist diplomacy, and the prospect of Hawaii bound more closely to the United States now was no more forbidding to many Republicans than to Democrats in the halcyon days of Franklin Pierce.

The imperial ambitions of the Secretary are well known, but of particular significance was his interest in Hawaii. As a member of the Senate prior to the Civil War, he had been an advocate of annexation

---

[21] Seward to McBride, March 18, 1863, *Instructions*, II.

at the time of the proffered cession under Fillmore. Indeed, no measure designed to promote American expansion in the Pacific had been without his support. During the Thirty-Second and Thirty-Third Congresses he had advocated measures to develop Pacific trade, and had even gone so far as to support Chinese immigration. Before the Senate on July 29, 1852, the then Senator had portrayed the decline of Europe and affirmed that "the Pacific ocean, its shores, its islands and the vast regions beyond, will become the chief theatre of events in the world's great hereafter."[22] The destiny of America was his favorite theme.

It was the fortune of Seward as Secretary of State to consider important propositions relating to Hawaii. The renewal of the reciprocity agitation provided the first of these. Minister McBride, motivated it appears in large measure by a fear that British interests might assume undue importance in Hawaii, had taken it upon himself in 1863 to renew the plea for a reciprocity treaty. He called attention to the act of 1852 by which Hawaii had proffered a mutual reciprocity to the United States. The acceptance of this offer was urged upon two grounds, the mutual economic advantage ensuing and the strengthening of political bonds. "Such a treaty," wrote McBride, "would be singularly beneficial to the States and Territories bordering on the Pacific Ocean."[23]

This move seems to have been upon the initiative of McBride alone and without direct inspiration from Hawaiian authorities, with whom the Minister was not upon good terms. It met with no success, for Seward was compelled to reply the following February 8 that the proposal would be given "earnest consideration" but that the circumstances made it impossible to give detailed attention at the time. Before the receipt of this discouraging reply, however, the Hawaiian Government manifested its direct interest by dispatching to Washington Elisha H. Allen, appointed in March, 1864.

Allen accomplished nothing of immediate importance. He was received by President Lincoln, who assured him of the "profound interest" of the United States in Hawaii. To Seward, Allen presented a declaration to the effect that Hawaii was solicitous "not only for the most friendly, but the most intimate commercial relations with the United States." A detailed argument in favor of reciprocity was advanced, involving emphasis upon the extent and importance of American economic interests in the Islands and their strategic geographical

---

[22] *Cong. Globe,* 32 Cong., 1 sess., 1973ff.; 33 Cong., 1 sess., 156ff., provide interesting samples of the Seward theories.
[23] McBride to Seward, December 10, 1863, *Dispatches,* X.

importance. The Hawaiian agent manifested a keen desire to present the most favorable terms possible and to satisfy any American objections to reciprocity which might have defeated earlier efforts in that direction.[24]

To this plea Seward was obliged to reply February 11, 1865, in much the same vein as before. The domestic situation was too troubled to enter into negotiations, but it was hoped that this difficulty would be temporary and the prospect for future conversations was held open.

Minister McCook was no less quick than his predecessor to become an advocate of the Hawaiian cause. Under date of September 3, 1866, he took early occasion to point out the value of the American stake both economic and political in Hawaii. The United States, he felt, might at any time be called upon "to arbitrate the future of this country." In the event of war with either France or Great Britain, the possession of the Islands would be "absolutely necessary to the United States." Annexation, McCook believed, could be easily accomplished should Washington desire to test the "Napoleonic conception in the way of territorial expansion."[25]

During the winter of 1866-67, Minister McCook, partly at the instigation of Hawaiian sugar planters, visited the United States and urged personally upon Seward the importance of heeding Hawaiian desires. As a result, he was authorized to undertake the negotiation of such a treaty. Hawaii appointed Finance Minister Charles C. Harris for the same purpose. Both President Johnson and Seward were interested keenly in the prospective treaty.

NEW PROPOSALS FOR RECIPROCITY

On January 29, 1867, the President had taken an important step toward friendly commercial relations with the Islands by a proclamation suspending all discriminating duties of tonnage or imposts upon Hawaiian vessels or products. This was done in accordance with information to the effect that similar action had been taken by Hawaii.

Seward moved with caution, and in January, 1867, he submitted to Secretary McCulloch of the Treasury a copy of the proposed treaty of 1855, noting the reason for its defeat. Reconsideration, Seward pointed out, was now desirable and he expressed the opinion that the possible increase in sugar imports resulting from reciprocity would not injure Louisiana. At the same time, "an important political consideration" made

---

[24] Allen to Seward, undated, *Notes, Hawaii*, II. Opposition of Oregon wool interests to free wool from Hawaii was noted by Allen.

[25] FR, 1894, 137f.

the treaty very advisable. The Treasury was asked for an analysis and opinion.

McCulloch replied January 26 with a detailed study of Hawaiian trade, and pointed out that the treaty proposed in 1855 had not provided sufficient advantages to the United States by failing to admit free such important exports as hardware, cotton, manufactures, clothing, boots and shoes, furniture, drugs, and similar commodities. A treaty based upon similar lines, if operating in 1866, would have resulted in the admission into Hawaii free of duty American goods worth less than $100,000 out of a total trade of $1,051,639. "But," concluded the Secretary, "the political considerations adverted to in your communication appear to me to be of such importance as to entirely overshadow the comparatively trifling interests involved in the commerce of these islands. . . ." Therefore, McCulloch endorsed the proposal for a new treaty, but urged that more care be taken to insure provisions satisfactory to American commercial interests.[26]

With this reply in mind, Seward formally had instructed McCook under date of February 1 to undertake the negotiation, with a care to a more equitable treaty and especial instructions to make it a water-tight measure which would leave few loopholes for Senatorial attack. It was with these admonitions in mind that the Minister met C. C. Harris. With both governments desirous of action, the treaty was shortly concluded, and by May 29 McCook was able to announce from San Francisco that the completed document as signed two days earlier was being forwarded by express to Washington. President Johnson submitted it to the Senate on July 5.

The new proposal represented a definite advance over that of 1855, and was negotiated so carefully as to insure in the minds of its sponsors little doubt of its acceptance. Great care had been taken to broaden the scope of the free list of American exports to Hawaii. It included agricultural implements, meats, boots and shoes, bread, building materials, cotton manufactures not over 160 threads to the square inch, fish, hardware, ice, iron, lumber, woolens other than ready mades, and petroleum. The value of the American goods to be admitted was estimated as $813,747 annually.

On the Hawaiian side, important goods to be admitted to the American market were listed as arrow-root, coffee, fruits and vegetables, furs and skins, rice, ornamental woods, tallow, unmanufactured cotton, and sugar not above the No. 12 Dutch standard of color. The latter pro-

---

[26] Correspondence in *Reports of the Committee on Foreign Relations*, 1789-1901, VIII. *Sen. Doc.*, 56 Cong., 2 sess.

vision was the work of McCook, anxious to protect Pacific coast refiners against competition from too high grade Hawaiian sugars. As
estimated by McCook, the value of free Hawaiian imports would reach
$629,385. This was less than the value of American goods to be ad-
mitted, but the fact that Hawaiian tariffs were much lower would
result in a larger remission of duties by the United States. While this
meant little in actuality, it was used later as a telling argument by
opponents of the treaty.[27]

From the standpoint of those supporting the treaty in the United
States, there is no question but that the ultimate interest was political
rather than economic. In his May 29 dispatch, McCook affirmed, "I
think that the consummation of this treaty will largely benefit the
commercial and manufacturing interests of this coast and of the country, and prove the initial step toward the acquisition of the islands
should this country ever want them." In a June communication, he
remarked even more directly, "When the Pacific railroad is completed,
and the commerce of Asia directed to our Pacific ports, then these
islands will be needed as a rendezvous for our Pacific navy, and a
resort for merchant ships, and this treaty will have prepared the way
for their quiet absorption."

From the economic standpoint, the treaty became a purely Pacific
coast measure, and more directly a California one. Keenly aware of
this, the Hawaiian agent, Harris, cleverly stimulated a wave of public
support for the measure in that area, working closely with California
trade organizations and members of Congress. The views expressed
were repetitious and the comment of the *Daily Alta* of San Francisco
under date of November 20, 1867, is typical. The financial and commercial stake of the United States in Hawaii was stressed. The *Alta*
went on to say, however, that, "Reciprocity with the Hawaiian Islands
would be the first step toward an eventual peaceable acquisition of that
territory, now regarded with covetous eyes by France and Great Britain."

Resolutions at about the same time by the San Francisco Chamber
of Commerce affirmed that the Islands were the "great highway of the
Pacific" and of the utmost strategic and economic value. Unless controlled by the United States, they would ultimately fall prey to British
or French influence. It is significant that following the Civil War the
political interest was assuming a somewhat different form, or at least
a new type of expression. New stress was placed upon the strategic

---

[27] See McCook to Seward, May 29, 1867, *Dispatches,* XII, for details as to the
negotiation; also John Patterson, "The United States and Hawaiian Reciprocity,
1867-1870," *Pacific Historical Review,* VII.

value of the Islands in relation to defense, and the theory was more or less constantly advanced that Hawaii was in danger of control by another power with consequent disaster to the United States. These ideas had been touched upon earlier but were now given added emphasis and meaning.

As a result, all those who looked with favor upon the idea that America was destined to become a great Pacific power were inclined to view closer relations with Hawaii as a national necessity. Those who looked more to the Caribbean and Latin America as a field for expansion were less enthusiastic. Support for the former idea was not lacking, however, in many quarters. The usually conservative *New York Times,* for example, editorially declared on July 22, 1868, "There is no question . . . that we are bound, within a short time, to become the great commercial, and controlling and civilizing Power of the Pacific."

The *New York Tribune* of April 17, 1869, after viewing the problem from every angle, concluded that the reciprocity proposal was a result of the inability for the moment to establish more intimate relations, and would be followed by further Americanization of Hawaii. The countering activity of the British was observed, and the Senate urged to consider it carefully when deciding upon the merits of the treaty. It was not a matter of dollars and cents alone, warned the *Tribune.* Similar views were expressed by resolutions of the Boston Board of Trade, voting unanimously for the proposal.

The favorable support accorded the treaty in the rather meager expressions of public opinion—for the general public was by no means as yet aroused to a widespread interest in Hawaii—did not facilitate the easy endorsement of the measure by the Senate. There it encountered such opposition as to result in nearly three full years of fruitless controversy before it was finally killed.

RECIPROCITY AGAIN DEFEATED

The suggested treaty was submitted to the Senate shortly after its completion in 1867 and referred to the Committee on Foreign Relations where it was not reported until a year later. Early in July, 1868, Senator Sumner, Chairman, presented the measure and defended it with an ardent speech. The opposition was led with powerful attacks by Senators Fessenden and Morrill. The latter became the most persistent opponent of reciprocity in the Senate on the technical ground of its unconstitutionality as involving an abuse of the taxing power by the Senate.

Following preliminary debate in executive session July 20, press observers agreed that despite the bitterness of the opposition and the rush of last minute business the treaty possessed excellent chances of passage. The opposition was led by Senators Fessenden and Morrill and recently admitted southern Senators were reported as averse to the measure. Senator Sumner delivered a vigorous supporting address. Considerable surprise was occasioned when on the twenty-fourth consideration was made impossible by a motion of Senator Morrill to table the measure, which was concurred in by a vote of thirty to twenty-one.[28]

Failure to consider the treaty more favorably, despite the vigorous lobbying of C. C. Harris, may be attributed to the strength of the constitutional argument and the general inability of those in support of the measure to dispel the impression that it was more favorable to Hawaii than the United States. Harris, who had been travelling about the country "for the most part under the patronage of the Rail-Road Companies," found that this view was so strong among Senators that "it takes no little showing to bring them to take a favorable view."[29] Several Senators, particularly Grimes of Iowa, strongly in favor of annexation opposed reciprocity as an obstacle to early acquisition of the Islands. This was a further influence against the treaty, and of course emphasized the political basis of the American attitude toward reciprocity. The opposition of Fessenden was viewed as especially damaging.

The end of the session without action on the treaty made necessary an extension of the ratification clause; and the desire 'of Hawaii for the advantages of reciprocity made this a matter of little concern. January 5, 1869, President Johnson submitted to the Senate an agreement signed the preceding July 28 to extend consideration of the treaty. Earlier in his message of December 9, 1868, the President had taken occasion "respectfully" to call the attention of Congress to the proposed treaty. "The attitude of the United States," affirmed Johnson, "towards these islands is not very different from that in which they stand toward the West Indies." Reciprocity was endorsed on the ground that "while it could not materially diminish the revenues of the United

---

[28] *Senate Executive Journal,* XVI, 334, 354-55. The *New York Times* and *Tribune,* July 21-25, 1868, contain the most extensive reports on the progress of the treaty, though little general comment was forthcoming. Hawaiian lobbyists for the measure, however, were not very confident of success from the start. See also Washington correspondence *San Francisco Evening Bulletin.*

[29] Harris to Allen, July 26, October 3, and December 8, 1867, Elisha H. Allen Papers. Senator Boutwell informed Allen on December 7, 1867, that a strong feeling existed against all reciprocity treaties. Patterson, *op. cit.,* stresses the opposition of the annexationists as defeating the proposal but constitutional objections were very powerful in prior and later considerations of reciprocity.

States" it would be a "guaranty of the good will and forbearance of all nations until the people of the islands themselves, at no distant day, voluntarily apply for admission into the Union." In this statement, the President placed endorsement of reciprocity upon a purely political plane.

While once more reported favorably to the Senate on April 7, 1869, the treaty failed again to secure active support, but its death was postponed another year. On July 16 Senator Hamlin reported to Allen that consideration had been delayed again without debate or expression of opinion. Doubts that it would ever be ratified were frankly expressed by the Senator. The desire for continued friendship with Hawaii, he informed Allen, was general, but fear of the loss of revenue and of the dangerous precedent created through such a breach in the protective system worked against favorable action upon reciprocity.[30]

Even earlier, on June 1, J. Mott Smith, who had assumed charge of the Hawaiian interests in the absence of Allen, reported to him that the treaty had no chance for passage, as it had been tabled. Fessenden was once more the unrelenting foe, but Smith complained bitterly that many friends of the measure had been more interested in securing confirmation of their appointments than battling for reciprocity. The "luke-warmness" of supposed friends had counted for much, as the treaty had been tabled by a margin of but nine votes.[31]

A last effort to save the treaty resulted in the hastened return of Elisha Allen to Washington in January, 1870. On January 20 Allen gained an audience with the new Secretary of State, Hamilton Fish, and urged strongly the ratification of the treaty. Allen sought to counteract the argument against it on the ground of its invalidation of the most favored nation principle by advancing the theory that the reciprocity treaty involved special concessions in return for special concessions and did not confer a *favor* upon Hawaii. Fish showed obvious unwillingness to listen to the long drawn out discussion and pointed out with some asperity that the temper of Congress was against any reciprocity measure.[32]

On February 3 Allen addressed the Secretary in writing, returning again to his interesting but involved argument as to the perfect feasibil-

---

[30] Hamlin to Allen, July 16, 1869, Allen Papers. Allen was now in Hawaii. C. C. Harris, who had remained in the United States at his own expense to lobby for the treaty, reported to Allen on February 2, 1868, that he had seen every Senator personally but because of preoccupation with reconstruction measures support was doubtful.

[31] Letter in Allen Papers. Smith insinuated that the personal antagonism of Fessenden towards Sumner, a great friend of the treaty, strongly influenced the attitude of the former. Morrill continued his constitutional objections.

[32] Account in MS Diary, I, Hamilton Fish Papers.

ity of reciprocity. "In this treaty there is no *favor* conferred—*a consideration* has been given," Allen urged. Even should the Hawaiian treaty be interpreted otherwise, the United States possessed no treaties with other sugar-producing countries which would involve danger, Allen pointed out.[33]

A week later Allen again presented personally his pleas; the Secretary again in his Diary manifested his growing impatience with the Hawaiian agent. On March 24 the conversations were again resumed, and on this occasion Fish injected into the issue the problem of increasing oriental immigration into Hawaii. He pointed out that this was viewed with increasing disfavor in the United States.[34]

At the same time Allen was pressing his views upon Fish, he was engaged in an active effort to secure Congressional support. Through the three months, the personal letters of Allen are full of stories of attending parties, dining, and meeting members of Congress, "especially Senators." Nor did the Hawaiian diplomat and lobbyist neglect the feminine angle, for he reported to Mrs. Allen that it was quite as important to influence the ladies as the members of Congress. The prospect for his treaty he thought to be promising, far more so than he had dared to hope.[35]

The hopes of Allen were without foundation. Without administration pressure, and this was not forthcoming, the treaty was doomed.[36] Considered in executive session on April 21 and May 31, final action was taken June 1, 1870, after a vigorous debate lasting from the opening of the afternoon session until six in the evening. Allen himself, acting upon the advice of Sumner who had become the great protagonist of the treaty, did not push for early action but played a game of drift. On May 10 when a vote could have been obtained, Allen was content to let it pass because he was not sure of his ground. In his letters he complained of the many interviews and the pressure of effort to support the treaty. Lobbying and jockeying were of no avail, however, for the treaty went down to defeat by a vote of twenty yeas to nineteen

---

[33] Allen to Fish, *Notes, Hawaii,* II.

[34] MS Diary.

[35] Letters in Allen Papers. That Allen was overenthusiastic, or Secretary Fish the perfect gentleman and better able to conceal his dislike face to face than in his Diary, is indicated by Allen's comment to his family that he was received with "great cordiality" by the Secretary of State. It is significant in the light of later developments, that Allen cultivated James G. Blaine closely.

[36] The Diary indicates a failure of both Fish and the administration to perceive the importance of Hawaii. As late as December, when Fish seems to have begun to manifest an aroused interest, he notes that when brought up in Cabinet meeting, the Hawaiian question was dismissed rudely.

nays after a vigorous assault by Senator Morrill based on his favorite theme—unconstitutionality.[37]

Various factors entered into the failure of the treaty, though the paucity of contemporary comment makes it difficult to unearth them. From scattered sources, however, it is possible to single out some of the more pertinent influences. From the beginning, it must be noted that the most persistent objection to reciprocity was the continued fear that the application of the principle in connection with the most favored nation clause in other commercial treaties with nations producing similar products would endanger the protected American market. This was emphasized by Fish in his discussion with Allen, and the proof of its importance is indicated by the efforts of the latter to overcome it with labored legal reasoning to the contrary. Minister Peirce, in explaining at Honolulu the defeat of reciprocity, likewise stressed this as the basic factor operating against such a treaty.[38]

A further objection called to the attention of Allen by Secretary Fish was the constitutional argument advanced and so strenuously upheld by Senator Morrill to the effect that a reciprocity treaty approved by the Senate would deprive the House of its constitutional prerogative of passing upon revenue measures. Press accounts indicate that this was a principal theme of both Morrill and Fessenden in their attacks upon reciprocity from the inception of the treaty.

Other influences which played a minor part were the preoccupation of Congress with reconstruction measures, a point noted by Allen as late as 1870; fears for the loss of revenue at a time when the Treasury was hard pressed; and the general apathy of the public which, outside the Pacific coast states, failed as usual to show active interest.

The theory formerly held that the opposition of the southern sugar interests was the basis for defeat of the treaty is without substantial support. While receiving some attention in the press at the time of the vote tabling the measure in 1869, comments on the treaty fight in 1870 make no mention of such opposition. Further evidence pointing against such a conclusion is provided by the failure of Allen or Harris to mention any such obstacle to the success of their cherished project. In fact, on the final vote on the treaty on June 1, 1870, not a single Louisiana Senator voted, and but five votes against the treaty were registered south of Maryland. Votes from Texas, Alabama, and Mississippi were recorded for the treaty. It also should be kept in mind that the states

---

[37] *Senate Executive Journal,* XVII, 466; *New York Times,* June 2, 1870. The Allen Papers contain many interesting letters on the fate of the treaty.

[38] Peirce to Fish, July 21, 1869, *Dispatches,* XII.

of the South were still in the throes of reconstruction and few of their members in Congress were truly representative of the interests of that section. The sugar industry of the section had been ruined by the war. It is questionable whether the South had any real influence on the reciprocity issue.[39]

In Hawaii the failure of reciprocity was a serious matter and threatened to raise grave issues. The economic disturbance with accompanying political unrest which characterized the Islands during the period of consideration of the treaty have been analyzed. Every new prospect that the treaty was going to meet defeat, as it dragged through some three years of consideration by the Senate, was a blow at the peace and quiet of Hawaii.

From the beginning of the consideration of reciprocity the possibility that revolution might overturn the King, or other causes threaten the sovereignty of Hawaii, remained a distinct possibility. The King himself appears to have been alarmed during the summer of 1867 at possible interference with his independence from American sources. This arose as a result of the visit to Honolulu of the American naval vessel *Lackawanna* in June and July, under the command of Captain Reynolds. The Captain had been a former resident of the Islands, and as such identified with the political group in opposition to the government. His peremptory and abrupt manner created a sudden fear that some assault might be undertaken and a repetition of the Paulet or De Tromelin incidents occur. The King utterly refused to sign the negotiated reciprocity treaty until the withdrawal of Reynolds.[40]

ANNEXATION REVIVED

Minister McCook expressed his opinion in August, 1867, that failure of the reciprocity treaty would mean revolution in Hawaii. This was a prospect not altogether displeasing, for McCook would have been happy to have turned the reciprocity negotiation into a scheme for annexation. He had suggested to Seward prior to his return to Honolulu in June, 1867, that the Islands could be purchased easily and requested the privilege of sounding out the project. The Minister had

---

[39] An examination of New Orleans newspapers for the key dates reveals no serious concern over reciprocity.

[40] McCook to Seward, July 23, August 5, and September 30, 1867, explain this affair, *Dispatches*, XII. The archives of the Navy Department reveal reports from Captain Reynolds hostile in tone to the Hawaiian Government and justifying the fears of the King. June 22 Reynolds reported American rights in Hawaii generally disregarded and referred contemptuously to the "insignificant" government of the Islands. October 21 he suggested to the Department that American relations with Hawaii "might *now* be properly modified greatly to our advantage."

also suggested to Seward the importance of discussing the matter with C. C. Harris before he returned to Hawaii. The views of Seward were sympathetic, and McCook was authorized to "sound the proper authority" on the matter while he himself promised to consult Harris.[41]

Further evidence of the intertwining of reciprocity with the larger issue of annexation was furnished in the dispatch in September by Seward of a secret agent, Z. S. Spalding, to Hawaii. According to later testimony by Spalding before the Senate Committee on Foreign Relations in 1894, his instructions were entirely oral and that he should make a careful survey of the possible effects of reciprocity upon the future relations of the two countries.[42] After viewing the situation, the confidential agent reported March 7, 1868, that should reciprocity fail, "the whole influence of the capital invested in Sugar on these Islands will go toward a change in the political status of the Kingdom, and demand some sort of connection with the United States to save themselves."[43] Upon this ground Spalding personally urged that the reciprocity measure should be allowed to die, as its passage "would perhaps impede or prevent annexation of that country in the near future."

The evidence seems clear that both President Johnson and Seward were highly favorable to the alternative idea of annexation. The correspondence of Seward indicates his belief that similar support was not lacking in Congress. In a communication to Minister McCook September 12, 1867, the Secretary emphasized the fact that circumstances "induce a belief that a strong interest, based upon a desire for annexation of the Sandwich Islands, will be active in opposing a ratification of the reciprocity treaty." In view of Seward's personal wishes, this may have been but wishful thinking. At the same time, however, McCook was informed that "a lawful and peaceful annexation of the islands to the United States, with the consent of the people of the Sandwich Islands, is deemed desirable by this Government; and that if the policy of annexation should really conflict with the policy of reciprocity, annexation is in every case to be preferred."[44]

April 14, 1868, Spalding reported to Seward upon the annexation excitement prevailing in Honolulu, and urged the importance of taking advantage of the situation to carry through the larger project. The Secretary, however, was compelled in a somewhat regretful tone to inform his agent that his ideas were impossible to fulfill. The public

---

[41] Correspondence in FR, 1894, 139ff. There is no evidence in the State Department as to possible contacts of Seward with Harris.
[42] FR, 1894, 59f.
[43] Spalding to Seward, *Dispatches,* XII.
[44] Seward to McCook, FR, 1894, 148f.

attention, wrote Seward, continued "to be fastened upon the domestic questions which have grown out of the late Civil War," and it refused to consider "the higher but more remote questions of national extension and aggrandizement." "Economy and retrenchment" were prevailing watchwords of the day, and in the political contest taking shape "the leaders of each party therefore seem to shrink from every suggestion which may involve any new national enterprise, and especially any foreign one." It is significant that this decision coincided with the determination of the administration to extend the convention for ratification of the reciprocity treaty.[45]

As consciousness of the fact that reciprocity was in doubt grew in the Islands, the restlessness of the American element increased. The special agent of Seward wrote April 14, 1868, to his father, R. P. Spalding, "The truth is that so long as there was a chance for receiving the benefits of free trade with the United States and escaping taxation, men who had capital invested here were generally opposed to annexation." The situation was now changing, wrote Spalding: "Men who have kept silent for months, guarding their words and actions, have openly expressed themselves of late as being in favor of annexation and begun to talk of forming an organization or party with that end in view."[46] The only influence needed to swing the balance, in the opinion of Spalding, was an assurance that they "will be backed up by the United States and its representatives here in all proper measures taken by them to secure a change in the political sentiment of the islands and their annexation at the earliest possible moment." Such an assurance was not forthcoming.

---

[45] Correspondence in FR, 1894.
[46] FR, 1894, 146f.

CHAPTER VI

Reciprocity Achieved

The inauguration of President Grant had marked temporarily at least a definite lapse in American official interest in Hawaiian affairs. The expansionist tendencies of the administration centered more largely in the Caribbean than the Pacific, and the problem of American policy relating to Cuba, San Domingo, and Canada attracted more attention in Cabinet meetings than did distant Hawaii. The rather brusque treatment accorded Mr. Allen by Secretary Fish during the reciprocity negotiations, considered in the preceding chapter, was typical of the early attitude of the administration toward the Islands.

One step taken, however, did augur favorably for the ultimate advance of Hawaiian-American relations. The Minister to Hawaii became Henry A. Peirce, native of Boston and former resident of the Islands with extensive mercantile interests at Honolulu prior to the Civil War. He had been a supporter of the reciprocity measure in 1867. Peirce arrived at Honolulu July 15, 1869, after pausing for some time at San Francisco to make a careful study of Hawaii's trade with the Pacific coast, where his appointement was greeted with enthusiasm. He had no sooner established himself in his new office than he began to promote a close relationship with the government and the American interests in the Islands, a policy made easier by his earlier residence.

The new appointee at once began to urge upon Washington the importance of more effective naval protection for the trade of the area. To this end, the establishment of a strong naval depot at Honolulu was urged. The prospect of political instability in the Islands, and the extent of American interests there and in the north Pacific were cited as justifying such action. This theory became of considerable significance in gradually developing an impression of the importance of Hawaii as a naval base. It properly may be regarded as an important turning point in the development of the American attitude toward the Islands. As has been noted earlier, it began to figure in the calculations of American opinion on reciprocity as early as 1869.

An immediate result was the dispatch of Admiral Turner to Hawaii in October, 1869, to discuss the matter thoroughly with the Minister. During November and December of the same year, Rear-Admiral Irwin of the Pacific squadron likewise visited the Islands, and it was the opinion of Peirce that these contacts did much to forward the "paramount" position of the United States in Hawaii. Out of them came as well the beginnings of American attention to Pearl Harbor.[1]

American preponderance in Hawaiian affairs progressed rapidly under the judicious guidance of Peirce. In December, 1869, a change in the ministry brought into power more definitely pro-American advisors. Through the American Minister, Hawaii was aided in negotiating a treaty with Japan, beginning established diplomatic relations with that power. The final defeat of the reciprocity treaty in 1870, however, was a severe blow to the program of "Americanization" so carefully fostered for over two decades.

HAWAIIAN NATIONALISM

The first reaction of Hawaii to the failure of the reciprocity negotiations of the sixties was a desire to return to a policy of national self-subsistence so far as practicable. Antagonism toward further fawning dependence upon the United States and the prostituting of national honor by begging attempts to curry favors characterized even the American business interests. The *Pacific Commercial Advertiser,* leading voice of the commercial and planter groups, declared November 18, 1870, "Let us depend upon our own resources, and upon the markets of the world, and make the most of opportunities which we have, and of which no one can deprive us." Since this paper was formerly an advocate of annexation, this constituted a significant expression of the changed viewpoint. Further evidence of the same trend appeared in the passage by the 1870 Legislature of measures encouraging the establishment of local cotton and woolen manufactures.

Even more significant, and dangerous from the American standpoint, was the search for new sugar markets in New Zealand and Australia. The 1870 session authorized the creation of a subsidy of $50,000 for the establishment of a steamship line to those countries. This found favor with the *Advertiser* and the economic interests represented by it. The urge for self-sufficiency had been a temporary manifestation, and one which sober second thought found impractical. Hawaii must have a market for its dominant crop. Denied this on advantageous terms by the United States, it now turned elsewhere.

So definite was the new trend that Minister Peirce reported in alarm to the State Department July 30, 1870, that trade with British possessions in British vessels was increasing at so rapid a pace as to constitute

---

[1] Peirce to Irwin, December 12, 1869, Navy Department Archives, *Pacific Fleet, To the Department.*

a definite menace to American interests. An excellent and favorable market for Hawaiian sugar existed in New Zealand and Australia. The sugar of the Islands was wanted there and freedom from the high American tariffs as well as from domination of San Francisco refiners was promised. All of these factors were fully appreciated by Peirce, and he warned, "These islands have too much value to the United States, politically & economically to permit England or France to have control over them; at most beyond that enjoyed by ourselves."[2]

ANNEXATION AGAIN REVIVED

These warnings were renewed in later dispatches and the importance of a Congressional subsidy for a steamship line from San Francisco was urged as a necessary counteracting measure. At the same time, Peirce began to toy with the idea of annexation. As early as September 20, 1870, he informed the Department that while the political situation was for the present tranquil, a "crisis" might be expected at the death of the King. A powerful group in favor of a republic and annexation was in the process of formation, declared Peirce. When the crisis arrived, wrote Peirce, "the Minister Resident of the U. S. will doubtless become master of the situation—and able to give form and shape to the future of the Kingdom."

February 25, 1871, Peirce returned to the same topic and raised the question as to whether it were not "proper, wise and sagacious" to once more consider the possibility of annexation. Even the native population, he felt, would now be more favorably inclined. The adoption of the Fifteenth Amendment to the American Constitution had done much to end former suspicion as to the status of native rights under the American system of government. The commercial and strategic importance of Hawaii in view of its geographical position was such as to demand the most serious consideration. Purchase of the Crown lands and an annuity for the King and chiefs, which could be taken care of easily and cheaply, would make possible the acquisition of the Islands, thought Peirce.[3]

The death of Kamehameha V on December 11, 1872, created the crisis which Peirce had been predicting, and aroused him to demand immediate naval assistance. Like his predecessors, the American Minister had become afflicted with an anti-British phobia and saw lurking in every corner an intrigue by British interests. It was necessary, therefore, to use every means possible to promote the continued ascendancy of American forces. To this end he was willing to utilize American

---

[2] *Dispatches,* XIV.
[3] Dispatch in FR, 1894, 17f.

forces to quiet any popular demonstration against Prince William as the candidate to the throne most favorable to the United States. The peaceful election of the latter, however, and the popularity of his brief reign rendered extreme measures unnecessary.[4]

In the meantime, the efforts of Peirce to arouse the interest of the Grant administration in Hawaiian affairs had been but mildly successful. The failure of the reciprocity treaty without any administration support resulted in a complete lull in Hawaiian diplomacy until October 18, 1870, when Secretary Fish brought before the Cabinet the Peirce dispatch of September urging a more forward-looking policy. The Secretary records that there was no comment other than the playful remark by the President that "Sumner had better be consulted whether Annexation is desirable. Let him think that he originates it, and all will be well." The Cabinet as a whole seemed totally disinterested.

Two months later Fish read further dispatches from Peirce bearing on the same matter and invited discussion. Fish himself was impressed by the arguments of the American Minister, as is evidenced by his personal observation that "we are losing the trade of these Islands & influence there; the present King is the last of his dynasty; on his death the Islands will necessarily pass under some other form of Govt.; their tendency would be to us, but our indifference may turn them elsewhere." As for the Cabinet, however, Fish records: "No one responds & the subject is dropped. The indisposition to consider important questions of the future in the Cabinet is wonderful." Further evidence of the failure of the administration to be alive to the Hawaiian problem at this time is indicated by an attempt of the President, thwarted by Fish, to remove Peirce in favor of someone desirous of a political plum. It seems clear that Fish, personally, awakened to the potentialities of the situation earlier than did either the President or the other members of the Cabinet.

ANNEXATION OR RECIPROCITY

The attitude, however, changed rapidly within the following year. On April 7, 1871, the President submitted to the Senate for confidential consideration the Peirce dispatch of February 26. The President commented briefly, "Although I do not deem it advisable to express any

---

[4] The manner in which American forces would have been used if necessary is indicated by instructions to Rear-Admiral Pennock from Secretary of the Navy Robeson dated December 25, 1872. Pennock was ordered to proceed to Honolulu "as soon as possible," to contact Peirce, and "in concert with him use all your influence and all proper means to direct and maintain feeling in favor of the United States; and at least to secure the selection of a successor favorable to our interests." See Navy Department Archives, *Letters to Officers and Commandants*, No. 7.

opinion or to make any recommendation in regard to the subject at this juncture, the views of the Senate, if it should be deemed proper to express them, would be very acceptable with reference to any future course which there might be a disposition to adopt."[5]

Further evidence of a revived interest was provided by the authorization in 1872 of a confidential mission by Major-General J. M. Schofield and Lieutenant-Colonel B. S. Alexander of the United States Army to examine the commercial and naval facilities of the Islands. Acting under secret instructions from Secretary of War, William W. Belknap, in June, the two military agents left for Honolulu in December and made a careful survey, reporting May 8, 1873.[6] It seems fair to assume that the changed attitude of the administration was influenced largely by the advice of Minister Peirce and the growing respect for the importance of Hawaii manifested by Secretary Hamilton Fish.

Further developments in Hawaii served still more to press Hawaii upon the attention of Washington. By 1873 the prospect for calm evident after the election in 1872 was at an end. Neither the economic nor the political situation had changed for the better. A vigorous debate over the respective merits of reciprocity and annexation as solutions to the difficulties of Hawaii raged at Honolulu. Henry Carter of C. Brewer and Company expressed the feeling of many in the business field when he wrote late in 1872, "I feel like throwing up my hands and letting things drift." Drift toward annexation by the United States was believed by Carter to be the only solution to Hawaiian difficulties.[7]

In the minds of most citizens of property it was certain that something must be done to remedy the distress of the sugar interests. While a majority undoubtedly favored a further attempt to secure a reciprocity treaty as the best solution, there was not wanting a group favoring annexation. The conservative *Pacific Commercial Advertiser* of February 15, 1873, was forced to admit that "there is unquestionably a large party, respectable in point of wealth and position, that is now openly and earnestly advocating the offering of the sovereignty of the country to a foreign power—in short, the annexation of these islands to the United States of America." Analyzing the situation for the *New York Tribune* of March 19, 1873, Charles Nordhoff reported from Honolulu that the

---

[5] FR, 1894, 16. There is no record of any action by the Senate. The Fish Diary provides no clues as to the reason for the action of the President. It was probably one of the characteristic impulses of Grant. See also Allan Nevins' biography of Hamilton Fish for background on the diplomacy and politics of Grant's administration.

[6] Report in FR, 1894, 154-58. The report was favorable in general to the acquisition of Pearl Harbor. See also "Report on Pearl Harbor, 1873," *American Historical Review*, XXX.

[7] Cited, Sullivan, *History of C. Brewer and Company*, 130-31.

substantial planters were being driven to support annexation in preference to economic prostration. The most speculative element, both politically and economically, was strongly for such a program.

The principal argument advanced for this procedure was that only by such means could the permanent prosperity of the Islands be maintained. Reciprocity the United States would not grant, argued the annexationists, because there was no advantage to be gained by that power justifying the favor extended to Hawaii. Annexation would place the economic interests of the Islands upon the most favorable basis, attract further foreign capital and immigration, and lead to benefits for the entire population.

The most fundamental opposition to annexation came from the more conservative propertied interests, as usual at all times afraid of change, and the native population. Nordhoff hit upon an important distinction when he differentiated between the speculative and the more substantial economic groups in their attitude toward annexation. It was true, however, that even the most conservative were forced by circumstances of the time to consider the prospect with some favor. The opposition of the natives flowed from the intense spirit of nationality which pervaded the dying Hawaiian race. This feeling was frequently played upon with success by those desirous of perpetuating their political power. It was not without accident that the "ins" politically in Hawaii were uniformly opposed to annexation.[8]

TRIUMPH OF THE RECIPROCITY IDEA

Those concerned with defeating annexation concentrated upon reviving the reciprocity movement, despite the rebuffs already received from the United States. That the more conservative propertied interests of the Islands, as well as those in governmental authority, turned to this power in spite of the unfavorable reception accorded their previous overtures was a remarkable testimonial to the extent to which Hawaii had come under the control of American influences. Despite the inviting prospect for new markets in the British possessions developing during the early seventies, the distressed business interests of Hawaii still turned in a last gesture designed to secure American assistance. As early as January, 1873, a memorandum favoring a renewal of the reciprocity proposition was placed in the hands of the King by planter representatives. Heavily in debt, and with no other prospect for improvement of their status, such action was inevitable.

---

[8] The *Pacific Commercial Advertiser*, February 15 and 22; March 1 and 8, 1873, provides valuable comment on these issues. See also *Hawaiian Gazette*, July 16. See also Charles Nordhoff, *Northern California, Oregon and the Sandwich Islands.*

As a further inducement to the favorable consideration of reciprocity by the United States, it was suggested that the government offer a proposal for the leasing of Pearl Harbor for future development as a naval rendezvous in the Pacific. Three principal arguments in favor of reciprocity were advanced: (1) the economic advantages to be gained, which would be greater than could possibly be secured elsewhere; (2) the development of Pearl Harbor as a distinct asset to Hawaii; (3) the defeat of annexation. A month later a committee of the Honolulu Chamber of Commerce presented a similar request to Minister Peirce. Peirce replied favorably but indicated that he lacked instructions from Washington.[9]

The full pressure of the planter and mercantile interests was brought to bear upon the government. "We believe that the time and the circumstances, are today more than ever before, favorable to the accomplishment of the one and only national measure that can turn the tide of adversity that is now advancing upon the country, into one of unexampled prosperity—the negotiation of a Treaty of Reciprocity with the United States," declared the *Pacific Commercial Advertiser.* By May the *Hawaiian Gazette* reported petitions pouring in upon the King from all quarters to the same end. Those favoring reciprocity urged upon the monarch a personal visit to the United States as an aid to the project.[10]

So rapidly did the agitation advance, with the bulk of conservative influences leaning more and more to reciprocity and away from annexation, that on February 10, 1873, Minister Peirce reported to the State Department his expectation that proposals to reopen reciprocity negotiations would shortly reach him. "The subject now uppermost in the thoughts of Hawaiian officials, planters, and merchants relates to the measures needed to be taken to stop the decline of the Kingdom in its population, revenue, agricultural productions, and commerce," wrote Peirce. "The principal panacea for the cure of these evils, in their opinion," he continued, "is to be had by effecting a reciprocity treaty with the United States."[11]

Ten days later Peirce reported further, and affirmed that annexation and reciprocity were still twin subjects of discussion. Annexation, he

---

[9] Charles R. Bishop to Peirce, February 26, 1873; Peirce to Bishop, February 27, *Foreign Office File,* Archives of Hawaii, hereafter AH. This reference and others following from the Hawaiian Archives were made available through the courtesy of Dr. Ralph S. Kuykendall.

[10] The *Advertiser* for February 8 and the *Gazette* for February 26 and March 5, 1873, provide interesting editorials. Charles Nordhoff reported that the planters were willing to spend $100,000 lobbying for a treaty.

[11] FR, 1894, 152f. It is important to note that the pressure for reciprocity came from this planter and merchant class. Nordhoff found that the "mass of the people are not uncomfortable" and little concerned.

felt, would never come from governmental action. "The glitter of the crown, love of power, and emoluments of office have too many attractions to prevent it," thought the Minister. He continued, however, "Should the great interests of the country . . . demand that 'annexation' shall be attempted, the planters, merchants, and foreigners generally will induce the people to overthrow the Government, establish a republic, and then ask the United States for admittance into the Union." To the Department, he suggested once more the feasibility of acquiring the Islands by satisfying the financial necessities of the ruling power.[12]

The suggestion of Peirce regarding annexation did not meet with enthusiastic endorsement by the State Department. On March 15 Fish informed the American Minister that such suggestions were "premature" and a violation of the "good faith with which we profess to regard the independence of those Islands." Peirce was informed that no consideration favorable to such proposals should be shown, but that reports from time to time on the developments connected with them would be proper.[13]

Ten days later the Secretary instructed Peirce more at length. Regarding the prospect for territorial expansion, he wrote: "The acquisition of territory beyond the sea outside the present confines of the United States meets the opposition of many discreet men who have more or less influence in our Councils. It cannot be entered upon without very grave deliberation and in full view of all the advantages or disadvantages that may result."[14]

RECIPROCITY AND PEARL HARBOR

Peirce informed Washington on February 28 that he had been approached officially by the Hawaiian authorities intimating a desire to reopen the reciprocity negotiations. The need for such a measure upon the part of the Islands was so great, wrote Peirce, that terms even more favorable than those proffered in 1867 might be secured. The cession of Pearl Harbor and a limitation of sugar imports to a No. 15 Dutch color standard could be included. That quick action must be taken was the view of the Minister, lest Hawaiian trade drift into the possession of British colonies with ultimate control from that source. The sugar duties of the United States were from 2½ to 3½ cents a pound as contrasted with 2 cents for British Columbia and New Zealand; ¾ to 1 cent for Australia.

---

[12] *Ibid.* Nordhoff indicated that the popularity of the King was such that there was "not even a glimmer" of annexation sentiment among the natives. See letter to the *New York Tribune*, March 11, 1873.

[13] Fish to Peirce, *Instructions*, II.

[14] *Ibid.* This dispatch is published in part in FR, 1894.

These more favorable tariffs and the prospective steamship connections "are likely to give the British interests in the trade and navigation
of this ocean, superiority over those of the United States, unless we
take measures soon to prevent it," warned Peirce. The attention of the
State Department was called further to the essential unfairness of existing trade relations between the United States and Hawaii. Figures were
cited from the *Hawaiian Gazette* showing that the United States collected annually $400,000 in duties from Hawaiian goods as contrasted
with $100,000 by Hawaii on American products.[15]

Despite this approach in February, the Hawaiian Government hesitated
to actually request direct consideration of a treaty. Such a proposition
was not forthcoming until July. Major reasons for the delay appear to
have been unwillingness to compromise dignity by taking the initiative
in new negotiations following two rebuffs, and controversy over the
advisability of including the Pearl Harbor project in any proposition
presented. Of the two, the latter was more important. From the beginning of the renewed discussion of reciprocity, rumors of the proposed cession had aroused vigorous opposition upon the part of the
native political leaders and the native populace. David Kalakaua led the
protest on the ground that it was inconsistent with the dignity of the
government and a dangerous step toward the alienation of Island
sovereignty. Indeed, there developed a strong objection in these quarters
against any renewal of the reciprocity negotiations.[16] In the somewhat
prejudiced opinion of Peirce, the British and French interests were not
averse to utilizing this feeling to spike the projected overtures to the
United States.[17]

Notwithstanding the delay, an official request to begin the negotiations
was received early in July, following further preliminary approaches in
June. At this time the government officially announced its intention to
seek a new treaty and to proffer control of Pearl Harbor to the United
States. Peirce informed the State Department that by now annexation

---

[15] Peirce to Fish, *Dispatches,* XV. It was suggested that a provision might even
be inserted in the treaty providing for cession of the Islands upon the death of the
King. In June C. R. Bishop queried Consul Severance at San Francisco suggesting
a No. 16 standard which the planters very much desired.

[16] See address by Godfrey Rhodes, member of the Privy Council, to a native
audience June 30 as reported in the *Hawaiian Gazette* for July 12, 1873. Peirce
informed Bishop on June 3 that Hawaii must initiate the negotiations and expressed
doubt that the proffer of Pearl Harbor would favorably influence the United States.
See *Foreign Office File,* AH.

[17] Peirce to Fish, March 7 and 17; July 3, 1873, *Dispatches,* XV. See also letters
of Charles R. Bishop to Elisha H. Allen on the controversy over Pearl Harbor,
Allen Papers.

was out of the question, and that the only proper course was to accept recripocity with a grant of Pearl Harbor and then "to await events."[18]

Early in November the Hawaiian Government was forced to reverse itself on the Pearl Harbor proposition, and Minister Peirce was informed by Minister of Foreign Affairs Bishop that fears for ratification of a treaty containing such a proposal dictated the change in suggested terms. While Peirce chose to attribute the change more largely to foreign intrigues against the United States, Bishop spoke with truth.

The native population, already aroused by rumor, was swept with a wave of indignation when the proposition was announced to the public. Native mass meetings in protest were widely held. In the words of the *Hawaiian Gazette* of July 30, 1873, "A general feeling of profound patriotism seemed to prevail at the idea of ceding to a foreign power any part of the island; and many declared that, their money and skill to develop the resources of the country were welcome, but any cessions of territory must be unalterably opposed."[19] Peirce himself reported that fears of popular uprisings had swayed the government during the month after July.[20]

Withdrawal of the Pearl Harbor proposal so dimmed the hopes of those supporting reciprocity as to create further political unrest. The expected death of the King and the uncertainty attendant upon the succession contributed further to the same end. The climax of nearly a year of extreme unrest was reached with the elevation of Kalakaua to the throne in February, 1874. The combination of native opposition and intrigue by British partisans of Queen Emma was such that it cannot be questioned but that the landing of a force of one hundred and fifty American marines at the request of the King on February 13 became a decisive factor in maintaining the peace against the threat of revolution. While the force was used at the request of Kalakaua, the fact remains

[18] Peirce to Fish, July 7, 1873, *Dispatches,* XV. Bishop had made it clear to Peirce that the decline in sugar prices was the basis of the desire for reciprocity. Attempts to further develop markets at Sydney had failed. Bishop informed Peirce July 7 that he was authorized to negotiate a treaty based upon that of 1867 "subject of course to some changes and modifications, the most important of which will be, to raise the grade of sugar . . . from No. 12 to No. 16 Dutch Standard of color . . . together with cession of land for a Naval Station under such reservations, restrictions and conditions as the interests of the contracting parties may seem to require. . . . " *Foreign Office File,* AH.

[19] Statement in opposition to the cession in *Hawaiian Gazette,* December 18, 1873. This, of course, further emphasizes the fact that the reciprocity drive was promoted by the planters to better their fortunes and neither desired or needed by the mass of the population in Hawaii.

[20] Peirce to Fish, November 18 and 24, 1873. Bishop had written Peirce on November 14, "it has become evident that the general feeling in the country is so adverse to the measure; that even if the United States should acquiesce in it, a treaty on the basis of cession of territory, would not be ratified by the next Legislative Assembly." *Foreign Office File,* AH.

that it was in the interest of maintaining the "paramount" position of the United States.[21]

Once in power, Kalakaua proved an ardent supporter of reciprocity. Addressing the Legislature April 30, 1874, the new ruler declared that if the United States "hereafter consider a commercial treaty to be for its interest, my Government will not fail to open negotiations to this end." In June the King was presented with a petition signed by virtually every planter and merchant of importance on the Islands praying for reciprocity. The memorial emphasized that "serious disaster" threatened the plantation interests unless action was taken at once. Responding to the pressure, the new ruler recommended favorable action by the Legislature as "very desirable." In July enabling legislation empowering the King to ratify and complete a reciprocal trade agreement "with those nations having Territory bordering on the Pacific Ocean" was authorized.

By this time, Minister Peirce was leaving no stone unturned to forward such an agreement. This was in the face of the instructions from Fish in March, 1873, throwing cold water on the entire idea. At that time the Secretary had written that both branches of Congress were adversely disposed on the issue as a result of "deference due to the interests of those States who have or hope to have sugar as one of their staples, and also on account of an apprehension more or less well founded that if we admit Sandwich Islands sugar freely we shall, under treaties with other countries, be obliged to admit their sugar on the same terms, to the ruin of the producers here and to the loss of the large revenue now derived from the importation of the article . . . , also on account of the reluctance to regulate by a Treaty the establishment of duties, thus depriving the House of Representatives of its proper control over this class of questions."[22]

Undaunted, Peirce pushed on and in August, 1874, informed Washington of a proposed visit of the King to the United States and impressed upon the Department the importance of facilitating his desire. "The political and moral effect of such an action on the part of our Government, will tend to strengthen every American interest connected with the Archipelago," wrote the Minister. On September 10 he was able to inform Fish that the King would not only come, but also that he would

---

[21] Navy Department records reveal in the instructions to naval commanders preparations for nearly a year to hasten a naval force to Honolulu at an instant's notice with the frank purpose of forwarding America dominance. British forces were also landed.

[22] *Instructions*, II.

be accompanied by Elisha H. Allen, assisted by Henry A. P. Carter, as special agents to undertake the treaty negotiation.

In October, Allen and Carter departed for the United States, followed a month later by the King, accompanied by Hawaiian dignitaries and Henry Peirce, on board the American naval vessel *U.S.S. Benicia*. It was the first visit of an Hawaiian monarch to the United States, and, occurring exactly half a century following the famous visit of Kamehameha II to Great Britain, symbolized the shift of Hawaiian interests from that power to the United States. The tour of the King was a triumph in every respect, contributing through columns of newspaper space given over to the description of events connected with the reception of the Hawaiian monarch, a marked impetus to American attention toward Island affairs. When the King returned in February, 1875, the fundamental objective of his mission had been secured in the form of a reciprocity treaty signed January 30, 1875, the negotiations of which will now occupy attention.[23]

The way had been paved for a more favorable consideration for reciprocity upon the part of the Grant administration. It seems clear that the insistent pleadings of Peirce for a more careful consideration of the importance of Hawaii and the American interests there had struck home. The Fish diary indicates that the Peirce dispatches were read before the assembled Cabinet on several occasions and that while, as indicated earlier, they were at first received with little attention, the attitude gradually changed. By March 21, 1873, the Secretary was able to record that considerable "discussion ensues regarding the relative merits of annexation and reciprocity." As a result, Fish was instructed by the President "cautiously and informally to sound the Government as to their feelings on the question of annexation and the conditions on which it might be effected." Ways and means of improving commercial relations were also to be considered.

"The position of the Sandwich Islands as an outpost fronting and commanding the whole of our possessions on the Pacific Ocean, gives to the future of those islands a peculiar interest to the Government and people of the United States," wrote Fish in a dispatch dated March 25. Their transfer to a foreign power was unthinkable, he declared, and careful consideration of the future of the Islands in relation to the United States would characterize administrative policy. Thus Fish reshaped to the needs of the time the fundamentals of what Tyler had asserted as the American policy.

---

[23] The tour of the King may be followed in leading newspapers, attracting as it did widespread comment and attention. The MS Diary of Hamilton Fish provides interesting details as to the official arrangements.

The consideration of further commercial ties with Hawaii continued to attract official attention. October 2, 1873, Fish noted that the Cabinet considered the original proposal presented through Peirce for a reopening of the reciprocity negotiations with the cession of Pearl Harbor. Much interest was indicated in trade conditions developing in Hawaii and the danger to American interests embodied in the expanding relations with the British colonies, as well as the disturbed political situation. The President, Fish wrote, declared he would bring the problem to the attention of Congress. Lack of enthusiasm for a reciprocity convention was revealed, however, because of the state of the treasury and currency of the United States. It seems clear that fears aroused as to the relation of the Islands to other than American contacts and the strategic danger to American position in the Pacific involved provided the basis for an awakening realization of the importance of Hawaii.[24]

THE RECIPROCITY NEGOTIATIONS OF 1874

The new attempt at negotiation of a reciprocity treaty began with the arrival of the Hawaiian representatives in Washington in November, 1874. The Hawaiians suffered no illusions as to the ease with which their task might be accomplished. Allen himself had gone through the bitter and fruitless struggle of an earlier date, yet he had been an earnest advocate of reopening negotiations.[25] "A reciprocity treaty, unless there is something material offered the U. S., will not be a success in the Senate, I fear," he wrote his wife. A member of the ministry had extended his sympathy to Carter "in the almost hopeless task which you have undertaken."[26] Bishop had written in January, 1874 that "the present prospect is not favorable."

This discouraging situation, however, did not appear to deter the Hawaiian envoys. Allen opened the conversations with Fish on November 18, declaring that reciprocity was absolutely necessary to the salvation of the Islands. According to Fish, he represented "the business & population" of Hawaii to be "languishing." A strenuous effort

---

[24] Vol. III of the Fish Diary is a valuable record of these conversations.

[25] J. Mott Smith wrote Allen June 18, 1882, ". . . I remember well the meeting of the Privy Council, in which your courage and zeal inspired new hope, and set afoot a new resolve. . . ." Allen Papers. See also Green to Allen, August 19, 1874, in same collection.

[26] Correspondence cited in Allen Papers. Interesting conjectures as to why Allen and Carter devoted themselves to the task may be raised. Both were ardent pro-Americans and were undoubtedly influenced by their zeal for closer relations with the United States. The supporter of the economic interpretation of human motives will find significant the fact that both men were bitter complainants as to their personal fortunes in the period preceding the reciprocity negotiation. Allen had written May 1, 1874, "Oh, how I wish that affairs here were prospering. I would sell my property at auction & close my business in thirty days." Both were actively interested in the larger planting interests of the Islands.

ensued to convince the Secretary of the satisfactory nature of terms which could be arranged. Neither rice nor wool would be demanded as free imports, declared Allen. The possibility of any evil consequences to American sugar interests was decried. Allen pointed out that Hawaiian sugar was consumed only on the Pacific coast where competition from eastern sugars was impossible because of transportation costs.

The reception accorded the Hawaiians was not overly warm. The diary of Secretary Fish fairly bristled at every mention of Allen, even at this date, while at the first interview he refused to recognize Carter as a formal diplomatic agent. Undaunted, Carter and Allen appeared once more at the State Department on November 25. Allen renewed his plea against the application of the most favored nation principle to an Hawaiian treaty. He proposed to enlarge the free list for American goods over that of 1867 and to reduce the number of Hawaiian commodities if necessary. Reciprocity at any price, appeared to be the Allen slogan. Fish continued to evidence boredom and wrote in his diary, "Allen begins generally on the relations of the two Countries, the prevalence of American sympathies in the Islands, & the preponderance of ownership of plantations &c by Americans; that their trade is being drawn away from the U. S., between which & Hawaii, the traffic is diminishing rather than increasing."

December 5 was devoted to a discussion of arrangements for the visit of the King, which Fish had opposed in 1873 when originally suggested, but now appeared to favor as desirable. The conversation veered inevitably to reciprocity. Fish pointed out the persistence of the same general objections to "any Reciprocity Treaty" which had prevailed since the Civil War and cited the failure of Canadian reciprocity proposals as evidence.

On December 16 Fish again returned to an analysis of the opposition to reciprocity, leaving the Hawaiians under no illusions about the difficulties of the task which confronted them. Once more the example of Canada was cited, and Fish pointed out that many not opposed on general principles "expressed the opinion that it would be unwise to attempt this negotiation at the present time, when the currency of the U. S. was still unsettled . . . ; they state also that the depressed conditions of business in the country would make the negotiation of a Treaty at the present time impolitic."[27]

---

[27] All references to the views of Fish not otherwise cited are from the MS Diary, V. The narrow view of Congress was further illustrated by a notation of Fish that a request for funds for entertaining the King led Garfield and Orth of the House to be "very solicitous that I make the amount as small as possible." Carter informed his government on December 5 that he believed Fish to be favorably inclined. *Foreign Office and Executive File*, AH.

Allen and Carter were not to be dissuaded. December 24 Fish was again pressed for early action and promised to consider terms in general without any official commitments. Allen asked as to the advisability of going before the Senate Committee on Foreign Relations to secure support, and Fish scouted the idea. A week later on the 31st, Allen having left Washington, the ambitious Carter took the matter in hand and approached Fish with the statement that he had prepared a tentative treaty draft. The Secretary was informed that Carter had "seen and conversed with a number of Senators who encouraged him to believe that his treaty will be favorably acted upon, and urge an early submission after the assembling of Congress."[28]

According to Carter, he was informed by those approached that much objection to the proposed treaty could be removed if a clause were inserted prohibiting the levy of any export duties by Hawaii. Carter also pointed out to Fish that a proposal pending in Hawaii for a seven million dollar British loan would be killed by adopting a reciprocity treaty, with consequent protection to American interests. It is evident that Carter was not without skill as a lobbyist or in placing pressure upon the State Department.

Carter appeared to meet with more success than Allen in approaching Fish, and by January 4, 1875, he was able to present a draft for a treaty and the following day his proposals were presented to the Cabinet by Fish. The result was favorable, and the President, wrote Fish, "expresses a desire for the negotiation of the Treaty." This the Secretary agreed to do, provided the full support of the administration were placed behind it. "The President states he will give it his positive, active and official support," Fish recorded. Similar views were expressed by the Cabinet as a whole and the stage was set.[29]

Further support was marshalled by a report from the Secretary of the Treasury, Benjamin Bristow, endorsing the measure. In a communication to Fish, Bristow called attention to the languishing trade with Hawaii and the need for its improvement. The advantageous nature of Hawaiian trade with the United States was emphasized in view of the demand for its sugar and the high consumption of American

---

[28] Allen reported to his government that Fish was unwilling to act until assured of Senate support and that opponents of reciprocity controlled the Committee on Foreign Relations. Allen to Green, December 24, 1874, *Foreign Office and Executive File,* AH.

[29] Carter informed his government January 7 that he was attempting to force Fish into action by influencing Senators and Cabinet members. By January 14 he felt Fish to be more favorably inclined. On December 17 Allen expressed his belief that the House would act favorably. See Carter to Green and Allen to Green, *Foreign Office and Executive File,* AH.

manufactures in return. The Secretary found little to criticize in the proposed draft other than that the sugar schedule be made to exclude all other than "unrefined" sugars. The Hawaiian free list was declared very satisfactory and included virtually every product entering into American export there.

In addition to the economic gains, the head of the Treasury found political advantages. His report declared: "In addition to the particular articles of commerce affected by the treaty, there are general commercial advantages likely to follow, which can only be alluded to here. The rendezvous so long afforded at these islands for the sailing fleets of the Pacific is still needed; and with the increasing commerce of all the seas bordering the Pacific, the demand increases for such aids and facilities as would be afforded through the better establishment of American interests in the Hawaiian Islands proposed by the treaty."[30]

Formal endorsement having been secured from the Treasury, the Cabinet proceeded to consider the draft article by article. Agreement with the Bristow suggestions as to the sugar schedule was forthcoming, and it was decided that coffee and hemp should be removed from the American free list and the Hawaiian list further expanded. The Cabinet was determined to drive a hard bargain, and the President had been won to full support of the proposal. "The President expressed himself as warmly advocating the Treaty and advised its early signature and submission," wrote Fish. Further consideration on January 19 resulted in no further important changes.

On January 20 Allen, who had returned to Washington early in the month, Carter and Fish went over the draft with all the suggestions of the Treasury and Cabinet in mind. Agreement to remove coffee from the free list, due to the desire of the Treasury to restore tea and coffee duties generally as revenue measures, and the abolition of hemp, flax, and other textiles to quiet possible opposition, was quickly reached. The sugar schedule remained the chief bone of contention. The Hawaiians objected to the term "all unrefined sugars" as too vague and it was finally decided, after further Cabinet consideration, to make the treaty read "muscavado, brown and all other unrefined sugar, meaning hereby the grades of sugar heretofore commonly imported from the Hawaiian Islands and now known in the markets of San Francisco and Portland as 'Sandwich Island sugar.' . . . ." This matter out of the way, the measure was signed by the negotiators January 30 and submitted to the Senate by the President on February 1.

---

[30] Confidential Executive Document. Copy in *Notes, Hawaii,* II.

POLITICAL CONSIDERATIONS BEHIND RECIPROCITY

One of the most important questions arising during and after the negotiations was the possible inclusion of some political consideration for the United States in return for the economic favors extended to Hawaii. Allen firmly believed personally that some such bribe must be offered the Senate to secure the endorsement of any treaty. That this belief was rather common in Hawaii also is indicated by the general desire of the proponents of reciprocity to include some provision on Pearl Harbor in a treaty.

On the other hand, it was necessary to consider the bitter opposition to any compromising terms evidently to be expected from native Hawaiians. In view of that fact, Carter and Allen were in no position to offer such inducements. The evidence indicates that both Minister Peirce and Secretary Fish were interested in securing some political guarantees along with the commercial arrangement. It also appears that the Hawaiian agents, both of whom had been supporters of annexation at different stages of their careers, were not averse personally to some such terms. They were held in check, however, at all times by the sober realization of what would happen to such a proposal at Honolulu.

Correspondence exchanged during the negotiations does indicate that several informal discussions must have occurred in reference to such propositions among the parties drafting the treaty. A letter from Carter to Fish dated January 5 refers to suggestions evidently advanced by Carter himself as to "any privileges outside of a purely commercial Treaty" which might be included. Carter hastened to explain that whatever "suggestions" had been made by him should not be regarded as a "proposition." Such privileges, he wrote, could probably be better secured "after the operation of the Treaty was understood by our people." "The influence of the simple reciprocity Treaty would enable you perhaps to obtain whatever privileges you want," wrote Carter.[31]

Peirce, now in the United States, remained in the background throughout the negotiations, but wrote Fish January 11 regarding a suggestion made by the latter the preceding Saturday "about some insertion in the proposed Treaty, one that would give the U. S. a firm hold over the Isles." Peirce himself suggested a guarantee of independence as a bar to foreign aggression, and at the same time not forbidding further American overtures. He had considered the matter with Carter and enclosed a pencilled note from him declaring that both he and Allen were "anxious to discuss freely with him any points he may

---

[31] Correspondence in Fish Papers.

consider in regard to securing for the United States all proper influence in the islands and anything within our powers to lead to such a result."[32] One is led to conclude from these exchanges that Fish was desirous personally of extracting some political control over the Islands as a guarantee that the advantages conferred by reciprocity would be kept under American control.

No such provision found its way into the treaty as originally completed and approved by the President. Other than a simple prohibition against export duties, it consisted of a list of the products concerned. The Hawaiian list of products to be admitted free of duty into the United States consisted of: "Arrowroot; castor oil; bananas; nuts, vegetables, dried and undried, preserved and unpreserved; hides and skins undressed; rice, pulu; seeds, plants, shrubs or trees." The sugar clause already has been noted. The American goods to come into Hawaii without duty included virtually every product conceivably to be exported by the United States, with heavy emphasis upon wood, iron and steel, and textile products. It doubled the number of enumerated commodities in the defeated treaty of 1867.

THE ORIGINS OF ARTICLE IV

The process of treaty-making, however, was not over. When reported favorably in March by the Committee on Foreign Relations, the treaty included the addition of tobacco, starch, and leather manufactures to the already lengthy list of favored exports to Hawaii. Most important was the inclusion in Article IV, following the prohibition of export duties or charges, of the significant sentence: "It is agreed on the part of His Hawaiian Majesty, that, so long as this treaty shall remain in force, he will not lease or otherwise dispose of or create any lien upon any port, harbor, or other territory in his dominion, or grant any special privilege or rights of use therein, to any other power, state, or government, nor make any treaty by which any other nation shall obtain the same privileges, relative to the admission of any articles free of duty, hereby secured to the United States."

The importance of this sweeping inclusion was two-fold. In the first place, it assured the fact that while the United States had not secured any preferential territorial or political considerations as the price of reciprocity, no such advantages could be secured for the future by any other power. Secondly, the provision clearly cut the ground from under any possibility of furthering trade relations with British colonies, which,

---

[32] *Ibid.*

unable to secure reciprocity, would be doomed so far as any expansion of trade advantages were concerned. The provision thereby became a powerful lever for the establishment of complete political and economic control over the future development of Hawaii. As an alternative to annexation, it represented a perfect solution.

When reported favorably by the Committee with amendments, the general interpretation of the time, and since accepted, was to the effect that the new article and the additions to the free list were the price exacted by the Senate for approval. This view needs some correction. The Fish diary makes it clear that an expansion of the free list originally was proposed by Henry A. P. Carter with the feeling that it would strengthen the treaty. It appears equally clear that the limitation upon Hawaiian sovereignty was not the work solely of the Senate Committee as such. The Fish diary reveals that Senator Howe of Wisconsin raised the criticism that the treaty granted great privileges to Hawaii without insuring properly the American interests there. Thereupon it appears that Fish, probably with the support of the President, brought the proposed change to the attention of Carter. Understanding the overtures of the Secretary previously in this regard, it is reasonable to conclude that Fish was quick to press the matter with Carter.

That Carter and Allen were not overly enthusiastic about the clause is indicated by a telegram of Carter to Allen informing him that "you had better assume we considered the amendment alright and stand by it with me if you will do so."[33] According to Fish, Carter endorsed the proposed article and it was approved by the President and Cabinet February 12, and submitted to Senator Cameron, Chairman of the Senate Committee, three days later. Carter was informed of this fact by the Secretary and could not have been ignorant of what was happening.[34] It seems clear, therefore, that the limitations upon Hawaiian sovereignty included in the treaty were not the work solely of the Senate, but the result of decisions by the administration and the Hawaiian negotiators.

POLITICAL IMPLICATIONS OF THE RECIPROCITY TREATY

The addition of the single sentence to the reciprocity treaty embodied the most fundamental of American purposes in consenting to listen to the Hawaiian plea. The Senate Committee on Foreign Relations reporting in 1894 reviewed the history of Hawaiian-American relations and

---

[33] Allen Papers.
[34] Fish to Carter February 16, 1875, *Notes to Hawaii*, I. Other references are to the diary.

declared, "The Hawaiian treaty was negotiated for the purpose of securing political control over those islands, making them industrially
and commercially a part of the United States and preventing any other
great power from acquiring a foothold there which might be adverse
to welfare and safety of our Pacific coast in time of war."[35]

The Committee commented upon the evidence submitted at the time
concerning the danger of the loss of trade to the British colonies and
a political drift of the Islands in the same direction. "It was now felt
in the State Department," affirmed the Committee, "that the question
was assuming graver importance, and, as the political supremacy in the
islands must inevitably follow the commerce, it was recognized that
this country must make favorable concessions to them, or else let them
follow the inevitable tendency and drift slowly into the status of an
English colony."

A more lucid explanation of the final acceptance by the United States
of the long continued plea of Hawaii for reciprocity could hardly be
written. The views of Peirce as already presented and his importance
in the background negotiation and passage of the treaty, the attitude
of the Grant administration, and the character of the negotiations all
point to the validity of this analysis. It is safe to say that reciprocity
became a favored measure of the administration, with all its force
thrown behind it, primarily because of the political implications involved, despite some serious doubts of either its constitutionality or
economic value.[36]

The views of Washington at the time were not overdrawn, and the
reciprocity negotiation of 1875 was a turning point in Hawaiian-
American relations. There is no questioning the desperation of the
planter class. Some expansion of the market for sugar was vital. The
best outside the United States was in Australia, New Zealand, and
British Columbia. Under the aggressive leadership of the famous Pre-
mier Julius Vogel of New Zealand, the British possessions were prepared to make a vigorous drive toward the commercial and political
domination of the Polynesian world. Overtures in this direction upon
the part of Vogel early in 1874 had aroused the fears of the American
Minister, who had transmitted full information to the State Department.
There it had been deemed so important as to be placed before the
Senate Committee on Foreign Relations.[37]

---

[35] *Senate Reports,* 53 Cong., 2 sess., Appendix, No. 227.

[36] See previous reference by Fish. Allen wrote March 11, 1875, that the President
is "decidedly for us." The letters of Allen to his wife during the struggle over the
treaty are a most revealing record. See Allen Papers.

[37] See Peirce to Fish, October 20, 1874, with enclosures from *Hawaiian Gazette*
of September 9 containing extensive extracts from the declarations of Vogel in
Dispatches, XVI.

According to E. H. Allen, "a strong effort was made to induce the Government to enter in negotiations which would lead to more intimate commercial relations with all the British Colonies in the Pacific" which would have been successful but for opposition by American planters.[88]

While the American element in Hawaii was reluctant to establish connections outside the United States, it is not impossible that they might have been forced to such a program. The *Hawaiian Gazette* of August 13, 1873, had declared, "If we fail at Washington, then it may be advisable to make a similar effort with England, and one or more of her colonies, which, though not offering the same advantages, may be induced to negotiate with us for political reasons." As late as February 14, 1875, Allen was writing to his wife that if the reciprocity treaty were not approved, the British colonies must be tried. Allen was "tired of this kind of life" and "tired of dancing attendance upon Congress."[39]

The reciprocity treaty of 1875 was a momentous measure from the standpoint of its bearing upon the entire future relationship of Hawaii to the United States. Its economic significance was small as compared with the political implications involved. Contemporary public opinion seems to have been quick to sense this. It was rather frankly recognized that the importance of Hawaii as an American strategic outpost in the Pacific, and the danger that this vantage point might be lost were the reciprocity issue fumbled once more, were the important considerations behind the treaty.

NEW RECOGNITION OF HAWAII'S IMPORTANCE

The American public had been prepared gradually for a larger view of Hawaiian affairs. The westward thrust of the railroads and population following the Civil War aroused in many quarters a new conception of the position of the United States as a Pacific power. With it came a new view of the importance of Pacific islands such as Hawaii and Samoa. Reports of the turbulent political situation in Hawaii had been perused with some attention in the United States and were often a source of comment. Speculation as to the future of the Islands was engendered.

Typical of the comments which began to appear was the statement of the *Boston Daily Globe* for February 18, 1873, that, "No doubt the day is not far distant when the annexation of a number of groups of these

---

[88] Allen to Evarts, October 22, 1879, *Notes, Hawaii*, II.
[39] Allen Papers.

islands, in Central Polynesia, to the United States, will be effected through the simple agency of American ideas and influences." The Samoan and Sandwich Island groups, it declared, "must sooner or later become American property." A month later, March 18, the same organ affirmed that while there was no immediate need for annexation of these islands, it should be a subject for careful consideration. Even the conservative and generally anti-imperialistic New York *Nation* asserted regarding Hawaii, "They are sure to fall prey sooner or later to England or this country, but the method and time of acquisition are a matter of considerable importance to us."[40]

Those interested in the reciprocity question were quick to sense its importance to the protection of American interests. The Washington correspondent of the *Boston Daily Globe* informed his paper July 10, 1873, when the question first arose, "The United States have nearly a monopoly of both the import and export trade by way of San Francisco, and if Congress would be willing to concede reciprocity in return for a naval station, the commerce between the two countries would be stimulated to a still greater extent, and an appreciable step toward future annexation secured."

As the negotiation and debate over the treaty progressed, this point of view became even more clearly outlined. From the beginning, the California press dominated by Claus Spreckels and predominantly in favor of a treaty despite the opposition of the sugar refiners, stressed the commercial advantages to the coast, but was likewise quick to note the larger national significance of reciprocity. The *San Francisco Daily Morning Call,* for example, warned, "If we reject the treaty, the British Colonies are anxious to make a similar one, which shall practically exclude us from Hawaiian markets by admitting there British goods free of duty."

In the East a similar point of view prevailed upon the part of those favorable to the treaty. The dispatches of Charles Nordhoff to the *New York Tribune* early in 1873 aroused considerable interest in Hawaiian affairs. A keen analyst, Nordhoff stressed the economic difficulties of the Islands and the practical impossibility of their cure by means other than reciprocity. Annexation he thought to be impossible because of the opposition of the natives. The great mass of the people Nordhoff found to be content with things as they were. "Reciprocity would best suit our men of property," he wrote.

As the debate progressed, surprising support was developed in the East and a grasp of the national aspect of the problem evidenced. The

---

[40] July 24, 1873.

New York Post, for instance, supported the measure with such ardor that Representative James A. Garfield was led to read its editorial of April 5, 1875, during the course of the House consideration of enabling legislation. The treaty, affirmed the *Post,* "makes the Sandwich Islands ours without the expense and trouble of governing them." "Let the treaty go into effect," continued the editorial, "and American capital will accompany the migration of American adventurers to this new field, and these garden-isles of the Pacific will be essentially a part of our country . . . , there is a proposition to put into our hands without the payment of a dollar, a stronghold in the depths of the Pacific, in the very track of that power which threatens to be supreme in that quarter, and we hesitate at accepting the advantage."

Commenting upon the controversy, the *New York Times* of March 12, 1876, remarked that it was a well-known fact that the commercial aspect of the agreement was secondary to the political. The only important argument against reciprocity, the *Times* pointed out, was that of doubtful constitutionality, and the larger national interest involved should be sufficient to dismiss it. The New York organ found much force in the political arguments for the treaty, and little but feeble quibbling and special interest in opposition.

In New England a similar point of view was shared by the *Boston Daily Advertiser* in its comment of August 16, 1876. Opponents of the treaty in general found little comfort in the press and a broad view prevailed. Much strength was furnished to the Hawaiian supporters by the publication in 1874 of Charles Nordhoff's, *Northern California, Oregon and the Sandwich Islands,* which became a literal Bible of fact and figures for the proponents of an American policy for Hawaii. Without resorting to sensationalism, Nordhoff painted quietly a picture of the American domination of the Islands from the days of the missionary conquest. Hawaii was portrayed, quite correctly, as, to all intents and purposes, an American colony.

THE SUGAR REFINERS AND RECIPROCITY

One of the most peculiar aspects of the controversy over the treaty was the division of opinion on the part of California interests. The sugar refiners, contrary to the popular view in the East, were not uniformly in favor of the reciprocity proposal. Contemporary attacks upon the treaty to the effect that it was a measure of the sugar refiners are without foundation.[41] The principal basis of opposition developed from

---

[41] This was the view, for example, of the New York *Nation.*

the old fear of competition from the high-grade Hawaiian sugars with the refined product. This, it was believed, would raise the price of crushed sugars and weaken the Pacific coast refiners in their control of the market of that area. This control, it should be remembered, was still somewhat precarious, and it was not until about 1876 that the California refiners under Claus Spreckels' leadership had reached a position where they felt confident of their ability to meet the threat of competition from the East. Thus the peculiar situation was created of eastern refiners opposing reciprocity because of their belief that it would be advantageous to their western rivals by providing a cheap supply of raw sugar, while the western refiners trembled at the thought of being weakened by the measure.[42]

Late in April, 1875, the opposition of the Pacific coast refiners took the form of a protest to members of Congress against the treaty. In their memorial the view was expressed that greatly increased production of Hawaiian sugars would result. This surplus would be greater than could be handled by the San Francisco refiners, and serve to depress the price of sugar elsewhere with unfavorable consequences to American producers. In the Senate the cause of the western refiners was championed actively by Senator Booth of California. In discussing the treaty, he asserted that its passage would endanger valuable interests of the refiners and importers of his section through competition from high-grade Hawaiian unrefined sugars. Press interests favorable to the refiners took the same view with emphasis further upon dangers from overproduction and price declines.[43]

On the other hand, the lament of the refiners was counterbalanced by vigorous support from commercial and general business interests standing to profit from increased trade. San Francisco merchants united March 3, 1875, in addressing California Senators in favor of the measure, and were followed a month later by the Chamber of Commerce. The San Francisco memorial for the treaty stressed heavily its

---

[42] The *San Francisco Daily Morning Call,* March 7 and 19, 1875, and March 6, 1876, provides an excellent analysis of the problem. See also the *New York Tribune,* March 13, 1875.

[43] *San Francisco Daily Morning Call,* March 7, 1875; *San Francisco Commercial Herald and Market Review,* March 4, 1875. Andrew Welch, San Francisco merchant and planter, informed Allen in December, 1875, and January, 1876, that he had talked with many importers and found them uniformly opposed to reciprocity. Their opposition was so strong that the San Francisco Chamber of Commerce delayed endorsing the treaty until April. Letters in Allen Papers. The Spreckels' interests were on the verge of achieving a monopoly of the west coast sugar market and especially frightened. Foreseeing the inevitable, Spreckels withdrew his opposition and, as will be seen later, sought to become a producer of raw sugar in Hawaii as well as a refiner.

value to consumers through expanded commerce and cheaper sugar. The refiners were attacked directly for their opposition. "The refiners of San Francisco . . . while advocating protection for Eastern interests and consumers, are endeavoring to make contracts with the Hawaiian planters, with a view to defeating this treaty, and establishing a monopoly to crush out Eastern competition and advance prices here," declared the mercantile petition.

Political advantages to be gained from the treaty were also stressed. It declared: "The treaty, if ratified, will give the United States Government a foothold which will prevent any other nation from obtaining control of the Islands. The Hawaiian Islands strategically command the trade of this coast with the rest of the world, and if in possession of an unfriendly nation, would afford a refuge and basis of operations for our enemies to destroy our commerce in time of war."[44]

THE RECIPROCITY TREATY BEFORE THE SENATE

Despite the favorable point of view expressed publicly and the ardent support of the Grant administration, final assurance that the treaty would be endorsed by Congress was long delayed. Reported favorably by the Committee on Foreign Relations March 11, 1875, the treaty received important support from both Minister Peirce and Elisha Allen. In January Peirce appeared before the Committee and presented the case for a more forward Hawaiian policy. The economic advantages of reciprocity were duly stressed, but especial emphasis was placed upon the necessity for maintaining the advantage gained by the United States. Failure to deal more generously with Hawaii was bound to throw the Islands toward the British colonies, Peirce asserted. He also cautioned the Senators against attempting to extort favors directly by treaty lest it meet with defeat through the popular reaction at Honolulu. His arguments carried considerable weight.[45]

In February Allen appeared before the Committee and presented his now well-rehearsed argument to the effect that reciprocity was thoroughly constitutional and in no way menaced the most favored nation commercial system. This argument carried conviction and produced the administration support necessary to transmit the treaty to the Senate.

The endorsement was accompanied by a detailed explanation of the advantages of the measure by Senator Hamlin, who, in the opinion of Allen, did "nobly." Early reports indicated, however, that the treaty

---

[44] Cited, *San Francisco Daily Morning Call,* March 6, 1875.
[45] *New York Tribune,* January 15, 1875.

might have a thorny path. Active opposition by Senator Booth of California was indicated, and the southern sugar interests were marshalling their forces. The sugar industry of that section, recovering slowly from the effects of the war, was especially sensitive to the threat of Hawaiian competition. The defeat of Canadian reciprocity in February and the cry for governmental economy presented a most unfavorable aspect for the Hawaiian treaty in the opinion of contemporary analysts.[46]

Active debate came March 16, 17, and 18. During an extended discussion, Senator Morrill proved to be the most vigorous opponent with his traditional constitutional argument on the grounds of violation of the revenue power. Behind him was a resolution by the Vermont Legislature supporting his stand. Booth of California presented arguments against the treaty, while Senator John Sherman questioned it as a matter of policy in view of the condition of the Treasury. Senator Whyte of Louisiana took up the case of the Louisiana planters.[47]

In favor of the measure, and leading the fight for adoption, were Senator Hamlin for the Committee on Foreign Relations and Senators Kelly and Mitchell of Oregon together with Sargent of California. Their principal argument centered around a complete denial of unconstitutionality, pointing to the necessary enabling legislation to be passed by the House and precedents in the form of previous reciprocity treaties. Passing from the strictly legal phase, proponents of the measure drove home with telling effect the idea that to deny the Islands the advantages provided by the treaty was to throw them into the arms of the British possessions in the Pacific. Such able and respected figures as Senators Boutwell and Frelinghuysen, aided also by Senator Cameron, joined with them and presented in strong terms the issue of national interest. On March 18, late in the afternoon, the debate was brought to an end and the vote taken. Fifty votes were registered for the treaty and but twelve in opposition. Senators Booth, Edmunds, Ferry (Michigan), Hamilton, Hitchcock, Howe, McCreery, Morrill, Robertson, Sherman, Whyte, and Withers were the dissenters. The victory had been decisive.[48]

There is little reason to doubt that the success of the treaty in the Senate was due entirely to the political considerations involved. The final vote in favor of the measure was larger than expected by its proponents. In view of the evidence as to the questionable future of the Islands should reciprocity be denied, there were few willing to let con-

[46] *New York Times,* March 12, 1875.
[47] The *San Francisco Daily Morning Call* and the *Boston Evening Transcript* present the best reports on the debates.
[48] *Senate Executive Journal,* XX, 41f.

stitutional prejudice or sectional interest stand in the way. The *San Francisco Commercial Herald and Market Review,* along with other papers which widely adopted the same view, was undoubtedly right when it affirmed, "The national consideration appears to be the one which carried the most weight, as those referring to trade and commerce were treated as mere appendices."

RECIPROCITY BEFORE THE HOUSE

Ratification by the Senate, however, was not enough because the treaty involved the revenue power. Enabling legislation by the House was now necessary. Years later, the son of Elisha Allen wrote, "I remember my father's telling me that the most strenuous year of his life was the fight he had to wage to secure the assent of the House. . . ."[49] In the words of J. Mott Smith, the Senate struggle was a mere "parade drill" as compared with the battle to be waged in the House.

Nearly a year elapsed before the necessary legislation was even brought before it. On January 6, 1876, the needed act was presented by Representative Luttrell of California and referred to the Ways and Means Committee. On March 2 the Committee presented a majority and minority report which revealed sharp cleavages of opinion as to the desirability of a reciprocity arrangement with Hawaii.[50]

The majority report favoring the bill placed stress upon the letter of Secretary Bristow the preceding year endorsing the Treaty. The commercial advantages presented by the Treasury analysis were deemed sufficient justification for reciprocity upon economic grounds. The majority emphasized further its belief that failure to extend reciprocity to Hawaii would result in an inevitable shift toward British influences. "The English government and people are always on the alert to increase their commercial advantages," it declared. It further affirmed that their vast Pacific possessions with their requirements for sugar were bound to lead to connections with Hawaii. Should the Treaty be a failure economically, the majority yet declared its conviction that "there are political reasons of sufficient magnitude to warrant us to make it." "Private interests should be subordinate to national interests and commercial security and advancement," announced the majority.

Representatives Morrison of Illinois, Thomas of Maryland, Tucker of Virginia, and Kelley of Pennsylvania joined in vigorous dissent. The economic values to be gained were disputed. A heavy loss to the Treasury with no compensating gains was decried. Some forty or fifty

---

[49] Memorandum for Franklin D. Roosevelt, dated June 6, 1934, in Allen Papers.
[50] *Cong. Rec.,* 44 Cong., 1 sess., IV, Part 2 presents the report.

Hawaiian-American planters were to be the beneficiaries. The danger that the way might be opened to importations from other countries was pointed out. The minority declared that the alleged expansion of American markets was illusory and noted that some articles listed in the Treaty, such as coal, were already admitted into Hawaii without duty.

Passing from the economic foundations to the political argument of national interest, the minority was no less critical. The opponents denied the necessity for any further American control over Hawaii. "The neutrality of the commercial nations as to these islands, the hospitable *entrepot* for the Pacific commerce of the world, their healthful civilization and development under the common protection and liberal policy of all, and an open but firm diplomacy, which claims only equal but no exclusive rights to this place of refitment and refuge for the wayfarer of the sea, will do more to expand our commerce and secure our peace than the possession of the sovereignty of the islands, and for a much stronger reason than the illusory provisions of this treaty," argued the minority.

This opened the way to a thorough debate of the entire project before the House. Supporting the majority view, Chairman Fernando Wood of New York presented the case for reciprocity. His remarks were largely a repetition of the arguments stated in the majority report. The Pacific he characterized as "that vast sea which in the not distant future will be more essential and indispensable to the prosperity and material interests of this great nation than the Atlantic ocean twice over." Every Secretary of the Treasury since Walker had endorsed Hawaiian reciprocity, asserted Wood.

On March 6 Wood returned to the debate, and, attacking the arguments against the Treaty, he marshalled the statements of Elisha Allen presented previously to the Senate. The support of the proposal by General Schofield of the Army and the admonitions of Admiral Porter of the Navy, who declared England to be driving America from every point of vantage in the Pacific, were cited.[51]

The case for the opposition was best presented by Representative Morrison. He contended that in effect the measure contemplated an extension of the protective system to Hawaii and would produce the same evils of special privilege for a few as characterized its operation in the United States. No possible advantage to American sugar consumers could result, declared Morrison, because of the small amount produced by Hawaii. That it would prove a stepping stone to annexation was denied. Rather, he affirmed, it would have an opposite effect

---

[51] Debate in *Cong. Rec., op. cit.,* 1420ff.; 1488ff.

by providing certain economic advantages which would enable Hawaii to exist longer on an independent basis. The supreme issue before Congress, Morrison asserted with feeling, was to make living costs cheaper for the common man in the United States. A decline in governmental revenues and a bounty for Hawaiian planters from the Treasury were violations of that trust. Mills of Texas and Kelley of Pennsylvania warmly endorsed these views.

On March 9 Wood secured consideration of the act as a special order of business and Representative Luttrell defended it on both economic and political grounds. Rather frankly, he informed his colleagues, "It is a Pacific-coast measure, and we do not want to have you send us home defeated and mortified." Leavenworth of New York, Page of California, and Dunnell of Minnesota likewise defended the bill, while Reagan of Texas presented the anti-protectionist view.[52]

Further consideration followed on April 6 and 10. One of the most powerful addresses in support came from Representative Garfield of Ohio. The future President took the ground that the Treaty was the best possible means of establishing an "alliance" with Hawaii capable of protecting the vital national interests of the United States without resort to the pitfalls of annexation. Congress was further duty bound, urged Garfield, to give due heed to the interest of the Pacific coast in the measure. By this date the San Francisco refiners had withdrawn their earlier opposition, having come to terms with the Hawaiian planters, and a united front in favor of the measure was presented from that section.

The final debate was concluded on May 8 and a vote secured. Tucker of Virginia and Gibson of Louisiana voiced opposition, the latter emphasizing the protest of southern rice and sugar producers against a measure threatening their security. Tucker for the last time presented the strict constructionist view. The final vote, however, resulted in a close victory for reciprocity with 115 favorable ballots and 101 opposed; 74 members failing to register an opinion. An analysis shows that midwestern and southern votes were principally represented in the opposition.

RECIPROCITY TRIUMPHS

Yet another hurdle had to be overcome, however, before the Treaty was safe. The Senate must now agree to the House legislation, and here the last stand of the opposition concentrated. "The South has come up in force," wrote Allen June 1, 1876, though he still expressed the opinion that "we shall triumph." Referred to the Committee on Foreign

---

[52] *Ibid.*, 1600-04.

Relations, the House bill was reported without modification June 29, after the application of considerable pressure from the administration. June 14 Allen had warned Fish: "The delegations of the rice and sugar interests are active in their opposition."[53] Fish had called the attention of Grant on June 20 to the delay and urged him to bring personal pressure to bear. On June 26 and 27 Fish personally approached Senators Conkling, Cameron, and Hamlin and urged them to make haste.[54]

Once reported, the success of the measure was threatened immediately by a clever move of that ancient foe of reciprocity, Senator Morrill. The Vermont Senator suggested reference of the bill to the Committee on Finance. This was opposed by Cameron, but Morrill secured adoption of a motion to that effect. The following day, Senator Sargent, leading the fight for the act, secured a reconsideration and thus rescued the measure from a doubtful fate at the hands of the Morrill committee.[55]

Further consideration was delayed until August 11, much to the concern of both Fish and Allen. July 13 the latter approached the Secretary with his fears that the Senate delay would defeat the entire project by extending completion of the pact beyond the eighteen month limit provided for ratification by the Treaty. Fish took the ground that the enabling legislation could not be construed as a part of the Treaty, but urged the President to bring pressure to bear upon Cameron for speedy consideration. On July 18 the Secretary noted, "The President says he has spoken to several Senators asking for its consideration." So important were the moves made by Fish that Allen was led to express personal appreciation for the pressure applied to the Senate.[56] To his wife the redoubtable Hawaiian agent expressed his personal feeling: "I am annoyed by delay, and the weather continues hot and disagreeable."[57]

The Senate returned August 11 to consideration of the act, and Sargent was able to secure the discharge of the Committee on Finance from any consideration of the measure. This was accomplished with Senator Morrill's aid, who consented to the move though insisting still that the bill should have been considered by his Committee where it would "undoubtedly" have been altered. Sargent then moved for immediate consideration. Logan of Illinois moved for a special order, but

---

[53] Fish Papers.

[54] Fish Diary. Cameron and Conkling appeared disgruntled over patronage.

[55] The parliamentary history of the act may be followed in *Cong. Rec.*

[56] Allen to Fish, July 20, 1876, Fish Papers. Fish wrote Allen July 18, "You are not more desirous than I am for the passage of the Bill. . . . If you can suggest anything effective to secure the action of the Senate, I shall be glad to consider it. I have been making & shall continue to make efforts to that end." *Treaty Docs.*, AH.

[57] Letter dated July 17, Allen Papers.

this Sargent quickly opposed on the ground that if the bill assumed this status unfinished business would have precedence over it and the Hawaiian bill might die through failure to consider it.

The following day Sargent briefly defended the bill, pointing out the commercial advantages to the Pacific coast. He then turned to the larger question of national interest, declaring that the Islands represented an outpost in the Pacific. "They will soon be a mere waif, to be seized by the strongest power or the power which shall have political influence over them." The example of the Civil War, and the dangerous threat to the United States in case of foreign war, were pointed out. France, Great Britain, and Germany were all "looking toward these islands," he asserted.[58]

In response to questions from Senator Norwood of Georgia about the influence of the Treaty upon the American position in Hawaii, Sargent proceeded to express his faith that reciprocity was a stepping-stone to control. "The influence of the United States is strengthened by this treaty by these close relations, by the encouragement of Americans to go to the islands and settle and enter into business there," he declared. "The effect of the treaty," continued Sargent, "is to encourage Americans to go there and make it an American colony, and therefore it will cost us nothing to buy it by and by, because it will be in our possession as Texas was in our possession by the American population supplanting in influence and in numbers the Mexicans or Spaniards, by this influence which follows the trade and inducements to go there, making it an American colony." Thus accurately, if somewhat incoherently, did Sargent predict the future.

Sargent was followed by Senator West of Louisiana, spokesman for the sugar and rice interests of the South. West denied vigorously the alleged benefits of reciprocity to the coast. He declared it to be a "collusion existing between the sugar planters of the Hawaiian Islands and the refiners of San Francisco." Trade with Hawaii was characterized as "miserable" and "picayune." Stress was placed cleverly upon the use of Chinese labor. Citing statistics to prove his point, the Louisiana Senator sought to prove that $750,000 in duties might be sacrificed to secure a possible $500,000 in trade. The bill should be labelled, he declared, "A bill to give the Sandwich Islands $3,000,000 per annum for a lease of sufferance for seven years." Strategic necessity behind the control of Hawaii was denounced as a fiction of the imagination. West closed by attempting to secure consideration of the bill as a special order. Sargent avoided the trap and refused as well to permit post-

---

[58] *Cong. Rec., op. cit.,* V, 5461ff.

ponement in favor of other business, denouncing the devious means used to defeat the measure.

On August 14 consideration was again resumed, and Norwood of Georgia took the floor with essentially the same arguments as those of West. A new element was injected, however, by his prediction as to the evil consequences to the South should the measure pass. In lurid tones, the Georgians declared that "three hundred thousand blacks to run as savages through the wilderness" would be turned loose should the Treaty become operative.

Further support for the attack came from Morrill who advanced again his legalistic approach. Serious losses to New England traders in the West Indian trade were predicted, providing the key to much of the Vermont viewpoint. "I consider this one of the worst possible bargains that ever was presented to the American Senate," declared the Vermont statesman. To prevent frauds, Morrill suggested amendments enabling the Treasury to take especial care to verify Hawaiian imports, and providing for termination of the treaty by the President should frauds be revealed.[59]

Senator Boutwell, former Hawaiian lobbyist, followed with a vigorous defense, and dismissed the arguments of Morrill as lacking in sincerity, attributing his opposition to the fears of Vermont that reciprocity with Hawaii might open the door to a Canadian treaty. Concluding his arguments, Boutwell served notice upon the Senate, "If we reject this treaty we transfer these islands either to France or Great Britain, and we diminish our markets, we diminish our political power, we limit the influence of our institutions, we circumscribe American ideas, we retard the progress of American civilization."

After further remarks in support of the bill from Logan, and rebuttal by West, the Morrill motion for amending the act was voted down 30 to 7, all Southern votes other than that of the Vermont Senator. Senator Gordon of Georgia made a last effort to check action by a motion for postponement until December; this was lost with but 8 votes favorable. Thereupon, by a vote of 29 to 12 the Senate endorsed the enabling legislation. With the exception of votes of Booth and Morrill, every opposition vote was from the South.[60]

Thus ended the immediate struggle over reciprocity. To his wife Allen wrote with a sense of labors well done: "Is it not Glorious that the Bill has passed to carry the Treaty into effect. . . . You have no idea of the labor & anxiety I have had on this business, but if it is of

---

[59] *Ibid.,* 5567ff.
[60] *Ibid.,* 5572.

value to the Islands, I am rewarded that I have done them some good."
How much of this gratification was furthered by a sense of improvement of his own fortunes, it is impossible to determine. It is interesting to note, however, that his associate in the Hawaiian sugar interests congratulated him upon the "glorious victory" and lost no time in informing him that "Princeville crop will have the benefits of the Treaty."[61]

The final vote on reciprocity reflected the general apathy with which the project had come to be regarded as it dragged out into an apparently interminable proceeding. Final inauguration of the Treaty attracted no important comment. The Senate and House debates reveal fully the extent to which political interest dominated the entire affair. Even at that, it is perhaps doubtful as to whether the enabling legislation would have been passed without administration intervention. Reciprocity had been an Hawaiian measure from the beginning to the end. Its final success was due almost entirely to the national interest which the United States had come to associate with the Islands due to their strategic commercial and naval importance in the Pacific.

---

[61] Letters from Andrew Welch in Allen Papers dated August 14 and September 6, 1876. Since April, Welch had been jockeying with Allen as to whether their sugar should be sold or held awaiting passage of the treaty enabling legislation. Allen was to telegraph at the earliest prospect of final adoption and its provisions as to sugars in bond. This was a matter of much speculative concern.

CHAPTER VII

RECIPROCITY AT WORK

Sought by the Hawaiian Islands as a means of securing economic and political stability, the Reciprocity Treaty of 1875 proved a turning point of the utmost importance in their history. Rather than forestalling the disintegration of the native monarchy, it hastened its end. Instead of quieting political unrest, it generated influences which tended to intensify it. Its effects upon the development of Hawaii were indeed revolutionary. The workings of the Treaty, therefore, are deserving of careful attention in order that further diplomatic developments may be viewed in proper perspective.

THE EFFECT OF RECIPROCITY UPON HAWAII

All authorities are agreed upon one point in regard to reciprocity. It gave a tremendous impetus to economic and social changes in progress since the rise of the Hawaiian sugar industry. A contemporary Hawaiian historian, William D. Alexander, in a review of the period prepared in 1893 asserted, "The first effect of the reciprocity treaty was to cause a 'boom' in sugar, which turned the heads of some of our shrewdest men and nearly caused a financial crash."[1] Production of sugar expanded between 1876 and 1880 from 26,072,429 to 63,584,871 pounds and the value of the crop from $1,272,334.53 to $4,322,711.48, showing the immediate nature of the Treaty's effects. During the following five years production further increased to 171,350,314 pounds with a value of $8,356,061.94. Expansion was continuous until 1889 before it reached its fullest extent.

Speculative characteristics in this new development of the sugar industry were noticeable at once. Sugar exports to the United States increased within four years after 1876 from some twelve thousand to nearly forty-seven thousand short tons. Immediate price increases equalling the remitted duties made increased production attractive. Sugar rose 2.81 cents a pound immediately upon ratification, while molasses increased 6.25 cents a gallon. Profits on well-conducted plantations were admitted by no less an authority than Claus Spreckels to run as high as fifty per cent. The changed outlook for the planters was voiced in the

---

[1] Statement prepared for Commissioner Blount. See FR, 1894, 647.

sentiment with which C. Brewer and Company closed its books in 1876: "So ends the year, 1876, Praise God." To Elisha Allen, the planter and treaty negotiator, his compatriot J. Mott Smith wrote on March 10, 1878, "All our planters through it are riding the crest of the waves, and are getting out of the trough of the sea, where for so many years they were engulfed."[2] Thoughtfully he added that it would be unwise to "parade our profits" before the United States.

As a result of this situation it was inevitable that many would seek to engage in sugar production. Sales of land at high prices and other manifestations of speculative activity were quickly observable. The American Consul reported in 1876, "Lands are being freely purchased or leased." Thrum reported by 1878 a large increase in land sales the preceding year, while the *Hawaiian Gazette* noted on March 7, 1877, the founding of eight new plantations and plans for several others. Interestingly enough, one of the new enterprises was called the Reciprocity Sugar Company. Between 1872 and 1892 the number of sugar corporations nearly doubled. Great increases took place in the total acreage devoted to sugar growing.

Equally significant was the further tendency toward concentrated capitalism. The cost of land, expensive machinery, and the need for large labor forces continued as in the past to make for large holdings. The difficulty of producing sugar profitably on small holdings was even greater than before reciprocity. The new expansion, therefore, took the form of large enterprises. The capital investment ranged, as a rule, from $250,000 to half a million or more dollars. Capital invested in sugar production in 1872 had been estimated at about four million dollars but by 1889 it had increased six times.[3] While in the early stages of the boom it appears that the bulk of the new capital came from Hawaii and was represented by investments from profits in previous sugar enterprises as well as investments by commercial interests, it was controlled by those of American descent.

---

[2] Allen Papers. Smith reported he himself had made $18,000 in sugar dividends in 1877. Not all planters were thus favored. William Allen informed his father in 1879 that several plantations were still in debt from $200 to $450,000. With good management an Hawaiian planter could produce sugar at some $35.00 a ton as compared with $75.00 in the United States and $40.00 in the West Indies. The yield in Hawaii was four tons to the acre, about three times that in the United States and nearly twice the West Indian yield.

[3] Thrum's *Almanac and Annual* is a good source in which to follow economic developments of the period. In 1893 Thrum compiled a detailed analysis of the sugar companies for Commissioner Blount. It reveals that by this date the smallest sugar corporation was capitalized at $120,000 while the largest was $10,000,000. Three corporations alone accounted for nearly one-half the total for all enterprises. Non-incorporated small enterprises represented a capitalization of only $3,000,000. See FR, 1894, 1081-1105.

The largest single development in Hawaii became the operation of Claus Spreckels of California. Born in Germany and coming to the United States in 1830, Spreckels came to California with the gold rush and became first a grocer and then a sugar refiner. By 1876 he had become the largest refiner on the West coast with a virtual monopoly. Originally an opponent of reciprocity because of fear of competition from Hawaii's high grade sugar, Spreckels saw its inevitability because of the national interests involved and sought to take advantage of it by investment in Hawaiian sugar production. He obtained under somewhat questionable circumstances special water rights from the Hawaiian government to develop an irrigation system for his plantations in the Islands. Taking advantage of his control of refineries on the Pacific coast which were the indispensable market for other planters, Spreckels achieved quickly a position of great power. In addition to producing sugar, he was a heavy buyer and came virtually to control the market and price for Hawaiian sugar.[4] The political implications of this situation in terms of the reciprocity agreement will be noted later.

Important social consequences flowed from this rather autocratic economic system. The life of Hawaii shortly came to resemble that of the ante-bellum South in the United States with a small and powerful planter aristocracy in full possession of economic and social privileges. So dominant was the planter that he came to overshadow completely the mercantile element which had played so leading a role in the early history of foreign enterprise in Hawaii. The remaining merchant class was absorbed into and closely connected with the planter overlordship, as an examination of Hawaiian corporate holdings will clearly demonstrate.

The natives came to occupy a lowly position in the social scale. Considered unsatisfactory and insufficient in numbers for a plantation labor supply, they were unable to benefit from advantages which might otherwise have come to them. Not only did they occupy an inferior position, but their numbers continued to decline from 51,531 in 1872 to 40,622 in 1890.

THE LABOR PROBLEM

Faced with the need for a labor force over twice that used before reciprocity, a sharp labor shortage developed which produced a revived

---

[4] See sketch of Spreckels in *Dictionary of American Biography*, XVIII, 478; also Herbert Myrick, *The American Sugar Industry*, 230f., and George T. Surface, *The Story of Sugar*, chap. xv. The Allen Papers contain many valuable letters from William Allen and J. Mott Smith relative to Spreckels' activities. On September 29, 1879, William Allen wrote his father that Spreckels had purchased virtually the entire sugar crop for 1880. "We were completely in his hands, he would have all or none, and as Spreckels controlled all the refineries, we could not send our sugar to an open market," wrote Allen.

demand for foreign immigration. Much of the new supply became cheap contract labor, mainly Oriental. The attitude of the planters toward this more or less servile labor element came to resemble the Southern philosophy of slavery days toward the negro in the United States. A Planter's Convention in 1882 declared frankly, "No country is expected to prosecute industries which are not profitable, and the experience of sugar growing the world over, goes to prove that cheap labor, which means in plain words servile labor must be employed in order to render this enterprise successful."[5]

An organization of the planting interests into something resembling a trade association was accomplished in 1882 with the emergence of the Planter's Labor and Supply Company. Through this medium the planters brought pressure to favor importation of cheap labor. A fundamental conflict of interest quickly appeared. The native government was desirous of a high type of immigration capable of repopulating the Islands upon a substantial basis, while the planter cared most for servility and cheapness in a labor supply.

As a result of this pressure, the government expended increasing sums for assistance in importing labor. A report prepared for Commissioner Blount in 1893 showed an expansion of such expenditures from $16,098.23 for 1874-76 to a high of $473,050.86 for 1882-84. The report affirmed frankly, "The amounts so expended were in aid of our sugar planters, who were in need of cheap labor for their plantations."[6]

The resulting conditions became a matter of considerable controversy. In the United States the contract labor system was viewed with disapproval. In 1873 when the importation of Japanese coolies was considered, Secretary Fish did not hesitate to express disapprobation. To Minister Peirce, he expressed the view that it was but "the slave trade under another name." Criticisms of the condition of the sugar laborer as amounting to "slavery" and "peonage" were common in the United States, and used with effect by opponents of reciprocity. The planters resented these attacks, and Hawaiian agents in the United States spent much effort to combat them. So resentful was the business community of Honolulu that on January 11, 1882, the Chamber of Commerce was led to memorialize the King against such charges in the American press. It is but fair to note that in 1890 only 10,991 out of 20,536 plantation laborers were employed under a contract system.

---

[5] The *Planters Monthly* argued that cheap contract labor was a necessary evil. The number of plantation laborers increased from 4,772 in 1872 to an estimated 12,000 in 1883. Claus Spreckels expressed his belief in 1893 that sugar production could not be carried on profitably without cheap labor.

[6] FR, 1894, 1139.

THE RACIAL PROBLEM

Whatever the merits or demerits of the general program of immigration, the dangers to the native Hawaiian race and its political system were beyond controversy. From 1877 to 1890 over 55,000 immigrants were added to the Hawaiian population. So large a number of these were Chinese as to arouse alarm and lead to an attempt to encourage Portuguese instead. This was not viewed originally with favor by the planters. In 1886 an immigration convention with Japan resulted in increased numbers of this race coming to the Islands. By 1890 the Japanese numbered 12,360, as compared to 15,301 Chinese and 8,602 Portuguese. A definite preference for Japanese labor was reported by the Inspector-General of Immigration.

The immediate effect was a weakening of the native race. By 1878 this trend was indicated when census reports disclosed a decline since 1878 of 4,023 in the native population, and an increase of 5,111 in foreign residents. By 1890 native Hawaiians numbered but 41,000 out of a total population of nearly 90,000. Declining in numbers and forced into an inferior position in the labor system, the natives devoted themselves to agriculture on a small scale, fishing, and maritime activities. Their small holdings, however, were of little significance in the new economic dispensation. While in 1890, 3,271 natives out of a total of 4,695 landholders held real estate, this was but a meager portion of the valuable land in Hawaii. In 1882 the American Minister declared that not a single sugar plantation was owned by a native Hawaiian.

Further evidence of the limited place of the native in the new economy is furnished by the fact that in 1893, according to information furnished United States Commissioner Blount by the Minister of Finance, he paid but $71,386.82 in taxes as contrasted with $274,516.74 contributed by American and European residents. Native landholdings upon which taxes were collected represented 257,457 acres to 1,052,492 for foreigners. Half-caste Hawaiians owned nearly twice the amount of property possessed by natives.[7]

At the same time the native enjoyed advantages not possessed by the imported foreign laborers. The average pure blood Hawaiian was characterized by a spirit of independence and pride of race, the product of elevation to a Christian civilization, which little conditioned him for the acceptance of a backward role in the life of his country. He was possessed likewise of a rather good educational background. Over sixty per cent of the natives were able to read and write in 1890, while 12,053 out of 12,360 Japanese, 13,277 of 15,301 Chinese, and 6,276 of 8,602

---

[7] FR, 1894, 542f. The term "native" is used to designate pure blood Hawaiians of the old native stock.

Portuguese were illiterate. While possessing little land as compared with the planter aristocracy, the average native owned a small holding which gave him a degree of economic security and independence not enjoyed by a contract laborer. All of these factors made the pure Hawaiian better able to appreciate the disturbed future for himself and his country inherent in the changes taking place.

Circumstances further gave the natives an opportunity to control the political destiny of the Islands. A literacy and property-holding qualification for suffrage, and its limitation prior to 1887 to "subjects" of the King, assured this result. Under the revised Constitution of 1887 "every male resident" was permitted to exercise the suffrage, subject to an oath of support to the Constitution in addition to literacy and tax qualifications. Orientals, however, were still excluded from voting. Though the new Constitution increased the political power of the large foreign property-holders in various ways, as will be observed later, the suffrage was still in native hands.

This situation provided the basis for much of the political disturbance in Hawaiian history. The natives, as demonstrated, were not possessed of extensive property and paid but 13.52 per cent of the taxes as compared to 51.98 per cent by Americans and Europeans, and 34.5 per cent by others, yet they were in the main those who voted the taxes. Commenting in a report to Commissioner Blount in 1893, Minister of Finance Porter wrote that "the pure Hawaiian pays $1.01 in $7.39 of the taxes, owns 1 in every 7.02 acres of the taxable land, and holds two-thirds of the offices and positions under the Government." Out of this grew racial antagonism and constant rumblings of republicanism or annexation.   •

FURTHER AMERICANIZATION OF HAWAII'S ECONOMY

Especially important from the standpoint of American policy was the place of American capital in this picture. Reciprocity provided the final impulse toward an Americanization of Hawaii already under way for some decades. The almost miraculous economic development previously described was American in every fiber. By 1883 the value of sugar properties in Hawaii owned by those of American extraction was assessed at $10,180,164, about two-thirds of their actual value, and much of it built up after 1876. In 1885 the Hawaiian agent at Washington, H. A. P. Carter, estimated the value of the properties at $10,500,000 and affirmed that six-sevenths of it had been created under the Treaty.[8]

---

[8] Quoted *New York Tribune*, January 5, 1885. The term "American" is used in the sense that those investing were American born or their descendants. It does not necessarily imply that the capital came from the United States, and Hawaiian observers contended that little capital was actually imported.

There is little reason to doubt the accuracy of the observation. A careful analysis by Thomas Thrum for Commissioner Blount in 1893 showed that out of a total capital stock of $28,274,000 in Hawaiian sugar corporations, $18,594,695 was controlled by native Americans and $2,-960,280 by Hawaiian-born Americans. In addition, those of American nationality controlled another $915,000 in non-incorporated enterprises.

American capital was not lacking in other fields, though nowhere so dominant as in sugar. H. A. P. Carter claimed seven millions invested in the transportation system. Thrum estimated in 1893 that the total of American controlled capital in Hawaii on the eve of the revolution was $25,194,166. Z. S. Spalding, appearing before the Senate Committee on Foreign Relations in 1894, claimed total commitments amounting to $50,000,000, and if loans, mortgages, and other advances to planters are considered the figure is perhaps not too high. An 1881 analysis of commercial relations with the United States under reciprocity indicates that by that date well over one million dollars in freights, cargo insurance, and commissions was going into American pocketbooks.

The serious problems to be created by reciprocity were little realized when it first became a possibility and then a reality. News of ratification of the Treaty by the United States Senate resulted in great jubilation in all quarters in Hawaii. Despite earlier misgivings, all appeared to sanction even the amendment prohibiting alienation of territory. "This clause will only render the treaty more popular . . . ," declared the *Hawaiian Gazette* on April 14, 1875. It was recognized frankly that the American motives had been political. The jubilant American Minister informed the State Department that while reciprocity was not yet complete, it "has nevertheless inspired the Planters and Merchants here with hope and confidence in regard to the benefits hereafter to be derived."

Enthusiasm was somewhat dulled and hopes threatened by the slow procedure by which the Treaty received final endorsement. This was reflected as usual in political unrest and by August, 1876, the King personally expressed to Minister Peirce his concern over the situation. Fears were at an end with the receipt in September of news of final adoption of necessary enabling legislation. A royal proclamation announced the result to the people and declared, "This country has now its way opened to flourish like a green bay tree; capital and immigration will be attracted to it; and the rich bounties which God and nature have bestowed upon these beautiful islands will be developed under a good government and able ministry." Foreign Minister Green affirmed that the measure should be accepted as a virtual guarantee of Island independence. Celebrations and torchlight processions through the streets of Honolulu on the evening of September 26, 1876, signalized the advent of the new arrangement from which both planters and the government expected so much. In the words of the *Hawaiian Gazette* for the following morning, the populace was "alive with joy."

HAWAIIAN POLITICS UNDER RECIPROCITY

Even prior to news of the final result, discontent and unrest disturbed the Islands. Sober realization of the consequences of reciprocity in terms of the influx of foreign capital and labor led many natives to begin to question its benefits. Others were doubtful about the limitations on Hawaiian sovereignty and argued that the ultimate loss of independence was presaged. The discontent mounted to such proportions in early 1876 as to lead Minister Peirce to declare that the presence of the Navy's *Lackawanna* alone preserved the country from serious outbreak. During July a naval force was retained at Honolulu at the expressed desire of the King, who feared a conspiracy of native nationalists supporting Queen Emma. By mid-August it was found necessary to increase the Palace Guard and the number of government troops.[9] This agitation was almost entirely from native sources.

The publicly expressed declarations of the King in favor of good government and his early moves in that direction, combined with the glow of good feeling upon the part of the planters in the midst of a rising tide of prosperity, aligned them for a time behind the monarchy. With this support the native administration enjoyed a few years of quiet characterized by a powerful pro-American dominance in the ministry and counsels of the King. In December, 1876, Peirce informed the State Department of the reorganization of the ministry with men of "talents, ability and integrity" noted "also for their pro-American proclivities" at its head. Elisha Allen resigned as Chief Justice and Chancellor to assume the post of Hawaiian Minister at Washington. On January 29, 1877, Peirce boasted that the Islands were "an American colony in all their material and political interests."

The American influence in the Hawaiian Government was further expanded by the resignation of Henry Peirce as American Minister June 29, 1877, and his later appointment as Hawaii's Foreign Minister. He continued to be an American in sentiment and actions, as is indicated by his statement to his successor, James M. Comly, that his services were as much in the interest of the United States as of Hawaii.[10] Comly him-

---

[9] Cf. Peirce to Fish for February 3; April 24; August 10 and 16, 1876, for analysis of the situation, *Dispatches,* XVII. This desire of the King for support was partly due to personal fears of the political opposition.

[10] Comly to Evarts, March 11, 1878, *op. cit.* Peirce served as Foreign Minister for but three months.

self reported in March, 1878, "The Ministry as it is now composed, is entirely American in sentiment, and three-fourths so by birth." This very fact, he later observed, was a cause of growing criticism.

By this date a native reaction against the alarming expansion of American interests began to take form. Aided, apparently, by other national interests opposed to the United States, an impression began to gather popular acceptance that reciprocity was leading directly toward annexation. Native leaders began to press the question in the Legislature and protests against the growing Americanization of the Islands became so common as to alarm the American Minister. Criticism of the King's American controlled ministry grew in volume and a legislative committee on foreign relations went so far in 1878 as to adopt a majority report declaring the reciprocity arrangement a violation of agreements with Great Britain. The Treaty itself drew increasing fire of critics on the ground that it favored American interests unduly as opposed to Hawaiians. A definite result of the agitation was the reorganization of the ministry with stronger native representation.[11]

THE TURBULENT EIGHTIES

During the following two years the unrest mounted to revolutionary proportions with the emergence once more in Hawaiian politics of a strong native nationalist movement. Minister Comly reported to Washington on February 6, 1880, that the legislative body had come to be controlled almost entirely by natives and that "rumors" and rumblings of revolution were prevalent. At the same time important American interests were seething with protest against the trend of governmental affairs.

Foremost among their objections was the rising debt of the monarchy and the consequent increase in the burden of taxation. Viewing in retrospect the situation the preceding year in his *Annual* for 1881, Thrum noted a "peculiar unrest and anxiety" upon the part of the business classes. The elections, he pointed out, showed a general defeat of "men of experience and worth" for public offices, and a consequent rise of those "who would be pliant to schemes of crafty lobbyists."

The familiar factor of depression likewise influenced the situation. As always, a period of rising prosperity of boom proportions produced little attention to expenses of government. By 1880 some of the evil results of the overexpansion created by reciprocity were beginning to make themselves felt. Thrum noted a dulling of general business activity and commented upon the growing constriction of credit as a result of

---

[11] See Comly to Evarts, July 8, 1878, for detailed account, *Dispatches,* XVIII.

overexpansion. Economic conditions remained prevailingly unstable through the early eighties. As the period for expiration of the reciprocity agreement drew at hand, the uncertainty created by the issue of its renewal added to the difficulties.

The problem of an adequate cheap labor supply for the planters also remained, according to Thrum, "yet a vexed and unsolved question." The increasing tendency of the King to accumulate a large national debt through wild financial schemes aroused the fears of the propertied classes. A growing preponderance of natives in control of the politics of the Islands was itself a cause for further concern. By August, 1880, Minister Comly reported to the State Department that conditions were so alarming as to cause an appeal by American residents for the use of his personal influence with the King in restoring more satisfactory government.

Promises to this end resulted in the restoration of comparative quiet until the meeting of the Legislature in the spring of 1882. Schemes for enlarged expenditures then once more attracted opposition. "There is such a state of anxiety in the minds of foreign residents," Comly informed the State Department, "that a number of the most prominent planters and business men have pressed me earnestly for some assurance that the United States Government would protect American citizens against such native legislation as might amount to practical confiscation of a large share of their estate in the Islands."[12]

At the same time, the Minister noted the emergence of "what is just beginning to be called here the Young Hawaiian Party—embodying a Hawaiian 'Know-Nothing' sentiment of opposition to the foreign influence in the government." This group, he emphasized, represented an "extreme" native point of view and was "looked upon with apprehension and dread by the foreigners who do the business and pay the taxes of the country."[13] Similar information was provided the State Department by Comly's successor, R. M. Daggett, who arrived at Honolulu in August, 1882. Reviewing the work of the recently adjourned Legislature under date of September 20, Daggett emphasized the extent to which it had been dominated by native interests. Upon the part of American residents he observed two conflicting reactions. One group represented the "young American" annexationist movement, supported in the main by younger persons without extensive property holdings. These persons were favorable to radical political agitation and even the defeat of reciprocity in order to embarrass the government and promote revolution and annexation.

---

[12] Comly to Frelinghuysen, May 8, 1882, *Dispatches,* XX.
[13] *Ibid.,* June 5, 1882.

Another source of unrest relative to existing conditions was provided by the older, more conservative and propertied class represented by the larger planters and merchants. The opposition of this element, Daggett reported, "is less to the form of government than to the manner of its administration." The inevitable result, in view of the dominant position occupied by American business in the Islands, was a tendency to look to the United States for protection and security.

By 1884 and 1885 conditions were still more disturbed. The declining price of raw sugar, coupled with the heavy burden of debt incurred by a majority of the planters with high interest rates ranging from eight to twelve per cent, produced serious difficulties. Increased competition from European beet and Mexican cane on the sugar market contributed to the planter's woes. The price of raw sugar on the San Francisco market had fallen from $130 and $140 per ton in 1882 to less than $100 by 1884. An overconcentration upon sugar production left the Islands little escape from the declining profits. Those planters fortunate enough to be free from debt, and they appear to have been few in number, were able to stand the strain, but others were faced with ruin. Increased governmental expenditures and a threat of silver coinage inflation, coupled with reports of political corruption, were viewed uneasily by those in such a position.

THE REVOLUTION OF 1887

The culmination of the mounting unrest and depression was a revolutionary outbreak in 1887 against the Kalakaua regime, a prelude to the more serious upheaval to come six years later. The Revolution of 1887, as it is known in Hawaiian history, is to be understood in the light of the combination of racial unrest and economic disturbance which followed upon the heels of the boom caused by the Treaty. The pages of Thrum for 1885 to 1887 reveal clearly the growth of these tendencies. The year 1886 was characterized by Thrum as "a trying one for the commercial and planting interests of the islands," and the situation had not improved by 1887. Gross irregularities in the elections and an extravagant and dissolute session of the Legislature voting appropriations of $4,552,477 in the face of a budget of $2,583,170 added to the bitter feeling.

As if this were not enough, the legislators proceeded to further affront the surviving Puritan instincts of the American element by licensing the sale of opium. The nationalistic fervor of the natives and the unscrupulous political leadership of one Walter Murray Gibson as head of the ministry increased the alarm of the planter and mercantile group.

The climax was reached in 1887 with the King personally involved in a gross scandal in connection with bribery in the issuance of opium contracts.[14]

By this date the opposition of the foreigners produced the formation of the Hawaiian League. In the words of one of its leaders, Lorrin A. Thurston, it was "an outgrowth of a revolt in the public minds of Hawaii against the aggressions, extravagances and debaucheries of the Kalakaua regime."[15] If the word "foreign" be inserted before the words "public mind" in the Thurston statement, a fairly lucid expression of the origins of the League is forthcoming. Its membership exceeded four hundred. It was interested merely in the "reform" of Island affairs. This reform Z. S. Spalding interpreted to mean that "the rights of property and the rights of the white people should be more respected and observed." This statement is revealing of the fundamental racial basis for the movement.

Foreign residents, and Americans in particular, were driven to some organized means of protecting their interests against what they regarded as dangerous political, financial, and moral excesses upon the part of the government, headed by a dissolute and corrupt sovereign. The *Honolulu Daily Bulletin* for May 23, 1887, summed up the prevailing view of this class in declaring that while the reign of Kalakaua had begun "full of promise" it had been "exceedingly disappointing in its later aspects." "The people," declared the *Bulletin,* "aroused to a sense of their wrongs, have resolved to assert their sovereignty."

In June, 1887, the foreign residents did indeed assert their sovereignty. Commenting later and reviewing the immediate circumstances leading to the revolt, the American Minister wrote, "During the month of June there was evident a quiet determination on the part of those met in business houses, or on the streets of Honolulu, that, sooner or later some change for the better must be made in Government affairs." Rumors of resistance by the King led to the importation and distribution of arms among the foreign population. The Hawaiian League itself was divided as to just what policy to pursue. The more radical members preferred open revolt. "Many favored dethroning the King, framing an entirely new Constitution, proclaiming a republic, electing a president and taking entire charge of the Government," wrote the Min-

---

[14] William D. Alexander, *History of the Later Years of the Hawaiian Monarchy and The Revolution of 1893,* together with the State Department dispatches from Hawaii and the annual surveys provided in Thrum, furnish an authentic and contemporary account of the political and economic situation from which this sketch is drawn.

[15] Lorrin A. Thurston, *Memoirs of the Hawaiian Revolution,* edited by Andrew Farrell. Chapters seven and eight present the full story.

ister. The prevailing view, however, was that sufficient pressure could reform the monarchy.

Pressure was applied in the form of a general indignation mass meeting on June 30 at Honolulu. Presiding over the meeting was Sanford B. Dole, head of the later republic. Resolutions were presented by Lorrin Thurston, principal leader in the more complete revolution of 1893. Actual revolution, however, did not prove necessary. The Thurston resolutions, adopted vociferously, declared the existing government of Hawaii "had ceased through corruption and incompetence adequately to perform the function and afford the protection to personal and property rights for which all Government exists." This blanket indictment was followed by a demand for a new ministry, constitutional amendment, and guarantees against personal interference with elections or legislative processes by the King.[16]

By the following week the intense feeling developed behind the demonstration had begun to cool and a reorganization of the ministry was accepted in good faith by the potential revolutionists. Following ministerial changes, the King proclaimed a new Constitution abrogating the somewhat arbitrary one of 1864. The new charter provided important limitations upon the power of the native government, and extended vastly the possibilities for foreign control over governmental functions. Most significant changes were those establishing the responsibility of the ministry to the Legislature, limiting the power of the King by requiring Cabinet approval for all official acts, popular election upon a limited suffrage basis of the formerly appointed House of Nobles, and extension of suffrage to American and European residents willing to take an oath of allegiance.

The new document marked the definite weakening of the power of the ancient nobility and royalty of Hawaii and indicated the end of the era of independent and absolute monarchy which had been subject to gradual alteration for decades. There is no doubt but that the constitutional changes wrung from Kalakaua prevented immediate overthrow of the monarchy. Once the power of the monarch was as definitely weakened as it had been by the new Constitution, any attempt to regain it could produce but one probable result—revolution and a republic.

AMERICA'S NEW IMPERIALISM

While these important developments were taking place in Hawaii, what of American policy relating to the Islands? In analyzing this subject properly it is important to notice that the inauguration of reciprocity

---

[16] Cf. *Honolulu Daily Herald,* July 1, 1887. Enclosure Minister Merrill to the State Department, *Dispatches,* XXIII.

with Hawaii was coincident with the beginnings of some shift in the attitude of the people of the United States toward matters of foreign policy. As has been noted previously, the public generally, as was observed so correctly by Secretary Seward, was not during the reconstruction era inclined to concern itself with problems of foreign affairs or imperial expansion. This period, however, may be said properly to have come to an end with the administration of President Hayes and the withdrawal of Federal forces from the South in 1877.

With the gradual passing of concern with serious internal problems, the late seventies and the eighties became the period during which the seeds of a more vigorous foreign policy and a tendency toward imperial expansion were sown. In fact, the political considerations behind the original acceptance of Hawaiian reciprocity fairly may be said to have indicated something of this new consciousness. The roots of the expansionism of the nineties were established in the preceding decades.

In the interest of the United States in Latin American affairs, the Congo, and the Far East, especially as related to Samoa and the Congo Conference, the beginnings of some abandonment of isolationist traditions of earlier years are observable. Perhaps more important than actual participation in international politics or the scramble for territorial position as indicating the trend of American policy, was the tone of the press, business journals, and general public utterances. From this angle, there are many indications of a broadening horizon of interest upon the part of the United States.

Americans followed with interest the exploits of European imperialism in Africa, and especially the adventures of Henry M. Stanley in the Dark Continent. "Let the procession of explorers go on. Many of them may be lost, but others will follow, and in the end the indomitable energy of the white man will conquer and hold this mysterious land and all its treasures," exclaimed the *Atlanta Constitution* of August 24, 1888. The religious press in particular approved and extolled the achievements of European imperialism in Africa.[17] Americans also were conscious of French and British expansion in the Pacific and such incidents as the occupation of the Fiji Islands in 1874 and the protectorate proclaimed over the Solomons in 1893 by the latter power.

A quickening sense of American economic destiny was also evident. The astounding business expansion of the United States following the Civil War, producing a new realization of economic power and its possible needs, was bound to influence foreign policies. *Bradstreet's* for April 12, 1884, sensed the situation and declared editorially: "It is now

---

[17] Cf. especially New York *Independent*, November 13, 1884, and other issues for interesting examples of such reactions.

coming to be perceived that it is no longer possible for us to dream of industrial or commercial isolation. . . . We are not free to say whether or not, or to what extent, we shall come within the range of foreign influence in commercial affairs." Later, the *American Manufacturer* was led to observe that "this subject of foreign markets is one that arises and will constantly arise in looking into the future of our industries."

Chambers of commerce in important eastern cities as well as on the Pacific coast began the organization of committees to study the feasibility of expanding Pacific trade. The government itself looked to the development of improved trade relations with Japan, Korea, and China. The Hayes administration in particular emphasized the need for an expanding commerce and scarcely a presidential message in that and succeeding administrations failed to point out this necessity. The idea that the United States might and should outdistance Great Britain in its Pacific trade and interests began to appear in many quarters.

If Americans did suffer any illusions as to the meaning of such activities, Europeans were not slow to catch their importance. In London, the *Pall Mall Gazette* declared: "The American republic is now at last beginning to have a foreign policy. The doctrine of complete isolation so long maintained by American statesmen has perished."[18] Commenting upon America, a writer in the English *Contemporary Review* for March, 1888, pointed out, "The whelp of former days has become a lion; and this alone signifies an immense change in the attitude of Europe." America, he affirmed, was a power to be reckoned with in the future by European nations.[19]

HAWAII AND AMERICAN PACIFIC INTERESTS

These influences are observable to some extent in the evolution of American policy toward Hawaii following the inauguration of reciprocity. The immediate policy of the Hayes administration was dictated by a scrupulous regard for the preservation of independence and the protection of all advantages gained through reciprocity. Informed by Minister Comly of native fears that reciprocity would lead to annexation, Secretary of State William M. Evarts made haste to instruct him to "disabuse" the Hawaiians on this matter. At the same time, Evarts was firm in pointing out that the United States could not adopt the view that the rights granted the United States under reciprocity were susceptible of extension to any other power. Hawaii's controversy with Great Britain,

---

[18] Cited in *Bradstreet's*, February 7, 1885.
[19] G. T. Bettany, "Europe vs. the United States."

France, and Germany over the rights of those powers under the Treaty made necessary some such statement of American policy.[20]

The brief period of the Garfield-Blaine diplomacy revealed an even more direct interest in Hawaiian affairs upon the part of the United States. The ambition of Blaine to inaugurate a "vigorous foreign policy" is well known, and it was but natural that reflections of this in Hawaiian policy were observable. Furthermore, the Secretary was backed by the President, who manifested a keen interest in Hawaii. As a member of Congress, James A. Garfield had participated actively in the debates as a supporter of reciprocity and the closest possible union of the two countries without actual annexation. His appreciation of the Hawaiian situation was revealed in an effort to secure his personal friend, B. A. Hinsdale, as ministerial appointee. One of the early Cabinet meetings on June 7, 1881, considered at some length matters of Hawaiian policy, and the diary of the President shows his careful attention. Garfield considered Hawaii as closely linked with the problem of an isthmian canal and the probable future expansion of American commerce in the Pacific.[21]

Almost immediate occasion was presented for a full exposition of the Garfield-Blaine point of view as a result of the growing difficulty of Hawaii in adjusting its commercial relations with Great Britain and rumors of a proposed convention with that power by which "coolie" labor would be imported from British possessions. From the first Britain had viewed with concern the negotiation of a reciprocity treaty and, if Minister Peirce is to be believed, sought to checkmate it.

Once the Treaty was negotiated, the British presented a vigorous protest through Consul-General Wodehouse at Honolulu, though somewhat against the will of that gentleman. The objection was based upon the ground that the reciprocity measure was a violation of existing commercial agreements between Hawaii and Great Britain.[22] A special mission by H. A. P. Carter to the major European powers concerned resulted in 1878 in a satisfactory agreement with Germany, but Great Britain for some time continued an aggressive objection to reciprocity. The British stand was made the stronger because of championship by the native elements in the Hawaiian Government increasingly antagonistic toward the United States.

---

[20] Cf. Comly to Evarts July 8, 1878, for resumé of difficulties over the Treaty, *Dispatches,* XVIII. Also Evarts to Comly, *Instructions,* II.

[21] Theodore Clark Smith, *The Life and Letters of James Abram Garfield,* 1167f.

[22] Peirce to Evarts, June 13, 1877, *Dispatches,* XVII. Wodehouse informed Peirce that he "would take all proper measures" to lead the British to withdraw their demands.

By the date of the elevation of Garfield to the Presidency, the threatened importation of British East Indian coolies for Hawaiian labor had become a live issue. Minister Comly called the matter to the attention of Washington and termed it "one of great and increasing danger to both Hawaiian and American interests." Comly believed that Hawaii was being subjected to British pressure to force such an arrangement, which would provide "innumerable opportunities for meddlesome interference with the internal affairs of this government."[23]

On June 30, 1881, Blaine took occasion to emphasize to Comly the opposition of the United States to any extension of the advantages of reciprocity to any other power. The Treaty, he declared, had been made "at the continuous and urgent request of the Hawaiian Government," and its provisions limited to the two powers. Any "pressure" by a third party to secure similar concessions would find the United States not "unobservant of its rights and interests," nor would it be "unwilling or unprepared to support the Hawaiian Government in the faithful discharge of its treaty obligations." Blaine thus reaffirmed more strongly the policy of Evarts, and placed the United States squarely behind Hawaiian efforts to protect itself from the demands of any other power for reciprocal trade advantages.[24]

November 19 of the same year, Blaine replied fully to the Comly notes on the proposed Coolie Convention, as it had come to be known. Such an agreement giving British representatives semi-judicial supervision over British subjects imported for labor purposes, as was contemplated, was declared to be an unjustifiable extension of extra-territoriality and in violation of Hawaiian sovereignty. The United States, Blaine emphasized, had sought at all times "the real and substantial independence" of Hawaii, and "has always avowed and now repeats that, under no circumstances, will it permit the transfer of the territory or sovereignty of these Islands to any of the Great European Powers."

A little later, on December 1, both an official and private communication to Comly extended the Blaine view. In a formal note for the view of Hawaiian officials, Blaine reviewed the history of American relationships with the Islands and the rise of "a legitimately dominant influence in the North Pacific, which it can never consent to see decreased by the intrusion therein of any element of influence hostile to its own." The dangers resulting from the decline of native population and increased Oriental immigration were emphasized. The preservation

---

[23] Comly to Blaine, August 29, 1881; Comly to Frelinghuysen, April 10, 1882, *Dispatches*, XX.
[24] *Instructions*, II.

of independence and neutrality remained the goals of American policy, Blaine affirmed. Hawaii had become the "key to the dominion of the American Pacific," and should its independence be threatened from "any cause" the United States, declared Blaine, "would unhesitatingly meet the altered situation by seeking an avowedly American solution for the grave issues presented."

Privately, Blaine referred to the Islands as "a part of the productive and commercial system of the American States" and "practically members of the American zollverein, an outlying district of the State of California" so far as commercial life was concerned. Their political structure, however, was "as remote from our control as China." The soundness of the choice made by the United States in early years when it chose "commercial assimilation" in preference to "material annexation" was praised by Blaine. It was a policy which must be adhered to. The great threat to it, the Secretary felt to be the declining native population and the incentive toward importation of low grades of foreign labor transforming the entire character of Hawaiian civilization. To solve this problem, Blaine suggested the careful cultivation and development of some form of assisted American immigration.

Further evidence of the care with which Blaine viewed Hawaiian affairs is provided by his strenuous objections to a proposed international tour by the King. This, reported the British Minister at Washington, the Secretary regarded as very dangerous and apt to result in unsatisfactory commitments by the monarch to European powers.[25] While Blaine had no further opportunity to oversee Hawaiian relations until 1889, he had, with the limited precedents provided by Evarts, succeeded in relating new developments in Hawaii to the former fundamentals of American policy.

Alice Felt Tyler in her study of Blaine's foreign policy has tended to magnify the importance of his Hawaiian policy as an extension of the Monroe Doctrine into the Pacific. Actually Blaine was merely voicing the fundamentals of the original Tyler doctrine as developed over some decades when he included Hawaii within the American system of paramount interest. His contribution consisted of the emphatic statement of American policy in relation to the peculiar advantages secured as a result of reciprocity. Any other secretary of state would likely have pursued a similar policy.

Blaine's successor, Frederick T. Frelinghuysen, manifested a keen interest in the internal affairs of Hawaii so far as they affected the

---

[25] Thornton to Granville, April 12, 1881, "Private Letters from the British Embassy in Washington to the Foreign Secretary Lord Granville, 1880-1885," *Annual Report American Historical Association*, 1941, I, 73-189.

United States. Reports of continued political unrest from R. M. Daggett, Arthur appointee as Minister, and emphasis upon the difficulties of American capitalists led the Secretary to an unusual step. Under date of May 31, 1882, Frelinghuysen instructed the Minister to present a "very urgent request in all proper quarters" against measures "subversive of the material interests of so many of its citizens who, on the faith of international comity, have given their wealth, labor and skill to aid in the prosperity of Hawaii." The United States, declared Frelinghuysen, in view of the consideration that a large part of the "operating capital and mechanical enterprises of Hawaii has been contributed by citizens of the United States" as well as the "traditions of past intercourse" could not hesitate to protest "the adoption of a shortsighted policy which would be alike harmful to existing vested interests and repellant of the further influx of capital from abroad."[26]

In many respects this represented a more significant departure from past precedents than anything advanced by Blaine. While American diplomatic agents had never hesitated to bring pressure to bear in order to protect or advance American interests, this was the first time the State Department itself had recognized officially the investment of American capital in Hawaii as justifying a protest against the domestic policies of Hawaii. The Frelinghuysen note represented a brief expression of what came later in American expansion to be termed "dollar diplomacy." Reciprocity, therefore, had set the stage for further significant developments in the relations of Hawaii with the United States.

---

[26] FR, 1894, 1162.

CHAPTER VIII

PEARL HARBOR AND THE RENEWAL OF RECIPROCITY

By far the most important issue involving Hawaii during the eighties was the renewal of the reciprocity agreement due to expire at the end of seven years from its inception. Without its extension it was inconceivable that the planting interests would not force the Hawaiian Government to turn elsewhere for similar advantages. The inevitable shift in economic attachments would have seriously weakened ties with the United States. On the other hand, there was little incentive upon the part of the United States to renew the Treaty unless further concessions were made by Hawaii. The trade involved was too meager and advantageous for too small a section of the country to provide a strong economic motivation for a continuation of reciprocity. Political favors were needed to strengthen the drive for renewal. That such favors could be extended by the Hawaiian Government with safety to itself was doubtful. Thus the entire problem was a perplexing and difficult one.

In Hawaii, following the first wave of enthusiastic endorsement of the Treaty as representing a new era in its development, considerable opposition to reciprocity appeared from native and anti-American sources. With the natives, fears that reciprocity meant the ultimate absorption of Hawaii by the United States were uppermost. British and other competing business interests were not averse, naturally, to sabotaging the arrangement in order to promote their own trade. With few exceptions the American propertied groups swung into line behind the proposition to renew the Treaty.

CLAUS SPRECKELS IN HAWAII

The situation was complicated by the position of Claus Spreckels in relation both to the production of sugar in Hawaii and refining in California. A dominant factor by 1881 in the entire sugar industry, the monopolistic practices of the German-born sugar baron made his attitude of peculiar importance. During the early stages of the attack upon reciprocity in Hawaii and the United States, he worked for the continuance of the Treaty. In 1879 Spreckels had a representative in Washington working on behalf of the measure. The very fact, however, that Spreckels saw in reciprocity an advantage to his interests served to antagonize the independent planters who were struggling against his growing stranglehold on both the production and marketing of sugar. The independents were willing to make use of his influence despite this and on January 28, 1881, J. Mott Smith wrote Allen, "I think you will find in Washington that those who have his [Spreckels] confidence will sustain and second your efforts and arguments."[1]

By 1882 Spreckels appears to have become less vigorous in defending the Treaty and his interest reported as shifted to showing "a strange indifference." He declined to finance further lobbying, choosing rather to work directly through Senator Miller of California and other friends. This decision appears to have been influenced by Spreckels' decision to lessen his Hawaiian sugar interests in favor of American beet sugar development. The Planters Labor and Supply Company, representing the independent planters, now took up the burden of the support of the reciprocity measure. Despite some opposition from native nationalists, these planters secured the appointment by the government of J. Mott Smith as Special Commissioner to assist Elisha Allen at Washington. In his capacity as Hawaii's Minister, the latter had been combating assiduously since 1877 any and all attacks on the Treaty. As early as September of that year Allen had informed his government that opposition was to be expected and must be fought "with all the vigor and power we command."[2]

Late in 1882 Allen was informed by Foreign Minister Gibson of the desire of Hawaii to negotiate for renewal of the Treaty. Gibson emphasized that it should be done without further encroachment upon Hawaiian sovereignty and that if at all possible even Article IV of the existing agreement should be voided. Similar views and instructions were communicated to J. Mott Smith. Gibson was desirous also of some clause in the new treaty which would release Hawaii from its obligations should the American sugar tariff be reduced thereby lessening the Hawaiian advantage under reciprocity.[3] Such proposals had little chance of success in view of the attitude of the United States.

---

[1] The Allen Papers contain many very important letters on this situation. Spreckels was urged at one time to give a contract for ships to John Roach of Chester, Pennsylvania, to influence Pennsylvania Congressmen in favor of reciprocity. Hawaiian representatives were fearful, however, that the Spreckels monopoly prejudiced reciprocity generally.

[2] On November 14 of the same year Allen wrote, "I have reports of every day's doings in Congress the same evening and I shall write you instantly of all matters of interest." In 1879 Allen prevailed upon New Englanders with investments in Hawaii to employ Senator Boutwell to support the Treaty. An unsuccessful effort was made to get similar aid from San Francisco. Allen Papers. See Dozer, D.M., "Opposition to Hawaiian Reciprocity, 1876-1888," *Pacific Historical Review*, XIV, for a careful study of the propaganda against reciprocity.

[3] See letters in Allen Papers and also Gibson to Allen and Gibson to Smith in *Foreign Office and Executive File*, AH.

There a battle was looming over reciprocity by the time Hawaii indicated its desire to renew the Treaty. Opposition to the measure had developed within a short time after its adoption and was a cause of concern to the Hawaiian Minister at Washington. As early as May 1879, Representative Gibson of Louisiana had introduced a resolution calling for termination of the agreement. This was the opening gun in the Southern sugar industry's attack on reciprocity. An unfriendly report by the Secretary of the Treasury, John Sherman, in 1878 also had caused concern to those interested in reciprocity.[4] Sherman indicated that the remission of duties was in favor of Hawaii at the expense of the Treasury.

Antagonism toward the reciprocity measure came from several quarters. On the Pacific coast the operations of the Spreckels refinery monopoly created a reaction which did the Treaty no little harm. Those struggling against the Spreckels combination were at least lukewarm if not opposed to a measure which, as a result of his shrewd manipulations, had furthered a sugar monopoly. Popular feeling against the sugar monopoly was very strong. Hawaiian promoters of reciprocity found, therefore, the San Francisco press in 1882 indifferent if not in opposition. In Oregon, opinion was "positively hostile." In that state the antagonism was based in part on opposition to the Spreckels interests, and more definitely on the feeling that the Treaty had worked to the advantage of San Francisco at the expense of commercial interests of the Pacific Northwest.[5]

THE BATTLE OF THE SUGAR TITANS

By far the most serious opposition to reciprocity came from the eastern section of the United States from both sugar refiners and producers of sugar cane. The early eighties witnessed the maneuverings which resulted in 1887 in the creation of the Sugar Trust, one of the

---

[4] Gibson wrote Senator Bayard of Delaware in 1876 regarding the injury reciprocity occasioned the sugar industry of his state. Sherman's statistical analysis of the results of the Treaty in his report for 1878 was highly unfavorable and interpreted by Hawaiians as indicating his desire to please southern interests and secure support for his presidential ambitions. See Severance to Allen, October 13 and October 27, 1879. It was suggested that pressure be brought to bear upon him. Allen Papers.

[5] See letters from J. Mott Smith in Allen Papers, especially for June 18, 1882. Mott Smith hinted that the use of "coin" might change the tone of the San Francisco press, an indication of the methods used by the planters in promoting their case. The *San Francisco Chronicle* was especially vigorous in its assaults upon reciprocity. Oregon's views were influenced by the fact that cold figures showed San Francisco exports to Hawaii had increased from $47,000 in 1875 to $221,000 in 1881.

most powerful of the several combinations then under way in the American business world. A three-way struggle among the refining groups of the East, led by the Havemeyer interests which ultimately dominated the Sugar Trust, the brown sugar producers of the Gulf coast relying upon the reviving cane sugar industry in the South, and the Spreckels controlled refiners in California relying on Hawaiian sugar was reaching a critical stage just at the moment renewal of the Hawaiian Treaty became an important issue. Southern sugar growers and refiners, as was indicated previously, were fearful that the increasing production of Hawaiian sugars constituted a threat to their midwestern sugar market. Every dollar of remitted duties for the Hawaiian planters was a discrimination against their industry. The now reconstructed South was in a better position than formerly to protect its interests and its opposition to reciprocity was therefore more serious.

More threatening to renewal, however, was the battle between the eastern refiners and the Pacific coast titan, Claus Spreckels. The Hawaiians themselves were aware of this, and J. Mott Smith early expressed the feeling that the crux of the reciprocity problem was "the antagonisms of Mr. Spreckels and the eastern refiners." *The Planter's Monthly* in February, 1883, expressed the same view and noted that the contest was ". . . daily narrowing down to a difference between the eastern sugar refiners . . . and those statesmen who look at the treaty as a simple and effective political expedient for giving the Government at Washington a paramount influence in Hawaiian affairs." The eastern trust builders feared both the resistance of Spreckels to a national combination of refiners and his power, aided by abundant supplies of Hawaiian raw sugar, actually to invade their domain.

Voicing the views of this group, the New York *Journal of Commerce* on March 2, 1882, attacked the Treaty as one-sided rather than reciprocal and supported by "free trade theorists." Eastern importers and manufacturers, it pointed out, were becoming alarmed increasingly at the great expansion of Hawaiian sugar production and fearful of its bid for the eastern market as well as that of the West coast. Hawaiian sugar, it asserted, already was invading the mid-western market. It was further contended that Hawaii was being utilized as a way station for East Indian sugar which thus escaped the duty. The steadily improved quality of Hawaiian sugar, which rendered refining less expensive and even unnecessary for a part of the market, was an added cause for antagonism.[6]

---

[6] Elisha Allen, Jr., analyzed the nature of the conflict in several letters to his father. See especially that of April 26, 1882, in the Allen Papers. See the "Preliminary Report on Trusts and Industrial Combinations" in *Reports of the Industrial Commission,* 1900, I, for the background of the Havemeyer trust. Spreckels

The eastern refiners were aided by allied business and commercial interests including the wholesale grocers who had formed a combination to control the marketing of sugar and cooperating with the Trust. A fair example of the way in which influence was exerted is provided by the National Board of Trade. Prior to 1882 the *Proceedings* of this national and influential business organization show a consistent endorsement of the reciprocity idea. That year a resolution was offered by a New York member petitioning Congress to abrogate the Treaty. Loss of revenue to the Treasury, the fostering of a sugar monopoly on the West coast, and the encouragement of coolie labor in Hawaii in competition with free American labor were offered as the objections. The true basis of the complaint was indicated, however, in a simple statement that the Pacific coast sugar monopoly was "greatly injuring our merchants and refiners of the East." The Executive Council of the Board refuted these allegations and it was not until 1883 that the National Board followed in the footsteps of the New York Board and adopted a formal resolution protesting the Hawaiian Treaty.[7]

HAWAII'S RESPONSE TO ATTACKS ON RECIPROCITY

The Hawaiian agents entrusted with meeting attacks upon the Treaty both in the press and in Congress and with forwarding its ultimate extension were under no illusions as to the seriousness of the task before them. The letters exchanged among J. Mott Smith, Henry Severance, the Hawaiian Consul at San Francisco, and Elisha Allen are replete with references to the situation which indicate a high degree of realistic thinking. The independent planters in Hawaii were ready and did contribute considerable sums to promote their cause both in the press and at Washington. Mott Smith expressed the view that they faced "an organization for the defeat of the Treaty more determined than has hitherto assailed us, and one which probably is spending money."[8] The Hawaiians were determined to fight fire with fire and references to the use of "coin" to change the tone of the California press and expressions of determination to "carry the fight" to the enemy appear increasingly in their correspondence for the time. "It will be for us to marshal the facts, urge on the defense, and by our zeal and constant activity to stir

---

actually started a refinery in Philadelphia and fought the Trust almost single-handed in the late eighties, a struggle continued by Claus Spreckels, Jr., after his father had capitulated. The Trust retaliated by starting a Pacific coast refinery. See also letters from Elisha Allen in *Letter Copy Book, Foreign Office File*, AH.

[7] See *Proceedings of the Annual Meeting of the National Board of Trade*, 1876-1884.

[8] See letter dated January 28, 1881, Allen Papers.

up and quicken our United States friends," wrote Mott Smith. "We shall have to make even our California friends believe that our Treaty is absolutely necessary to their own progress and prosperity," he continued. Facts and figures designed to justify the Treaty in Oregon were marshalled. The Planters Association took steps to raise funds to promote an "educational" campaign.

The Hawaiians met with excellent success in their effort to secure early the necessary executive endorsement of the renewal of the Treaty. The letters of the resourceful Elisha Allen indicate that he was in close touch with the State Department as early as 1881, and that his strong and constantly reiterated argument for the continuation of reciprocity rested upon political rather than economic grounds. The necessity for the protection of established American interests in the Islands as an essential part of the national policy of the United States in the Pacific in terms of the promotion of commerce was emphasized again and again.

In December, 1882, President Arthur called attention in his annual message to the importance of renewing the Treaty. "While certain provisions of this compact may have proved onerous, its existence has fostered commercial relations which it is important to preserve," he commented. The following year the President called attention to the fact that the question of renewal was now before Congress, repeated his admonition of the preceding year, and went so far as to state, "I am convinced that the charges of abuses and frauds under that treaty have been exaggerated. . . ." Again in 1884 the matter was called to the attention of Congress, and on June 9 the advice of the Senate was requested as to extension. Ten days later Senator Miller unexpectedly reported from the Committee on Foreign Relations a resolution advising renewal of the Treaty and suggesting that Hawaii be requested to permit the establishment of an American naval base at Hawaii. Consideration of the resolve was blocked by Senator Morrill.

CONGRESSIONAL OPPOSITION TO RECIPROCITY

In the meantime attacks upon the Treaty had multiplied. Sessions of the first meeting of the Fifty-seventh Congress were hardly under way before on January 9, 1882, when two resolutions were presented to the Senate. One, offered by Senator Hill of Georgia, requested the Committee on Foreign Relations to consider termination of the Treaty. Senator Jones of Louisiana sponsored a joint resolution to terminate the measure. Both, of course, represented the growing concern of southern sugar producers. In the Senate, however, the matter was in the friendly hands of Senator Miller, a strong champion of the Pacific expansion of the United States.

In the House also, the opposition was active. On January 16 Darrall of Louisiana seconded his colleagues in the Senate by introducing a measure to abrogate the Treaty. Hardy of New York, inspired by the refiners of that area, sponsored a resolution to terminate the agreement with Hawaii. Protests against reciprocity were presented from citizens of Georgia and Louisiana, and memorials against it were submitted from the New Orleans Chamber of Commerce and the Cotton Exchange, the Produce Exchange, and the Merchants and Traders Exchange of the same city. Behind these was the Louisiana Sugar Planters Association which also protested against the Treaty. The refiners were no doubt responsible for a variety of petitions from "citizens" of New York, New Jersey, and Pennsylvania, the Baltimore Chemical and Fertilizer Exchange, the New York Chamber of Commerce, the New York Maritime Exchange, and several seaboard Boards of Trade.

On March 10, Senator Gibson of Louisiana delivered an extended condemnation of the Treaty. He echoed the general line of attack of opponents of reciprocity. Attention was called to the report of the Secretary of the Treasury for 1878 which showed that the total increase in American trade with Hawaii since inception of the reciprocity agreement had mounted to $15,661 less in value than the remitted duties on Hawaiian imports into the United States. The Treaty was not reciprocal at all, declared Gibson, but pro-Hawaiian and a subsidy at the expense of American taxpayers for the benefit of a few planters in a distant island. The surrendered duties in 1881 alone, he emphasized, amounted to $2,400,000. The dangers both to the sugar growers of the South and refiners in the East were stressed, indicating the merging of the interests of the two groups. The peculiar unrest of Louisiana was explained in statistics offered by Gibson which showed that the sugar production of that state now represented but ten per cent of the total consumed in the United States as contrasted with forty-seven per cent before the Civil War. His state felt that its drive to recover its former position had been dealt a deadly blow by the Reciprocity Treaty.[9]

The second session witnessed no respite in the war on reciprocity. In the Senate, Morrill, as usual, proved the most persistent foe. A bill introduced in January, 1883, to terminate the Treaty was referred to the Foreign Relations Committee and then transferred to Morrill's own Finance Committee together with a resolution to the same purpose.

[9] Facts drawn from *Cong. Rec.*, 47 Cong., 1 sess. Louisiana's sugar production in 1855 had reached 177,000 tons; in 1875 it was 60,000 tons, but a drive for its recovery was under way.

The Committee submitted a report proposing a thorough investigation of the workings of the Treaty. On January 9 Morrill defended his report and declared the Treaty had not benefited the natives of Hawaii but "people who have gone there for the purpose of making a speculation," a charge which could be directed only at Spreckels. The use of coolie labor was condemned. The Vermont Senator also went to some lengths to denounce the political motivation of the Treaty, and spoke caustically of "a sort of jingo empire in the Pacific Ocean" which would be of little value and a problem to defend. Miller of California warmly defended the measure but the Morrill proposal to review it was adopted by a vote of 31 to 20.[10]

In the House, Belmont of New York presented a resolution on February 19, 1883, calling upon the Treasury to report upon the operation of the Treaty. On February 24 this resolution was reported favorably and adopted, after which a second motion to reconsider the previous action was passed by friends of the measure. Blount of Georgia, who was to figure prominently in Hawaiian affairs ten years later, vigorously attacked the whole scheme of reciprocity and favored its abolition. Belmont, despite his previous action, attempted to present a more favorable view and supported it with reservations. No further attention was paid to Hawaii in that session.

The first session of the Forty-Eighth Congress in 1884 witnessed a definite weakening of the strength of the Congressional opposition to reciprocity. This was due in part to an approaching reconciliation of the conflicting interests of the eastern and western sugar refiners and to some growth in the conception of American national interests in the Pacific and Hawaii. No doubt the aggressive campaign of the Hawaiians to influence opinion undertaken two years earlier also had something to do with the tightening resistance to attacks upon the Treaty. Resolutions in the Senate against the agreement presented by the Louisiana Senators were reported unfavorably by the Committee on Foreign Relations. In the House similar resolutions met with a cold reception. It was noticeable that the peak in opposition to reciprocity had been reached the preceding year and occasional outbursts from the Louisiana members were the only expressions of Congressional opposition.

---

[10] *Ibid.*, 2 sess., XIV. The Senate report spoke of the "great inequality, and the conspicuous injustice to our government and the people" involved in Hawaiian reciprocity. It declared it represented greater concessions than would now be demanded by Hawaii and "that nothing less than its abrogation affords a sufficient remedy." *Senate Reports,* 47 Cong., 2 sess. A minority report placed further stress upon the constitutional objection to the Treaty that, as a revenue measure, it had not originated with the House.

The report of the Senate Committee on Foreign Relations took sharp issue with the earlier report of the Finance Committee. It failed to discover that charges American trade and revenues were not adequately compensated by reciprocity were valid and pointed to "higher considerations" involved. The expansion of world commerce in the Pacific and the importance of the Islands to the American participation in this trade were cited as demanding a policy of dominant American influence in Hawaii. The transcontinental railroads of the United States and the proposed Isthmian canal were pointed to as evidence of future American commercial development in Pacific areas. Increased American population and capital in Hawaii were results of reciprocity which helped make the Islands an outpost of the United States.

A minority report, presented by Senator John Sherman, took issue with the majority as represented by Senator Morgan and summarized the basic charges which had been advanced against reciprocity. Extensive improvements in the quality of Hawaiian sugar were defeating the intent of the Treaty. It was charged also that there were extensive re-exports of Chinese and East Indian sugars through Honolulu which thus escaped the full sugar duty. This loss, the minority charged, amounted to $12,795,578 since the inception of reciprocity. Losses on rice imports which were following similar channels were pointed out. "We require no fortified Gibraltar, no halfway houses on any of the highways of the ocean leading to colonial dependencies," the minority argued.

It is questionable whether the charges against Hawaii presented by the minority members were substantiated by facts. It is true that reciprocity was producing results which were more important and advantageous to Hawaii economically than to the United States. The few million dollars involved, however, were certainly outweighed by the impetus reciprocity gave to strengthening American interests. On a dollars and cents basis it was possible to prove that the United States was getting the worst of the bargain in many particulars, but this was a minor consideration.

Matters were brought to a head through the negotiation with Hawaii by Secretary of State Frelinghuysen of a convention signed December 6, 1884, providing simply for the extension of reciprocity for another seven year period. It was submitted to the Senate three days later with full administration endorsement. Its final approval, however, was not a simple matter. One difficulty, of course, was the almost immediate change in administrations at Washington including a shift in party alignments.

There is no evidence, however, of any important break in Hawaiian policy as a result of the election of Grover Cleveland to the presidency. As early as December following the election, H. A. P. Carter, placed in charge of the negotiations for reciprocity renewal the preceding April, was in touch with Senator Thomas Bayard of Delaware, already understood to be the incoming Secretary of State. The Senator was by no means unfriendly to the Hawaiian desires and had been an active supporter of the Treaty at its inception. His attitude had not changed.[11] While the new executive quickly withdrew several pending treaties from the Senate and indicated in his inaugural address his desire to return to the policy of the founding fathers avoiding "any departure from that foreign policy commended by the history, the traditions, and the prosperity of our Republic" this did not result in any attempt to change existing relations with Hawaii.

On March 18, 1885, Carter was able to inform Gibson at Honolulu that a new Committee on Foreign Relations had been organized and in an early conference extension of the Treaty "found warm favor with the Committee as now constituted." At the same time, he wrote that Bayard "told me they have no objection to the Senate taking action upon it." Further occasion for optimism was found in the fact that at the reception tendered the diplomatic corps President Cleveland himself had spoken to Carter and said "he wanted to assure me of his very friendly disposition toward Hawaii." On the same evening Bayard affirmed "that no steps would be taken so far as he was concerned to amend the Treaty, or in any way affecting the Treaty without having my views fully before him."[12] On May 18 Bayard further informed Carter that the administration contemplated no modification of the sugar tariff. "Mr. Bayard," he wrote, "seems to grow more and more friendly and to speak with greater freedom regarding matters than at first."[13]

During the short session of Congress action on the renewal of the Treaty was not pressed for several reasons. Among them were preoccupation with problems confronting a new administration, and the illness of Senator Miller, chairman of the Committee on Foreign Relations. The administration's interest in the matter continued and early in 1886 Secretary Bayard communicated to Senator Miller his desire to "take counsel" with the Committee as to the growing importance of the commerce of the Pacific "and the group of Islands which seems just

---

[11] Charles C. Tansill, *The Foreign Policy of Thomas F. Bayard, 1886-1897*, has many details on Bayard's Hawaiian policy. Cited hereafter as Tansill.

[12] Carter to Gibson, March 18, 1885 (Confidential), *Foreign Office and Executive File*, AH.

[13] *Ibid.*

now to be in great demand with some of our Commercial rivals. . . ." At the same time, he was debating by letter with that vigorous opponent of reciprocity, Representative Morrison. Bayard's views on the importance of Hawaii were set forth clearly and decisively. "The vast importance, and our close and manifest interest in the commerce of the Pacific Ocean upon which we now hold the most important seaboard, renders the Hawaiian group of essential importance to us on every score, and as a member of the political organization now charged with the administration of our National affairs and interests, I trust you will not allow a commercial question to outweigh political consideration so important as I believe the control of these contiguous Islands on our Pacific Coast to be now, and still more to be in the near future," wrote the Secretary of State.[14]

THE PEARL HARBOR AMENDMENT

On April 14, 1886, the Committee on Foreign Relations reported the Frelinghuysen-Carter agreement favorably but with an interesting and significant amendment providing for exclusive rights to the use of Pearl Harbor on Oahu Island as a coaling and repair station. Though it was supported by leading Senate Democrats, the State Department appears not to have known of the existence of the amendment or to have been conversant with the text of the reported agreement until its publication in full by the *New York Tribune*. Consternation reigned among the Hawaiians, as is evidenced by the somewhat frantic communication of Carter to his government on April 23: "Have made no proposal or given any assurances regarding Pearl Harbor. Text of amendment in Senate unknown. Trust will be defeated. Satisfactory interview with secretary yesterday. He opposes any changes. Think shall come out right."[15] The key factor in the renewal of reciprocity became, therefore, not the advantages or disadvantages attached to it as an economic measure but the desire of certain Senators further to consolidate the political position of the United States in the Pacific.

The origins of the proposed amendment have long been in doubt. It was not a new idea. As has been indicated earlier, it originated in Hawaii itself in 1873 as a possible bait to make the original Treaty more attractive. It had been withdrawn because of immediate nationalistic opposition. The proposition now presented threatened, therefore, to upset the entire negotiation. The background of the proposal, as it appeared in 1886, is most completely provided in a lengthy and confi-

---

[14] Letter dated March 16, 1886. Tansill, 373f.
[15] Carter to Gibson, *Treaty Docs.*, AH.

dential communication from Carter to Gibson in 1885. Carter reviewed
the background of the idea with care:

In response to your request to be informed as to the origin of the talk regarding
Pearl River, I would say that much of the information I have has been imparted
in confidence & I therefore mark this as confidential.

The first intimation I had was in the fact that some Senators, Messrs. Miller of
Cal., Morgan, Ex Senator Gwin, & others remarked to me that they had heard
of such a harbor & asked if any use was made of it, whether it was private
property &c. This was during last session, and I thought but little of it as the
parties did not speak of it as if attaching much importance to it. When this session
opened the Supplementary Convention was in the State Dept. unsigned, as I was
in some doubt about having it go in with the other Treaties, when I heard that
a resolution was being proposed asking the President to take steps to secure Pearl
River Harbor, I went to several friends at once and told them that the Hawaiian
Legislature would not consent to such a Cession and that I did not think the King
& Government would entertain the proposition, and further that the United States
did not need it, and Congress would certainly refuse to entertain the project. Most
of them agreed with me. Mr. Morgan while declining to say anything in regard
to what had transpired in Committee took my view of the case as regards Congress, though he thought that some time in the future the needs of the United
States might lead them to wish the harbor. He said he would oppose the project
as not now desirable. In a few days I was told that the project was being pressed,
and that there was danger that those who favored it, might join with those who
advocated abrogation of the Treaty of '75 and make Pearl River the price of non-
abrogation. Discussion with our friends followed, and I was advised to get the
Supplementary Convention sent to the Senate as soon as possible with a strong
letter from the Secretary of State stating that the administration was convinced
that the Treaty was deserving of extension & continuance on its own merits. This,
it was thought, would aid the advocates of continuance pure and simple, and in
any event furnish new basis for any amendments, and thus put away the question
of abrogation of the original Treaty. I think it has served this purpose already,
and I think any amendments will be successfully resisted. . . .[16]

It appears certain that neither the Arthur nor Cleveland administrations had anything to do with the proposal. Carter informed Bayard
that no such proposition had been discussed with Secretary Frelinghuysen, and it is very definite that Secretary Bayard was not aware
of the Pearl Harbor amendment until it was called to his attention by

---

[16] Carter to Gibson, March 18, 1885 (Confidential), *Foreign Office and Executive File,* AH. In a memorandum written by Bayard following a conversation with
Carter on May 7, 1886, the point is made that Senator Edmunds was perhaps the
earliest proponent of the Pearl Harbor proposition and that other members of the
Committee on Foreign Relations were opposed until fears of British and German
expansion changed their views. See Tansill, 376f.

Carter and published by the *New York Tribune* on May 6, 1886. Carter informed his government April 27 and again on May 7 that alleged amendments were "without knowledge or concurrence" by Bayard.

The demand for special concessions could not have appeared under more inopportune circumstances. As noted previously, Foreign Minister Gibson had impressed upon his Washington representative as early as 1882 the fact that Hawaii was desirous even of securing modification of Article IV of the 1875 convention as an encroachment upon her sovereignty. These views were repeated to Carter on January 31, 1884. On February 21 Carter had informed Gibson that he would press for extension of reciprocity upon a basis of amending Article IV with its limitations upon Hawaiian sovereignty, and on February 29 Gibson had again pressed upon Carter the importance of some "saving clause" in this regard.[17] Hawaii was desirous, therefore, of eliminating existing restrictions upon its freedom while the expansionist Senators in the United States were demanding even greater privileges as the price for reciprocity.

RECIPROCITY AGAIN ATTACKED

The fortunes of reciprocity were further complicated at the moment by a vigorous attack upon the existing Treaty in the House, led largely by Representative William R. Morrison of Illinois. Hearings on the measure had been held by a sub-committee of the Ways and Means Committee in February and evident hostility to its continuance revealed. The Committee held that reciprocity had not produced promised results. This Carter attributed to the general trade depression and antagonism produced by increased trade with Hawaii. Bayard had expressed to him, however, his regret that such action had been taken "without due consultation with the Executive" but emphasized that "speaking personally" he thought that "the Treaty should be maintained & that it would be."[18]

The position of the Treaty was made more insecure by the fact that a special representative of the Treasury Department, John E. Searles, investigating trade conditions with Hawaii had reported adversely upon the general commercial situation and was strongly opposed to reci-

---

[17] See Gibson to Allen, December 21, 1882, and Gibson to Carter, May 5, 1883, *Foreign Office and Executive File*, AH. Also Carter to Gibson, February 21, 1884 (Private and Personal), and Gibson to Carter, January 31, 1884, enclosing draft of changes, *Treaty Docs.*, AH.

[18] Carter to Gibson, February 20, 1886, and March 19, *Treaty Docs.*, AH. See also *House Reports*, 49 Cong., 1 sess., Vol. 6 for Morrison report which showed Hawaiian exports to the United States had increased over 10 per cent while American exports to Hawaii declined about that amount.

procity. His views were so pleasing to Senators Gibson of Louisiana and Nelson Aldrich of Rhode Island, representing the sugar interests of the East, that they referred him to Bayard in the hope that he might win the Secretary over to the opposition. Searles emphasized that the better class of Americans was leaving the Islands and that those remaining were "not a class of whom we may be proud nor whose loss we need mourn."[19] Searles asserted that American exports over a nine-year period had amounted to $22,870,000 while duties remitted were $22,808,000. These views were shared by Morrison, who asserted that the Treaty was one-sided and had produced no economic advantages. The political argument for reciprocity, Morrison dismissed with the statement, "If we have any political rights in the Pacific they should be ours without hiring or paying for them."[20]

CLEVELAND AND BAYARD SUPPORT RECIPROCITY

Bayard remained firm in his adherence to support of the original Treaty and its renewal. Arguments against the economic benefits were refuted ably by Carter. The Secretary, as noted earlier, was adamant in his beliefs that the considerations of national interest involved were more important than a dollars and cents balance in trade relations. The prospect that the proposed amendment to the supplementary convention by the Committee on Foreign Relations might threaten the very existence of the Treaty by arousing Hawaiian opposition, therefore, became a matter of major concern to the State Department.

The day following the publication of the text of the agreement in the *Tribune,* Carter waited upon Bayard and a careful statement of the official attitude of the State Department was presented to the Hawaiian Minister. Bayard disclaimed any knowledge of the amendment prior to the time it was called to his attention by the *Tribune* representative on May 6. Bayard's memorandum states that:

I said to Mr. Carter that . . . the importance of the Sandwich Islands to the United States since the opening and settlement of the Pacific Coast . . . did not require to be stated by me; that it was an open and admitted fact that those Islands could never be allowed to become a menace or source of danger to the United States. . . . I said that I . . . thought it was . . . our policy to strengthen the autonomy of the Islands and do anything we could to promote the mutual prosperity of that Government and our own people.[21]

---

[19] See Tansill, 374.
[20] *Ibid.* See also *House Reports, op. cit.*
[21] Tansill, 377. It should be noted that the new treaty was reported in executive session of the Senate and yet the *Tribune* knew more about it than the State Department.

By May 13 Carter had been able to study the purported text of the renewal treaty as published in the *Tribune* and informed Bayard that it was not as bad as he had feared. He stressed that temperate and prudent action would be necessary to secure approval in Hawaii. To his Foreign Minister he reported on May 26 that he had done everything in his power to point out the dangers in the Pearl Harbor amendment, but that it looked very much as if the renewal convention could not pass the Senate without it. Gibson promptly informed Carter that the views of the Hawaiian Government had not been modified and, that the "people and Government alike will resolutely decline to listen to it, and will unhesitatingly meet whatever difficulties the refusal may entail."[22] Carter replied he would continue to press objections.

In his annual message on December 6 President Cleveland expressed his "unhesitating conviction that the intimacy of our relations with Hawaii should be emphasized," and called attention to the fact that as a result of reciprocity the Islands had become "virtually an outpost of American commerce and a stepping stone to the growing trade of the Pacific." Failure to renew the Treaty would, he warned, mean a loss of "paramount influence" difficult to regain and the emergence of a stronghold for "our commercial competitors." These statements reflected a growing concern of the administration that the failure to approve the renewal of reciprocity might lead to Hawaiian entanglements in other quarters.

Bayard had been very much disturbed by comment in London to the effect that reciprocity negotiations might be opened with Canada. Accounts in San Francisco papers of a proposed Hawaiian loan of $2,000,000 to be floated in England were also disconcerting to Bayard and the President. In November Bayard expressed frankly to Carter his concern over this matter and the threat to impairing preferred rights of the United States. It was these events which prompted Cleveland's expression of views in his December message.[23]

Favorable assurances from the Hawaiian Government that no loan was to be floated which obligated its revenues and left the way open for political influence by another power, led Bayard to urge upon the President official opposition to the Pearl Harbor amendment. The Secretary pointed out that the Midway Islands, acquired by the United States in 1867, offered the same advantages as Pearl Harbor. Use of Midway for naval purposes "would not involve us or Hawaii with the other treaty powers." In view of this and the known opposition of

---

[22] See Carter to Gibson, May 13, 1886; Carter to Gibson, May 26; and Gibson to Carter, June 12, *Treaty Docs.*, AH.

[23] Tansill, 378f.

Hawaii to the amendment, Bayard stated, ". . . I am opposed to engrafting such an amendment upon a treaty which as at present framed, merely gives a longer life to the present favorable status." To Carter, Bayard likewise reiterated his objection to the amendment as reported in the press, though as late as January 22, 1887, he himself was unaware officially of its exact content. Carter again emphasized the fact that there was no chance that the amendment would be accepted by Hawaii.[24]

THE TREATY BEFORE CONGRESS

The views of Bayard and Carter were without avail, however, and the renewal treaty was debated on January 10, 11, and 20 in the Senate and approved on the latter date by a vote of 43 to 11. The Pearl Harbor amendment was accepted by the narrow margin of 28 to 21. Principal objections raised to reciprocity renewal were upon constitutional grounds. Much of the opposition was notivated by the self-interest of Louisiana sugar planters and incidental allies. Most prominent opponents were Senators Morrill of Vermont and West of Missouri, together with that old foe of reciprocity, John Sherman. The validity of a Senate approval of a measure affecting the revenues was again raised by Morrill, who lost by a vote of 41 to 11 a motion to require another House enabling act. Louisiana Senators were united in opposing renewal, and Senator Dolph of Oregon voted with the opposition. Meager accounts of the debate reveal that the dominant consideration behind approval was the political interest of the United States in Hawaii. The matter received little attention in the press.[25] It was the opinion of Carter that approval of the Pearl Harbor amendment was aided by the votes of some who believed that this would ultimately cause the defeat of the principal treaty.[26]

Ratification by the Senate did not end opposition. In the House a vigorous protest developed. On April 15, 1886, the Ways and Means Committee reported by a 9-1 vote a resolution favoring abrogation. Two days following Senate ratification, a resolution was introduced requiring the House Judiciary Committee to report whether the purported renewal of the reciprocity treaty by the President and Senate "can be

---

[24] See Tansill, 379f.

[25] Vote from *Senate Executive Journal*, XXV, 691ff. See *San Francisco Morning Call* for scattered information on the debate. Such papers as the *New York Times* and the *Chicago Tribune* paid scant attention to the issue.

[26] In a note to Gibson on February 3, Carter wrote, "The vote was carried in the Senate by the aid of those who thought that if Hawaii gave it to the U. S. she could not give it to any other power, & by those who wanted to make the treaty obnoxious to us. . . ." *Treaty Docs.*, AH.

valid and binding without the concurrence of the House of Representatives, and how far the power conferred on the House by the Constitution of the United States to originate measures to lay and collect duties can be controlled by the treaty-making power under said Constitution." The President was requested to furnish a copy of the new agreement.

While the President complied on February 1, 1887, thereby making public the new treaty, the Judiciary Committee on March 3 proceeded to produce a blistering condemnation of the whole negotiation. The exercise of the revenue-making power by treaty "would virtually surrender the domain of tariff regulations to the treaty-making authority of the President and Senate," it was declared. This would make a "mockery of the power of the House" and constitute a "radical change in the equilibrium of the Constitution." The Committee recommended formal resolutions condemning the exercise of the power by the President and Senate and called upon the former to withhold final ratification pending enabling legislation by the House.[27]

Such measures were of course ineffective. Approval by the Senate completed, the fate of the treaty shifted to Honolulu. At the same time, conversations between Bayard and Carter in Washington were of the utmost importance in adjusting the situation created by the Pearl Harbor proposal. On February 3, 1867, Carter reported to Gibson that Bayard had suggested an entirely new treaty might be the answer to the problem and that particularly it might provide for termination of reciprocity only after two or three years notice rather than the twelve months originally provided. This would make the treaty more attractive to Hawaii by providing greater surety.[28]

INTERPRETING THE PEARL HARBOR AMENDMENT

Up to this time it is evident that the administration was definite in its opposition to the Pearl Harbor amendment and anxious to avoid its implications. Conditions developed, however, which served to convince Bayard that the renewal treaty should be ratified and completed, in spite of what he considered a "mischievous" amendment. These conditions were associated with growing anxiety in Washington over reports of vice and corruption in the Hawaiian Government as well as certain of its expansionist ambitions which threatened complications with other powers.

---

[27] Cf. *House Reports,* II, 49 Cong., 2 sess.

[28] *Treaty Docs.,* AH. In a memorandum dated January 28 Bayard indicates that his discussions were "informal and personal and involved substituting the administration proposal for that of the Sen."

On March 20, 1887, King Kalakaua concluded a "political confedera-
tion" with Samoa which promised to be the beginning of a Polynesian
League in the Pacific. The designs and activities of the rather unscrupulous Gibson, and suggestions that Claus Spreckels and others had secured by corrupt means control over Hawaiian affairs, had disturbed
many in Washington interested in American influence in Hawaii. Especially alarming were the rumors of fraud and corruption connected
with the approval of the sale of opium which were reported to Bayard
by Minister Merrill in April.[29]

Bayard was so greatly concerned that he not only urged Merrill to
report completely upon these activities, but was impelled as early as
February to comment to Carter upon Spreckels. News of the Samoan
arrangement was disturbing especially in view of the fact that the
Secretary had already informed the German Minister that rumors of
this were all nonsense. Carter was informed that this step was unwise
and ill advised.[30]

By May Bayard definitely was interested in pressing for completion
of the treaty arrangement. On May 13 Carter called at the State Department and mentioned debates in the British Parliament which revealed increasing ambitions in the Pacific. The visit of Queen Kapiolani
and Princess Liliuokalani to England to attend ceremonies connected
with the celebration of the fiftieth anniversary of the elevation of
Queen Victoria to the throne did not add to the comfort of the State
Department, in spite of the fact that they were to pass through Washington and receive official courtesies.

In his conversations with Carter, the Secretary emphasized he did
not feel upon reflection that the terms of the Pearl Harbor amendment
were such as to impair seriously the value of the treaty. The point was
made that it was very questionable whether the United States would
expend any money upon the development of such a harbor. Bayard
aptly pointed out that, "We have no navy to put in it in the first place
and that our Merchant shipping did not need it."[31]

While Bayard's own report of his conversations does not put it in
exactly the same light, Carter's report to the King indicates it was at
this time that he broached to Bayard the matter of some statement from
the State Department which would indicate officially that the proposed
right to use Pearl Harbor would not interfere with the sovereignty of

---

[29] Merrill to Bayard, April 11, 1887 (Private), cited in Tansill, 384. See also
earlier discussion of internal conditions in Hawaii in the preceding chapter.
[30] This subject is covered very fully in Tansill, 382ff.
[31] Memorandum in Tansill, 389. See also Carter to the King, May 16, 1887,
Treaty Docs., AH, for Carter's version.

Hawaii. According to Carter, Bayard indicated his belief this could be arranged.[32]

It was evidently the understanding, therefore, of Carter that Bayard had agreed to some type of exchange of notes, similar to that employed following the Clayton-Bulwer treaty with England in 1850, which would further clarify the status of Pearl Harbor in terms of its impact upon the sovereignty and independence of Hawaii. On this assumption, Carter urged strongly upon the King the ratification of the new convention. His attention was further called to the fact that "three of our worst enemies" had been returned to the Senate and "I do not think we could again get renewal on as good terms and I truly feel that we are taking a very great risk in letting such a chance slip by."

In June Carter again called upon Bayard on different occasions and urged that the matter of the ultimate status of Pearl Harbor be clarified. On June 10 Carter reported to Gibson that he had again conversed with the Secretary, who still "regretted" the interpolation of the amendment without consulting the Executive department and saw no particular advantage in it, but that "he was also surprised that there should be so much objection on our part as he did not see that any concession was made by us." Bayard indicated it was his belief that the United States already had the right to enter Hawaiian harbors for coaling and repair services, and "to grant an exclusive right to enter an estuary which was not now a harbor, & could only be made one at great expense, he did not think a valuable concession. . . ." Bayard's objection to the Senate amendment, according to Carter, was "based upon the way it was interpolated, and its crudeness, which he did not think creditable, and he did not like to accept it for the President, but in view of the peril in which the Treaty of 1875 was left with all the interests involved, and in view also of the desirability of a greater stability in the relations of the two countries looking to other questions of mutual interest, he thought if our objections were removed the Treaty could be ratified, and the Treaty of 1875 would be renewed for 7 years more and put beyond the reach of the selfish interests which assail it."[33]

---

[32] Bayard's memorandum is indefinite on this point and refers to conversations as to an understanding that use of Pearl Harbor would terminate at any time the treaty came to an end and his point of view that "no additional guarantee would be given" in any case. Carter reported, however, "I asked him if in case you were willing to accept it a paper could be signed showing that we understand it as not interfering with Hawaiian sovereignty and that it would last as long as the Treaty was maintained and he thought he could do so."

[33] Carter to Gibson, June 10, 1887 (Confidential), *Treaty Docs.*, AH.

Despite Bayard's assurances, Carter pointed out "that even if no objection existed *per se* to the use of Pearl Harbor there was a feeling in our country that, in some way, the Sovereignty of Hawaii was involved and further that there might be a question whether on the termination of the Treaty of 1875 the Pearl Harbor article would continue to have any force. . . ." According to Carter, ". . . Mr. Bayard thought I was right on both points, and I asked him if he thought a declaration covering these points could be signed if our Government considered that such a declaration removed their objections, and he said he would consider the matter." On resuming the conversation later, Bayard indicated that ordinarily an executive officer could not make a "declaration of the intent of a legislative act" but in the case of the Clayton-Bulwer treaty a communication of the British Minister had been replied to by the Secretary of State in such a way as to influence the interpretation of the treaty.[34]

Carter strongly urged upon his government the early approval of the treaty. The fact was pointed out that any idea of modification was absolutely useless. "There is no question but that the proposition to abrogate the Treaty of '75 would pass the House of Representatives by a large majority and that the recent elections to the Senate have placed very strong enemies of the treaty in that body, therefore Mr. Bayard is quite right in thinking it useless to propose any modification of the amendment," wrote Carter.

During June further conversations between Bayard and Carter did not clarify the situation. Carter on June 3 again emphasized his wish that the status of Pearl Harbor following termination of the treaty might be settled, and once more Bayard patiently explained his belief that Hawaii had nothing to fear. Bayard again took occasion to warn Carter against the ambitions of the King relative to the Samoan alliance, and called attention to the dangers in terms of difficulty with Germany. A week later, Carter again pressed for a definite statement to the effect that the amendment was not to be considered as an abridgement of Hawaiian sovereignty. The Secretary again repeated he did not consider it within the power of the Executive to do this and the United States was unlikely to make any use of the concession during the seven years of the treaty's tenure.[35]

The revolutionary outbursts in Hawaii late in June resulting in a new constitution and ultimate reorganization of the ministry produced added

[34] *Ibid.* Bayard's personal view still was that the amendment was unfortunate. An undated note in *Notes, Hawaii,* III, contains the statement, "I was sure that the Pearl Harbor amendment was mischievous depriving us of a *certainty* and attempting to pull fruit before it was ripe."
[35] See memorandum by Bayard cited in Tansill, 389ff.

complications. On July 12 Carter informed Bayard that the internal situation was such that ". . . it would not be wise at this time to press the acceptance of the Senate amendment for Pearl Harbor; that it might arouse the jealousy of the natives."[36] He further advised that he had been informed that British officials had advised against ratification. By August, Bayard was definitely alarmed at the trend of events and recorded his foreboding, based upon certain confidential reports, that revolution in Hawaii might produce "a scramble for the domination of the Islands by the great Commercial Powers. . . ." Fears that reduction of the sugar tariff in the United States might lead to new Hawaiian trade arrangements with Germany or Great Britain also were expressed.[37]

The situation was indeed a trying one. Carter informed Bayard on August 19 of his alarm that the treaty might now fail through national feeling against the Pearl Harbor concession and his belief that consideration should be postponed until after the fall elections. A little later he returned to the suggestion of exchanging notes to interpret the amendment. Bayard again emphasized that it was not within his power to do this, but suggested that Hawaii accept the treaty and "that they could accompany that acceptance with a statement of what they held to be an interpretation of the Pearl Harbor amendment. . . ."[38]

Carter used every influence possible with the new ministry at Honolulu in attempting to press the treaty ratification and accepted Bayard's views as to the urgency of the matter. On July 17 he wrote Godfrey Brown, new Minister of Foreign Affairs, that Bayard had not been disposed originally to "do anything further" regarding the treaty "but subsequent events have led him to think that further delay may be dangerous to the continuance of the Treaty of '75 and he thinks it had better be put beyond danger by accepting the amendment of the Senate. . . ." On August 16 Carter again urged action and suggested the possibility of further interpretation by exchange of notes.[39]

On August 23 Brown replied privately to Carter's communication and said he appreciated "the force of Mr. Bayard's reasoning, but until after our elections which are set for the 12th prox. the Cabinet will not take action in the matter." He expressed his opinion that it was the private view of the Cabinet that ". . . the vital necessity of the treaty to us must be apparent to anyone acquainted with our circumstances, and its abrogation would simply mean bankruptcy to our only industry,

---

[36] *Ibid.*
[37] *Ibid.*, 393.
[38] See communication from Carter to Bayard, *Notes, Hawaii,* III; also Tansill, 394.
[39] *Treaty Docs.*, AH.

which even with the advantages which it now derives cannot be said to be in a very flourishing condition."[40]

On September 27 Carter was informed by Brown that the King at a Cabinet meeting the preceding day had approved the amendment "on the condition that the note explaining our interpretation of the interpolated clause, namely, that Hawaiian Sovereignty and jurisdiction are not impaired, that the Hawaiian Government is not bound to furnish land for any purpose and that the privilege to be granted is co-terminous with the treaty is accepted by Mr. Bayard."[41]

THE PEARL HARBOR ISSUE SETTLED

In the meantime, in Washington, Carter had taken steps to clarify the situation, though he did not go as far as the King evidently desired. On September 22 Bayard, at the request of Carter, transmitted a formal note setting forth the status of the pending treaty and enclosing a copy of the amended convention. In reply Carter gave a detailed interpretation of the scope of the Pearl Harbor amendment. This emphasized his belief that "the question of Hawaiian jurisdiction is left untouched by the article" and that in case the United States availed itself of the opportunity to develop Pearl Harbor, "the autonomous control of the Hawaiian Government remains the same as its control over other.harbors in the group where national vessels may be, except that the Article in accordance with Article IV of the existing convention prevents the Hawaiian Government from granting similar exclusive privileges during the continuance of the convention to any other nation." It was pointed out furtkcr by Carter that the Senate had no intention "to invade the autonomous jurisdiction of Hawaii and to transfer the absolute property in, and jurisdiction over, the harbor to the United States. . . ." It was indicated that the term of the amendment would be the same as the life of the treaty.[42]

The same day Bayard acknowledged the Carter note briefly:

. . . the amendment relating to the harbor of Pearl River was adopted, in its executive sessions, by the Senate, and I have no other means of arriving at its intent and meaning than the words employed naturally import. No ambiguity or obscurity in that amendment is observable, and I can discern therein no subtraction from Hawaiian sovereignty over the harbor to which it relates, nor any language importing a longer duration for the interpolated Article II than is provided for in Article I of the supplementary convention.[43]

---

[40] *Ibid.*
[41] *Ibid.*
[42] Carter to Bayard, September 23, 1877, *Notes, Hawaii,* IV.
[43] Bayard to Carter, September 23, 1887, *Notes to Hawaii,* I.

Upon receipt of the communication from Foreign Minister Brown setting forth the Hawaiian position, Carter conferred with Assistant Secretary of State John Bassett Moore, and informed his government of his opinion that the sweeping character of the notes already exchanged with Bayard was sufficient to answer any anxiety at Honolulu as to the meaning of the treaty and amendment.[44] On November 5 he was able to inform Bayard that he had received full powers to exchange ratifications. Four days later he conveyed to the State Department "the great satisfaction felt by the King and by the Government in forming closer relations with the United States."[45]

It is important at this point to note the extent to which final settlement of the treaty problem had been influenced by internal politics and external foreign pressures. The peaceful Hawaiian revolution of June and July, analyzed earlier, resulted in a coalition of Hawaiian propertied interests into a political organization known as the Reform Party. The abolition of all unnecessary offices and curtailment of expenditures and taxes with preservation of "autonomy and independence" were principal credos of the group. Its backers, according to Minister Merrill, "are generally men identified with the business interests and welfare of the Kingdom." A bitter political battle with factions already in control of the government came to a head in the September elections.

The elections resulted in a decisive victory for the Reform Party and "men of property and fully identified with the progress and prosperity of the country," according to Merrill, were placed in power. The shift in control also represented ultimately at least the ascendancy of a pro-American coalition in contradiction to a relatively anti-American policy as exemplified by the opposition. It was this situation and the prospect for change which explains the desire of friends of the treaty to delay its consideration.

INTERNATIONAL COMPLICATIONS

Equally important was the international aspect of the problem. Opposition to American interests generated by native nationalists had resulted in attempts to develop association with other powers and created conditions which, as we have seen, alarmed the State Department as far back as the brief regime of James G. Blaine. By 1887 the American Minister was emphasizing strongly to Washington that early action to clinch the reciprocity agreement was necessary. Announced plans of the Canadian Pacific Railway to extend a steamship connection with

---

[44] Carter to Brown, October 12, 1887. *Treaty Docs.,* AH.
[45] *Notes, Hawaii,* III.

Hawaii and British colonies in the Pacific were disturbing as offering a possible development of new trade connections.

British unrest over the consequences of reciprocity in terms of its influence upon Hawaiian union with the United States had been expressed in the seventies. By 1885, however, this view seems to have shifted to the theory that reciprocity would provide some guarantee of Island independence by checking other aspirations.[46] News of the Pearl Harbor proposal caused a rude shock to this theory and aroused marked concern.

Merrill reported shortly to Washington that the British representative at Honolulu was "very sensitive" on the subject and in August, 1887, a request for information had been addressed to the Hawaiian Government. On October 22 the British government firmly protested at Honolulu the proposed concession as a violation of the neutrality convention of 1843. The opinion was expressed that this would "infallibly lead to the loss of its independence and the extinction of Hawaiian nationality." In London, Lord Salisbury expressed to Germany his belief that "we must keep a sharp watch on American fingers."[47]

From the American standpoint, however, the power which needed watching was Germany. The concern of Secretary Bayard that Hawaiian machinations under Kalakaua endeavoring to promote a Polynesian League with Samoa would bring the Islands into direct conflict with Germany has already been noted. Beginning about 1884, Prince Bismarck toyed with the idea of developing an ambitious colonial policy with particular reference to the Pacific area. Bayard had hardly assumed his duties as Secretary of State when involved diplomacy resulting from these ambitions arose to perplex him. While the new Secretary could not be said to have been an expansionist, he early concerned himself with opposing the development of German imperialism in the Pacific. As early as 1885 he expressed his conviction that the "moral interests" of the United States with reference to Pacific islands "would counsel us to look with concern on any movement by which the independ-

---

[46] See dispatch of Sackville-West to Salisbury dated November 7, 1885, informing him that H. A. P. Carter felt that under "the present temper of the United States" reciprocity was a guarantee of Island security. Cited in Allan Nevins, *Grover Cleveland, A Study in Courage,* 250.

[47] See Merrill to Bayard, August 29 and October 22, 1887, and enclosures for British protests, *Dispatches,* XXIII. See R. G. Dugdale, *German Diplomatic Documents,* I, 24 for Salisbury comment. Commander Graham of the U.S.S. *Alert* reported to the Secretary of the Navy rumors that the King planned to turn to British protection and that an agent had been sent to London to make the arrangements. Bayard took this seriously enough to speak to the Hawaiian Minister about it and was assured that there was little foundation for such rumors. See Tansill, 402f.

ence of those Pacific nationalities might be extinguished by their passage under the domination of a foreign sovereign."[48]

Naturally, Hawaii was a subject of more concern to the United States than Samoa. In numerous conversations with Carter, Bayard expressed his fears that internal difficulties in Hawaii might provide an opportunity for foreign meddling in her affairs. In May Bayard called Carter's attention to the expansion of German interests in Hawaiian sugar planting and, as noted earlier, he had been disturbed at prospects of new commercial connections with British possessions and the possibility of an Hawaiian foreign loan. There can be little doubt but that these factors in the international situation had much to do with both the Senate demand for the Pearl Harbor concession and the ultimate belief of Bayard that the reciprocity treaty must be extended without delay.

Actual exchange of ratification was something of a stroke of state so far as opposing foreign interests were concerned. Carter on November 9 read to Bayard a communication from the Hawaiian Minister of Foreign Relations, Godfrey Brown, in which pleasure was expressed that the King had signed the treaty in spite of influence exerted against it and that "the British Lion did not know that the treaty had already been signed. . . ." Brown also expressed his fear that conclusion of ratification might "give pretext to Germany for making some trouble if she could with Hawaii. . . ." Carter indicated that he had been queried by the British Minister and had informed him that no actual cession of Pearl Harbor had been made but a mere agreement for its use had been reached.[49] According to Carter, the Minister had expressed himself as "perfectly satisfied."[50]

The German representative, Baron Zedtwitz, was not so pleased. On December 7 he visited Bayard for a discussion of matters. Since Bayard had already expressed to the American Minister at London, Edward J. Phelps, his concern at German ambitions in the Pacific and had remarked that his thoughts "are turned anxiously toward the Sandwich Islands where we have very important rights and interests to preserve," his reaction is understandable.[51] Bayard rather curtly informed the Baron that he could not understand Bismarck's Hawaiian policy; that the treaty was merely a commercial agreement of advantage to even German citizens in Hawaii. The Secretary made it clear to the German

---

[48] Bayard's Pacific policy, and especially the Samoan question and German relations, are treated with new materials at hand by Tansill. Germany in turn complained of the American tendency to "interpret the Monroe Doctrine as though the Pacific Ocean were to be treated as an American Lake. . . ." Dugdale, *op. cit.*

[49] Tansill, 396.

[50] Carter to Brown, November 8, 1887, *Treaty Docs.*, AH.

[51] Bayard to Phelps, October 20, 1887, Tansill, 396n.

Minister, however, "that we considered our interest in Hawaii was manifestly much greater than that of other powers, and our treaties had been made with that view. . . ."

To the Secretary of the Navy, Bayard suggested that in view of the Hawaiian situation and of the movements of Germany in Samoa, it might be well to send a naval vessel to the Midway Islands to erect a flag and make a landing to demonstrate publicly the authority of the United States. This would mark an assertion of American Pacific interests. It is quite probable that the presence of three American naval vessels at Honolulu during the autumn of 1887 was influenced by the same consideration.

Both British and German concern over Hawaii was furthered by other developments. In the first place, admittedly the success of the Reform Party heightened the strength of pro-American tendencies. The ultimate reorganization of the ministry found Jonathan Austin, a native New Yorker and Civil War veteran, in charge of foreign affairs. A cable line was projected to San Francisco and a proposed mission to Canada to consider commercial relations cancelled. By early 1888 it seemed apparent to many that the authority of the King was rapidly weakening and that the monarchy itself might fall. Bayard was visited by Carter and Samuel G. Wilder of Honolulu suggesting that the protection of the United States was desirable. Wilder said he had suggested to the King that the Islands be disposed of to the United States. Fears of German or British interposition were expressed.[52]

In February the British Consul-General at Honolulu delivered a stiff protest to Austin against the Pearl Harbor cession as a violation of the treaty of 1852 by which the ships of all nations were guaranteed equal access to Hawaiian ports. Austin furnished the American Minister with a copy and was assisted by him in his denial of the British claim, and declared that the growing importance of Hawaii was directly attributed to the reciprocity treaty.[53] The same view was set forth to Sackville-West, the British Minister in Washington, by Bayard. The Minister expressed himself as being satisfied and hinted strongly that the British protest was provoked by German representations.

By its vigorous support of the reciprocity convention as renewed with the Pearl Harbor amendment, the Cleveland administration contributed measurably to strengthening American control over Hawaii. All efforts to neutralize American influence in the Islands had been resisted sturdily. In many ways there was much truth in the German complaint that the American policy toward Hawaii was an extension of the Mon-

---

[52] Tansill, 397f.
[53] Merrill to Bayard, February 24, 1888, and enclosure, *Dispatches*, XXIII.

roe Doctrine. More strictly, it was a continuation of the Tyler doctrine. On more than one occasion, Bayard reaffirmed his belief that American interests were paramount and that the Islands held a peculiar relationship to the United States which no other nation might threaten or oppose. At the same time, the familiar twin principle that Hawaiian autonomy and independence should be cultivated and protected was asserted. Whether later developments would force new interpretations of American policy could not have been foreseen in 1888.

CHAPTER IX

Manifest Destiny and the 1893 Revolution

"The Hawaiian pear is now fully ripe, and this is the golden hour for the United States to pluck it," wrote the American Minister, John L. Stevens, in an oft-quoted letter to the State Department, February 1, 1893. The ripening process was indeed rapid following the renewal of reciprocity and the constitutional changes of 1887 in Hawaii. Six years of turbulence and racial conflict, reflected in kaleidoscopic changes in the political situation, ended in a revolution which went a step beyond that of 1887, overturned the native monarchy, and erected a republic. Meanwhile, events in both Hawaii and the United States had set the stage for what seemed to be an immediate realization of a new manifest destiny in the form of annexation. The era of crucial political unrest in Hawaii was paralleled in the United States by four years of a new political administration under Benjamin Harrison as President with James G. Blaine as his Secretary of State. This administration was dedicated to a forward foreign policy and not disinclined to look with favor upon the prospect for absorption of Hawaii. The stirring events of this brief period are so important as to deserve a full chapter for their consideration.

EFFECTS OF THE RENEWAL OF RECIPROCITY

The extension of the reciprocity agreement in 1887 for another seven-year period did not work any further startling economic transformation in Hawaii. Its most noticeable effect was the temporary relief of the uncertainty about renewal which had operated as an unsettling factor in Hawaiian economic affairs. Rather than contributing any radically new influences to the Americanization of the Islands, it simply served to continue the steady operation of existing forces generated after 1876. The exports of sugar to the United States increased but slowly, rising from 216,223,516 pounds for 1886 to 274,983,580 for 1891, while the value actually decreased slightly due to lower prices and adverse effects of the McKinley tariff. While exact figures are not available, it is doubtful whether any important additions to the capital investment in sugar or other enterprises from American sources were made, though a small number of new plantations were developed during the period.

The *Hawaiian Gazette* for November 4, 1887, had declared, "The definitive extension of the Reciprocity Treaty with the United States . . . removes from our chief industry an element of uncertainty that has for several years hindered the development of our agricultural resources." This bright prospect, however, suffered shortly a sharp reverse. Hardly had the agreement been renewed than the Island economy fell prey to the evil consequences of a change in American tariff policy. The return of the Republicans to power March 4, 1889, resulted in immediate revision of the tariff under the direction of William McKinley. In October, 1890, that masterpiece in the art of political logrolling, the McKinley Tariff Bill, became law. The diplomatic significance of this will be treated later, but it is important to note here the economic results. The new tariff placed raw sugar upon the free list, and placated struggling sugar interests in the United States by a two cents a pound bounty on domestic production. The bounty was a tribute to the political pressure exerted by representatives of the newly developing beet sugar industry in the western states and cane sugar producers of the South.

CONSEQUENCES OF THE MCKINLEY TARIFF

The danger to its sugar industry involved in this measure was appreciated in Hawaii even prior to its passage. When the bill was reported by the Ways and Means Committee and news of its provisions reached the Islands, a degree of uncertainty was created far greater than any prior to 1887. Minister Stevens contributed his own alarm and that of the planters to the State Department on May 20, 1890, in a long communication reviewing the probable effects of the measure. "In the opinion of all well-informed persons here," he wrote, "to place sugar on the free list would be the virtual annulment of the reciprocity treaty and the destruction of the prosperity of the islands." The "deep anxiety" of Hawaiian business interests and their feeling that "it is a matter of life and death to the Hawaiian kingdom" were emphasized by the Minister. Stevens himself agreed that the result would amount to a "calamity" as far as the economic life of Hawaii was concerned.[1]

Predictions as to the effects of the new tariff were not exaggerated. Its passage produced a severe decline in the value of sugar equal approximately to the loss of the tariff advantage enjoyed earlier in the American market. The American Consul-General estimated this loss in 1891 as at least $5,000,000, and wrote that it was only by the closest economy that the larger planters were able to make a profit, while some of the smaller ones were being forced to abandon their plantations to

---

[1] FR, 1894, 319f.

other uses. Stevens reported that the sugar industry had been dealt a "very severe blow, and with the most favorable estimate it now looks as though bankruptcy must be the inevitable fate of more or less of the sugar-planting firms and corporations."[2] Property values declined an estimated $12,000,000.

The business depression continued in 1892 before any partial recovery was noticeable. The production and export of sugar declined for the year 1892 some 2,832 tons under 1891, and the continued abandonment of some plantations was reported, though more daring individuals undertook three new enterprises the same year. Summarizing the economic situation November 20, 1892, the American Minister declared that the loss to the planters and mill owners from declining prices for sugar and the general depression in property values since the new tariff amounted to fully $12,000,000. Efforts to correct the situation by developing a more diversified agriculture, including the culture of coffee, fibrous plants, rice, and pineapple were but partially successful. The continued high cost of labor, combined with these other factors, made the period a precarious one indeed for the American interests in Hawaii.

POLITICAL TUMULT IN HAWAII

As usual, the disturbed economic situation was reflected in the political affairs of the Islands. This took the form of intensification of the struggle for political control between the native factions and the Reform Party of property-holding foreigners which had engineered the peaceful revolution of 1887. As has been emphasized previously, this political *coup d'etat* had been followed by a sweeping victory for the perfected political organization representing this group. The victory, however, did not produce all that had been hoped for by the Reform Party leaders. "Five years of bitter experience under the new regime have proved that the revolution of 1887 had one fault. It did not go far enough," declared a revolutionary pamphlet in 1893. This adequately summarizes the background of the political situation after 1887.

Native nationalists had not accepted the renewal of reciprocity and the obnoxious Pearl Harbor amendment with equanimity. Their views were fairly reflected in the sincere diary notation of Princess Liliuokalani under date of September 26, 1887. "Today a day of importance in H. history. King signed a lease of Pearl Harbor to U. States for eight [sic] years to get R. Treaty. It should not have been done."[3] The

---

[2] Stevens to Blaine, September 5, 1891, FR, 1894, 350. All of the dispatches from Stevens of any importance are from this source unless otherwise indicated. Virtually all received were published.

[3] Cited in reproduction from original in Ralph S. Kuykendall and Herbert E. Gregory, *A History of Hawaii*, 259.

King himself had resisted until the last, realizing fully the native op-position. To every native nationalist leader Pearl Harbor became the symbol of foreign control and a growing threat to the sovereignty of the native monarchy.

Further causes of discontent outside the ranks of the Reform Party group added to the complications of the political scene. One important cause of this was the growing unrest of many among the older foreign laboring population at the influx of Chinese. There were not wanting ambitious political leaders, some natives but more frequently Hawaiian-Americans or even Americans, who represented a radical fringe seeking political advantage for the position and power which it might give them. For the most part these leaders were revolutionists by instinct and in-capable of cooperating with established political organizations. Their purposes varied from a desire to repudiate the King and proclaim a monarchial constitution more autocratic in tone and with more regard to native control, to thoughts of complete overthrow of the monarchy and establishment of a republic.

In his *Memoirs,* Lorrin A. Thurston, leader in the Revolution of 1893, observes that "the diverse nationality and numerous conflicting interests of the population render Hawaiian politics kaleidoscopic to the last de-gree, resulting in the most unexpected changes and combinations." This declaration, made in 1892, fairly summarizes the maze that was the political history of Hawaii during the last days of the monarchy. In a general way, the principal basis of the growing conflict continued to be racial. S. M. Damon, participant in the revolt of 1893, declared to Com-missioner Blount that the "clashing of two nationalities for supremacy" was the foundation of the revolution.

THE UPRISING OF 1889

The first important rift in what had appeared on the surface as a secure control of the monarchy after 1887 by foreign property holders utilizing the Reform Party appeared in an abortive uprising in 1889 led by Robert Wilcox. A harmonious legislative session in 1888 was followed by serious political disturbances in 1889. On July 15 the American Minister learned of the organization of a scheme for rebellion by half-castes and natives seeking to dethrone the King in favor of his sister, Princess Liliuokalani, and to promulgate a new constitution. The following day Stevens was informed of official cognizance of such a movement, and a request was made for the retention of the U.S.S. *Adams* at Honolulu. On July 30 the rebellion occurred under the leadership of Robert W. Wilcox, ambitious half-caste educated in Italy, and Robert Boyd, half-caste publicist and nationalist leader. At the request of the Hawaiian Government, marines were landed from the U.S.S. *Adams* and the revolt ended with little excitement and its leaders were captured.

During the trial of the conspirators, evidence was produced indicating that the King himself had not been unsympathetic toward the movement. Its purpose was simply to overthrow the constitutional arrangement which had been forced upon Kalakaua in 1887 and to restore a more strongly nationalist government capable of preserving the sovereignty of the Islands against the foreigner. It appears to have been poorly organized and with little popular support, other than a vague native restlessness upon which the ambitious Wilcox and a few others hoped to capitalize.

The failure of the revolt did not end the unrest. It was accompanied by the organization of a political society among the natives known as *Hui Kalaiaina*. The gradual evolution of a party working for the restoration of royal power and native control in the government was under way. This movement ultimately developed sufficient power to cause the Reform Party, weakened by internal dissensions, to lose its legislative majority. Rumors of a proposed new treaty with the United States aided in arousing native opposition.

Failure to convict Wilcox and his fellow conspirators further aided in opposition to the existing political control. As early as November, 1889, the situation had become so tense as to lead Minister Stevens to ask the State Department for additional naval forces "for the prompt protection of American interests, should occasion arise." By the February elections in 1890, the political alignment had become fixed. The Reform Party, in a vigorous campaign, pleaded to continue responsible government under the Constitution of 1887 with economy and honesty as its watchwords. Closer relations with the United States were presented as its foreign policy.

The opposition, made up of natives with a liberal sprinkling of whites opposed to the planter aristocracy, presented an organization known as the National Reform Party. In general this party represented, as its name indicated, a nationalistic movement. Its watchwords were the revision of the constitution in the direction of greater power for the King and the native people, and it appealed to opposition to growing American domination. A racial and economic conflict was involved.

February 7, 1890, Minister Stevens hastened to inform the State Department of the results of the election held two days earlier. While a "very heated and determined" contest and "extremely bitter and unscrupulous" in many of its aspects, he believed it to have been conducted with fairness. "An election conducted in the most intelligent and moral of American rural towns could hardly have been more orderly," he reported. The results were such as to insure the probable overthrow of the Reform Party ministry when the new Legislature should be organized in May. The National Reform Party had won a narrow control which was interpreted correctly by Stevens as representing an anti-American trend for the future.

In keeping with expectations, when the new Legislature convened on May 21, the Reform Party soon found itself in the minority and the offices and committees in the hands of the nationalists. The new National Reform Party was strengthened by the desertion of the Reform Party's Canadian-born Attorney General, C. W. Ashford. The following month the Reform ministry was forced from office and replaced by a moderate coalition with two representatives from each of the contending factions.

GROWING NATIVISM IN HAWAII

A further cause of disturbance during the year became the effort of the King and his supporters to take further advantage of their political strength and secure a revision of the Constitution. The limitations upon his authority provided in the 1887 charter, and the means by which it had been extorted from him, had never pleased Kalakaua or his native followers. Proposals for a constitutional convention were presented to the King in August, 1890, by a native meeting. Without referring the matter to his Cabinet, he commended the petition to the Legislature. The result was a furor among the propertied classes at the prospect of modification.

The idea of a popularly elected convention for revision, in view of the demonstrated weakness of the Reform Party, frightened the substantial business interests. "The business men and the more responsible citizens of the islands are greatly disturbed," reported Stevens on August 19. Reform Party members of the ministry and Legislature approached both Stevens and the British diplomatic agent seeking cooperation in advising the King. On August 18 both Stevens and his British colleague followed the suggestion and united in urging the King against any such move. Legislative consideration of constitutional changes continued, but without action. Had the King persisted, it is likely that revolution would have come before 1893.

Any questions as to the future course of Kalakaua, however, were ended by his death, January 20, 1891, while on a visit to the Pacific coast of the United States. Nine days later, the Princess Liliuokalani ascended the throne. Despite the fact that her reputation was later besmirched liberally by those connected with the revolutionary movement in 1893, contemporary opinion from all quarters at the time of her ascension was agreed that she was a woman of talent and broad culture. Now over fifty years of age, she had taken a keen interest in the politics of the kingdom over a long period and was known for her strongly nationalist views. Since the revolt of 1887, which occurred while she was in England, Liliuokalani had been increasingly critical of the growth of foreign influence in Hawaii and the limitations upon the power of the monarch. Kalakaua had been urged by her to strengthen his resistance to inroads upon his power. To Minister Stevens her views were those of "extreme notions of sovereign authority" and provocative of future trouble.

The forebodings of the American Minister were such that upon the occasion of his formal presentation to the Queen on February 16, 1891, he took it upon himself to urge her to make her reign "strictly constitutional" and regard with care the rights of her ministry and its responsibility to the Legislature. The Queen paid little attention to these warnings, and proceeded, after a political controversy in which her contentions were upheld by the Supreme Court, to appoint a new ministry, on the ground that the former one expired with the death of the King. The result was another coalition, and after some little confusion political affairs quieted. The sanctioning by the Queen of renewed efforts to secure a new commercial agreement with the United States to rescue the country from the evils produced by the McKinley tariff added to an apparent growing approval of her reign by the conservatives.[4] Until the February elections in 1892, Hawaiian politics appeared to have resumed a relatively quiet trend.

HARRISON, BLAINE AND HAWAII

In the meantime, developments of the utmost importance in Hawaiian relationships to the United States were taking place on the diplomatic front. The appointment of James G. Blaine as Secretary of State under Benjamin Harrison announced in January, 1889, brought into power not only a proponent of a "vigorous" foreign policy but one long interested in Hawaii. The interest of Blaine was seconded closely by that of the President, who assumed a larger responsibility for foreign affairs than has been popularly attributed to him.[5]

---

[4] The dispatches of Stevens to the State Department Archives with enclosed newspaper clippings, and the analysis and information in the *Annual* of Thrum, provide excellent contemporary materials for a general survey of the politics of the period and have been relied upon for the most part.
[5] Cf. sketch of Blaine by Joseph B. Lockey, S. F. Bemis, *American Secretaries of State* series. Albert T. Volwiler, Harrison authority, confirms these impressions.

The interest of the Harrison administration in a close check on Hawaiian affairs was indicated quickly by the appointment of John L. Stevens, former associate of Blaine in his Maine journalistic ventures and ex-minister to Norway and Sweden, as diplomatic representative at Honolulu. In the absence of any detailed written instructions, or any later extensive comment in State Department communications to him, it must be supposed that a close personal understanding existed with Stevens as to the nature of his duties and the policies to be pursued.

The views of Secretary Blaine were definitely favorable to ultimate full American control over Hawaii. On August 10, 1891, he wrote to President Harrison that the three places valuable enough outside the continental United States to deserve acquisition were Hawaii, Cuba, and Porto Rico. The two latter, he felt were not of immediate concern, nor would they be for "a generation." However, Hawaii "may come up for decision at any unexpected hour and I hope we shall be prepared to decide it in the affirmative . . . ," declared Blaine. The views of the President were perhaps not quite so definite, but that the United States should further its hold upon Hawaii was an accepted policy.

MINISTER STEVENS' ACTIVITIES

Diplomatic relations of the tiny kingdom with its powerful neighbor were conducted upon two levels. On one there flowed a continuous stream of communications from the American Minister to Washington, which were cryptically acknowledged without comment. The new Minister, Stevens, lost no time in reporting upon Hawaiian affairs and seldom were his observations quieting. Fears of British influence, and especially of intrigues of the Canadian Pacific Railroad, and to a lesser degree expressions of hostility toward the French commissioner, and the growing preponderance of Asiatics in the Islands were his chief concerns. The belief that all of these represented a constant threat to the security of the American position in Hawaii was reiterated.

Out of Stevens' observations and impressions emerged shortly a strong support for a policy of vigorous assertion of American interests in Hawaii which was urged continuously upon the State Department. So long as the Reform Party remained in power, the worries of Stevens were not so observable. In exact proportion to the rise of native nationalism, the number and intensity of warnings flowing from Stevens at Honolulu to Blaine in Washington, increased.

See review of D. S. Muzzey, *James G. Blaine,* by Volwiler, in *American Historical Review,* April, 1936. See also Albert T. Volwiler, *The Correspondence Between Benjamin Harrison and James G. Blaine, 1889-1893,* for several Blaine and Harrison letters relative to Hawaii.

March 20, 1890, was the occasion for a particularly long dispatch emphasizing the historical background of American interests in Hawaii and their preponderance. "But a change of facts and circumstances in recent years is bringing near the time when this well-sustained power must be strongly reinforced," wrote Stevens. A "drifting policy" toward Hawaii would no longer suffice. "To hold an assimilating control over the largely preponderating Asiatic and native Hawaiian population there must be maintained an American policy, strong, conservative, but not costly, if adopted in time," he affirmed. A cable to Honolulu and the improvement of Pearl Harbor would be salutary steps to undertake, together with modifications of the existing reciprocity treaty to further favor the influx of American interests. Some new treaty arrangement to negative the evil consequences of the new tariff was absolutely necessary, in the opinion of Stevens.

By 1892 the views of Stevens had ripened still further and a new treaty, he now felt, would not be enough. The business class, as well as an important element in the native population dissatisfied with the existing administration, was reported as increasingly favorable to annexation. On February 7, 1892, Stevens informed the State Department he would comment shortly upon the necessity for a "new departure" in the policy of the United States. He voiced the opinion in this connection that a protectorate "is impracticable and that annexation must be the future remedy, or else Great Britain will be furnished with circumstances and opportunity to get a hold on these islands, which will cause future serious embarrassment to the United States."

Just what influence the views of Stevens had upon the policy of the United States it is difficult to determine with any exactness. His dispatches were acknowledged very briefly, but with frequent emphasis upon the fact that they had been reviewed with "interest." That they became a principal source of the information and ideas upon which the administration based its Hawaiian policy is probable, and there is every indication of the confidence of both Harrison and Blaine in their Hawaiian agent. In September, 1891, the President wrote Blaine of his feeling that American "interests" in Hawaii "are in jeopardy" and spoke of "the schemes of those who are seeking to bring the islands under the control of European powers." These were views undoubtedly influenced strongly by the dispatches from the Minister. Stevens, however, was kept very much in the dark about conversations carried on with Hawaiian representatives at Washington and there is no record of any information forwarded him regarding the important negotiations under way during 1889 and later.

Direct negotiation with the Hawaiian Minister at Washington was the principal channel through which the really important developments in diplomacy flowed. Until his withdrawal was forced by illness late in 1891, the ambitious and imperious H. A. P. Carter filled this post for Hawaii. J. Mott Smith, American-born Bostonian, active in the reciprocity fight and but recently appointed Minister of Finance at Honolulu, then was appointed to the post. Both Carter and Smith were definitely pro-American and inclined over a long period of their official service with the Hawaiian Government to favor the closest possible relations with the United States. Both were connected with the larger American propertied interests of the Islands and represented the point of view of that group.

Two factors combined after 1889 to forward the prospects for still closer economic and political ties between the United States and Hawaii than had been produced by the reciprocity conventions. One was the evident desire of Harrison and Blaine to tighten measurably the bonds of American control on the Islands, due in part to fears of possible German or other designs. The second was the excitement produced in Hawaii by the threat of loss of the benefits of reciprocity through a change in American tariff policy. As usual, the Hawaiian desire to protect its economic interests, especially the sugar industry, created a willingness to bargain and extend privileges to the United States.

THE PROPOSED TREATY OF 1889

In early March, 1889, Honolulu transmitted to Minister Carter at Washington a protest against impending tariff changes in the House. Carter passed this on to the State Department with added emphasis of his own. The Hawaiian dispatch spoke of the existing "pro-American feeling" in Hawaii and the danger to it should tariff modification result. A cleverly worded threat was presented in the declaration: "If it should become necessary for us to seek . . . markets outside the United States for our products, intimate associations with foreign purchasers would tend to the alienation of our feelings for the United States." To drive the barb home, Canada was mentioned directly as the possible new market. Carter took the same ground and emphasized to the State Department the "destruction" of benefits created by reciprocity and the "diversion" of Hawaiian trade to other channels should tariff modification prevail.[6]

Blaine was stirred to action, and in early April Carter and the Secretary began conversations on the subject of a new treaty. On April

---

[6] See correspondence in *Notes, Hawaii,* III, Austin to Carter and Carter to Blaine. Hawaiian fears were first aroused by the Mills bill, Democratic tariff bill passed by the House.

11 Carter confidentially transmitted to Blaine a copy of a proposed treaty "of the nature as I understood it, of the propositions discussed between us personally. . . ." In brief, the proposal extended complete commercial reciprocity to Hawaii as well as providing for mutual application of provisions of any bounties or other favors of either power. This meant that a sugar bounty adopted in the United States would apply equally to Hawaii. In return, Hawaii would agree to what amounted to the establishment of an American protectorate, similar to that later created in Cuba by the Platt amendment. A positive and efficacious American guarantee of Hawaiian independence and autonomy, long an Hawaiian desire, was agreed upon. The United States, as a safeguard, was given a guarantee that Hawaii would not enter into any foreign treaty without the approval of the United States. It was also to have the right to land armed forces at its discretion to repel attack upon Hawaii or preserve domestic order.[7]

As to the responsibility for the initiation of these proposals, there is no clear evidence. Defending the negotiations in Hawaii in 1890, Foreign Minister Austin asserted that he himself had undertaken the project to insure the development of Pearl Harbor, which officials were convinced would not be done under existing agreements. The desire to guard Hawaiian independence was also stressed by Austin. At the same time, L. A. Thurston emphasized that the desire for a guarantee of independence and to share in any sugar bounties were important considerations. Austin, Carter, and Thurston implied that the return of Blaine to the State Department had been taken as a favorable moment for the accomplishment of their ends.[8]

On the other hand, Carter in September, 1890, defending his negotiations before a new ministry, asserted that Blaine had opened the negotiations as a result of a wish to cement more closely American control in Hawaii. The protectorate clause of the proposed treaty had resulted from Carter's request for privileges for Hawaii.[9]

It is likely, however, that the negotiations were opened upon a somewhat mutual basis resulting from the original note of March 29 dealing with the tariff problem. Blaine personally was inclined to regard complete free trade with Hawaii and a guarantee of its independence by the United States as an excellent foundation for protecting the American interests there. As to Harrison, the evidence indicates that his mind as

---

[7] *Ibid.* Both Bayard, as noted earlier, and Blaine were fearful of possible development of new trade relations with British possessions. The check on treaty making would have provided a safeguard.

[8] *Report of Proceedings of Committee on Foreign Relations to the Legislature of 1890, in regard to the Investigation of Treaty Matters.*

[9] Cf. Note in Julius W. Pratt, *Expansionist of 1898,* 38n. Hereafter cited as Pratt.

late as 1891 was not made up as to specific terms of any agreement with
Hawaii, but he was deeply interested in preserving the American position. There is doubt as to whether the negotiations were taken seriously
at Washington, for Carter himself emphasized the fact that no pressure
for a treaty was applied by Blaine and when consideration was resumed
in 1890 he seemed very nonchalant as to the whole affair.[10]

In general, ardent pro-American interests in Hawaii, as usual, seem
to have been more eager to press matters than was Washington. As to
the particular provisions of the suggested treaty, the desire for complete reciprocity was a natural result of the danger to Hawaii involved
in a revision of American tariff policy. Fears of such a development
had appeared in the negotiations for the renewal of reciprocity. The
clause guaranteeing Hawaiian independence was a long-standing aspira-
tion of the Islands. From the days of Wyllie, Hawaii had attempted to
draw the United States into such an agreement. It had been desired as a
part of the original reciprocity treaty. The limitation upon Hawaii's
treaty power was hardly more than an extension and broadening of the
clause in the Treaty of 1875 limiting alienation of territory. The most
serious proposition was that permitting armed intervention by the United
States in Hawaii.

Both these latter two propositions apparently originated with Blaine.
Hawaiian public opinion was opposed to alienation of sovereignty in any
form. Carter, from his own experience, certainly must have appreciated
this sentiment and it is most unlikely that he would have suggested such
provisions. Like the Pearl Harbor proposition, these were the prices to
be exacted by the United States for its commercial favors. Intervention
likewise was a price for the assumption of binding guarantees as to the
independence of the Islands. As an alternative for annexation benefiting
the capitalists of Hawaii, it was an ideal solution to the problems of
Hawaii.[11]

When Carter returned to Hawaii in the summer, however, the proposals met with immediate difficulties. The King vigorously opposed
them, obviously fearing their effect upon his subjects, and refused to
sign instructions to negotiate a formal treaty. At a Cabinet meeting on
September 24 Carter was instructed, nevertheless, to negotiate for a

---

[10] Cf. correspondence cited in *Report, op. cit.* Blaine's attitude was no doubt
influenced by knowledge of Hawaiian opposition to the proposal.

[11] Sereno Bishop in the September, 1891, *Review of Reviews* affirmed that Blaine
was responsible for the concessions to the United States involved in the proposed
treaty. A digest of this article appearing in the *New York Tribune*, September 15,
1891, was clipped by Blaine and sent to President Harrison with the statement,
"The facts between Carter and myself are told with exactness." This item from
the Harrison Papers was furnished the author through courtesy of Albert T.
Volwiler.

formal treaty upon a basis of the inclusion of Hawaii in any bounty system, extension of full reciprocity except on opium and spirits, a simple guarantee of independence with no strings attached other than the obligation to notify the United States of treaties with other powers, and an indefinite tenure subject to abrogation or modification by mutual consent. Obviously, in this form the proposed treaty represented tremendous concessions to Hawaii which could hardly be approved in the United States.

FAILURE OF THE NEGOTIATIONS

Upon this somewhat peculiar basis, with a Cabinet supporting him against the will of the King, Carter left for Washington in September. In the meantime native nationalists had become aware of the proposals and aroused a furor of opposition. The ministry was led to defend the negotiations, pointing out in a somewhat misleading fashion that no treaty actually had been drawn. The importance of extending the commercial advantages of reciprocity upon a permanent basis was stressed. Minister Stevens attributed the opposition to British and French interests. The issue became an important one in the political campaign of the following February with the Reform Party advocating permanent reciprocity and a guarantee of Hawaiian independence as twin objectives of its foreign policy. The opposition circulated ugly rumors as to the intent of the treaty negotiations and played upon native hostility to the United States.

The exposure of the plans and their capitalization by the nationalists strengthened Kalakaua and December 20, 1889, he refused to sign instructions for Carter to negotiate. In April, 1890, he again refused and on May 3 Austin was forced to notify Carter that "His Majesty and the Cabinet Ministers have not decided to authorize the negotiations. . . ."[12] In the meantime, while some informal discussions appear to have taken place, the State Department demonstrated little interest. The Behring Sea controversy and the Pan-American Conference were monopolizing the attention of Blaine. The effect of the proposed tariff on the sugar industry was left problematical until its passage, and Hawaii remained therefore, temporarily in the background.[13]

---

[12] *Treaty Docs.*, AH. Earlier dangers to Hawaii from Germany, which had been dissipated largely by 1890, probably created a more independent attitude upon the part of Hawaii.

[13] Bishop, *op. cit.*, attributed Hawaiian opposition to the proposed treaty mainly to Ashford and Canadian Pacific Railroad interests, as did Stevens. It is probable that this view was accepted by Blaine. Austin, however, felt the opposition was due to political factionalism.

HAWAIIAN REACTIONS TO THE MCKINLEY TARIFF

The urgency of some means by which Hawaii might escape from the danger of American tariff tinkering was again demonstrated even before the discussions in 1889 had ended. The McKinley bill now under consideration proposed to place raw sugar on the free list and provide a two cents a pound bounty for American producers. In a "Private and Personal" communication to Blaine dated April 25, 1890, Carter expressed his desire to discuss the tariff changes. As proposed, he pointed out, it would prove "very disastrous to all the interests between Hawaii and the United States, and to the commercial and industrial interests which have been built up and fostered by the admission of Hawaii into the protective policy of the United States."[14]

At the same time Carter publicly criticized the suggested changes and indicated they might justify Hawaii in abrogating the reciprocity treaty. In Hawaii news of the proposed tariff measure created consternation and on May 28, 1890, Stevens reported Americans there as depressed and alarmed, while the situation was playing into the hands of the foes of the Reform Party ministry. Eight days earlier he had transmitted a long protest against the new tariff both on the ground of its evil consequences to Hawaii and its doubtful wisdom as domestic policy. The news from Stevens and the protests of Carter were unavailing, though they appear to have been viewed with sympathy by the administration. The McKinley bill was passed, and with disturbing consequences to the economic life of the Islands, as has been noted earlier.

Hawaii, however, did not relinquish its struggle to escape the results of the new tariff. While the House had included originally a clause providing that the bill should in no way change or impair existing treaty obligations, the Finance Committee struck out this safety clause and as passed it hit directly at Hawaii.[15] This clause would have saved other Hawaiian products such as rice and tallow from the operations of the tariff, the schedules of which now fell upon them. Carter pointed this out and declared that Hawaii might be forced to abrogate the Treaty and attempt to secure similar advantages from Canada or Australia. He further suggested that the Pearl Harbor concession might well be withdrawn on the ground that the bargain through which the United States secured rights there had been broken.

The following day, in another confidential note, Carter renewed his contention. Agreeable to "your personal request," Carter sketched his

---

[14] *Notes,* Hawaii, III.
[15] Cf. Memorandum of conversation of Blaine with Carter, January 6, 1891, *Notes, Hawaii,* III. Carter attributed this to a clerical error, but the memorandum specifically declares that it was eliminated by Committee.

ideas as to how Congress might be stirred to action on the matter. Carter suggested that the State Department should stress the advantages gained by the United States in Hawaii through reciprocity which possibly might not be granted again. The acceptance of the original Reciprocity Treaty by Germany, which might now refuse to sanction such liberal advantages for the United States in the Pacific, and the possible opposition of other powers were cited. The possible loss of Pearl Harbor, Carter thought, should also be stressed to the Congress.

On February 1 Carter once more communicated with Blaine. This time a proposition before Congress to establish a coaling station at Pearl Harbor excited his attention. It would create "a painful impression" in Hawaii, Carter informed Blaine, should Congress pass legislation designed to assume for the United States advantages coming from reciprocity "while denying the legislation necessary to give to Hawaii the advantages accruing to that country by the same treaty." By March 3, 1891, Congress, influenced no doubt by the campaign engineered jointly by Carter and Blaine, passed legislation providing that nothing in the tariff act should affect existing reciprocity agreements. This restored the limited advantage to Hawaii of exporting duty free a small number of commodities, mainly rice, affected by the tariff. It was a meager concession to the Islands.

ANOTHER TREATY ATTEMPTED IN 1890

Hawaii sought once more to secure a new agreement which might aid the Islands to recover from the blow inflicted by the McKinley tariff. On November 13, 1890, the Legislature passed a resolution authorizing negotiations with the United States with a view to extending the reciprocity principle. The spirit which had defeated the original negotiations in 1889, however, manifested itself in the precautionary injunction that this would be done "while guarding zealously the freedom, autonomy, and independent sovereignty of the Kingdom of Hawaii. . . ."[16] Carter believed the negotiations might be undertaken.[17] He felt this to be the case especially as a result of the favorable action of Congress in March 1891, and on March 10 he was instructed formally to begin the negotiation.[18]

By April 6 Carter was able to forward to his government a copy of a draft for a treaty which included complete reciprocity and extended it indefinitely until terminated by mutual consent. The illness and ultimate death of Carter in November led Hawaii to dispatch J. Mott

---

[16] FR, 1894, 339.
[17] Pratt, 45.
[18] *Ibid.,* 47.

Smith in October to complete the task. Smith presented a new treaty draft to Blaine on November 18, 1890, which contained important proposed modifications of the 1875 and 1887 agreements. It was suggested that the United States agree to forego rights to Pearl Harbor unless it was improved and utilized within five years. This represented a desire prompted in no small measure by a speculative boom which had gained momentum in 1890 for the development of the Pearl Harbor area. Smith likewise attempted to secure definite assurance of the construction of a cable, a project which Foreign Minister Parker had urged Carter to press the preceding September. The extension of the bounty system and other advantages to Hawaiian sugar were desired. Naturally, the extension of complete reciprocity, except for opium and liquors, was included.

The finally negotiated draft provided for the extension of the reciprocity principle, a time limit on the Pearl Harbor development, and an article binding the President and the Queen mutually to urge construction of a cable. For obvious reasons the other demands of Smith, extreme as they were without compensating advantages to the United States, were dropped.[19] Within a few days the proposed treaty was in the hands of the President where it remained as late as November 30, in spite of gentle prodding from Blaine, urged on by Smith, for its return so that it might be sent to Hawaii. In October the President had expressed himself as undecided how far the United States might go in extending its trade relations with Hawaii though "the necessity of maintaining and increasing our hold and influence in the Sandwich Islands is very apparent and very pressing." It appears that his indecision was never overcome. Fears for the fate of the proposed treaty in the Senate because of the breach in the protective system, the threatened reopening of the tariff question, the impending elections, and pressure by California fruit and sugar interests were cited by the Hawaiian Minister as reasons for the ultimate failure of Harrison to sanction the treaty.[20] Democratic success in the election ended the entire negotiation.

AN IMPASSE IN HAWAIIAN-AMERICAN RELATIONS

By 1892 proposals for closer relationships between Hawaii and the United States had reached an impasse. Hawaii desired definite advantages from any new treaty. At the very least she insisted upon complete reciprocity, while the wish to secure extension of the sugar bounty was ever present. Desires for the improvement of Pearl Harbor and a cable to Hawaii were becoming almost equally urgent. These

---

[19] Cf. drafts and correspondence in *Notes, Hawaii,* III.
[20] See explanation offered by Smith, Pratt, 48.

demands were those which the planting interests literally forced the monarchy to seek as the price of their peace and allegiance. They were the necessary guarantees of economic security and political quiet for any native government.

From the American standpoint, however, such demands were exorbitant and hardly of such a nature, in view of past battles over reciprocity in a limited form, as to win support and probable passage. No administration could afford to engage in a battle for a treaty containing such concessions to Hawaii without very material compensating advantages. It is important to recall that the original Treaty of 1875 and its renewal in 1887 had been won only by what amounted to bribes extended to the United States. Yet the rise of native nationalism in Hawaii had created such a situation that no ministry which countenanced any further grants of privilege could hope to weather the political storm and secure ratification of such a treaty.

It is probable that a new treaty could have been pushed through the United States Senate prior to the McKinley bill, had it been submitted promptly. But, as has been shown, nationalist agitation in Hawaii made it impossible for the Austin ministry to secure early approval to undertake such a treaty with its favorable concessions. Without them, and following the McKinley bill, the United States was not interested in the purely theoretical advantages of reciprocity any more than it had been in 1875 or 1887. Thus the prospect for some protectorate status for Hawaii failed under Blaine and Harrison. Such a protectorate would have prevented the political disorders of 1893 and probably defeated for decades any prospect for annexation.

While these maneuverings were taking place in the diplomatic field, the cauldron of Hawaiian politics once more began to boil. Under the system of biennial elections which prevailed, the peak of disturbance was reached every two years in connection with the political campaign. The foreign property holders struggled on these occasions to maintain their position politically despite their disparity in numbers, while native and other opposition leaders sought to capture the support of the masses.

THE ELECTION OF 1892 IN HAWAII

In the February 1, 1892, election, three political groups appeared. The Reform Party based its chief campaign appeal upon the support of proposed new treaty arrangements with the United States and pledges of economy and honesty in government. The National Reform Party continued to support the cause of the ruling dynasty, having been transformed from the "King's Party" to the "Queen's Party." The cause of strong monarchy, the preservation of independence, and full autonomy were the principal appeals which it presented to the populace. By 1892 still a third political grouping had emerged in Hawaii in the form of a new Liberal Party, supported in the main by half-castes and a few ambitious whites, mainly Americans outside the larger propertied interests.

The unity of this new group was achieved through common opposition to the existing administration. A new constitution and a more definitely nationalist policy were its original objectives, though political expediency led its leaders to vacillate so greatly as to make it difficult to ascertain with certainty the basic principles of the party. Headed by Robert W. Wilcox, leader of the ill-starred insurrection against Kalakaua, and C. W. Ashford, ambition for personal power upon the part of its leaders seems to have constituted the principal excuse for its existence. Alternately it opposed and then favored the proposed treaty. By the time of organization of the new Legislature, the Liberal Party was favorable to revolution and annexation. A group of radical opportunists, the new Party added further complexity to an already muddled situation.[21]

The elections resulted in placing eighteen members of the National Reform Party, seventeen of the Reform Party, fourteen of the Liberal Party, and three independents in the newly constituted Legislature. Two of the independent members invariably supported the National Reform Party program, giving it a voting strength of twenty, while one followed the Reform Party, giving it eighteen votes. The National Reform Party succeeded in organizing and controlling the Legislature and ministry. The old Reform Party was blocked completely at the moment in any program which it sought to forward.

The result of this situation was an alliance between very strange political bed-fellows—the Reform and the Liberal parties. During the summer of 1892 the two factions worked in harmony and succeeded, after a second attempt, in voting out of power the National Reform Party ministry. Leader of the coalition appears to have been the now ardent annexationist, Lorrin Thurston. The common ground upon which the group operated was agreement in opposition to the Queen and the desire for closer relations with the United States, even to the point of annexation.[22]

---

[21] Stevens reported with his usual care the nature of the campaign and elections. Cf. FR, 1894, 353ff. For a statement of the political program and ideals of the Liberals see the interview of Wilcox with Commissioner Blount, April 18, 1893, in FR, 1894, 1005f.

[22] The analysis of the Legislature prepared for Commissioner Blount by E. C. MacFarlane is valuable; also the interview with Wilcox and the dispatches of Stevens. All are contained in FR, 1894. See also discussion by Pratt, 63-67.

The coalition secured, after considerable wrangling, a victory over the Queen. Both the Liberal and Reform parties demanded a ministry responsible to the dominant coalition, while Liliuokalani attempted to secure one under her influence. After the overthrow of two such royally controlled ministries in November, 1892, a Reform Party Cabinet headed by G. N. Wilcox, conservative business leader, came into power at the close of the session. The Liberal Party was left without a single ministerial position, a fact which led to difficulty and in no small manner influenced the later revolution.

CONSERVATISM AND AMERICANISM SEEM TRIUMPHANT

The final success of the Reform Party was a triumph for the wealth and power which it represented. To the State Department, Stevens reported with some pleasure that its leaders were "the responsible men of the Islands, none of them needing the salaries, all being of comparative wealth, their aggregate property being estimated at nearly one million of dollars." It was likewise a triumph for the American influence. Stevens pointed gleefully to the fact that three of the Cabinet were "strong in American feeling and purposes." "The success of the Legislative majority," he wrote November 8, "and the appointment of this cabinet are regarded as the triumph of the better citizens of Hawaii over the worst, and especially a proof of American ascendancy over ultra-English and other anti-American elements and sentiments."[23]

What this political development ultimately presaged for Hawaiian-American relations can only be surmised because a new political upheaval drove the Reform Party from power January 12, 1893, and thereby precipitated a revolution. Pratt is inclined to adopt the view that the Reform Party triumph favored a move for annexation upon the part of the interests behind it.[24] The fact is certain that the economic disturbance produced by the McKinley act had increased the strength of the annexationist movement. Stevens declared in his famous November 20, 1892, dispatch, "it is a well authenticated fact that the American sentiment here in 1890, the last year of the great prosperity under the sugar provisions of the reciprocity treaty, was much less manifest than before that treaty had gone into effect." The annexation desire he now found "much stronger" than in 1889 or 1890. For more than a year previously he had reported the steady increase of annexation sentiment.

---

[23] FR, 1894, 376f.
[24] Pratt, 63f.

THE ANNEXATION CLUB AND ITS PROGRAM

That this was not a vagary of the American Minister is proved by the secret maneuvers of some of the more important Reform Party leaders in Hawaii. About 1892 there had been organized in the Islands a secret Annexation Club. The exact purposes of the Club, despite its name, are not clear and are in dispute. Its principal leader, Lorrin A. Thurston, declares in his *Memoirs* that its object was not to promote annexation but merely to act should the Queen precipitate the issue. The existence of the organization was known to Rear Admiral Brown in charge of the American naval force at Honolulu as early as September, 1892, and he reported to the Navy Department that its object was to change the government peacefully with the consent of the Queen and established authorities.[25]

One of the most mysterious aspects of the existence and activity of the Club is the complete absence of any mention of it in the correspondence of Stevens with the State Department, in spite of frequent references to annexation sentiment, and specific reference to the plotting of Liberal Party leaders for revolution and annexation. Furthermore, in all of the voluminous testimony taken from both friend and foe of the revolution before Commissioner Blount, and later before the Senate Committee on Foreign Relations, there is no mention of the Annexation Club. Of its existence, however, there is no doubt. It was known to the naval officers at Honolulu, as has been indicated. The correspondence included in the *Memoirs* of Thurston indicates further that Stevens was aware of the aims of the group, if not of its complete organization.

Its activities were confined to about seventeen members. These represented the more radical of the American element at Honolulu, impatient at the slow development of the drift toward the United States. It is important to recall that such a faction had usually appeared in every crisis in Hawaiian affairs. Lorrin Thurston, chief inspiration of the movement, was not by any means the most outstanding figure in the Reform Party; nor did he represent the larger economic interests of the Islands. Primarily a lawyer and a small planter with some other minor business connections, he would not come under the classification of the "planter interest" in any important sense. There is little doubt that the Club represented an American element with limited property holdings, and therefore more prone to support radical measures than was true of the larger capitalists. In many respects, Lorrin Thurston

---

[25] Cf. note by Pratt, 55n. See also dispatch of September 6, 1892, FR, 1894.

in the history of the Hawaiian revolution compares with the Samuel Adams type of patriot in the American struggle for independence.

The Club did have a program. Two principal procedures for achieving the peaceful annexation of Hawaii to the United States were adopted. The first step, and perhaps most important as a preliminary move, was to sound out the possibility for favorable acceptance. On May 5, 1892, therefore, the indefatigable Thurston arrived at Washington, partly to arrange for the Hawaiian cyclorama exhibit at the World's Fair. Actually, according to his *Memoirs,* his other purpose was to approach American leaders and get their views as to annexation. Within the month Thurston managed to canvass the situation with some thoroughness. James H. Blount, chairman of the House Committee on Foreign Affairs, the Secretary of State, Mr. Blaine, and Secretary of the Navy Tracy were the principal persons approached. The President declined to be interviewed, preferring to allow any policies he might endorse to originate through the State Department. Thurston appears to have received considerable sympathy from Blaine and Tracy, and gained the impression that annexation would not be denied should the ground work for it be prepared. Before returning to Hawaii from San Francisco on May 29, Thurston prepared a careful memorandum for Blaine in which he detailed the favorable prospect for annexation in view of conditions in the Islands as he believed them to be at the time.[26]

The second objective of the annexationists, once the favorable situation in the United States was made known, was a peaceful and careful maneuvering of the Hawaiian political situation to insure the presentation of a definite proposal. To Blaine on May 27, prior to his return to Hawaii, Thurston outlined his political program. The securing of a favorable ministry, education of the populace, and an early adjournment of the Legislature so that it might be subject to its own recall should the situation remain favorable in the United States by the following December, constituted the outlined procedure. Thurston and his cohorts proposed to arrange for a modified plebiscite on annexation or, should this not prove feasible, force action through a favorable legislature and send an annexation commission to the United States.[27] In order to keep in touch with the Washington situation, Archibald Hopkins, a clerk in the Court of Claims, was selected as permanent agent

---

[26] See the personal account of Thurston in his *Memoirs,* 230ff., and the careful discussion by Pratt, 54ff., for further reference. It should be noted that Secretary Bayard earlier had come to adopt the view that annexation was more or less inevitable.

[27] The Thurston Memorandum in the State Department Archives was discussed in an article by Julius W. Pratt, "The Hawaiian Revolution: A Reinterpretation," *Pacific Historical Review,* I.

to inform the annexationists of developments and to represent them in necessary contacts in the United States.

The chief significance of the Thurston mission lies in its forecast of the probable future trend in Hawaiian-American relationships. It indicated the existence of a small but ambitious and aggressive element in the Islands willing to work consistently to take advantage of every opportunity to force the issue of annexation. While Thurston emphasizes in his *Memoirs* the peaceful and legal methods by which this objective was to be sought, his memorandum for Blaine shows that extra-legal methods were acceptable should the schemes of the group fail of realization through regular channels. A relatively ruthless and unscrupulous conspiracy existed in 1892 against the autonomy of the kingdom.

HARRISON AND ANNEXATION

The nature of the reception accorded Thurston, coupled with certain other developments, demonstrated the willingness of the Harrison administration through its most important representatives and spokesman to seize full advantage of the opportunity presented for the realization of manifest destiny in Hawaii. According to Thurston, Blaine had informed him directly that should Hawaii apply for annexation, "he did not see how the application could be rejected."[28] Similar assurances undoubtedly were received from Secretary Tracy. It is significant that a few months later, December 30, 1892, Tracy, in response to a direct question from Admiral Skerett about to depart for Hawaiian duty, declared the United States would be very glad to annex Hawaii if ordinary legal means could persuade the people to desire it.[29]

Both American diplomatic and naval representatives on the scene were inclined to the same views. By 1892 Minister Stevens had become a confirmed annexationist. On February 8 of that year he wrote, "The present political situation is feverish and I see no prospect of its being permanently otherwise until these islands become a part of the American Union or a possession of Great Britain."[30] On April 2 he asserted that the annexationists "would carry all before them, provided the latter could get any encouragement that the United States would take these islands as a territory." November 20, 1892, Stevens sent his oft-cited dispatch in which he reviewed the economic and strategic basis of American interests, the chaotic political situation, and the dangers from

---

[28] *Memoranda of Conversations with the Secretary of State, 1893-1898.*
[29] See FR, 1894, 476. Tracy had ordered Admiral Brown, August 28, 1890, to proceed with all despatch to Honolulu "keeping his movements secret."
[30] FR, 1894, 353f.

English, Canadian, and Asiatic sources to the American position in the Islands. The remedy must be an "implied" protectorate and a cable and virtual customs union with Hawaii—or annexation. The latter was regarded as the sensible policy, and the former would but delay the matter a possible twenty-five years. "I cannot refrain from expressing the opinion with emphasis that the golden hour is near at hand," declared Stevens. Eight days later, the Minister sent a duplicate of this dispatch, requesting that it be shown to the President and Secretary Tracy as well as Senators Morgan, Thurman, and Frye and "such others as you deem expedient." "I am not sure that our statesmen are yet ready to grapple boldly with this Hawaiian question. I am, however, very confident that the sooner it is firmly taken hold of, the better it will be for the United States as well as for Hawaii," he wrote.[31]

In view of this flow of information, it is small wonder that the administration at Washington grew more and more to feel that the "hour" indeed had arrived. The reports of American naval officers to the Navy Department, quickly relayed to the State Department, were of much the same tenor, if somewhat less aggressive in urging a positive policy. Through 1890 and 1891 the tension in Hawaii had produced a series of urgent dispatches to naval officers to make haste in reaching Honolulu and remain until affairs "are settled and absolutely safe."[32] This meant one thing—the fullest possible protection of American interests against any political shift which might endanger them. Stevens more or less continuously bombarded the authorities at Washington with requests for one or more naval vessels, asserting that they frequently checked by their mere presence uprisings against the government.

Frequent reports from the naval representatives since the autumn of 1890 had commented upon the disturbed political situation, and the more or less constant threat of revolution. The officers agreed with Stevens that their presence acted as a check upon violence during this period. The naval commanders kept in close contact not only with Stevens but also, in the words of Rear-Admiral Brown, with "many of the leading American merchants and lawyers. . . ."[33] The tone of these communications reflected fully the point of view of the American capitalists in much the same fashion as did those of Stevens. McCurley, for example, declared that "the Anglo-Saxon race here,

---

[31] *Dispatches,* XXV.

[32] A series of these cryptic notes are contained in *Cipher Messages Sent,* Navy Department Archives. The one cited is for January 24, 1891, and due to uncertainty of results from the death of the King.

[33] See Brown to Tracy, July 29, 1890; McCurley to Tracy, August 22, 1890, FR, 1894, 1173f. and *Cipher Messages To* in Navy Department Archives.

with intelligence and civilization behind them, move irresistibly forward on their march to democracy. . . ." Any attempt of the monarchy to strengthen its power in the form of increased native rights for the ruler would result in revolution and a republic, he declared with some note of prophecy.

Similar reports came from Captain G. C. Wiltse during late 1892. On October 12 he noted the growth of annexation sentiment but added: "I am informed that the leaders do not think an opportune moment will arrive for some time to come. However, everything seems to point toward an eventual request for annexation." On November 1 he reported the prospect of a crisis because of the conflict of the Queen with the Reform Party. Eight days later, he expressed the view that the presence of his vessel had checked the prospect of revolt.[34]

To appreciate fully the nature of the point of view of the naval representatives it is important to keep in mind the fact that from early days the Navy had played an important role in Hawaiian-American affairs. Naval officers serving at Honolulu circulated in the society created by the more wealthy American residents. They absorbed inevitably the political views of this group, and were ever inclined to present these views to their superiors in official reports. The high diplomatic importance of their service over a long period of time tended as well to give the naval officers a sense of responsibility for supervising and reporting upon the affairs of the Islands second only to that enjoyed by the American Minister. As representatives of a more powerful nation dealing with a much weaker and insignificant power, they likewise developed a sense of superiority and condescension which in some cases, as that of Captain Reynolds and the *Lackawanna,* had produced open difficulty. The reports from such a source as to conditions in Hawaii during the nineties must have had an important part in leading both Tracy and Blaine to sense that the issue of annexation was likely to be raised.

AMERICAN PUBLIC OPINION ON HAWAII IN 1892

Further encouragement, both for supporters of the Annexation Club in Hawaii and for those at Washington who sympathized with their purpose, must have come from the new interest in Hawaiian affairs displayed in the United States by this date. In former years only a few news items appeared in leading American newspapers with scattered editorial comment, but both were so limited as to make it im-

---

[34] FR, 1894, 184-88.

possible to assert that the public was deeply interested in Hawaii as a matter of established national interest.[35] By about 1891, however, this attitude began to change somewhat and there emerged a more active concern for the destiny of the little Pacific kingdom. How much of this was inspired it is impossible to say with accuracy.

One of the first evidences of this appeared in an article in *Review of Reviews* for September, 1891, under the pen of Sereno Bishop. This is an excellent example of inspired publicity.[36] The editor of the publication, Albert Shaw, was an ardent exponent of Anglo-Saxon expansion, while Bishop was former editor of the old missionary publication *The Friend* at Honolulu and one of the leaders of the annexationists. The article devoted some attention to the character of the Queen and the native kingdom in general, after which it proceeded to play upon every device which might excite American attention. The strategic importance of Hawaii as the "cross-roads of the North Pacific" was much emphasized. The familiar foreign bogey was also dragged out. Bishop declared, "There will grow up a pressure, not now existing, for Great Britain to take possession of the Islands, in order to provide the security of her growing commerce across the Pacific." The instability of the kingdom politically received attention and the entire article was designed cleverly to arouse attention. In this it was successful, and it was widely noticed throughout the country.[37]

American papers began to take notice of Hawaiian political conflicts at about the same time, and not infrequently items on the situation explained the nature of the party controversy in Hawaii and its significance.[38] The *New York Tribune,* that perfect expression of Republican viewpoints, found occasion during 1891 to comment on Hawaiian affairs no less than three times. Each stressed the importance of American interests. Typical was the editorial of December 11: "The growth of our Pacific States, the fact that 90% of Hawaii's trade comes into and goes out from their ports, the enormous investments of American capital in Hawaiian enterprises, the position of the islands in the path of our Chinese and Australian commerce, their strategic importance and their political and commercial relation to the Nicaraguan Canal combine to render it absolutely necessary for us to take such steps as will insure us against their absorption into a foreign colonial system."

[35] A check through the index to the *New York Tribune* for the seventies and eighties will quickly establish this fact. The usually rather inclusive comment in *Public Opinion* has scarcely anything on Hawaii. The author has examined many newspapers of the period as well and found little worth noting.

[36] The article was entitled, "The Hawaiian Queen and Her Kingdom."

[37] *Public Opinion* considered it worthy of extracting its more significant portions. See also *New York Tribune,* October 11, 1892.

[38] Cf. *Public Opinion* during 1891 for some citations.

The visit of Thurston in May, 1892, provoked general comment on Hawaii. Appreciating the methods of Hawaiian agents, it is not difficult to suppose that much of it was carefully stimulated by Thurston and his friends. *Bradstreet's* for May 14, 1892, noted that there was "more or less talk" about Hawaiian annexation. Newspapers in every section of the United States commented upon the prospect, and for the most part in a favorable vein. Typical perhaps was the *Kansas City Times* observation, "Should Hawaii conclude that she would like to become one of the States of the Union and should she see advantages to herself equal to what she can confer, and Congress can see equal mutual benefits, let her come in."[39]

During November and December of the same year further rumors of the political crisis appeared in the American press, and resulted in considerable comment favoring annexation, should it be proffered. Once more the fear of foreign influence, obviously British or British colonial, was stressed as the major justification for such action. Reports by the *San Francisco Examiner* that the business interests of Hawaii were overwhelmingly in support of annexation received wide publicity in the United States.[40] It has been reasoned with some validity that many of these rumors may have been inspired by the State Department, a view accepted by the contemporary New York *Nation*.[41] The whole does seem to bear the familiar ring of the clamors as to British designs upon California and Texas which preceded the Mexican War. It is probable that a not unfamiliar device was being utilized to set the stage of public sentiment.

With the existence of an organized minority in Hawaii determined to take advantage of any opportunity to force the issue of annexation, a favorable administration at Washington, and built up opinion supporting the idea that annexation was not to be unexpected or deprecated, the prospect for some *coup d'etat* by which Hawaii might be joined to the United States indeed was bright. The two chief obstacles were the difficulty in securing peaceful adherence to any such proposition in Hawaii, and the question as to whether President Harrison might continue in power in the United States.

THE HAWAIIAN POLITICAL SITUATION IN 1892

As to the situation in the Islands, Thurston himself was doubtful and in December, 1892, informed his agent, Hopkins, at Washington

---

[39] Cited *Public Opinion,* May 28, 1892. See same for June 11 and Pratt, 55n. for other comments of similar purport.
[40] Cf. *New York Tribune,* November 20 and December 1, 1892.
[41] See comment November 23, 1892.

that he questioned the possibility of an endorsement of his proposals by the Legislature. Opposition from the natives desirous of preserving national autonomy, and fears of planters that contract labor and Chinese immigration would be prohibited by the United States should Hawaii come under its jurisdiction, were the main barriers.[42]

The early alliance of the Liberal and Reform parties had broken down in late 1892. The conservative Reform Party leaders failed to continue the flirtation established by Thurston and excluded Liberal Party representatives from the Reform Party ministry. An abortive conspiracy of the Liberal Party leaders against the Crown in May had been cut short, as has been noted, by the arrest of important leaders. This had served further to weaken the Wilcox-Ashford faction, and lead the natives to swing more solidly behind support of the Queen and her policies. The Queen and her supporters were in a stronger position in 1892 than at any previous time.

Furthermore, in the United States all was not well with the schemes for annexation. The Harrison administration was in the midst of a national election and struggling to keep in power. Foreign policy had some importance in the campaign, for the swashbuckling tactics of Blaine had aroused the bitter opposition of such organs as the New York *Nation,* the *Evening Post,* and the *Herald.* Whatever the result in prospect, the exigencies of the campaign tended to obscure interest in Hawaii and keep it at a low ebb despite some efforts, as indicated earlier, to arouse such an interest.

As it proved, however, it mattered little what men had planned in the way of Hawaiian-American relationships. Fate stepped in to the picture in a most unpredictable fashion and shifted the entire stage of events. By November, 1892, the "responsible" men of the Islands had triumphed over the Queen and a Reform Party ministry of conservatives was in power. The position of this ministry and its support in the Legislature seemed so secure that the American Minister, always looking for trouble, was lulled into a sense of security and deserted his post for a short rest tour to Hilo aboard the naval vessel stationed in the harbor. At no time since 1890 had it seemed that a conservative government might be more apt to persist.

Had this state of affairs persisted, the entire history of Hawaiian relations with the United States might have been changed. Some close students of Hawaii are inclined to support the conclusion that the Wil-

---

[42] *Memoirs,* 235f. This letter is of great importance in view of later developments. Claus Spreckels had been liquidating his Hawaiian holdings anticipating such a result. It is quite clear that the large planters were fearful of annexation because of its influence on the labor problem.

cox Reform Party ministry was committed to annexation and would have pushed such measures had it continued in power. This conclusion seems of doubtful validity in view of the past history of Hawaiian politics. The most conservative business interests, as had been demonstrated time and again since 1850, were not interested primarily in annexation. Thurston himself was keenly aware of this and so expressed himself in his famous December 14 letter to Hopkins.

The principal cause of rising annexation sentiment had been the combination of the threat of arbitrary native government and the economic disorganization prevailing in 1890 and 1891. Both these influences appeared to have changed by late 1892. Economic conditions were improving slowly due to some improvement in sugar prices and more diversification of Hawaiian agriculture. The conservatives seemed firmly in power. Reasoning upon a basis of the past experiences and reactions in periods of crisis and recovery in Hawaii, there is every support for the view that a reasonable prosperity and substantial control over the government would have quieted every alarm of the conservative propertied interests after 1892.[43]

However, this state of affairs was radically changed. Shortly prior to the adjournment of the Legislature in January 1893, the supporters of the Queen staged a political uprising which not only drove the Reform Party ministry from power but secured the passage of legislation licensing the establishment of a lottery. Following closely upon the heels of licensing the opium traffic the preceding December, this measure was an affront to the surviving Puritan consciousness which was about the only remaining vestige of the missionary influence in Hawaii. More than that, the Queen appointed a new ministry of a decidedly anti-Reform character and subject to easy manipulation by the Crown. Once more the political cauldron began to boil furiously. The conservatives were aroused to vigorous protest. The *Pacific Commercial Advertiser,* perfectly reflecting their views, began to warn the Queen that her actions threatened the security of her throne, and the business interests of Honolulu would not quietly sanction a revival of the drive for increased royal power. The situation was once more critical.[44]

---

[43] Julius W. Pratt emphasizes correctly and strongly the conservative planter opposition to annexation in January and February 1893; a fact which contradicts his previous observations as to the probable course of the Reform Party representing those interests.

[44] The dispatches of Stevens with enclosures provide a perfect picture of the alarm of the conservatives.

THE ATTEMPTED REVOLUTION BY QUEEN LILIUOKALANI

Had the nationalists stopped at this point, it is doubtful as to whether serious consequences would have obtained. The strong willed Liliuo-kalani, however, on January 14, 1893, attempted to promulgate by royal edict a new constitution closely resembling that of 1864 and restoring the control of the monarch over the House of Nobles, as well as limiting the suffrage to actual subjects. It was a definite challenge to those who had forced the Constitution of 1887 upon Kalakaua. No more serious or radical affront to them could have been conceived. Kalakaua earlier had attempted the same move but flaring discontent and the pressure of foreign diplomats had influenced him to back down.

The motives, however, behind the action of the Queen are not difficult to understand. Always an ardent nationalist and a strong-minded person, she had opposed consistently the rise of influence obnoxious to her concept of a royal Hawaiian monarchy. The Queen had become convinced that the time was now ripe to take action. There is little doubt but that she felt her policy fully justified in terms of the desires of her native subjects. According to her own statements, the new constitution was under consideration for some time and was not hastily conceived.

The radical act of promulgating it by edict was the product of circumstances. The original purpose had been to secure a convention for constitutional revision at the call of the Legislature. Proposals to this end were unsuccessful, for the authors of the Constitution of 1887 had framed it deliberately in such a fashion as to enable a minority to check its revision. It is doubtful whether any proposals legally to change the Constitution contrary to the wishes of the Reform Party would ever have succeeded. Unable to work through the document, the Queen determined to work around it, and the political change of January undoubtedly encouraged her. That she expected some difficulty is indicated by the fact that preparations for trouble were made, but that she expected to be sustained by her ministry and people is unquestioned.[45]

THE QUEEN'S PLANS THWARTED

Carried virtually to the point of final consummation, the desire of the Queen was thwarted at the last by the timidity of her supposedly complaisant ministry. J. F. Colburn, Minister of the Interior, hearing

---

[45] The statements of the Queen and her ministers to Commissioner Blount in 1893 are the best possible record of her intentions and desires. A majority of one Legislature and two-thirds in the following one was necessary to amend the Constitution.

of the impending action of the Queen early on the morning of the 14th, proceeded to the office of his friend A. S. Hartwell with the news. Hartwell, in turn, requested that Thurston and W. O. Smith, later an annexation commissioner and member of the Provisional Government, be notified. One may imagine the satisfaction with which Thurston must have received news of a development which promised to turn a defeat for his aims into victory. Colburn was instructed to resist the Queen and carried others of the ministry with him. The Queen relented and informed the populace that the promised constitution would be postponed.[46]

Thus far nothing more than a threatened constitutional *coup* had developed. The action of the Queen had been averted, and later developments showed that very shortly the calmer advice of her ministers was sufficient to extract from her by evening assurances that she would not again resort to such an attempt. Consulting with representatives of the foreign population the following day, her advisors were able to win by the 16th an official announcement from Liliuokalani that she would not again attempt to modify the Constitution except by regular means. Despite this promise, revolution ensued.

The explanation for this lies in the fact that the Queen's action had played into the hands of the more radical supporters of annexation. Her effort to countermand her error, which under ordinary circumstances might have been as successful as that of Kalakaua, was negatived by the swift movements of an opposition which took full advantage of her mistake. The plans of the Queen had failed, but those of her opponents were to be successful. That a complete revolution was either necessary or justifiable is questionable. That it would have occurred, had it not been for the existence of a well-organized minority, also is open to question.

Every evidence indicates that the Queen presented this vulnerable opening at a time when the radicals themselves least expected to be successful in their schemes. The *Memoirs* of Thurston indicate that there was no expectation in December, 1892, or early January of the following year that the carefully nurtured scheme of annexation would prevail. The American Minister, the American naval representatives, and in fact everyone, felt in early 1893 that the Hawaiian scene was as calm as a summer sea.[47]

---

[46] Cf. testimony by Colburn before Commissioner Blount. FR, 1894, 496f.

[47] Cf. especially the testimony of Lieutenant Young of the U.S.S. *Boston* before the Senate Committee in 1894. In contemporary debate, and since, it has been charged that Stevens left Honolulu to encourage revolution. This is not logical in view of his oft-repeated assertions that the presence of naval forces checked disorders, and the opportunity to have removed them at any time and encouraged revolt by so doing had always been available.

THE SUCCESSFUL REVOLUTION OF THE ANNEXATION CLUB

As a result of the indignation aroused and the lack of confidence promoted by the unconstitutional strategy of the Queen, leaders of the dormant Annexation Club were enabled gradually to assume full control of the situation and move for revolution. According to C. Bolte, German born and most reliable of the members of the Committee of Safety to present evidence on affairs in 1893, from the beginning of the protest meetings held by foreigners in the office of W. O. Smith on January 14, sentiments were freely expressed by himself, W. C. Wilder, and other members of the later Committee that the action of the Queen was a good thing, and would hasten annexation.[48]

At a second protest meeting held the afternoon of the 14th, a Committee of Safety was organized consisting of thirteen members. In the words of George N. Wilcox, head of the former Reform Party Cabinet, it was organized "to take steps to preserve the public peace and secure the maintenance of law and order against the revolutionary acts of the sovereign." It was supported by many of those who had been active friends of the monarchy and it is doubtful whether they conceived of this committee as a revolutionary body.[49] Even pro-revolutionary accounts of the early protest movement emphasize the fact that it represented those "of every political complexion" and that the purpose was to "resist the revolutionary encroachments of the Queen."

According to W. O. Smith, and his account for the benefit of Commissioner Blount is supported by the admission of Thurston in his *Memoirs,* the Committee of Safety early took steps, however, on the 14th to promote a complete revolution against the Queen and to establish a provisional government replacing the monarchy. A motion introduced by Thurston to this effect was unanimously adopted by the Committee. The Annexation Club, leaders of which now dominated the Committee, was moving rapidly toward its long desired objective. Two things were now necessary—the sentiment of the American Minister as to the possible landing of troops to create a "protectorate" must be

---

[48] Cf. affidavit dated December 14, 1893. Bolte declared that at a second meeting sentiments that "this is a splendid opportunity to get rid of the old regime, and strong demands for annexation, or any kind of stable government under the supervision of the United States were expressed." W. D. Alexander told the Committee likewise that Thurston declared, "Must we continue to live in this way, with this peril hanging over our heads, uncertain whether we may not wake up any morning and find our liberties gone?"

[49] Cf. affidavit of Wilcox and the pamphlet, "Two Weeks of Hawaiian History," published by the Hawaiian Gazette Company (Honolulu, 1893) included in FR, 1894, 777-93.

sounded, and a further testing of public opinion of the foreign community must be secured.

Thurston, W. C. Wilder, and H. F. Glade of the Committee were appointed to confer with Minister Stevens and preparations made for a meeting Sunday, the following day, for further plans. So anxious were the leaders to hasten their program, however, that still another meeting was held at the Thurston home Saturday evening. Thurston told those present that Stevens had informed him that the American authorities would land troops "any moment to prevent the destruction of American life and property, and in regard to the matter of establishing a Provincial Government they, of course, would recognize the existing government whatever it might be." Thurston further declared he had informed Stevens of the plans for a new government and asked him concerning his attitude. Stevens had replied that "whatever government was established and was actually in possession of the Government building, the executive departments and archives, and *in possession of the city,* that was a *de facto* government proclaiming itself as a government, would necessarily have to be recognized."[50] At the same meeting a general outline for the proposed Provisional Government was created. Thurston continued as the guiding genius of the movement.

The following day, Sunday the 15th, the committee which had waited upon Stevens reported to the entire Committee of Safety at a meeting at the home of W. R. Castle. At this gathering it was decided to take the second step necessary to bulwark the revolutionists. Arrangements were made for a mass meeting Monday afternoon, and once more the importance of the position of the annexationists was emphasized in that they prepared the program for this meeting. At the same time a formal request to Stevens to land troops was prepared for presentation to him, but was not to be acted upon until further notice from the Committee.

Whether the mass meeting of Monday, January 16, could be taken as an authorization for a revolutionary program seems doubtful upon a basis of contemporary reports. Furthermore, the revolutionists seem to have concealed the true purpose of their activity from those attendant upon the meeting. The meeting itself must be regarded as essentially similar to the demonstration staged by the foreign population in June, 1887, which had forced under threat of revolt a new constitution from Kalakaua. It is doubtful whether it was considered by a majority of those attending as anything other than a demonstration in favor of sound government. In fact, Wilder, active on the Committee, declared

---

[50] Statements those of W. O. Smith in his affidavit for Commissioner Blount. This has been accepted as a reliable account for the general activity of the annexationists.

in opening the meeting that it was similar in intent to the demonstration of 1887 and for the same purpose. "We do not meet as revolutionists, but as peaceful citizens who have the right to meet and state their grievances," he declared to the accompaniment of loud applause. One wonders what Mr. Wilder would define as revolution in view of the activities already under way by his Committee, including plans for a new government and use of armed force and foreign aid to support it.

The report of the Committee of Safety to the public was equally evasive. It stressed that it had been created "for the maintenance of the public peace and the protection of life and property." It presented a series of six resolutions endorsing its own activities and protesting the action of the Queen as "unlawful, unwarranted, in derogation of the rights of the people, endangering the peace of the community, and tending to excite riot, and cause the loss of property." The report did not tell of the really secret work of the Committee, however, and it is significant that, despite an apparent early intention to do so, the prepared petition to Minister Stevens for the use of the forces from the *Boston* was not circulated for signatures. The Committee was authorized to "further consider the situation and further devise such ways and means as may be necessary to secure the permanent maintenance of law and order, and the protection of life, liberty and property in Hawaii." No mention of ways and means already undertaken was forthcoming. While there were two incendiary speeches by a J. Emmeluth and R. J. Greene, those of the Committee who spoke did so as moderates and seemed definitely unwilling to expose their hand. The meeting, however, was taken by the leaders as an endorsement of the projected Provisional Government.[51]

Further ground for considering the revolution as a staged uprising rather than vitally necessary to the salvation of foreign property and liberties, as it was so freely portrayed by its proponents, is to be drawn from a consideration of the activity of the Queen and her advisors while these events were taking place. The friends of the Queen were quick to realize the seriousness of her actions. While personally loyal, her ministers had strenuously combatted her wishes and were responsible, as has been seen, for persuading her to forego actual promulgation of the proposed constitution. The annexationists chose to dismiss this as but a gesture, and regard her desires as unchanged and still menacing. That such was the case seems questionable. Every evidence indicates that, whatever the inner wishes of the Queen, the influence of

---

[51] Reliance for facts concerning the mass meeting has been placed mainly upon the contemporary pamphlet history of the revolution already cited.

her closest advisors would have been sufficient to have prevented a recurrence of unconstitutional procedures. The Queen herself seems to have learned her lesson and to have been willing to listen to her friends.

Despite efforts of the revolutionary leaders to secure the support of Colburn and Peterson, members of the Cabinet, the ministry remained loyal to the Queen and took vigorous steps to reassure the public and to stave off the impending disaster. By the morning of January 16, members of the ministry sought to assure the Committee of Safety that Liliuokalani had forsaken her original purpose. They displayed copies of a proposed proclamation publicly repudiating any desire ever again to resort to unconstitutional means to void or evade the Constitution. Prepared Sunday, it had been signed by the Queen, and was distributed prior to the mass meeting on Monday afternoon. In addition, a native mass meeting was staged by her supporters at which speakers attempted to quiet any popular passions aroused by the incident, and secured an endorsement of the intention of the Queen to abandon her attempted action.

It is difficult to see what more could have been done to quiet popular unrest, which constituted the only real threat to foreign property or liberties. It is significant that in an effort to further ease the tension, the government made no attempt to arrest the members or to interfere with the activities of the Committee of Safety. A neutral observer viewing the situation from the vantage point of today is apt to conclude that little excuse existed by January 16 for any overt action by the Committee. The just and fair procedure would have been to have accepted the conciliatory gestures of the Queen at their face value and abandon any attempt to destroy the monarchy, unless later events proved the utter insincerity of the Queen's protestations.

The rejection of her overtures indicates but one thing—the determination of certain persons connected with the annexation movement to push their program to its ultimate conclusion. The Thurston faction could not be placated or deterred from its chosen course of revolution and attempted annexation, the vision of which had grown increasingly full of promise since January 14. The annexationists were determined to exact their pound of flesh from the Queen and to destroy her sovereignty.

THE EVENTS OF JANUARY 16 AND 17

Following the mass meeting on January 16, events moved rapidly toward the consummation of the revolutionary movement. At five o'clock

Minister Stevens effected the landing of forces from the *Boston*, despite the fact that the revolutionists had requested that such action be delayed until the following morning. This peculiar action resulted from the fact that Captain Wiltse had already decided to land forces prior to the request by Stevens, and so informed him at three o'clock.[52]

Thurston and his followers, who had urged earlier that the force be landed that afternoon, had later changed their minds and requested postponement. It seems apparent that the reason for the desired delay was the failure of the leaders to complete their plans for establishing a provisional government. Stevens had emphasized to them earlier that he must recognize the government in power and the revolution had not as yet progressed to the point where a new government existed. The leaders were desirous evidently of perfecting their Provisional Government before American intervention. As events developed, it appears that the landing was a source of assistance to the revolutionary forces. The American forces offered no protection to the existing government, but were located in such direct proximity to the government buildings as to intimidate the royalists.

The evening of the 16th was spent by the revolutionists in hastily perfecting their plans for the establishment of a Provisional Government. By the following morning Judge Sanford Dole had been persuaded to head the executive council of four, which was finally established as the executive agent of the new government. In addition, an advisory council of fourteen was created, and by the afternoon of January 17 a commander of the armed forces of the revolutionists had been appointed and proclamations drawn up announcing the overthrow of the monarchy.

At 2:20 o'clock the leaders proceeded to the government buildings. After having taken the precaution of finding out that it was not occupied by any royalist forces, the proclamation was read and the Provisional Government began to function, pending recognition. The Queen, acting upon the advice of her friends, surrendered the government property under protest. The signed declaration of the Queen significantly stated that she yielded her authority "until such time as the Government of the United States shall, upon the facts presented to it, undo the action of its representative and reinstate me in the authority which I claim as the constitutional sovereign of the Hawaiian Islands." The Queen further asserted that she surrendered "to the superior force of the United States of America, whose minister . . . has caused United

---

[52] Cf. testimony of Lieutenant Young.

States troops to be landed at Honolulu, and declared that he would support the said Provisional Government."

MINISTER STEVENS AND THE REVOLUTION

This emphasis upon the influence of Minister Stevens in forcing the capitulation of the monarchy makes necessary some consideration of the much controverted question of his actual role in the events which led to the successful overthrow of the Queen. It is the carefully reasoned conclusion of Julius W. Pratt that Stevens may be indicted upon at least three counts for his activities in connection with the revolution. In the first place, his early relations with the revolutionists were of an "entirely improper character"; and secondly, his recognition of the Provisional Government was hasty and not justifiable upon the grounds which he later defended it. Thirdly, every evidence indicates that the early landing of American forces from the *Boston* and their station in proximity to the government buildings gave undue aid and comfort to the revolutionists and discouraged the existing monarchical government from effectively coping with the situation.[53]

There is little to be added to this indictment. The relationships of Stevens and the Thurston annexationists were unquestionably improper from the standpoint of ordinary conduct by a foreign diplomat accredited to a friendly government. While Thurston asserts in his *Memoirs* that his acquaintance with the Minister "was slight and most formal," this statement is contradicted by correspondence cited in the same volume. In replying to the annexationist agent Hopkins regarding proposals forwarded by him, Thurston wrote in December 1892, "The American Minister, *with the fullest knowledge of the facts,* and himself an enthusiastic advocate of annexation, concurs in this opinion."[54]

It appears clear that Stevens was not only in close touch with the annexationists prior to the revolution, but the testimony of the leaders of the Provisional Government before both Mr. Blount in 1893 and the Senate Committee on Foreign Relations in 1894 reveals the numerous visits paid to Stevens during the period after his return to Honolulu and prior to the actual overthrow of the Queen. Stevens was well aware of every activity of the annexationists. The accounts by supporters of the Queen likewise reveal clearly their belief that throughout the crisis the revolutionists had the aid and comfort of Stevens.

---

[53] Cf. Pratt, 94-109, for his careful analysis of the problem.

[54] Italics mine. Cf. *Memoirs*, 235f. Hopkins had informed Thurston that the United States would pay $250,000 to secure the assignment of Hawaiian sovereignty.

In explanation, rather than in justification of his attitude, it must in fairness be recalled that the administration at Washington likewise had given every evidence of sanctioning the activity of the Thurston faction from the date of his 1892 visit. When Thurston replied to the Hopkins communication previously referred to, he raised the question whether annexation might be best promoted by action of the Queen, Queen and Cabinet, the Legislature or the voters, and endeavored to find out whether contract labor and Asiatic immigration could be permitted under the United States. This letter was communicated to Secretary John W. Foster, who had become Secretary following the death of Blaine. Foster thought it would be "useless to attempt to bring matters to a head during the short time which remains to this administration," but expressed the belief that the incoming one might favor the project. As noted earlier, Secretary Tracy in December 1892, frankly expressed the favorable attitude of the administration toward annexation and the tone of the reports of naval officers reflects that attitude. In short, while, as in the case of Stevens, the Harrison administration had little reason to expect any crisis in early 1893, it had sanctioned consideration of the idea of annexation by a faction in the Islands and indirectly given comfort to that group.

However, as this survey of Hawaiian-American relations has shown, close contact between American ministers and malcontent leaders had not been unusual. From the time of Commissioner Brown, American diplomatic agents had shown a tendency to intrigue freely in Island politics and endeavor by every means possible to promote all movements and influences favorable to the United States. In connection with the unrest in 1874, the landing of American forces had advanced the American interest; though the action had been in cooperation with British forces. American naval vessels for decades had visited Hawaii with the obvious purpose of stimulating American interests. Stevens happened to confront a somewhat more serious crisis and a more crucial issue than his predecessors and his action, while in accordance with traditional practice, had more serious implications. It must be admitted, however, that no other diplomat had gone so far in extending sympathy to revolutionary forces within Hawaii. The same facts must be kept in mind in understanding other phases of the indictment.

According to Lieutenant Young, and there is little reason to doubt his statement in view of the nature of the instructions ordinarily possessed by every naval officer of the United States at Honolulu during the period, Captain Wiltse took quite as keen an interest in Hawaiian political affairs as did Stevens, and independently of him. Likewise, acting upon instructions, Wiltse was prepared to land forces and would have landed them whether or not Stevens had presented a request. The recent naval policy as to Hawaii had been that of prompt display of force whenever the protection of American property and citizens was demanded. The use of the naval forces to exert a "quieting" or "stabilizing" effect upon Hawaiian affairs was common practice.

WAS REVOLUTION INEVITABLE?

Whether revolution as it developed under leaders of the Provisional Government could have been successful without the comfort given by Stevens to Thurston and his aids is problematical. Pratt is inclined to the view that it would not have been, and there is much evidence to support such a conclusion. The testimony of adherents of the Queen tends to show that the annexationists, whether truthfully or not, asserted loudly from the beginning that they were supported by Stevens and that American forces would back them in their moves. This must have had a restraining effect upon any action taken by the government of the Queen. The problem of importance, however, is not whether the revolution would have been successful, but as to what form it would have taken had it not been for the armed intervention. The action of the Queen had in itself constituted a revolution.

There might merely have been such an assertion of the foreign protest movement as to have still further weakened the monarchy, as in 1887, and yet preserved the shell of the ancient government of Hawaii. On the other hand, an independent republic might have been established without any movement for annexation, controlled by the property holding classes, utilizing contract labor and Asiatic immigration, and angling for favorable trade relations with British possessions or the United States. There were not lacking those who favored such a course of action. These were two alternatives to the annexationist solution of the radicals, who captured control and established the Provisional Government.

Furthermore, it is hardly a correct interpretation of the events of January, 1893, to argue whether a revolution in the general sense would have been successful. The events of January 14 to 16 constituted a revolution in themselves. This uprising had been successful in its most original purpose of checking the development of absolutism upon the part of the Queen. Victory was won when almost hysterical assurances were forthcoming from the ministers of the Queen by Sunday evening and during Monday that Liliuokalani would never again attempt to resort to her schemes for personal power. Further evidence of the success of the uprising is demonstrated by the failure of the Queen's government to make any attempt to suppress the revolt or seize its leaders, and the staged mass meeting of the natives accepting the new intentions of the Queen.

The real question is what might have happened following the citizen's protest meeting on Monday. As has been demonstrated, actually the activity of the Committee of Safety had been directed toward the complete overthrow of the monarchy and application for annexation to the United States. It is significant, however, that this was concealed carefully from the general body of foreign citizens at the Monday mass meeting. Two reasons seem to have been behind this: in the first place, the radicals were not entirely sure whether such a move would receive general endorsement; secondly, their own plans were not fully developed.

The most revealing source of the actual purposes of the Thurston faction is the testimony of C. Bolte before Commissioner Blount.[55] According to Bolte, the Committee early decided "the only perfect safeguard against future occurrences of this kind would lie in annexation to the United States, or in a protectorate, or in anything of that kind, but that we could not go on with the form of government as it was then." When members of the Committee spoke of seeking ways and means of preserving law and order they meant through changing the government. *"What the people meant I cannot say . . . ,"* Bolte revealingly told Blount in speaking of the resolutions at the Monday mass meeting.[56]

Asked by Blount why the Committee did not reveal its annexationist desires, Bolte replied that it "might be going a little too far." He further declared that ". . . we did not know whether the action of the committee would be indorsed by the large majority of the people at the mass meeting. We thought it would." The radicals, then, were not sure of popular support and therefore were unable to reveal their hand fully at any time before the 17th.

Symbolical of the difference of opinion which existed as to the significant purposes of the revolt up to that time is the attitude of Sanford Dole. When Thurston, on the ground that he was recognized as too radical, refused to accept the presidency of the executive council of the proposed new government, he demonstrated again that his followers were not in the majority. A conservative was then sought to accept the post and Dole was approached. When informed of the revolutionary plan

---

[55] FR, 1894, 715ff.
[56] Italics mine.

of the Committee, Dole, according to Bolte, "was utterly surprised at it." He consented to attend the Sunday afternoon meetings of the Committee and listened to their discussion. Even then he declared, according to Bolte, that "he felt it was his duty, as well as the duty of any other citizen of these islands, to do all they could to get pure and stable government, but he was not quite convinced then that it was necessary to take so radical a step as to overthrow the old Government." Dole revealed what was probably the majority opinion as late as January 16.

In view of this situation, the radicals did not feel fully able to develop their plans. They knew what they wanted, but did not know as yet actually how to achieve it. The mass meeting was designed to bolster their cause, but even then they dared not submit to it the question of landing American forces, and so, continued to work secretly. In the meantime, the peace overtures of the royalists were such as to tend to quiet the situation. Had matters remained as they were the afternoon of January 16 it is doubtful whether the events would have had any other result than to have forced some further constitutional checks upon the Queen. That annexation, or even republicanism, was the watchword of a majority is very doubtful. As usual in revolutionary movements, the majority possessed little more than a sense of indignation against the existing government.

The uncertainty of the radicals was further revealed by their last minute decision to request delay in landing the American marines. Later events, however, indicate that the debarkation of the force from the *Boston* brought matters to a head and enabled the radical leaders to push through the final achievement of their objective—overthrow of the Queen and application for annexation. The fears of those who might have been held back by thoughts of danger to their own safety were quieted and many hearts undoubtedly emboldened. One cannot help but sense, in reading descriptions of how the revolutionists marched to the government building on the 17th, that they were more comforted by the existence of a body of American marines sworn to protect American lives and property and prevent rioting than by their own straggling and meager force. Nor can the fact be disputed that it was the American forces which assured the radicals of the security necessary to push their plans for the Provisional Government the evening of the 16th and boldly to proclaim their purposes on the morrow.[57]

In view of these facts, it is probable that had it not been for the intervention, and its indirect coercion of the established government,

---

[57] Bolte declared the Committee did not consider itself safe or able to mature its plans until troops landed. FR, 1894, 723.

and the virtual assurance of recognition and protection by the United States, the radicals would not have been able to push their plans to a climax. Insecure in respect to full support from the foreign citizens, and possessed of no military power at any time prior to the American intervention sufficient to protect them in any open effort to overawe the Queen, it is difficult to perceive how the radicals could have accomplished her overthrow. It is doubtful on the contrary whether the Queen would have used any force against the radicals, for to have done so would have played into their hands. Had the supporters of the Queen continued their attempts to quiet the natives, to drive home their assurances that she had abandoned her unconstitutional program, and avoided open conflict with the Committee of Safety, it is altogether probable that the agitation which gripped Honolulu would have passed within a matter of days and peace would have been restored. Brief periods of intense excitement and demonstration were common aspects of Hawaiian politics, and always followed by a cooling off process.

In fact, by late Monday prior to the landing of the marines this appears to have been exactly what was happening. J. O. Carter told Commissioner Blount that on Monday Honolulu was "the most peaceful, law-abiding community you would see anywhere." According to Bolte, the purpose of the Committee of Safety in desiring troops was to insure its own safety rather than to quiet any disorders actually existent. Pratt expresses the view that the quiet was due to the fear of the Queen's forces to take action because of the belief that American support was forthcoming. It is more likely that it was due to the strategy of allowing the unrest to burn out by itself. A display of force by the Queen against even the radicals would have been most unwise. The advisors of the Queen were clever men and apparently sought every means to restore harmony and to preserve the power of the Queen. If the past serves as a basis for judgment, it is likely that this strategy would have proved successful, had not the opposition become emboldened by outside assistance. The revolution then moved forward into the more radical stage of overthrow of the government and application for annexation.

What happened in 1893, however, was bound to have taken place sooner or later. Viewed in its proper perspective, the revolution was but a culmination of the forces of disintegration which had long afflicted the ancient kingdom. The power of the proud Hawaiian noble and the imperious monarch had gradually declined with the rise of foreign capital. By the end of the American Civil War, as we have seen, the forces of economic progress had created the basis for a new capitalism which came increasingly to demand the promotion of its interests as the price for the perpetuation of the trappings of Hawaiian monarchy. In the belief that reciprocal trade relationships with the United States, even at the price of some limitations upon sovereignty, would provide security for this capitalism, which would in turn provide security for his throne, the Hawaiian sovereign had sought and secured reciprocity.

Reciprocity, however, had but further undermined the kingdom. It brought a startling economic expansion of that capitalism, and it became ever more insistent in demands for control in the government. These demands, and the gradual loss of sovereignty as the price of reciprocity and its continuance, against a growing native nationalism provided the basis of conflict which served as the principal source of agitation in Hawaiian politics. In 1887 the peak of control over the monarchy by the foreign element was reached by the new constitution forced upon the King. At the same time the renewal of reciprocity further protected the growing economic interests of the planters.

Could the situation as it existed at this date have been continued, the monarchy might have been perpetuated. Two factors intervened, however, to prevent it. A rising native nationalism, aided by the discomfited half-castes typified by Robert Wilcox, and further augmented by white foreigners of the non-propertied classes willing to fight the battle of the under-dog, constituted a perpetual menace to the precarious controls gained by the foreigners in 1887. Neither group was able to gain a position of decisive advantage, producing a series of crises which shook the foundations of the monarchy.

The other factor was the insecurity of the reciprocal trade advantages with the United States and the consequent fundamental instability of invested capital in Hawaii. The disastrous consequences of the McKinley tariff have been demonstrated, and it should be clear that this caused much of the political tension after 1890. A prosperous mercantile and planter community would have been much less inclined to listen to the advocates of annexation in 1892. Proof of this lies in the quieting of that agitation by the latter part of the year as some signs of better times appeared.

Neither of these conditions, however, stood to be remedied. The racial conflict tended to become more taut rather than to relax. It was but a matter of time before some native nationalist leader would have emerged to direct a native rising against the foreign interests which had won economic control of the Islands and steadily encroached upon the political power of the monarchy. Liliuokalani became that leader.

What she attempted in 1893 was what someone was almost certainly bound to attempt sooner or later. The results inevitably must have produced immediate foreign reaction against the monarchy.

Nor would the nature of the political conflict permit further bargains with the United States by which the planters could have secured more permanent protection for their economic interests through the only means by which it could have been achieved—a virtual protectorate status for Hawaii. As a matter of fact, from the 1850's this had been the real goal of those interests. The planter oligarchy was never anxious for annexation, not even in 1893, except as the last possible resort. A protectorate would have provided maximum economic advantages and free opportunity for American intervention in domestic political disorders, which would have been to the advantage of the American capitalists. Contract labor could still be preserved. The attempted arrangements of 1889 would have provided that, but native reaction killed the attempt and would have continued to do so.[58]

Thus the struggle was left to go on. A possible way out would have been closer commercial relations with British possessions providing markets independent of the United States. The dominant concept of American national interest in Hawaii would hardly admit of such a development. A virtual impasse in the diplomatic and political life of the Islands had been reached, therefore, by the nineties. While it has been indicated that republicanism and annexation were the desires of a minority and had not favorable circumstances aided that group they would not have been realized in 1893, it is doubtful whether an independent Hawaiian monarchy could have been perpetuated much longer. What happened in January, 1893, as the result of the conniving of a small group of determined men, was but the logic of Hawaiian history for some fifty years.

---

[58] See William S. Russ, Jr., "The Role of Sugar in Hawaiian Annexation," *Pacific Historical Review,* XII, for an excellent analysis of the planter philosophy.

CHAPTER X

The Annexation Fiasco

The revolutionary overturn of 1893 in Hawaii was led by men of strong determination. As has been made evident, their basic objective was annexation to the United States. Having canvassed the situation at Washington with some care in 1892, there is little doubt but that they expected an early and favorable response to their offer to deliver the Islands. The fact that they were checkmated temporarily was not due to lack of energy upon their part but to the late date on which the revolt took place. The new Provisional Government of Hawaii, even prior to completing its organization, had taken steps to secure passage to the United States for annexation commissioners. By January 18 the necessary instructions and credentials had been completed. The following day, Lorrin A. Thurston, William C. Wilder, William R. Castle, Charles L. Carter, and Joseph Marsden embarked for San Francisco. An effort of the deposed Queen to send a representative was blocked. By January 28 the commissioners were on American soil and news of the revolution flashed over the wires to the people of the United States.

AMERICAN REACTIONS TO THE HAWAIIAN REVOLUTION

Americans were not unprepared for the issue. As has been noted earlier, an increasing amount of attention had been directed by the press to Hawaiian affairs. The growing trade of the Pacific and the importance of Hawaii to its control, the increased investment of American capital in the Islands, and their strategic value were points which had received attention. There were not lacking hints that annexation might not be a too far distant prospect, and the prediction of the *San Francisco Examiner* to that effect received considerable and favorable comment late in 1892.[1] The *New York Tribune* in an editorial on November 20, 1892, had declared: "Events are occurring in the Hawaiian Islands which should lead Americans seriously to consider the policy of forming a closer political tie with that interesting little Kingdom. . . . Hawaii must become an American territory." Much of this information and sentiment, as has been indicated in the preceding chapter, was connected with the activities of Lorrin Thurston in the United States.

---

[1] See the *New York Times,* December 1, 1892; *Brooklyn Daily Eagle,* November 21, 1892. Also *Bradstreet's,* May 4, 1892, and *Kansas City Times,* May 19, 1892, for earlier comment.

Not only was American opinion conditioned at least mildly for an understanding of the issue presented by the Hawaiian commissioners, but sentiment generally favorable to expansion and imperialism was not lacking in the early nineties. The utterances of many statesmen, as well as opinions freely expressed in the press, magazines and other journals of the time, were full of the spirit of a new American destiny. It was a spirit which sensed for the first time the fact that the old frontier was passing and that the further development of manufactures and economic opportunity in general must be more dependent upon conditions and contacts outside the continental limits of the United States. Harry Pratt Judson, a dean of the new University of Chicago, echoed the sentiment of many when he wrote in the *Review of Reviews* for March, 1893: "The United States has nearly twice as many people as France and Germany. We are one of the richest as well as one of the largest powers . . . and the United States cannot help being one of its foremost states, even if it would. It is no longer the island that it was; the oceans have been bridged; the wilderness has filled up, *and America must move on,* touching elbows with the rest of the world. . . ."[2]

Of course there were those who did not agree with this viewpoint. They not only did not agree with it but were highly alarmed by the vigorous and aggressive ideas which it provoked among many statesmen and publicists. There also were those isolationists who opposed a departure from what they regarded as the old and safe, tried and true policies of the founding fathers who had counselled for so many decades against foreign entanglements and dangerous experiments in foreign policy. It is only by appreciating this situation that it is possible to understand the extent of the debate provoked by the proposal to annex Hawaii, or how fundamental an issue it posed in American foreign policy. All of the basic differences of opinion over the future expansion of the American republic which had been accumulating since the wounds of the Civil War had been healed were brought now into sharp conflict, symbolized by a live issue. The Provisional Government at Honolulu presented the United States in 1893 its first opportunity for a full dress debate on the "new imperialism."

During the last three days of January, 1893, and the first two weeks of February, the press of the nation was emblazoned with the story of Hawaii. The fact that the revolution meant immediate prospective annexation was made known. Whether by accident or design, it was accompanied by a clever play upon the alleged opposition of Great Britain to the revolutionary government and surrender of the Islands to the

---

[2] Julius W. Pratt very effectively analyzes this spirit in the first chapter of his *Expansionists of 1898,* "The New Manifest Destiny."

United States. Loyal American hearts had never neglected a challenge from this quarter and it added to the heat with which the early discussion of Hawaii was surrounded. "We must plant the stars and stripes in Honolulu," declared the *New York Press*. "Shall we take Hawaii and thereby prosper and magnify ourselves, or shall we let England take it, and thereby enfeeble and humiliate us," dramatically questioned the *Washington Star*.[3] Unanimous denunciation of any British interference with either Hawaii directly, or any action the United States might wish to take, was virtually universal. However, there was a recognition of the seriousness of the situation even by the most ardent supporters of quick annexation. The *New York Tribune* on January 31, for example, felt that questions "of a most delicate, complicated and momentous nature" were posed, and that America was "close upon the time when the traditional hostility in the United States toward an expansion of authority, if not also of territory, among the islands near our coasts must to some extent give way to the necessities of our increasing commerce." By February 5 it was ready to declare: "The popular verdict is clear, unequivocal and practically unanimous. Hawaii is welcome."

NEGOTIATING THE ANNEXATION TREATY

On February 3 the annexationists arrived in Washington, having given out several interviews and statements on the way designed to fan favorable public opinion. Minister Stevens already was bombarding the State Department with messages urging that the commissioners represented the best intelligence and influence in Hawaii, while the opposition should be ignored as members of a lower class led by ignorant and corrupt leaders. At the same time, he cleverly hinted that failure to accept annexation quickly would throw Hawaii into the waiting arms of Britain and her colonies.[4] Washington was further informed of his action in raising the American flag over the Government Building and the announcement of a protectorate.

In view of what Thurston had learned on his earlier visit to Washington, there is doubt that urgings from Stevens were necessary to

---

[3] *Public Opinion,* February 4, 1893, provides a good review of the reaction at this time. The *Washington Star* editorial of February 1, 1893, is rather typical. The British opposition story appears to have been almost entirely rumor. The *New York Times* reported on January 31 that Sir Julian Pauncefote had received a protest for presentation, though the same issue carried news from London questioning any such action. Liliuokalani was reported to have sought British aid. By February 3 the *Times* was able to assert definitely that there would be no protest, though the furor was kept alive for some time. It bears the marks of manufactured rumor to expedite the annexation.

[4] Stevens had long been fearful of the Canadian Pacific Railroad's interest in Hawaii and the commercial ambitions of that company in the Pacific.

secure a favorable reception at the State Department for the revolutionists. As early as January 28 Secretary Foster had approved Stevens' recognition of the new regime, and on February 1 informed foreign governments of the "paramount interest" of the United States in Hawaii as "an essential and important element in our commercial system. . . ." He did, however, repudiate the protectorate so far as it might place the authority of the United States above that of the Provisional Government.

If annexation were to be consummated as a part of the accepted foreign policy of the Harrison administration, swift action was imperative. On February 14, therefore, Foster signed a treaty providing for such action. According to Thurston, the President, the Attorney General, and several other Cabinet members and administration leaders did "little else but devote themselves to this question" after February 4.[5] The anxiety for quick action led to arbitrary decisions to disregard Hawaiian demands for provisions in the treaty to provide for a cable, the improvement of Pearl Harbor, and a generous sugar bounty, as well as protection against the application of Chinese exclusion laws. Obviously, the administration feared these might prejudice the chances for ratifying the treaty.[6] President Harrison was troubled by the failure to include some provision for a plebiscite which would give the appearance of popular sanction of annexation by Hawaii. In view of the situation there, one may imagine the popularity of such a suggestion with the Thurston group.[7]

The treaty, as submitted hastily to the Senate on February 15, provided simply for annexation of the Islands as "an integral part of the territory of the United States," cession of all government buildings and property, and continuance of existing laws and government until Congress should otherwise provide. Importation of Chinese labor into Hawaii was prohibited, and all revenue and customs acts of the United States were to be applied within one year. The debt of Hawaii was to be assumed by the United States and an annuity of $20,000 for life provided for the Queen, together with a $150,000 grant to Princess Kaiulani. This was a gesture toward satisfying opposition to annexation from the native leaders. The treaty was accompanied when pre-

---

[5] Thurston to Dole, February 9, 1883. Cited, Pratt, 117f. The *New York Herald* on January 29 reported hastily held conferences regarding Hawaii. Its Washington correspondent reported that the revolution was not a surprise but "anticipated several weeks ago." See also *New York Times,* February 2.

[6] These Hawaiian demands reveal clearly how closely the annexation interest was tied in with the desire of the sugar planters for protection.

[7] Pratt, 118f., cites valuable material from the University of Michigan's Spaulding Collection of photostats and copies of original documents from the Archives of Hawaii concerning details of the negotiations. See especially R. S. Kuykendall, "Negotiation of the Hawaiian Annexation Treaty of 1893," *Fifty-First Annual Report of the Hawaiian Historical Society* for documents and stenographic record.

sented to the Senate by strong supporting statements from both the President and Secretary Foster. Counterbalancing these, was a letter of protest from the deposed Queen pleading for just consideration of her claim that she had been deprived of her throne by "some of my subjects, aided by aliens."[8]

ANNEXATION BEFORE THE SENATE

In the Senate, the Hawaiian question already had received attention. On the afternoon of January 28 Senator John Sherman, chairman of the Committee on Foreign Relations, moved for an executive session and for nearly four hours the Senate discussed the issue. The trend of sentiment, as reported in the *New York Times* the following day, was favorable to annexation, or at least the declaration of a protectorate. Difference of opinion quickly developed as to the proper method—joint resolution or the slower process of treaty negotiation. By January 31 the *Times* reported some opposition developing from both Democratic and Republican quarters and more sentiment for less hasty action, though general opinion in Washington continued to be pro-annexation, and aggravated by rumors of British opposition. Senators Butler of South Carolina and Platt of New York gave out statements favoring annexation.

On January 30 Senator Chandler introduced a resolution authorizing the negotiation of a treaty for annexation and asked for its immediate consideration. While a majority of the Republicans appeared to favor it, consideration was blocked and it became evident that most Democratic leaders were unwilling to be stampeded into action on the eve of the inauguration of Grover Cleveland. On February 8 Senator Morgan, ardent southern expansionist Democrat, introduced a bill to empower the President to provide the necessary territorial government over any newly acquired territory, subject to Congressional approval. This measure was believed to have administration support.[9]

Despite administration approval and a prompt favorable report by the Committee on Foreign Relations, the attempted *coup* was unsuccessful. Regardless of assurances from such Democratic stalwarts in the Senate as Senator Morgan, sufficient Democratic votes were not obtainable to insure ratification. Upon submission of the treaty, Morgan delivered a brief speech in favor of speedy action, emphasizing the value of the

---

[8] Text of proposed treaty in FR, 1894, 197f. It is interesting to note that Paul Neumann, representative of the Queen, informed Secretary Foster that annexation might be acceptable if reasonable compensation were provided.

[9] *New York Tribune,* February 9, 1893. See *New York Times,* January 31, 1893, for further details concerning Senate action and opinion.

Islands as the key to the Pacific. Little outspoken opposition or criticism was reported immediately, though a few Southern and Western senators appeared fearful of the effects of annexation upon the sugar and rice interests of their sections. A motion by Senator Teller to consider the measure in open session was defeated.

Opposition gradually developed, however, and by February 18 the *New York Times* reported that a combination of Democrats including Senators Gray, Brice, Blackburn, White of Kentucky, Caffery and White of Louisiana, Pugh, Vilas, Daniel, Berry, and Palmer, assisted by Republican Senator Pettigrew of South Dakota, had decided to prevent consideration of the treaty until the incoming Cleveland administration. Paul Neumann, attorney for the deposed Queen, had arrived in Washington on the 17th and was reported in close touch with this group. There were rumors that President-elect Cleveland himself was in conference with the opposition Senators. When the treaty was reported by the Committee on Foreign Relations, Senator Gray, stern anti-expansionist Democrat, was notable as the only dissenter.[10] In the House, Democratic members also took steps to block the final conclusion of annexation. The *Times* reported on February 19 and 24 that Representatives Springer, Turner, and Cochran were ready to force a House resolution opposing annexation.

AMERICA DEBATES ANNEXATION

In the meantime, the first salvos in the battle of words throughout the nation between supporters and opponents of annexation were fired. There were rabid partisans on both sides, while others attempted to preserve some balance and to weigh the matter with care. In the first place, the annexationists served to arouse suspicion by the very haste with which they endeavored to jam through the treaty. In general, Americans were not well informed in January and February, 1893, on just what had happened and many wished to know more of the facts before making a decision. This point of view was adequately expressed by the *New York Times* in an editorial on February 15: "It has not seemed to us that the information regarding the situation there and the cause by which it was produced was sufficiently complete for a full

---

[10] The *New York Times* is a valuable source for Washington developments. It is asserted by Matilda Gresham in her *Life of Walter Quintin Gresham, II,* 684f., that Cleveland conferred with Gresham, designated as the new Secretary of State, and John G. Carlisle at Lakewood, New Jersey, on February 22 and that it was decided to delay consideration of the treaty. The *New York Tribune* declared on February 21, that Senators Vilas, Vest, and Brice would not be opposing the treaty "unless they had some reason to believe that in doing so they were performing a service agreeable to Mr. Cleveland."

understanding of the case, without which such important action as that ought not to be taken. . . . There has been an appearance of undue haste in all the proceedings. . . . Each step taken was calculated to commit our Government to a preconceived policy without an opportunity for deliberation . . . our Government is not acting with a clear view of all the circumstances . . . in such a matter it is the permanent interests of the country that should be considered and not the prestige of a passing administration." The *Times* had earlier indicated its support of responsible interests of the United States in Hawaii and was not voicing obstructionism.

Further information was wanted by many, but on the other hand there were those with somewhat preconceived opinions. In the one camp was the vigorous isolationist press led by such papers as the *New York Evening Post,* which commented sarcastically on February 16 on the desire of Harrison to "give a sort of sunset glow to his dying Administration" through a "Snap-Annexation." It accused undue haste and hinted at fraud and violence as involved in the entire proceeding. It indicated its belief that the very haste with which the treaty was being pushed was serving to alienate many who might otherwise support it.

Those who favored annexation took the high ground of national interest and talked bravely of the expanding economic power of the United States, and even of the Anglo-Saxons as "nation builders of the world." The Protestant religious press, aided by letters from former missionaries, was not without a word of favor for annexation. The *Christian Union* of February 18 asserted: "The Anglo-Saxon race is the colonizing race, the civilizing race, the pioneer race. We cannot if we would escape the duty which our race characteristics and our local position combine to lay upon us . . . Hawaii's necessity is our duty." Perhaps the most complete summation of the new expansionist viewpoint was provided by the *New York Tribune* in its February 21 editorial on Hawaii:

The views of the American people have grown with their growing empire. So long as we were a small country, lying along a single seacoast and sparsely settled, there was every reason why we should keep to ourselves. . . . But when we became sovereign in trans-Mississippi territory, when the Gulf of Mexico became our southern border, and still later, when our dominion extended to the Pacific sea and vast cities arose on every coast and in all parts of the interior, the situation changed. Today we produce of manufactures more than any two nations of Europe; of agriculture more than any three, and of minerals more than all together. The necessity for new markets is now upon us, and with it the necessity of cultivating close commercial and political relations with the rapidly growing nations of South

America and Australia and with the newly awakened empires of China and Japan. As a prime condition of this extending influence, the duty of controlling the Isthmian routes is clear to every intelligent mind. . . . To render that control sufficient, the sovereignty of Caribbean territory and of Hawaii is absolutely necessary.

Added fervor was provided for such nationalistic views by the rumor of possible opposition by Great Britain. In early February, as noted previously, the press was filled with such reports, and attention was called to the reported failure of the British to recognize the Provisional Government. Expansionists from the Pacific to the Atlantic belched defiance in the face of any such attempt to check American interests. The *Atlanta Constitution* asserted that Hawaii must be taken as a further protection "against the aggressive and robber-like policy of monarchial Europe." The clamor for annexation came from representative papers throughout the nation, regardless of party affiliation. Among the Democratic newspapers maintaining more or less consistent advocacy of such a policy were the *New York Sun,* the *Kansas City Times,* the *Denver News,* the *San Francisco Examiner,* the *Detroit Free Press,* and the *Atlanta Constitution.* Some were even more vociferous than administration organs and the *Kansas City Times,* for example, implied that a war to check the ambitions of any other power in Hawaii would be more justifiable than half the wars in history.[11]

Those who favored acquisitive tactics were not dependent alone, however, upon a single line of argument. The most frequently used of all the devices designed to arouse the public mind to the importance of Hawaii was that of stressing its vital strategic importance. The *New York Press,* for example, declared on January 31 that Hawaii was more important than Alaska and "absolutely requisite to the protection and development of the commerce of our great Pacific coast" as well as the proposed Isthmian canal. The *Washington Post* two days earlier had affirmed: "Hawaii is the natural and logical outpost of the United States in the Pacific. Its possession would mean the saving of incalculable millions in coast defense and the control of the commercial pathways of more than half the salt water on the globe." The editor of the *Review of Reviews* asserted in March, "We can protect our Pacific Ocean commerce, guard our Western coast line, and maintain our control of the prospective canal, at less than half the expense for fortifications and ships, if we hold Hawaii, that we should be com-

---

[11] The writer has made a careful examination of many of these newspapers but useful summations of editorial opinion are to be found in the periodical *Public Opinion.* See also Pratt, 146ff.

pelled to incur if without the islands in our possession." Captain Mahan entered the argument for annexation with an article on "Hawaii and our Future Sea Power" in the March issue of *Forum.*

Strong opposition to annexation was not wanting, and many sober minds were filled with foreboding as to the threatened new trend in American policy. The *New York World,* which on January 31 had announced that it was definitely in favor of annexation, turned an about face on February 7 and denounced it as neither necessary nor desirable. The *Chicago Herald* of February 11 charged it was a scheme of the sugar barons and jingoists. The United States was already supreme in Hawaii and there was little need for actually taking over the Islands. An interesting note was introduced by the *Charleston News and Courier* and other Southern papers, which poked fun at Republican interest in a government for Hawaii based upon white supremacy.[12]

The greatest unanimity in opposition to annexation came from the independent press. *The New York Evening Post,* the *Boston Herald,* and the *New York Herald,* together with such liberal journals as *The Nation* and *Harper's Weekly,* raised vigorous and frequent protests. They generally scouted the idea of any foreign interference in Hawaii. With this basis for the demand for haste disposed of, they proceeded to counsel a careful consideration of the facts and of fundamental American policy. The nation must not rush into the arms of the annexationists without knowing more about the revolutionary movement. It was doubtful whether any advantages were to be gained from annexation which were not already assured. There might be actual disadvantages in terms of political and defense problems involved in acquiring the Islands. This was the advice of these journals, based upon the assumption that American interests were so predominant in Hawaii that no hasty action was necessary to preserve them against any outside threat. "Go on, therefore, sending us your sugar and other tropical products, and sitting under your own fig-trees, in the full assurance that none will dare make you afraid," advised the *Evening Post* in an editorial repeated in *The Nation.*[13]

Interest was heightened as news of the proposed treaty and fuller information concerning what had happened became available. English opposition was stressed by the expansionist press as necessitating quick action, and such papers as the *New York Tribune* chided the Democrats for failure to support such a course due to alleged partisanship.

[12] January 30. See also *New Orleans Picayune, Baltimore Sun, St. Louis Post Dispatch* for same period.

[13] See February 3 issue *Evening Post* and February 9 *Nation;* also *New York Herald,* January 29.

The action of Minister Stevens at Honolulu in proclaiming a protectorate met with general approval from expansionists. Many state legislatures in session adopted or considered resolutions favorable to annexation. New York, California, Massachusetts, and Oregon were among those adopting memorials to Congress in favor of accepting Hawaii as an American possession.[14] Probably no issue relating to American foreign policy since the Civil War had attracted so much attention or controversy as was now shaping up relative to the Hawaiian question. By February 19 the *New York Times* was able to print a letter of protest from Hawaii against the revolutionists and the action of the American Minister, which added to the controversy. Prior to this time, statements of the annexation commission had constituted the principal source of information regarding what had happened.

HARRISON AND HAWAII

Regardless of popular feeling one way or the other, ratification of the treaty proved impossible. By February 25 the Hawaiian commissioners were convinced of this, so far as the present session was concerned. Even if it were theoretically possible, the margin would be so close that to press the treaty and to risk its defeat was deemed inadvisable. The question naturally arises, why the treaty had been pushed in such haste at the close of a repudiated administration. Opponents of Harrison attributed it variously to a desire to go out of office having performed a last bold stroke, and fears that the truth about what had happened in Hawaii would kill the proposal.

There is no conclusive evidence on the real motives involved. In his message accompanying the proposed treaty, President Harrison presented the matter in the light of an accomplished situation which could not be evaded. The revolt was "entirely unexpected so far as this Government was concerned," though information from Hawaii had indicated for some time that the seeds of revolution were sprouting from the political intrigue and turmoil in the Islands. The emphasis by both Secretary Foster and the President upon the point that the United States had in no way promoted the revolt in itself indicates a defensive state of mind and a realization that perhaps all was not well with the background of the treaty. The anxiety of the President to have some sort of an Hawaiian plebiscite on annexation points in the same direction.

---

[14] See *New York Times* and *Tribune* for the period; also *Cong. Rec.*, 52 Cong. 2 sess., 1563, 1605, 1608, 1170 for information concerning resolutions from the states.

In his *Diplomatic Memoirs,* Foster emphasizes that haste was made necessary by threats of anarchy and possible interference in Island affairs from other quarters. "It seemed apparent to me that if the Islands did not become American territory they would inevitably pass under the control of Great Britain or Japan," he wrote. In a letter to his friend John V. L. Findley written in December, 1893, Harrison denied that anything had appeared in the Hawaiian matter that would put him on the defensive. He undeniably was irritated by the later action of the Cleveland administration in pulling down the flag.[15]

That any ulterior motives were involved in the effort of Harrison to complete the annexation of Hawaii in his administration is doubtful. In the light of the known attitude and policy of his administration toward Hawaii and matters of foreign policy in general, his action was natural and more or less inevitable. Harrison, together with his Secretaries of State, Blaine and Foster, believed in a realistic and expanding foreign policy. A majority of those who were in close touch with Hawaiian affairs had believed for some time that ultimate annexation to the United States or some type of protectorate was inevitable. In February, 1893, the issue presented itself and Harrison attempted to meet it according to the best judgment and information at hand.

INTERNATIONAL REACTIONS TO ATTEMPTED ANNEXATION

The growing interest of both Great Britain and Germany in Pacific expansion, as well as the more recent awakening of Japan, made the future of Hawaii in 1893 potentially a matter of some international concern. Earlier objections upon the part of both Germany and Great Britain to the growing preponderance of American influence over the Islands already have been noted. As late as 1887, it will be recalled, Great Britain had gone so far as to revive the suggestion for a joint neutrality convention relative to Hawaii. That the Harrison administration expected some definite foreign reactions to the annexation proposal is indicated by the February 1, 1893, note which Secretary Foster addressed to the American ministers at St. Petersburg, London, Paris, and Berlin. The Islands "constitute an essential and important element in our commercial system, and their proximity and situation make them a potential factor, which we could never see transferred to any other control without the gravest concern," he had written. The American

---

[15] See John W. Foster, *Diplomatic Memoirs,* II, 166f. Foster also declared that annexation "had been the open policy of both parties in the United States for many years."

policy was characterized as the result of an "historical attitude" and was really an assertion of the old Tyler formula.[16]

In view of this background, surprisingly little immediate excitement was produced among the powers by the prospect of the United States absorbing so sizable and strategic a Pacific outpost. No German protest was forthcoming, and the German representative at Washington informed Secretary Foster at the February diplomatic reception that he expected no European reaction, his own government having come to regard the Hawaiian Islands as a "quasi protectorate" of the United States. Japan's Minister went to some lengths at the same reception to emphasize that his government "would look with favor upon the annexation of those Islands to the United States, as it would be assured that the interests of Japanese subjects and Government would be properly represented. It would not, however, look with any favor upon the annexation of these Islands by any European Power."[17] No expressions of opinion were forthcoming from Sir Julian Pauncefote at this time. From Paris, the American Minister had informed the State Department on February 3 that no opposition was to be expected. "I venture to add that in the present state of feeling in France toward England, no action or attitude of ours with reference to these Islands is likely to be looked upon unfavorably," he wrote.[18]

The incoming Cleveland administration also was desirous of sounding out European and Japanese sentiment. On March 16 Secretary Gresham received the diplomatic corps and secured certain reactions. The Japanese Minister again renewed his government's pleasure at the prospective American control of Hawaii. Sir Julian Pauncefote assured the Secretary that Great Britain's only interest in Hawaii was that a stable government should be maintained. He even appeared agreeable to removing the objectionable British consul at Honolulu, Mr. Wodehouse. From London, Robert Lincoln had informed Foster on February 3 and 17 that the Hawaiian affair was not likely to produce any official criticism and that questions raised in the House of Commons "caused not the least indication of interest in the crowded house."[19] Russia's Minister renewed previous warnings of British designs on Hawaii, but assured Gresham of Russian support and approval.[20] Much of the

---

[16] Text from *Instructions, France,* XXIII.

[17] See "Memorandum of Conversations," *Notes, Hawaii,* V.

[18] *Dispatches, France,* CVIII. The London *Times,* January 31, 1893, contains useful comment on European public reactions, which were similar to those expressed by the diplomats at Washington.

[19] Lincoln to Foster, *Dispatches, England,* CLXXIII.

[20] Dated March 16, 1893. From *Memoranda of Conversations with the Secretary of State, 1893-1898.* Only the Russian Minister appears to have been driven to ask

credit for the change in the attitude of the powers regarding Hawaii must be given to the firm diplomacy of both Bayard and Blaine who had left no doubt since the mid-eighties that the original principles of the Tyler doctrine of American "paramount interest" in the Islands must be regarded as a fixed and unalterable feature of American foreign policy.

BRITISH REACTIONS

The power most likely to have offered opposition was Great Britain, and for a variety of reasons. In the first place, the Hawaiian royal family had close British connections. The Hawaiian heir apparent, Princess Kaiulani, in her youth had been under the guardianship of an Englishman, T. H. Davies, and had been educated in England. The interest of British and Canadian capitalists in the commercial development of the Pacific following the completion of the Canadian Pacific Railroad to Vancouver also made the disposition of Hawaii a matter of importance. Likewise, the recent and prospective development of New Zealand and Australia in terms of Pacific commerce, steamship lines, and cable connections gave London further reason to regard Hawaii as a vital outpost. As indicated previously, these British possessions had been potential rivals of the United States since the inception of reciprocity in the possible development of Hawaiian commerce and the sugar industry.

In view of this situation, the British reaction to the prospect of Hawaii's annexation to the United States is of the utmost interest and significance. The Tory group in England assumed a somewhat truculent tone, but it was more in the nature of a criticism of the Liberals for sacrificing British interests generally throughout the world than an attack upon the United States. The London *Times* on January 30 pointed out that the geographical position of Hawaii gave the question of its disposition an international importance and one which could not be regarded with "complete indifference by other Powers." The possible conflict of annexation with the still existant Hawaiian neutrality

---

for an explanation of the later peculiar spectacle of a major power refusing an important territorial acquisition. In November, 1894, he queried Gresham apropos of his letter to the President on Hawaii, ". . . is it not a little singular that your Government, a Republic, should establish a Monarchy?" Gresham replied tartly that there were moral objections to the revolution and that governments "should have some regard for the principles of right and justice." The Russian candidly replied, "The moral code does not operate with the same force upon nations as upon individuals." Gresham replied, "That may do for imperialism, but a free Government takes a different, and I am glad to say, I think a better view of such things."

declaration by France and Great Britain in 1843 was pointed out. An extension of this to include the United States was suggested. The tone of the English conservative press was critical generally of circumstances under which revolution and the annexation move had been accomplished. References to "intrigues" and "American aggression" were common.[21]

The chief problem at Downing Street was created by the unquestioned opposition of Canada, New Zealand, and Australia to the prospect of American control of Hawaii. An early and formal protest was presented the Secretary of State for the Colonies by New Zealand. As early as February 1 Sir John Thomas stated in response to questioning upon the floor of the Canadian Parliament that Canada was opposed directly to annexation. A *New York Times* correspondent who interviewed members of the Parliament found them unanimously opposed to such action by the United States.[22]

The Canadian government organ, *The Citizen,* summarized adequately the Canadian viewpoint: "Canada's interest lies in the fact that the islands are situated on the direct route from Canada to Australia and on the line of commerce between this country and Chile. They are an important station in the British cable system, and it is desirable, from our point of view, that if they are not independent, England at all events should possess supreme influence there, so that Hawaii may serve as a center from which she can exercise surveillance of the Pacific Ocean, and also as a headquarters for her fleet. It is to be hoped that effective measures will be taken to prevent the United States from annexing territories which in the future are likely to be of so much importance to us."[23] A representative of British Columbian opinion declared that "neither our province nor Australia can afford to surrender the Key to the Pacific Ocean without a vigorous protest to the home government. . . . Are we to retire from Hawaii without a protest and surrender the most powerful mid-ocean rendezvous in the Pacific?"[24]

In the case of Canada, opinion was strengthened by a growing Canadian nationalism centering in the completion of the Federation of the provinces as well as the uniting of the country by the completion

---

[21] The *New York Herald,* January 30, and the *New York Times,* January 31 and February 4 contain many citations from the English press.

[22] See *New York Times,* February 7 and February 16, 1893, for citations from several sources relative to the attitude of New Zealand, Australia, and Canada; also London *Times,* February 3, 1893.

[23] Cited *New York Times,* February 4, 1893. See H. A. Innis, *History of the Canadian Pacific Railway* for Canada's plans for Pacific commerce.

[24] Cited *New York Times,* January 31, 1893.

of the transcontinental railway.[25] This political spirit, when coupled with the economic interests involved which unquestionably had definite ambitions in terms of Hawaii as a commercial outpost, made the Canadian reaction especially serious.[26]

Despite this feeling in the colonies, London did not see fit to protest the attempted annexation. Whether it would have, had the treaty early demonstrated prospect of endorsement by the Senate, is problematical but doubtful. It is interesting to note, however, that the incident provided the first major occasion for a demonstration of a decided improvement in Anglo-American relations and the growing entente of the two powers in the Pacific. It was indicated more strongly later in the Spanish-American War, but its first manifestations were in 1893 in connection with the Hawaiian problem. It is significant that the Liberal press in England assumed at once a very friendly attitude toward what appeared to be a major American move toward imperial expansion in the Pacific.

Commenting on the affair, *The Speaker,* formerly the *Liberal Review* and a spokesman for the Liberals in English politics, predicted the complete triumph of the forces of imperialism in the United States and urged that the step be taken with full British accord. On February 4 it editorialized: "We must stand by America in the course which the natural expansion of her interests and the interests of civilization prescribe to her as necessary; and this policy an entente with America should enable us to pursue, without jeopardizing or prejudicing in any way our own or our Colonies interests in the Pacific." On March 18 it continued with the statement that English statesmen must appreciate that American interests in Hawaii were far greater than those of any oher nation, and, despite colonial objections, acquisition of the Islands should be ". . . the first step, nay, the most important, binding and vital step towards the great British-American Alliance of the future. . . ." Still later on April 1 *The Speaker* indicated that settlement of the Behring Sea negotiation, the elevation of the British Minister at

---

[25] See W. W. Wallace, "The Growth of Canadian National Feeling," *Canadian Historical Review,* June, 1920, for a discussion of the growth of nationalism during this period.

[26] With some exaggeration in all probability, Minister Stevens had since 1890 warned the State Department concerning Canadian intrigue at Honolulu. Stevens believed C. W. Ashford, Canadian-born Attorney General at the time, implicated as well as T. H. Davies, guardian of Kaiulani, who had interests in British Columbia. As late as November 20, 1892, Stevens wrote of efforts to throw Hawaii into the "hands of Canadian and ultra-British schemers" and "to secure Canadian and British franchises, privileges and rights, entirely legal, to get rid of which would cause embarrassment and expense to the United States and her allies here." See Stevens to Foster, November 20, 1892, FR, 1894, 377f.

Washington to ambassadorial rank and support of the annexation of Hawaii would constitute three major steps toward an "Anglo-American Alliance." This point of view adequately explains the failure of Great Britain in particular to take umbrage at the threatened Hawaiian coup.

CLEVELAND WITHDRAWS THE TREATY

Five days following his inauguration Grover Cleveland withdrew the Hawaiian treaty from the Senate for "re-examination." Again the question of motives arises. Contemporary opinion unfriendly to the new administration naturally charged politics, but there is no ground for such a view. Both Harrison and Cleveland were motivated by a fundamental desire to do the right thing, with the views of each influenced by varying conceptions of governmental philosophy and foreign policy. As has been noted earlier, during his first administration Cleveland had indicated a genuine interest in Hawaii and its future. There is reason to believe that his withdrawal of the treaty was dictated in his own mind by no motive other than a desire to know more of the facts in the case, a viewpoint common to all who were not prejudiced by strong opinion either for or against immediate annexation. To Carl Schurz, the President wrote on March 19 that he was not opposed to annexation under any and all conditions but that "we ought to stop, look and think."[27] There is no reason to question the complete sincerity of this statement.

There is no doubt that Cleveland's decision was influenced strongly by his Secretary of State, Walter Q. Gresham. Gresham had recommended withdrawal of the treaty on the ground, as he later wrote to Bayard in London, that "it would lower our national standard to endorse a selfish and dishonorable scheme of a lot of adventurers." "I am glad to say," he continued, "that the President endorsed without hesitation the decision which I took in the letter addressed to him."[28] Regarding the motives behind Gresham's view, there has been much difference of opinion and a tendency to question his sincerity as affected by personal and partisan bias, a view which is given some credence in even the most recent scholarly accounts.[29]

There is, of course, no questioning the fact that Mr. Gresham had been a bitter opponent of Mr. Harrison and had every reason for

[27] Letter in Carl Schurz Papers, Library of Congress. Commissioner Blount found Cleveland motivated by the same feeling.

[28] Letter of October 29, 1893, Gresham Papers. In a letter of June 30, 1937, to the author, Robert Lincoln O'Brien says, "Mr. Cleveland was much influenced by Mr. Gresham but later somewhat changed his mind."

[29] See Pratt, 124.

antagonism toward the political leaders and thought connected with his administration. A careful perusal of the numerous letters between Gresham and the various persons to whom he explained at length the basis for his policy and indicated his deep moral and personal satisfaction at its support in many quarters, together with an appraisal of Mr. Gresham's views on other matters of contemporary public policy, should convince anyone, however, of his complete honesty and sincerity.

One finds it difficult, for example, to question the honesty of a statement such as that made by Gresham to Carl Schurz in replying to a letter commending him for his stand in the face of widespread abuse. Gresham expressed his hope that ultimately the people would see the light "but whether they do or not, I have done my duty."[30] To Noble Butler he wrote two days later: "I am opposed to annexation, especially of territory not a part of our continent. If I were in favor of annexation, however, I should oppose taking the Islands by force and fraud. . . . I think there is such a thing as international morality."[31]

Again and again, Gresham expressed his belief in international morality and his criticism of the circumstances under which the Hawaiian revolution had been consummated. Of his basic disagreement with the idea of territorial expansion outside the continental limits of the country, there can be no doubt. To Bayard he wrote on December 17, 1893: "If we enter upon a career of acquisition of distant territory, governing it as Great Britain and other European powers govern their dependencies, our republic will not long endure. Should we acquire the Hawaiian Islands with their population, we will have a hotbed of corruption."[32]

Further basis for belief in Gresham's sincerity may be gained from the fact that his views were by no means unusual upon the part of a large number of prominent men of the time, who agreed with him completely and commended him for his stand. If Gresham was impractical or political in his policy, he most certainly was not alone. One of the most vigorous supporters of Gresham was Carl Schurz, who shared his views both on acquisition of outlying territory and the nature of the Hawaiian revolution. From London, the hard-thinking Bayard, by no means unconversant with Hawaiian affairs, wrote a note of congratulation, saying, "Our country is too great and aspires to too high a place in civilization to stoop to the small arts of tricking or bullying a scanty and feeble set of Islanders out of their rights—whatever those

[30] Letter dated November 21, 1893, Gresham Papers.
[31] *Ibid.*
[32] *Ibid.* The Gresham Papers contain many such letters.

rights may be." Henry Watterson wrote of Gresham's position as "impregnable," both as to its justice and policy.[33]

Once he had withdrawn the treaty from the Senate, the action of the President was decisive. Desirous of ascertaining from his own representative the full story of the revolution, Cleveland on March 11 appointed James H. Blount of Georgia as special commissioner to investigate firsthand the causes of the revolt and condition in the Islands to "fully enlighten" the President. As Cleveland stated later, his one desire was to learn the truth and to vindicate the "national honor, conscience and love of justice." Commissioner Blount was instructed to exercise "paramount" authority in representing the United States on the Islands during the course of his mission. He arrived at Honolulu on March 29.[34] Refusing proffered accommodations by Stevens and representatives of the new government, he took up quarters at a hotel and set about his work entirely free from personal contact with the conflicting parties.

THE BLOUNT REPORT AND ITS AFTERMATH

One of the first acts of Blount was to terminate the protection afforded the Provisional Government by Minister Stevens and to withdraw American forces from Honolulu. By July 17 he had heard voluminous testimony from representatives of each side of the controversy and prepared a full report. It narrated in detail the background of the revolution, and the story of what had occurred in connection with it. It endeavored to assay the part of the American Minister in the revolutionary outbreak and the influence exerted by American armed forces in making it successful, as well as popular feeling in the Islands relative to annexation.

In regard to the role of Minister Stevens and the American forces, Blount concluded with finality that the revolution would not have been successful without this aid and comfort, and charged that pro-annexation sentiments had motivated collusion with the revolutionary

---

[33] Both letters from Gresham Papers. It should be noted also that Gresham took high ground on a majority of public questions. For example, he was much in advance of his time in his views on labor questions. Gresham was in reality an outstanding liberal of his day. See correspondence in Gresham Papers and also Matilda Gresham, *Life of W. Q. Gresham.*

[34] Blount had just finished serving as chairman of the House Committee on Foreign Affairs, and had some acquaintance with the Hawaiian situation as one of those approached by Thurston. In Congress he had opposed appropriations for enlarging the Navy and Isthmian canal projects, indicating a support of traditional isolationist foreign policy. The entire story of the mission and the testimony and interviews involved are contained in FR, 1894. See also Pratt, 130ff. for interesting sidelights and viewpoints. Also, Allan Nevins, *Grover Cleveland,* 549-62.

leaders. He likewise came to the unhesitating conclusion that native sentiment was overwhelmingly opposed to annexation. "The undoubted sentiment of the people is for the Queen against the Provisional Government, and against annexation," wrote Blount.[35]

Blount left Hawaii on August 8 and late in November his report was made public in the United States. It had been summarized and presented to the President by Secretary Gresham a month earlier with a letter asking, "Should not the great wrong done to a feeble but independent State by an abuse of the authority of the United States be undone by restoring the legitimate government?"[36] He had come to the definite conclusion that the Queen must be restored.

At this time it appears that, in considering a report to Congress on Hawaiian affairs, Cleveland began to depart from a strict adherence to the recommendations of his Secretary of State. Two other members of his cabinet, Carlisle and Olney, were responsible for a change necessitated by practical considerations. The intense idealism of Gresham led him to adhere vigorously to the idea that the only way to right the wrong done Queen Liliuokalani and the natives was to restore the kingdom, though he did admit that, "Wrongs may not always be entirely righted by individuals or nations."[37]

There were others who took a harder view. The most influential of these in shaping the President's policy after November was Richard Olney, Attorney General, who later, upon the death of Gresham, was to succeed him in the State Department. In an autobiographical sketch in his private papers, Olney indicates that both he and Carlisle advised a moderate course, and that an original message to Congress drafted for the President by Gresham following the Blount report was modified by him. Olney wrote that he had been asked by the President "to see what I could do with it," and that as a result he prepared a revision of the Gresham recommendations which was accepted by Cleveland "and forms by far the larger part of the message actually sent to Congress on the 18th of December."[38]

---

[35] FR, 1894, 598-99. The basic conclusions of Blount were supported strongly by an independent investigation conducted by Charles Nordhoff for the *New York Herald.* See *Herald* for April 17, 24, and 26, 1893.

[36] FR, 1894, 459-63. Publication of the Blount report was hastened by premature leaks to the press regarding its content.

[37] Letter to Noble Butler, November 23, 1893, Gresham Papers.

[38] Autobiographical Memorandum, Olney Papers. A comparison of Olney's draft with the message justifies his statement. Cleveland followed Olney's line of argument carefully, and some sentences were taken over in their entirety. In a letter to "My dear Agnes" on December 3 Olney wrote, "I thought that, while wholly right as to the wrong done by the U. S. in the deposition of the Queen, he (Gresham) did not fully realize the practical difficulties that might attend the

A further factor in modifying what appears to have been a policy aimed in the direction of restoring the Queen was the action of Liliuokalani herself. In September, Albert S. Willis had been named as Minister to Hawaii accredited to the Provisional Government. He was instructed that the President was agreeable to restoring the Queen, provided satisfactory assurances were obtained that she would grant amnesty to those participating in the revolt and assume all obligations of the intervening government. Willis met the Queen upon his arrival in November, and was somewhat shocked to hear her express her feeling that the laws of Hawaii would require death and confiscation as the punishment for revolution. Later meetings convinced Willis that restoration of the Queen would even mean overthrowing the Constitution of 1887, and a return to absolute government in Hawaii.[39] Delay in securing any different assurances made any thought of restoration at the moment appear impractical, and on December 18 the President dumped the entire problem in the lap of Congress.[40]

CLEVELAND'S HAWAIIAN MESSAGE

The Cleveland message on the Hawaiian problem ranks in clarity and vigor of expression with his best. Its major aspect was a complete review of the relationship of the United States to the revolution, which presented a vigorous indictment of the activities of the American Minister and the use of armed forces in such a manner as to constitute a protection for the revolutionary government. "The lawful government of Hawaii was overthrown without the drawing of a sword or the firing of a shot by a process every step of which it may be safely asserted, is directly traceable to and dependent for its success upon the agency of the United States acting through its diplomatic and naval representatives," commented the President. The entire message breathed something of a moral fervor, which must have been injected into it through Gresham's original draft. Declared Cleveland, "I suppose that

attempt to restore her." Regarding the Blount report, he also wrote, "The President wanted information—wanted to know exactly what the facts were about this remarkable revolution; the way it was brought about and the wishes of the people as respects annexation." This Blount secured "and no one in Washington pretends that this report is not the result of his honest convictions after as thorough and impartial verification of the facts as he could make." Charles Nordhoff wrote Gresham on December 2 commending the Blount report for its fairness and accuracy. See letter in Gresham Papers.

[39] See dispatches in FR, 1894, 463ff.

[40] On the same day, however, Willis wrote the State Department that the Queen had at last agreed to full acceptance of the conditions for her restoration. On December 20 Willis announced to the Provisional Government that it was expected to relinquish its authority, a proposition which was "respectfully and unhesitatingly" declined on December 23

right and justice should determine the path to be followed in treating this subject. If national honesty is to be disregarded and a desire for territorial expansion, or dissatisfaction with a form of government not our own, ought to regulate our conduct, I have entirely misapprehended the mission and character of our Government, and the behavior which the conscience of our people demands of their public servants." The proposal to annex territory more than two thousand miles from our shores "contemplated a departure from an unbroken American tradition," according to Cleveland. The haste with which the preceding administration sought to conclude such a proposal was condemned and contrasted with the refusal of President Jackson to recognize the Texas Republic in 1836. Stating that "unfortunate public misrepresentation of the situation and exaggerated statements of the sentiments of our people" had made it impossible to settle the question by executive action, Cleveland referred the problems to "the broader authority and discretion of Congress, with a full explanation of the endeavor thus far made to deal with the emergency and a statement of the considerations which have governed my action."

The President, of course, accepted in full the indictment of Stevens and the revolutionary leaders provided by the Blount report. The facts in this indictment were unquestionably true and agree with independent analyses from other sources. The report and the administration erred, however, in failing to understand the fundamental and long developed causes of the Revolution of 1893. Viewed in proper historical perspective, the revolt was inevitable. The actions of the revolutionary leaders, the American Minister, and the naval commander were those which probably would have been taken by any others facing the same situation. A proper understanding of the forces at work in Hawaii for half a century would perhaps have tempered the moral indignation aroused by a hasty view and cursory examination of the immediate circumstances connected with the revolt.

PUBLIC REACTIONS TO THE CLEVELAND POLICY

It is well at this point to return to the matter of public reactions to the Hawaiian problem. The withdrawal of the annexation treaty and the appointment of Blount did not meet with the condemnation from pro-annexationists that might be expected. In general they seem not to have regarded the move as one which would defeat their ambitions. It was viewed rather as a natural course of action for purposes of fuller consideration, and the issue of annexation was so inevitable as not to be avoided. The *Review of Reviews* declared in April, "There is no reason whatever to think that the natives would not heartily welcome the union with America." Therefore, investigation of the revolt would only strengthen the case for acquiring the Islands. The *New York Sun* thought that in his first administration Cleveland had been so much in sympathy with reciprocity and shown so keen an insight into the importance of Hawaii that his policy could not be unfriendly to the closer unity of the two countries. The *Philadelphia Public Ledger,* supposedly close to the administration, believed the treaty would be revised and returned, and asserted, "Let Hawaii come in, and let the Administration of Grover Cleveland have the glory of that magnificent acquisition." Both the *Inquirer* and the *Press* of the same city expressed similar views.

The *New York Tribune* Washington correspondent, reporting on March 10, expressed his confidence in the support of annexation by both Cleveland and Gresham, and indicated that a little "peanut politics" designed to secure administration credit was all that was behind withdrawal of the treaty. Even the Washington representatives of the Provisional Government seemed confident that an investigation would support their cause, if carefully handled, and that at least a protectorate status would be achieved under the new administration.[41]

It was generally assumed at once that withdrawal of the treaty would be followed by an investigation. The *New York Times* on March 10 declared editorially: "Mr. Cleveland undoubtedly intends to do precisely what President Harrison ought to have done, that is, devote enough time and care to the subject to be sure that he is doing what the best interests of the country require. It is in no sense a prejudgment of the case. It is, on the contrary, a definite step to prevent the case being prejudged." Similar statements appeared in the Washington correspondence of the *New York Herald* of the same day as well as in the *Evening Post*. The utmost secrecy surrounded Blount's mission, and while he gave an interview at San Francisco stating that he intended to hear both sides impartially, this attracted little or no attention.[42]

The first shock to such comfortable assumptions came with news of the ending of the protectorate upon Blount's arrival at Honolulu. The *New York Press* on April 17 characterized this action as "a gross and

---

[41] See Pratt, 128f., for comments by Thurston and advice to Honolulu on how to handle Blount. Thurston was anxious especially to get natives and half-castes to present views favoring annexation.

[42] The strength of expansionist Democrats such as Senator Morgan, the fact that several leading Democratic newspapers were pro-annexation, and Cleveland's Hawaiian policy in his first administration were important factors giving support to the idea that the treaty would not be rejected.

deliberate betrayal of American interests and a cowardly affront to the American name." By May the *New York Tribune* was convinced that something was wrong, and demanded the recall of Mr. Blount, asserting his appointment to be unconstitutional on the ground the Senate had not been consulted.[43] Not all of the annexationist press agreed with this view, however, and there were many who viewed withdrawal of the protectorate as necessary to a fair judgment of the issue.[44]

The general opinion of the more independent press viewed Blount's action with favor and as a logical move. The anti-expansionist press, which had viewed with misgiving for some time the trend of Republican diplomacy, was emphatic in praise and support of Cleveland's entire procedure. The *St. Louis Republic* lauded the administration for its opposition to imperialism and asserted that "there is an American Democrat in the White House," and that he was loyal to "the principles of American Democracy." The *New York World,* the *Herald,* and the *Times* of the same city, the *Chicago Times,* and the *Baltimore Sun* were unanimous in approving the President's early moves to untangle the Hawaiian knot.[45]

Gresham's letter to the President on Hawaii was made public on November 10, and on the 21st the Blount report was placed on the record for public consumption. This lifted the veil of secrecy as to the full intentions of the administration and led to a vigorous debate. Opinions were heated on both sides and there was little room left for a purely judicial view. The *New York Sun* on November 12 printed a burning editorial, declaring: "Never before has an American executive undertaken to stamp out republicanism and to set up monarchy in any part of the world. . . . Was there no American spirit in the Cabinet when this policy of infamy was decreed?" The *Atlanta Constitution* observed caustically, "The Democratic party has not been in the habit of restoring monarchies anywhere, and as Mr. Gresham is not a Democrat he may have made a mistake in this matter."

Later publication of the fuller story of the nature of Mr. Willis' mission and instructions relative to the restoration of the Queen added to the bitterness. The Washington correspondent of the *New York Times* probably expressed the true situation, when he wrote on November 11 that "it must be confessed that the proposed restoration was never understood as the question has been discussed by persons holding close relations with the administration." He commented further that

---

[43] May 8, 1893. This was the first time this issue was raised.
[44] See *New York Sun,* April 17; *Review of Reviews,* May, 1893.
[45] *Public Opinion,* XV, summarizes comment.

"a result of the protracted silence of the administration as to its policy in Hawaii has been to mislead its friends." If friends were thus misled, those who had been unfriendly but hoping for the best were doubly disillusioned.

The Washington correspondent of the *New York Tribune* reported on November 18 it was the intention of the President to restore the Queen "peacefully if possible, but by force if necessary." Until the complete instructions of Willis were made public, this assumption was common and did much to arouse antagonism. The handling of the entire Hawaiian matter in terms of the public was most inept on the part of the administration. The *New York Sun* declared that any attempt to unseat the Provisional Government would be an act of war and a violation of the presidential oath. Charges that the proposed action was unpatriotic, un-American, and unconstitutional came from such sources as the *Atlanta Constitution* and the *Chicago Tribune.*[46]

Even independent journals formerly friendly to the administration were led into criticism. The *Philadelphia Ledger* advised against hasty action while the *Washington Post* took a similar stand. The *Washington Star* characterized the administration policy as "indefensible," while the *Springfield Republican* thought it to be an effort to right one wrong by committing another. The *New York World* dismissed the whole affair as a "farce."[47] A policy of "hands-off" seemed the only way out to many observers.

Public opinion was further confused by publication of the Blount report, followed by news from Hawaii that the Queen was preparing for her restoration by ordering new finery and uniforms for her guard.[48] Later information concerned the alleged preparations of the Provisional Government to resist the restoration by force. Opposition to the administration concentrated upon an attempt to undermine confidence in the Blount report. The *New York Tribune* characterized it on November 22 as "a collection of stories told by the ex-Queen's corrupt clique backed by what he calls the 'admissions' of persons more or less associated with President Dole and the Provisional Government, disappointed office seekers, whose ambitions have been neglected and whose views of their own importance that Government had declined to share." The *Sun* spoke of "Paramount Commissioner" Blount and asserted his report was a mere lawyer's brief to support a preconceived case and afford "a working basis for the execution of the predeter-

---

[46] See quotations from *New York Tribune,* November 16.
[47] See *Public Opinion,* XVI.
[48] *New York Times,* December 9.

mined policy arranged and planned by Mr. Cleveland and Mr. Gresham and their Administration."[49]

The Protestant religious press entered the lists with caustic criticism of the proposed restoration as un-Christian and an attempt to contravene the Christian civilization of Hawaii built up by the missionaries. *The Congregationalist* asserted that the President was using "our national power and prestige to impose on decent people the authority they had overthrown of a vicious, immoral, irresponsible woman, surrounded by knavish advisers, to the destruction of guarantees of protection to life, liberty and possessions."[50] Similar views were expressed in *The Outlook.*

Rumor and innuendo were utilized to discredit the President. Persistent reports of dissension in the Cabinet over the Hawaiian policy were given credence to the point of suggesting resignations.[51] Another rumor was that efforts had been made to corrupt the Provisional Government to aid its overthrow. It was even reported that Minister Willis had ordered naval guns trained on Honolulu to coerce the Dole regime. Yet another story finding space in news columns was that Cleveland was cooperating with Japan and that strong Japanese forces had arrived at Honolulu. Emphasis was placed upon reported disorderly conditions in Hawaii threatening life and property, as a result of unrest produced by the President's policy. The *New York Tribune*, principal center for the propaganda reports, asserted on November 25 that this was the actual state of affairs and "Americans, blood of our blood, bone of our bone, flesh of our flesh" and the work of "Christians, of noble pioneers of civilization and human progress" were the innocent victims. Charges of personal and partisan motives were levelled at both the President and Secretary Gresham.[52]

The *New York Tribune* made much of the allegation that the President was flying in the face of general opinion as well as that of a majority of his own party. Attention was directed to the fact that the "great body of the Democratic press . . . is cold and silent, while many of the most powerful journals that usually support Democratic policies are sternly and resolutely declaring against this crazy Hawaiian re-

---

[49] Cited in the *New York Tribune*, November 23.

[50] Cited in *New York Tribune*, November 18.

[51] See *New York Tribune*, December 19.

[52] The *Tribune* on November 22 wrote editorially of the "bitter, vindictive, personal hatred, passionate, blinding, absorbing" upon the part of Gresham toward both James G. Blaine and former President Harrison. These charges were so assiduously disseminated as to color historical accounts of a later date. They do not take into account the fact that Gresham and former Secretary Foster, who directed the Hawaiian annexation treaty, were college mates and friends of long standing.

action."[53] The *Brooklyn Eagle,* the *New York Sun,* the *New York World,* the *Philadelphia Ledger,* the *Philadelphia Record,* the *Atlanta Constitution,* the *San Francisco Examiner,* together with such independent papers as the *Chicago Record,* the *Washington Post* and the *Star,* with the *Springfield Republican,* were all cited with telling certainty to support this conclusion.

The secrecy of the administration as to its intentions played into the hands of the opposition, and was utilized to allege sinister designs of an unconstitutional nature. The *New York Tribune* demanded that the people be acquainted with all the facts, a point which it had overlooked earlier in the year. "No matter how the scheme to unseat the Government of Hawaii and to create there another Government may be expressed, the first act that gives it meaning is an act of war, it declared. "Mr. Cleveland cannot lift his finger to injure President Dole or to upraise the besotted and broken throne of Liliuokalani without assuming powers which the Constitution expressly forbade to the President and reserved to the people themselves through their Congress," it asserted editorially on November 25. The President was sacrificing "our prestige and influence in the Pacific" and promoting the prostration of our commerce and surrender of the public rights "which every Administration for seventy years has jealously guarded."[54] It was statements of this type to which the President undoubtedly referred in his message of December 18 and which led him to place the problem before Congress, thus spiking most of the charges.

Quite naturally there were not lacking statements from those connected with the annexation effort, which provided ammunition for critics of the administration. George H. Dole, brother of the Hawaiian President, gave out an interview in California indicating that the Provisional Government might turn to England for recognition denied by the United States. Former Secretary Foster contributed a public announcement defending the Harrison administration and characterizing Cleveland's action as a "great blunder." Lorrin Thurston issued a long answer to assertions of Gresham and the Blount report which, in the opinion of the *New York Tribune,* "pulverizes" them. Former Secretary of the Navy Tracy denied that Harrison's administration had sanctioned revolt, and many letters and statements came from Honolulu from those active in the revolution, which were given space in the annexation press as antidotes to administration assertions.[55]

---

[53] November 23.
[54] *New York Tribune,* November 30.
[55] The *New York Tribune* was a repository for all these during November and December. Many of them were effective and struck at the weakest portion of the

Perhaps second only to appeals to moral sensibilities was the importance of charges that the Cleveland policy would throw Hawaii into alien hands. Reference has already been made to the Japanese scare. This was given impetus by a Rev. Mr. Oleson of Honolulu who wrote in the *Independent* of May 11 that "the present transition era offers Japan an opportunity in Hawaiian affairs that she would not be slow to avail herself of were negotiations pending with the United States to prove abortive." Captain Mahan added another peril in referring to the "comparative barbarism of China" as replacing European civilization if American influence were relinquished. The *New York Tribune* asserted on December 13 in one of its many editorials that Cleveland "had brought about a state of affairs in Hawaii so critical that armed resistance or the protection of another nation may be the only recourse of a friendly Power whose interests he has betrayed with ours." Former President Harrison gave out an interview calling attention to British designs in the Pacific and indicating that unless Hawaii were made secure "we shall be pretty much surrounded."[56]

Certainly the most interesting and one of the most vocal of the defenders of the legitimacy of what had taken place was Minister Stevens. His defense began with the arrival of Commissioner Blount and continued after his return to the United States. Attacks upon the Blount report and Gresham's letter to the President were presented through his *Kennebec Journal* and widely copied. On November 13 he answered the Gresham letter as "a grave offense against American civilization, justice and law," and spoke of its "cruel and untruthful words that strike at the noble band of men and women who have for ten months stood so resolutely and unitedly in defense of American civilization." On November 30 he gave a long and detailed answer to the Blount report which emphasized again the attack upon decency and Americanism in Hawaii. Blount was characterized as "a neophyte in diplomacy" and "caught in the meshes and snares adroitly prepared for him by the cunning advisers of the fallen Liliuokalani and by the shrewd, sharp, long experienced British diplomatic agent . . . without the least suspicion that he was aiding ultra-British interests even more than he was helping Hawaiian monarchists and the deposed Queen."

Gresham-Blount thesis that revolt could not have occurred without aid and comfort from Minister Stevens and American forces. Many utilized moral and missionary appeals. The well-known Sereno Bishop was a powerful proponent of this interest with references to the opium ring, the lottery, political corruption, and personal immorality of native leaders and their government. A letter to the *Hawaiian Gazette* (April 24, 1894) from the United States advised annexationists "to play the missionary for all he is worth."

[56] *The Nation*, November 23.

Those who had appeared before him were "corruptionists" and "notorious spendthrifts," and the entire Blount mission was "anomalous, un-American and most unfair."[57] In the December issue of the *North American Review,* Stevens presented "A Plea for Annexation" which placed the entire issue on a moral plane by declaring that an improper solution of the Hawaiian problem would deeply influence the moral standing of the United States before the world. "Will the American nation stand by its century's record in favor of republican government and free Christian civilization, or will it repudiate its past by using its power to murder its own offspring and to stamp out the reforming work of pure and noble men and women who have made the Hawaiian Islands what they are, thus following the once infamous example of the Austrian Hapsburgs in stifling the noble aspirations of Italy and Hungary?" he queried. A survey of the history of missionary activities in Hawaii, emphasis upon the decline of native population and rise of Oriental influence, with consequent dangers to the commercial and strategic importance of the Islands to the United States, were included in the article.[58]

The attack upon the Cleveland policy came to a focal point with his message to Congress, foreshadowed in the press some days before it was submitted. The *New York Tribune* felt that such action was indeed necessary in view of the fact that he had committed "a series of colossal blunders; he has transcended his constitutional authority; he has rejected an unparalleled opportunity; he has affronted Congress and the whole people by wrapping his proceedings in mystery; he had defied public sentiment, and finally he has brought about a state of affairs in Hawaii so critical that armed resistance or the protection of another nation may be the only recourse of the friendly Power whose interests he had betrayed with ours."[59]

ANTI-IMPERIALIST VIEWPOINTS

The presidential policy was not without defenders, however. The debate became more than a mere discussion of Hawaii's connection with the United States; the larger issue of America's position and policy

---

[57] See *New York Times,* November 13 and 30 for reprints of Stevens' letters.
[58] The *New York Tribune* found these arguments "strong and comprehensive" and naively added, "Besides, Mr. Stevens' statements are corroborated by Mr. Thurston, President Dole, Mr. Waterhouse and many other unimpeachable witnesses."
[59] November 30. Cleveland's message was reported under headlines "Diplomacy Gone to Wreck" and characterized as a "warming over" of Gresham's statements and "weak and disappointing" as well as an elaborate defense of a policy admittedly a failure.

in world affairs and expansion was inextricably bound up in the argument. Those who had viewed with distrust the tendency, especially under Republican auspices, to pursue a "vigorous" foreign policy were quick to support Cleveland in opposing annexation. Assertions that the changed conditions of American development were demanding territorial and commercial expansion and new world responsibilities, were met with rebuttals.

In New York, the *Evening Post* rejoiced at Cleveland's return to "the old gospel preached first by the founders of the Republic," and the *Nation* emphasized the importance of checking developments which since the day of Blaine in 1881 had constituted "a series of departures from the rules of international morality." *Harper's Weekly* asked the people, " Are we ready to alter the whole character of the government, with its beneficent traditional policies, to impose upon the people the burdens entailed by building up and maintaining of immense armaments, and to expose this republic to all the political and economic consequences which such a policy would bring in its train here as elsewhere, and for which we have been in the habit of pitying the nations of the Old World?"[60]

To those who adopted this view, Cleveland appeared as a knight in armor crusading against forces of evil. To them the Blount report, Gresham's letter to the President and his resulting policy, were factual evidence of intrigue of the basest type in Hawaii connived at by the Harrison administration. The *Evening Post* found Gresham's letter "a clear and straight forward statement of all the disgraceful episodes in this most un-American proceeding, showing . . . that the conduct of Mr. Stevens was indefensible in every particular and was sustained by him with misrepresentations and falsehoods." The only thing to do was "to put things back where they were before the marines were landed from the *Boston*." The Washington correspondent of the paper reported that the attempt at annexation had been hatched in Washington with leading members of Congress and the administration of Harrison concerned, and official sanction accorded the revolt.[61]

The *Post* was not alone, for the *New York World* had now concluded on November 21 that "The Harrison Administration may not have attempted to steal Hawaii, but it showed a great willingness to act as the receiver of stolen goods." The November 11 *New York Times* thought restoration of the Queen "an act of simple justice." The Cleveland policy, declared the *Times,* was "a sharp rebuke to the spirit of filibuster-

---

[60] See *Evening Post* of December 19, 1893; *Nation,* December 2; *Harper's Weekly,* March 18.
[61] See especially issues for November 11 and 13, 1893.

ing in this country," and Blount's report confirmed "in the most positive manner the conviction that the provisional Government was the product of a conspiracy and was forced upon the country by Minister Stevens, through an abuse of the authority of the United States."[62]

The attempt of the expansionists to utilize the missionary appeal was met with vigorous criticism of the missionary. The *New York Evening Post,* for example, scored Sereno Bishop's statements on the corruption and immorality of the natives with the statement that it was shameful that men supposedly evangelists should entertain such views of the people they were serving and suggested sugar planting as more nearly suitable to Bishop as a vocation. Attention was called to earlier reports of the growing worldliness of the missionaries in Hawaii, and the *Post* sarcastically commented that "in no other part of the world except Hawaii has the enormous scandal occurred of missionaries and their sons growing rich out of the property or resources of the natives." The moralistic tone of Stevens' defense was characterized as "pious black-guardism," and the Queen, affirmed the *Post,* was probably quite as moral as "Tom Platt or Crocker or Quay" and suggested that "a pure and wholesome government" in New York and Pennsylvania might be as desirable as in Hawaii. The *Nation* cleverly suggested that these charges against the Queen and her native followers were in themselves something of an indictment of the missionary activity.[63]

Likewise, assertions as to the strategic importance of Hawaii met with sarcastic comment from anti-imperialists. *Harper's Weekly* satirized the idea of so-called "keys" to the command of certain areas and emphasized properly enough that acquisition of one point of strategic importance usually created a necessity for another key position to defend the first and so on. The existing compact nature of the United States without island outposts was felt to be the best possible natural defense position. The weekly also pointed out that the proponents of Hawaiian annexation, with its large native and Oriental population were the same persons making an ado over South European immigration with its danger to American institutions.[64]

As the controversy developed over the presidential policy, the Catholic press generally rallied to its defense. The *Milwaukee Catholic Press* asserted that the President and Mr. Gresham were simply demonstrating

---

[62] See *Times* editorials of November 10 and 11. Similar opinions were expressed in the *World* of November 14. The investigation conducted for the *New York Herald* by Charles Nordhoff already has been cited and furnished much support for critics of the attempted annexation.

[63] See *Evening Post* editorials of November 18, December 1 and 10; *Nation* for November 30.

[64] March 18 and April 15, 1894.

a finer sense of justice than many were able to appreciate. The *Pittsburgh Catholic* felt that restoration of the Queen was just. Rancor of the Roman Church against attacks by Protestants upon the work of Father Damien had much to do with the attitude of the Catholic press.[65]

An interesting angle was the general support of the President from the Populist and labor press. The *Denver News,* a leading Populist journal, praised Cleveland's stand on Hawaii in spite of his erroneous philosophy on the currency. The Knights of Labor *Journal* also approved the President's policy.[66]

Opponents of imperial expansion used the current magazines as a most effective medium for the full development of their arguments, and several outstanding articles by notable persons were forthcoming. George Ticknor Curtis, in the *North American Review* for March, 1893, presented an extended brief proving that the annexation of non-contiguous territory was unconstitutional. He affirmed that the Constitution recognized but two conditions under which territory could be incorporated in the Union. It must be contiguous and there must be an impelling national necessity for its acquisition. These conditions had existed in the case of the Louisiana purchase, the annexation of Texas, and the Mexican cession as well as Oregon, but they were not applicable to Hawaii.

Judge Cooley, a constitutional lawyer of repute and first head of the Inter-State Commerce Commission, wrote in *Forum* for June, 1893, that the Constitution made no provision for territorial acquisitions without the expressed will of the people desiring to become a part of the United States. This situation, he argued with some reason, did not obtain upon the part of Hawaii, where the request for annexation came from a minority. In Congress, a constitutional objection was admitted even by proponents of annexation, but Speaker Sherman sought to avoid the illegality of acquiring a territory by proposing admission of Hawaii at once as a state.[67]

The sincerity of the objection to acquiring Hawaii because it involved a fundamental departure from accepted and traditional American policy was further indicated in several magazine articles. One of the most thorough and significant was Carl Schurz' article, "Manifest Destiny," in *Harper's Monthly* for October, 1893. Mr. Schurz called attention to the fact that the people were confronted with a new manifestation of the old spirit of manifest destiny which had motivated earlier expansion and one which now asked for acquisition of non-contiguous territories

[65] See *Public Opinion,* XVI, 189f., for Catholic opinion.
[66] *Public Opinion, op. cit.*
[67] *Cong. Rec.,* 53 Cong., 2 sess., 1311.

greatly enlarging the political and commercial sphere of American influence. Supporters of this new doctrine, he asserted, were politicians anxious for "effect," Americans with business interests or seeking them in foreign areas, ardent nationalists, and the "navy interest." Objections to such a program were many and included doubt as to its constitutionality and its consistency with the national ideal of a compact democracy largely self-sufficing in character. Attention was called to the danger of acquiring so-called "key" outposts which demanded protection. The difficulty of governing distant possessions with complicated internal racial and other problems was also cited. To men of the Carl Schurz school of thought, the proposed annexation represented a real danger, and they argued vigorously for a continuation of traditional policy and attention to the internal progress of America without regard to outside interests.[68]

THE HAWAIIAN ISSUE IN CONGRESS

The presidential message of December 18 brought to an end what might be termed the period of executive action in relation to the Hawaiian problem. It must be admitted that it had not been successful in any of its objectives. It had induced a strenuous debate over the merits of territorial expansion, however, which certainly did much to clarify and perhaps crystallize public opinion on both sides of a most important question. Time had been provided for a thorough review of the more recent history of Hawaiian relations with the United States, and for those who cared to do so to make up their minds whether or not the country should annex or otherwise more closely control the destiny of that group of Islands. Above all, the honor of the nation had not been tainted by annexation under questionable circumstances. What should be done was now in the hands of the Congress.

Even prior to the message, Congress inevitably had entered into the controversy. The opening guns in a long debate were fired after the President made a brief reference to the Islands in his first annual message, noting the appointment of a special investigator, and that the restoration of the former government was under consideration. Senator Dolph of Oregon launched a strong attack upon the constitutionality of the Blount appointment, charging an effort motivated by partisanship was under way to "roll back civilization in Hawaii." The Senator asserted, "Our national interests, the protection of our coasts, the interests

---

[68] The Schurz correspondence with Gresham as well as with Cleveland indicates that he had much to do with strengthening the administration's views and policy. William H. Springer's article, "Our Present Duty," *North American Review*, December, 1893, is also worth reading for the anti-imperialist viewpoint.

of our commerce, the requirements of our Navy all demand that the United States should not permit the sovereignty of the Hawaiian Islands to pass to any foreign country." Cleveland's entire foreign policy was characterized as "a snail-like policy that confines a nation within its own boundaries" and attention was called to his action relative to Nicaragua in 1885 as indicating a general opposition to the larger national interests of the country.[69]

The fundamental difference between the "snail-like" policy of Cleveland and the wishes of the expansionists was further indicated by Dolph's assertion: "We need an aggressive foreign policy. We need a reaffirmation of the Monroe Doctrine as it is popularly understood, applied not only to the continent of America but to those islands which are situated so near our coast as to be of great commercial and naval importance." America needed a foreign policy which "goes with our citizens and with our flag wherever they may lawfully go, and a policy which would give us a commanding position among the great powers of the world commensurate with our recognized situation and our wealth and power."

At the same time, Senator Hoar introduced resolutions calling upon the President to communicate to the Senate copies of instructions to any representatives or naval officers of the United States since March 4, 1881, relative to the maintenance of public order and the protection of American citizens in Hawaii. The President's policy was criticized and the Senator stated it as his opinion that the message contemplated war upon the existing government of the Islands. The following day, December 6, the resolution was debated, and Hoar declared that if the correspondence requested were submitted, it would show a consistent line of policy for three administrations which the President sought to abandon. The constitutionality of Blount's appointment was questioned, and the dictatorial attitude of the President in ignoring Congress castigated.[70]

Others entered the debate. Senator Vilas suggested that the proposed request was premature in that the President had announced his intention further to review the Hawaiian question. Vilas denounced the actions of the American Minister relative to the revolution as in themselves an act of war upon a friendly power. Senator Gray supported Vilas, while Senators Aldrich and Sherman supported the resolution and Hoar's views. Most active support for the administration came from Senator Mills of Texas, who pointed to the British action in 1843 in restoring

---

[69] *Cong. Rec.*, 53 Cong., 2 sess., 19f. Dolph referred to Cleveland's blocking of a proposed Isthmian canal treaty which had involved a rather unprecedented assertion of American control in Nicaragua.

[70] *Ibid.*, 61f.

Hawaiian sovereignty and repudiating a usurpation by its naval commander, Paulet, as precedent for Cleveland's action. Mills reviewed the revolution as attributable to the depression in Hawaii caused by the Republican McKinley tariff, and he indicated that the annexation resulted from a desire to extend the sugar bounty. With fine sarcasm he questioned, "Is that day coming when along Pennsylvania Avenue we shall see a Hawaiian queen, not loaded with golden chains, but weighted down with sugar sacks on her back, coming to the Congress of the United States pleading in behalf of her poor, miserable, ignorant people for the right that we claim to have come direct from God to us, inalienable in its nature—the right to institute a government for themselves."[71]

The Hoar resolution was agreed to, however, and transmitted to the President. A further step in the program to embarrass the administration was revealed in a second resolution by the Senator. This requested that the Senate be informed whether it was consistent with the public good that a commissioner be appointed to investigate the Hawaiian revolution without reference to the Senate. By this means Hoar attacked the constitutionality of the Blount mission. He called attention to the fact that the appointment of consuls, ambassadors, and "other public ministers" was vested in the President with Senate approval and that section 1674 of the Revised Statutes included "commissioners" among diplomatic officers. Attention was also directed to section 1751, providing that diplomatic officials should not correspond with private persons while engaged in duty, a point aimed at Blount's contacts during his investigation. Following upon this, Hoar indicated that Blount had been paid illegally by the Treasury because he was not appointed according to law. The President was called upon for evidence contradicting these charges.[72]

On December 13 debate on this phase of the resolutions resulted in a strong attack upon the administration by Senator Frye and a defense by Senator Vest. The latter sarcastically commented that the missionaries "have pursued the old New England fashion of taking possession in the name of God, and then dividing out under laws made by themselves." The New England Senator, he affirmed, was, like his friend Minister Stevens, "governed by the great truth that 'the earth belongs to the saints, and we are the saints.'" Vest called attention to the appointment of special agents by the President in connection with the fisheries negotiations as complete justification for such a practice. He denied that

---

[71] *Ibid.*, Cleveland wrote Mills a note of appreciation for "a manly, sincere assertion of true American sentiment."

[72] *Ibid.*, 127f.

force would be used to restore the Queen, and declared the issue at stake was "whether we are to quit now the traditional policy of this country established by Washington and carried out by Jefferson and concurred in by Madison and Jackson and Buchanan, and now by Cleveland, or are we to depart from that policy and now venture upon the great colonial system of the European powers." The resolution was referred to the Committee on Foreign Relations. The intention of the New England Republicans to make an issue of the Hawaiian question was evident.

Following the Hawaiian message, the debate was continued and on December 20 Senator Hoar renewed his charges of unconstitutional action. "If the present claim be allowed," he went on, "it is of no consequence that the Constitution invests in Congress the power to make war or peace." This issue of the presidential ability to dictate foreign policy he declared to be more important by far than the question of annexation.

The same day Senator Morgan secured approval of a resolution providing for a senatorial investigation of the diplomatic and other intercourse "in relation to the recent political revolution in Hawaii." A sub-committee of the Foreign Relations Committee began its work on December 27 with Senators Morgan, Gray, Frye, Sherman, and Butler as its members. Its composition was definitely friendly to the annexation with Gray the only genuine supporter of the administration.[73]

During the period of the Committee's investigation, the Senate was by no means quiet. On January 3, 1894, Senator Frye introduced a resolution providing that, pending the Senate review, there should be no exercise of moral or physical pressure to restore the Queen or maintain the existing government. The resolution was postponed for future consideration, due to objections. Five days later, Senator Turpie introduced a resolution that "from the facts and papers laid before us by the Executive and other sources, it is unwise, inexpedient, and not in accordance with the character and dignity of the United States to consider further at this time either the treaty or project of annexation of the Hawaiian territory to this country; that the Provisional Government therein having been duly recognized, the highest national in-

---

[73] Morgan was an ardent expansionist. While he had assured Gresham that he was with the administration and satisfied with the Blount report which his committee would uphold, it was soon evident that he was "insincere and that he means mischief." See Gresham to Bayard, January 21, 1894, Gresham Papers. Bayard agreed with this judgment. This is in contrast with Senator Vest who defended the President while personally expressing doubts as to the constitutionality of Blount's "paramount" authority. See Vest to Gresham, December 12, 1893, Gresham Papers. Gray felt that Morgan's conduct of the hearings was "very partial" and "unfair."

terests require that it shall pursue its own line of policy. Foreign intervention in the political affairs of these islands will be regarded as an act unfriendly to the Government of the United States."[74]

The following day Senator Chandler introduced a resolution calling upon the Judiciary Committee to report on the constitutionality of the Blount appointment and the general power of the President with regard to selection of special agents without advice and consent of the Senate. This was immediately objected to by Senator Vest as covered by the existing Senate investigation, a viewpoint concurred in by Senator Sherman and the motion was withdrawn.[75]

On January 10 Senator Davis of Minnesota, a member of the Committee on Foreign Relations, delivered a defense of American action in the revolution and denounced the Queen and Commissioner Blount. The following day Senator Turpie defended his resolution, and urged that Hawaii be maintained as an independent power under the protection of the United States. Later in the month, the resolution was the subject of further debate, and attracted considerable fire from the Republicans as implying an endorsement of the President's policy. As a result, action on it proved impossible.[76]

The report of the Senate sub-committee involved two months of hearings and testimony and resulted in a new volume of so-called evidence on the Hawaiian problem. Both Stevens and Blount had appeared before it, as well as various witnesses of the revolution. The testimony of several naval officers was heard and the report provided a rather thorough review of the circumstances connected with the February revolution. Presented on February 26, 1894, and written by chairman Morgan, it contained thirty-six pages of conclusions and a large volume of evidence. The Stevens-Thurston explanation of the revolution was accepted with consequent approval of landing of troops, though it skirted endorsement of the protectorate. It approved the action of Harrison in submitting the treaty and Cleveland's action in its withdrawal. Blount had been appointed legally, and performed his task well, but his conclusions were in error. The President was justified, without the use of force, in endeavoring to restore the Queen. Such an amazing series of contradictions could hardly have secured the complete endorsement of all the committee. Senator Morgan approved it in its entirety. Republicans Sherman, Frye, Dolph, and Davis agreed essentially, but refused to approve the endorsement of Blount and the

---

[74] *Cong. Rec., op. cit.,* 482, 523f.
[75] *Ibid.,* 567f.
[76] *Ibid.,* 621, 694f., 702f. The Turpie resolution was endorsed by the Committee on Foreign Relations.

presidential policy. Democrats Turpie, Butler, Daniel, and Gray did not endorse the approval of Stevens' action, while Butler and Turpie presented a statement approving annexation but not at the expense of internal disorder in Hawaii.[77]

While the Senate had been debating and investigating, the House was not idle. The trend of attack and defense was essentially the same. Representative Hitt introduced resolutions on December 6 calling on the President for information as to the instructions to the American representative in Hawaii. Following the special message, a very bitter debate ensued. In order to embarrass the Republicans, Representative Cochran introduced a resolution calling for an investigation of the powers of the House in connection with the annexation of territory. Boutelle of Maine supported a counter resolution asserting the rights of the House had been invaded by the President's action in sending a secret agent to Hawaii and that any intervention to restore the monarchy was contrary to the traditions of the Republic and the spirit and letter of the Constitution. Despite vigorous objection, it was referred to the Committee on Foreign Affairs.[78]

This was followed by several other miscellaneous resolutions, all of which were designed to embarrass the Democratic leadership, and were countered with success. The majority acted quickly, and by December 21 the Committee on Foreign Affairs had submitted a report sanctioning a resolution condemning the use of American armed forces in the revolution, commending the President, and declaring against annexation or a protectorate, as well as foreign intervention. The Republican minority submitted a report upholding Harrison and denouncing the Cleveland policy.

Formal debate on the majority resolution opened on February 2 with Republicans Hitt, Draper, and Morse leading an attack on the President and utilizing the familiar story of the destruction of the heroic labors of American missionaries who had rescued the Islands from "barbarism, cannibalism and heathenism of the most revolting sort." On February 4 the Republicans sought to force a vote on the resolution specifically endorsing Harrison's policy. It was defeated, as were several counter moves involving long arguments over House rules. Resolutions introduced by Representative McCreary of Kentucky condemning the action of Minister Stevens, approving non-interference and opposing annexation, were adopted by a vote of 177 to 78.[79]

In the Senate, a resolution of Senator Kyle expressing the sense of

---

[77] *Senate Report* No. 227, 53 Cong., 2 sess. But two members, Gray and Daniel, appear to have been opposed thoroughly to annexation.
[78] *Cong. Rec., op. cit.*, 397f. Also *House Reports*, I.
[79] *Cong. Rec.*, 53 Cong., 2 sess., 1814ff., 1849, 1967-68, 2001-2008.

that body as opposed either to the use of force to restore the Queen or the destruction of the existing government met with opposition and on May 31 was replaced with one submitted earlier by Senator Turpie. This latter resolution had the unanimous approval of the Committee on Foreign Relations, and declared that it was the right of the people of Hawaii "to establish and maintain their own form of government and domestic polity; that the United States ought in nowise to interfere therewith; and that any intervention in the political affairs of these islands by any other government will be regarded as an act unfriendly to the United States." The resolution was approved 55 to 0 with thirty members failing to register an opinion.[80]

THE IMPACT OF EVENTS ON HAWAII

Thus ended the period of legislative action on Hawaii. It can hardly be said to have been more satisfactory than the executive handling of the problem. The problem of Hawaii's future was still unsettled, so far as its relations with the United States were concerned. It seemed clear, however, that the majority sentiment in the United States was inclined to view the acquisition of the Islands with favor. It was not inclined, however, to accept control under dubious conditions which left in question the will of the Hawaiians themselves as to their future.

The impact upon Hawaii of all these events crowded into a few short months of hasty treaty making, hot tempered debate, investigation, and charges and counter charges, must now be given attention. It is interesting to note the insistence with which the Hawaiian representatives at Washington held to the idea that annexation or some type of American control would be forthcoming. They refused until the last to believe in the possibility of a policy of complete official nonintervention. Two factors were responsible for this view. In the first place, the Hawaiians realized the utter impossibility of getting along without the United States. On June 13, 1893, Thurston wrote President Dole with some feeling, "The simple fact is that we have got no market for anything except the United States." It was the United States or nothing, he pointed out, and Hawaii must hang on "until the logic of events shows them the utter futility of attempting to run the anomalous combination which is proposed by the protectorate advocates, and until we secure what we want from them or the succeeding administration."[81]

---

[80] *Ibid.*, 5499f. Cleveland was in accord with the Turpie resolution, and especially pleased by its emphasis upon the right of the people to determine their own polity.

[81] See Thurston to Dole in *Memoirs,* 291f.

Another reason was the steadfast belief that the Cleveland administration would not assume an unfriendly attitude, but would eventually give its support to some type of changed relations with Hawaii. This appears to have been encouraged by the indefinite early policy of the administration which left room for all sorts of wishful thinking. Thurston and Castle called on Secretary Gresham on March 10 to learn specifically whether withdrawal of the treaty meant opposition to annexation. Gresham would only say that it was withdrawn for "further consideration," and would provide no more definite statement. The Hawaiian envoys endeavored to impress him with the danger inherent in internal disorder within the Islands and possible foreign intrigue, unless action was hastened.[82] Reporting the same day to President Dole, Thurston expressed his belief that after the rush of office seekers was over, Gresham could be convinced that a government based on a popular plebiscite in Hawaii was impossible and that a protectorate was inadvisable.[83] The Hawaiians also appear to have felt that Mr. Blount as a Southerner would understand the peculiar racial problems in Hawaii and sympathize with the provisional regime.

On June 13 Thurston was still reporting to Dole that the utmost secrecy prevailed as to administration intentions. He wrote, "I believe that Mr. Gresham told me the simple truth when he said that the President did not know what he is going to do himself. I think he wants to do something different from what Mr. Harrison proposed, but what to do or how to do it without committing himself to some course which will eventually rise up to trouble him, he does not know."[84] In this assumption as to the presidential state of mind Thurston was not far wrong for on March 19 the President had written Carl Schurz, "I do not now say I should hold annexation in all circumstances and at any time unwise, but I am sure that we ought to stop and look and think. That is exactly what we are doing now."[85] Secretary Gresham personally and privately was much more definite in his opposition to either

---

[82] *Memoranda of Conversations with the Secretary of State, 1893-1898.*

[83] Cited in Pratt, 128. Thurston appears to have thought the administration would consider a protectorate and also to have leaned heavily on the idea that southern Democrats would understand the difficult position of the white minority in Hawaii. As late as April, J. Mott Smith and C. L. Carter asserted Gresham had no intention of restoring the Queen. It should be noted that even the Harrison administration had been desirous of some plebiscite, and this demand, therefore, did not impress the Hawaiians as hostile.

[84] Thurston to Dole, June 13, 1893, *Memoirs*, 291f.

[85] Cleveland to Schurz, March 19, 1893, Schurz Papers. The President was writing after reading an advance copy of Schurz' article, "Manifest Destiny," for *Harper's Monthly.*

annexation or protectorates anywhere in the Pacific.[86] In the midst of this unsettled state of thinking and partially conflicting administration opinion, it is little wonder that Mr. Thurston was confused.

Evidently the first real sense of disillusionment came in the autumn of 1893 with the definite recommendations of Secretary Gresham to the President following receipt of the Blount report. This revealed clearly the attitude of the State Department and the probable course of the administration. By November 14 Thurston, now acting as Minister, was able to report to Honolulu the results of an irate interview with Secretary Gresham in which the latter had made it clear that newspaper reports were true that the administration viewed favorably the restoration of the monarchy. Thurston was particularly irritated by Gresham's statement that if any bloodshed should result it would be the responsibility of the Provisional Government. The Hawaiian envoy asserted with heat that restoration of the monarchy would only lead to its overthrow again, and denied the right of the United States to thus interfere with Hawaii's internal political structure. Gresham justified intervention on a basis of appeal by the Queen, and the fact that the existing government had no permanence and by its very nature was conditional upon annexation. As to this, Thurston replied that the Provisional Government itself would be the judge.[87]

By this time there was no mistaking the intention of the administration, and the problem of Hawaiian relations shifted into the more regular channels of diplomatic relations. It was evident that annexation might now be a matter of some years.

---

[86] Gresham to Schurz, July 11, 1893, Schurz Papers. Writing with reference to Samoa, Gresham said the United States should not undertake alone or in cooperation with anyone else any protectorate "in the South Sea Islands or elsewhere." Gresham expressed himself at length to Schurz on his opposition to imperialism and his letters indicate the deep moral convictions on the subject which explain his Hawaiian policy.

[87] Thurston to Dole, November 14, 1893, *Memoirs,* 323f.

CHAPTER XI

Annexing a Republic

It is impossible to discount the unhappy situation produced at least temporarily in Hawaii as a result of the failure to achieve annexation, and the following repudiation of all overtures toward closer relations with the United States under the Cleveland administration. When the Cleveland appointed Minister, Albert S. Willis, arrived at Honolulu in November, 1893, he found the city "full of rumors and the excitement is increasing every hour."[1] A little later, he reported the prospective development of a move to organize a republic. The men at the head of this endeavor, he wrote, "are acknowledged by all sides to be of the highest integrity and public spirit." Rumors of possible revolution and disorder persisted throughout the autumn. Willis wrote: "It is impossible to exaggerate the unhappy condition of this people, nor can I in words, picture their pathetic surroundings. Almost every movement is under espionage, the most meaningless expression is given an important significance and speeches are quoted which were never delivered or thought of."[2]

ORGANIZING THE REPUBLIC OF HAWAII

While the storm of debate and propaganda of late 1893 and early 1894 was sweeping the United States as the Hawaiian question was paraded before the Congress and the public, events in the Islands were taking place which transformed the temporary government produced by revolution into a republic. Inevitably, the change was influenced strongly by the background of some three-quarters of a century of American civilization in Hawaii. It was this government which was to provide the stepping-stone for annexation.

On March 15, 1894, a constitutional convention was authorized by the Provisional Government. There is little doubt but that one of the principal factors behind the desire to organize a more permanent governmental structure was the belief that it would improve chances for annexation to the United States. Leaders of the movement were those who had led the Revolution of 1893, and they sought by every means possible to

---

[1] Willis to Gresham, November 6, 1893, *Dispatches,* XXVI.
[2] Willis to Gresham, November 13 and 18, 1893, *op. cit.* See also "The Present Hawaiian Situation," Thrum, 1894.

270

control the organization and development of the republic. The intent of the framers of the proposed constitution was well stated in the letter from Sanford B. Dole to the American political scientist, John W. Burgess, requesting advice in preparing a government with a strong executive, a limited membership in the upper house of the legislature, and other means to keep it "out of the control of the irresponsible element."[3]

With this thought in mind, the convention itself was designed to prevent any undesirable representation of turbulent elements. Its membership was composed of the five members of the Executive Council of the Provisional Government, fourteen members of its Advisory Council, and eighteen elected members. The elected representatives were required to be of Hawaiian, American, or European birth or descent, twenty years of age, taxpayers and residents for one year, and to have taken an oath of allegiance to the Provisional Government and to oppose the re-establishment of monarchy. Under this scheme, six native Hawaiians were members of the convention, together with seven persons of English extraction and three of Portuguese. All the others were of American descent. The principal objective of the voting arrangement was, of course, to prevent any possibility of Asiatic control.

The basic task of the convention, which met late in May, was to convert the same principle of control by the "responsible" element into an actual frame of government. The inalienable rights and cherished freedoms and liberties of English and American origin were all guaranteed by the new document. Executive power was vested in an Executive Council headed by the President and his Cabinet of four members. This was termed by Dole "a distinguishing feature" of the Republic of Hawaii in that the advantages of presidential direction were maintained and yet some of the features of English limitation of executive power retained. Members of the Cabinet were *ex-officio* members of both houses of the legislature without voting rights. "The result of this system," wrote Dole in 1897, "is that the power of the President is surrounded with more checks and balances than in the United States system, while he is not so shorn of powers as to become a mere figurehead relinquishing to a responsible Cabinet the administration of affairs with the logical result of such an arrangement of oft recurring efforts

[3] Henry M. Madden (ed.), "Letters of Sanford B. Dole and John W. Burgess," *Pacific Historical Review*, V. Dole and Lorrin Thurston were principal authors of the ultimate constitution. Donald W. Rowland, "The Establishment of the Republic of Hawaii, 1893-1894," *Pacific Historical Review*, IV, has many details. See also Sanford B. Dole, "The Constitution," Thrum, 1898, for an analysis by one of the authors of the document.

by the Legislature to unseat the Ministers." A six year term without the privilege of immediate succession was provided the President.

The legislative branch was composed of two houses of fifteen elected members each. Membership in the lower branch was encumbered with a one thousand dollar property ownership provision, or a six hundred dollar money income for the year previous to election. Members of the Senate were required to own three times as much property, or possess an income of twelve hundred dollars. Voters for a member of the Senate were required to own fifteen hundred dollars worth of real property, to have personal property worth three thousand dollars, or a money income of six hundred dollars for the year prior to exercise of the suffrage. Both voters and office holders were required to take an oath to support the Constitution of the Republic of Hawaii, and careful literacy qualifications were set up designed largely to bar Asiatics from the suffrage.[4]

The obvious purpose behind the establishment of the conservative Republic was the organization of such a government as would hold the turbulent racial and other forces in Hawaii in check until better relations could be established with the United States. The correspondence of President Dole with Lorrin Thurston indicates that the original theory of the latter that Hawaii must "hang on" until a change of opinion in the United States would permit annexation was never seriously modified. The constitution itself provided for a treaty of commercial and political union with the United States. It was with this thought behind its framing that the new constitution was proclaimed without reference to a popular vote and placed in operation on July 4, 1894.[5]

AMERICAN REACTIONS TO THE REPUBLIC

The relations of the United States with the Republic during the remainder of the Cleveland administration were upon a somewhat peculiar basis. In many ways the State Department appeared to seek to ignore Hawaii, although not always successful in this policy. On June 2, 1894, the text of the Senate resolution of May 31 declaring that the people of Hawaii had the right to establish their own form of government without interference from the United States or any other outside source was transmitted to Minister Willis by Secretary Gresham. "This declaration that the people of the Islands have the right to establish and main-

---

[4] See Donald Rowland, "Orientals and the Suffrage in Hawaii," *Pacific Historical Review,* XVII.

[5] See Donald Rowland, "The Establishment of the Republic of Hawaii, 1893-1894," *op. cit.* Rowland declares, "The frame of government devised effectually carried out the object of the party which sponsored it, which was to insure effective control until annexation could be attained."

tain such institutions as they think best adapted to their wants is entirely satisfactory to the President," wrote Gresham.[6] Throughout the remainder of the year completely noncommittal replies were forthcoming to information from Minister Willis relative to developments in Hawaii.

A rather grudging recognition was accorded the newly born Republic patterned so closely after the early American theory of aristocratic republicanism. At the same time, though unofficially, partisans of the deposed Queen were given audience in Washington.[7]

News of the political evolution going forward in Hawaii was received in the United States with varying comment. It was generally recognized from the beginning that whatever government was set up would represent the interests of the minority behind the Revolution of 1893. This provoked rather acid comment from the anti-annexationists and met with little defense from its proponents. The *Providence Journal* in late June declared, "Though the government they are now engaged in establishing may be called a republic, it is evidently enough going to be a small oligarchy based on property."[8] The *Nation* contemptuously referred to the Dole regime as "the most rascally and illegitimate little state in the whole world." The *New York Times* commented, "We have no doubt they have got a better form of government than they [the natives] preferred, but they did not establish it and it is not republican except in name only."[9]

The case for the Dole government was most fully presented in the United States through the columns of the *Independent* by the indefatigable Reverend Sereno Bishop, who reported the work of the constitutional convention as that of patriots of the highest degree. He defended minority control as rule by those "sufficiently enlightened to have a voice in the destiny of the country." The natives were pictured as thriftless, and "unreflecting and deeply in bondage to their Kahuna sorcerers." This was not too flattering a picture of the results of long years of American missionary endeavor.[10]

The full story of the nature of the new government arrived in the United States in late July and did not excite much comment. The *New*

---

[6] Gresham to Willis, June 2, 1894, *Instructions*, III.

[7] In August, 1894, Messrs. Cummins, Widemann, and Parker visited Washington in the interest of the Queen. A statement from the President was read them which absolutely denied "the least future or present aid or encouragement" to any effort to restore "any government heretofore existing in the Hawaiian Islands." Gresham, however, assured them the United States would not oppose any plans they might work out and thus, perhaps, indirectly encouraged their revolutionary designs. Withdrawal of all naval forces at Honolulu also pleased the Queen's partisans. See *Memoranda of Conversations with the Secretary of State, 1893-1898.*

[8] Cited *Literary Digest*, June 23, 1894.

[9] September 6, 1894.

[10] *Independent*, July 6, 1894.

York Herald expressed a rather common view when it declared, "We greet this new Republic of the Pacific, and trust that its birth will prove the final doom of the jingo annexation folly."[11] Its recognition was viewed by opponents of the President as proof of the utter failure of his original policy. The *Washington Star* asserted, "Mr. Cleveland has virtually acknowledged the error of the course pursued by his Administration in the Hawaiian matter by finally doing all that he was ever asked to do, and that was to give recognition to a government that was as properly constituted as any government ever was."[12] The *Independent* affirmed, "The Republic of Hawaii is now confessedly under the protection of the American Republic and we doubt if President Cleveland would do one thing to prevent before the end of his term of office a treaty of annexation."[13]

INTERNAL DIFFICULTIES OF THE REPUBLIC

At Honolulu itself the cauldron of intrigue and rumors boiled vigorously during the period prior to the inauguration of the new Republic. Threats of revolution were persistent early in 1894, though they quieted somewhat upon receipt of news of the Senate non-intervention resolution. During this period the relations of Minister Willis with the Provisional Government were upon anything but a cordial basis and sharp interchange of notes occurred. Here again matters improved with news of the Senate's action. American naval commanders reported at frequent intervals upon their conception of the dangers from foreign intrigue inherent in the restless political and racial situation in the Islands. Great Britain continued to be the perennial scapegoat. It is significant in the light of later developments, however, that the growing influx of Japanese into Hawaii began by this date to give rise to fears of its consequences.[14]

Temporary quiet following the establishment of the new government in July, 1894, was followed by new threats to the peace of the Islands in the form of plotting by royalists to restore the monarchy. As usual in Hawaii, it was impossible to keep anything secret. A revolutionary *coup* planned for January 7, 1895, was precipitated the preceding evening by the discovery by police of an armed band of revolutionists on

---

[11] Cited *Public Opinion*, July 26.
[12] August 10, 1894.
[13] September 3, 1894.
[14] See especially reports of Admiral Walker to the Secretary of the Navy in April, 1894, when he wrote, "Many people here, both in and out of the Government, think the Japanese possess a source of future danger." *Senate Executive Documents,* 53 Cong., 3 sess., I. The number of Japanese in Hawaii increased from 12,360 in 1890 to 24,407 in 1896, outnumbering the Chinese.

Waikiki Beach. Desultory fighting followed, martial law was proclaimed, and many suspects arrested. The revolt shortly was under control but provoked an outburst of intense feeling. The *Pacific Commercial Advertiser* demanded the full penalty of the law for the treasonable conspirators and accused the Queen of at least indirect complicity, asserting she should be banished.[15] The *Hawaiian Star* assumed a similar attitude and declared the rebels should be hunted down and killed or captured. The leaders should be shot.[16] This rather hysterical feeling was shortly calmed and replaced with one of confidence that the Republic had firmly demonstrated its power and was now secure. "There is now in power a strong, intelligent and just Government that has stood fiery test. Its purposes are to maintain law locally and to effect closer union with the United States," editorialzed the *Star* on March 10. Minister Willis maintained an attitude of detachment and as a result won the respect of the leaders of the Republic.

PRESIDENTIAL POLICY TOWARD HAWAII

This situation was bound to produce reverberations in the United States. News of what had taken place reached the State Department on January 19 and at an informal Cabinet meeting it was decided to make the Willis dispatch public. A later conference decided upon ordering the *U.S.S. Philadelphia* to Honolulu at once. News of the affair flashed over the country on January 20. President Cleveland made public the same day a statement announcing there was no cause for alarm and emphasizing that Hawaii was an entirely independent power. The sending of a naval vessel, the President said, must not be taken as indicating a change in policy. The instructions to Admiral Beardslee were also made public and contained a strong order to "extend no aid or support, moral or physical, to any of the parties" engaged in the civil disturbance. Any American citizen participating in the insurrection was warned of loss of citizenship.[17]

Further repercussions resulted from the ill-fated revolt. By the end of January wholesale trials of suspects were in progress in Honolulu and two allegedly American citizens active in Island politics were sentenced to death and another to life imprisonment. The Republic was

---

[15] See editorials on January 8 and 9. The revolt was reported to Washington by Willis in a dispatch dated January 11. See Willis to Gresham, January 11, 1895, enclosing copies of Hawaiian newspapers, *Dispatches*, XXVII. See also article, "Brief Record of the Rebellion," Thrum, 1896.

[16] January 8 editorial. The *Hawaiian Star* began publication in March, 1893, as an annexation advocate.

[17] See *New York Times*, January 20 and 21. The *Philadelphia* was requested by the Hawaiian Minister.

adopting a policy of ruthless extermination of the opposition. Further claims as to complicity of the former Queen were advanced and a store of bombs was alleged to have been found at her home. On January 16 she was arrested and forced to sign a complete abdication as the price for clemency for herself and associates. These developments were reported to the State Department by Willis, and produced quick instructions to protect to the fullest extent the rights of all who claimed American citizenship. The efforts of Minister Willis to do so produced a certain amount of irritation at Honolulu.

Late in February Secretary Gresham requested Willis to present a vigorous protest at Honolulu against "certain acts of its representatives in the United States of which this government has just cause to complain." Minister Thurston had given to the press on February 13 an interview in which he permitted the use of quotations from his correspondence accusing Willis of "unwarranted interference" with the conduct of the treason trials and harassing the government. A further and even more irritating statement was: "An analysis of the growth of the feeling and facts leading up to the insurrection showed that it is based almost wholly on the encouragement given to the royalists by President Cleveland and his announced and constantly reiterated opinion that the Queen ought to be restored, and a feeling which, rightly or wrongly, was disseminated throughout the royalist sympathizers, that upon the slightest opportunity Cleveland would take occasion to assist the royalists if they could get control to a sufficient extent to give him an excuse for so doing."[18] Thurston had acknowledged the impropriety of his statements verbally but had refused to present a written apology.

On February 25 Gresham was impelled to call the attention of the Hawaiian Government to the fact that some thirteen American citizens were still held in prison without charges or trial. Willis was instructed to insist that proper trials or immediate release be granted these persons. The entire problem of their citizenship was complicated by the fact that many persons had taken a voluntary oath of allegiance to the Constitution of 1887, as required by it, without renouncing American citizenship.[19] This tender situation was eased in July when the Republic

---

[18] Gresham to Willis, February 21, 1895, *Instructions*, III. The dispatch included the Thurston statement. Thurston also charged that arms for the revolutionists were furnished by San Francisco filibusterers. Thurston was recalled ultimately and replaced by Francis M. Hatch.

[19] The Constitution of 1887 had required an oath of allegiance as a suffrage condition. The State Department interpreted this at that time as not constituting a surrender of American citizenship. In connection with the somewhat similar oath required in 1894, Secretary Gresham had ruled to the contrary. This left the entire matter of citizenship in some confusion. The controversy over the rights of alleged American citizens was prolonged until the spring of 1895 after which it subsided.

suspended or commuted the sentences of a number of alleged conspirators. In September, and again on January 1, 1896, similar action was taken on others, including a full pardon for Liliuokalani.

The difficulties in Hawaii inevitably had their effect upon opinion and action in the United States. The question of official recognition of the new Hawaiian Republic received attention in the House, though it appears not to have merited Senatorial debate. On July 20, 1894, Representative Boutelle of Maine introduced a resolution demanding immediate recognition. The matter was referred to the Committee on Foreign Affairs where it occasioned some bitter wrangling between the Democratic majority and the Republican minority. Chairman McCreary announced on August 9 to the House that recognition was being extended. Boutelle took advantage of the opportunity to deliver an intemperate speech attacking the administration so vigorously as to lead to his suppression by Speaker Crisp.[20]

Withdrawal of American naval units in 1894 opened the way for another effort of the Republicans to embarrass the administration. On December 22, 1894, Senator Henry Cabot Lodge introduced a resolution calling upon the Secretary of the Navy to furnish information on the reasons for removing naval vessels from Hawaiian waters, and whether it was consistent with the interests of the United States. The correspondence of Admiral Walker, which rather unwisely had been made public, was used to indicate belief that a Royalist uprising was pending and that British interests in Hawaii were being aided by the administration policy.[21] When, on January 9, 1895, President Cleveland sent a special message urging Congressional assent to a lease of Necker Island by Hawaii to Great Britain as required by the Treaty of 1887, further impetus was given to this latter charge. Use of the Island was desired by the British as a cable station.

News of the January, 1895, uprising added further fuel to the flame and provoked a general renewal of debate in Congress on the entire Hawaiian policy. In the House at two o'clock on the afternoon of January 19, the fiery Boutelle seized the opportunity for a tirade against the President, charging him with indirect responsibility for the uprising. Objections were raised by Democratic members to the tenor of his remarks and considerable disorder ensued. Resolutions were introduced by Representatives Boutelle and Hitt deprecating the revolt and extending sympathy to the Republic, as well as urging an American

[20] *New York Times,* August 10, 1894.
[21] *Cong. Rec.,* 53 Cong., 3 sess., 555.

naval force for its protection. To it was added an objection to the use of any Hawaiian territory for any purpose by a foreign power.[22] On January 21 Breckinridge of Kentucky introduced a resolution declaring that the sense of the House was favorable to annexation. Resolutions of sympathy and requests to the President to submit all diplomatic correspondence connected with the insurrection were introduced. More important, as indicating the under current of opinion in Congress, was a resolution adopted on February 1 requesting the President to transmit any information on British activity in Hawaii promoting or aiding the revolt.[23] Whether these reiterations of British designs on Hawaii were sincere or merely put forward for their propaganda value it is impossible to determine. They were without foundation.

A similar furor was aroused in the Senate. On January 19 Senator Kyle introduced a resolution asserting the revolt had been encouraged by the policy of the administration and its withdrawal of naval forces. It demanded that a naval vessel be sent at once to Honolulu.[24] Senator Faulkner introduced resolutions of sympathy for the Republic. Two days later Senator Lodge asserted his belief that the American people "intend to take those islands and they will do so just as soon as they have an Administration which will not thwart their desires in that respect." Lodge introduced a resolution approving dispatch of a naval vessel to Hawaii, demanding a cable to the Islands, and declaring "immediate steps should be taken to secure possession of the Sandwich Islands by their annexation to the United States."[25] Under objection from Senator Vest the motion was postponed for future consideration.

Continued insinuations were made by Senators Frye, Aldrich, and Hawley that there had been a presidential conspiracy with the royalist representatives who had visited the United States the preceding August. Efforts to prove this, and that the withdrawal of naval forces had been intended to encourage the revolt against the Republic, led to a warm defense of the President's Hawaiian policy by Senator Gray. The Senator read in full the President's statement, and attacked vigorously those who sought to embroil the nation in the internal affairs of Hawaii. Senator George likewise delivered a scathing indictment of the Republic as aristocratic and out of touch with the will of the majority of the people in Hawaii. Senator Lodge took advantage of the occasion to return to his favorite theme of rapidly expanding British interests which were endangering the naval and commercial position of the United States in the Pacific.

---

[22] *Ibid.*, 1158f. This was provoked by the Necker Island proposal.
[23] *New York Tribune,* February 5.
[24] *Cong. Rec., op. cit.,* 1133.
[25] *Ibid.*, 1167.

The remarks of Senators Gray and Lodge were in particular contrast and highlighted the opposing policies at issue so thoroughly as to deserve citation. Senator Gray with deep sincerity declared: "I do not believe that the policy, the traditions or true interests of this country are consistent with annexation. I believe our policy is a continental one, and that we are not called upon by anything in our past history to step off this continent in a career of colonial aggrandizement."[26] Lodge countered with the statement: "I do not mean that we should enter on a widely extended system of colonization. . . . But I do mean that we should take all outlying territories necessary to our own defense, to the protection of the Isthmian Canal, to the upbuilding of our trade and commerce and to the maintenance of our military safety everywhere. I would take and hold the outworks as we now hold the citadels of American power."

On January 24 Senator Allen, Nebraska Populist, introduced a resolution affirming support of annexation. Senator Vest sponsored a counter resolution calling for absolute non-interference in Hawaiian affairs and on January 26 by a vote of 24 to 22, with 39 not voting, it was adopted. For the second time the Senate had declared for a policy of non-intervention in Hawaii.

While the annexation issue was under discussion, the possible construction of a cable to Honolulu again came to the front. On February 9, 1895, the regular appropriation bill for the consular and diplomatic services was amended in the Senate to provide $500,000 for this purpose, reviving a proposition dating back into the preceding decade and close to the hearts of those who sought to attach the Islands to the United States. The House refused to concur, however, and the Senate yielded the point thus blocking a further gesture toward closer contact with Hawaii. There is little doubt the President would have vetoed the measure. He had written Bayard at London, expressing his belief that cable building would strengthen the "annexation craze" and promote further departure "from our traditions."[27] Thus perished the last prospect for the closer union of Hawaii with the United States under Grover Cleveland.

THE AMERICAN PRESS AND HAWAII IN 1895

The somewhat spectacular developments in Hawaii surrounding the abortive revolt likewise aroused once more public controversy as to American policy. Supporters of the administration tended to minimize

---

[26] *Ibid.*, 1205f. President Cleveland held to similar views of course.
[27] Allan Nevins, *Letters of Grover Cleveland*, 377.

significance of the attempted revolt. The *New York Times* characterized it as a "Sunday afternoon riot" and denounced those who attempted to exaggerate its importance.[28] The opportunity was seized and exploited, however, by the proponents of annexation to promote sympathy for the Republic and undermine the Cleveland policy of non-intervention. The *New York Tribune* Washington correspondent wrote on January 20, "The sullen and peevish Hawaiian policy of President Cleveland and Secretary Gresham, long condemned and discredited by public opinion and barely tolerated by the Democratic leaders in Congress, has at last been openly confessed a failure by its Quixotic and self-deluded authors." Editorially the *Tribune* took up the same theme. "The Hawaiian rebellion is one of the logical consequences of the Cleveland conspiracy against civilization and progress in the Pacific Islands," it declared. "The revolutionary outbreak in the interests of the barbarous Queen would never have occurred if the Administration at Washington had not championed her cause with passionate fervor and indiscreet partisanship, and done everything in its power to weaken and discredit the Dole Government," it continued. Similar charges were echoed by the vociferous *Independent*.[29]

The debate in Congress was followed closely in the press. Partisans of annexation gave much space to the speeches of Lodge and others, praising their stand. The final reassertion of non-intervention was termed by the *New York Tribune* as "cautious and non-committal," and made possible only by Senator Pettigrew's desertion of Republican ranks.[30] Supporters of the administration were critical of the Congressional advocates of annexation, as might be expected, and returned to the usual charge of jingoism. A somewhat more sordid motive was insinuated as behind the New England support of the Republic when the *New York Evening Post* presented a letter from Hawaii which asserted that the Republic had issued depreciated bonds which had been purchased in considerable quantity by New England friends of Hawaii and now motivated their political actions.[31] "Christianity and a profit of 75%," was suggested as a motto for the New England Senators.

Activities of the expansionists in the Senate provoked increasing criticism from several Democratic and independent newspapers. The

[28] January 20, 1895.
[29] January 24, 1895.
[30] January 27, 1895.
[31] See *Evening Post*, January 21 and 22, 1895; also *New York Times* of January 22 and 24. In the Senate charges that the Sugar Trust was behind the annexation drive were presented by Senator Mills. Publicly at least, annexation was opposed by the Trust, and there is no evidence indicating any secret support. Eastern refiners were not interested in Hawaiian sugar.

Springfield Republican expressed its disgust at the "barking" of Lodge and suggested there were more important problems which might well occupy the mind of the junior Senator from Massachusetts. The annexationists were denounced by the *Boston Herald* as "Hawaiio-Americans." The *Baltimore Sun* called attention to the fact that problems of the tariff and currency vital to the national welfare were by-passed in favor of tirades on Hawaii and "sham convulsions over a domestic brawl."[32]

Following the second official assertion of the intention of the United States not to interfere in the internal affairs of Hawaii, there emerged a period of decided calm in Hawaiian-American relations. Hawaii almost entirely deserted the editorial pages of American newspapers during 1895 and only occasional news dispatches appear. These were devoted in the main to the usual crop of wild rumors, including in October a story that the Sugar Trust was sponsoring a filibustering expedition against the Republic.[33] Another claimed that the former Queen was about to marry a Japanese nobleman to promote Japanese intervention in her behalf.[34] None of these were taken seriously. Those who opposed annexation were content to leave well enough alone, while the ardor of its proponents had been shattered on the rock of Cleveland's stern opposition. Indirectly, however, the administration gave a boost to Hawaii's economic dependence upon the United States through the Wilson-Gorman tariff in 1894. This abolished the sugar bounty and restored the tariff on sugar importations, thus reacting very favorably for Hawaii which regained the original advantages of reciprocity.

INTEREST IN HAWAII QUICKENS

During 1896 there was a noticeable quickening of the current of Hawaiian affairs. This was due in part to the election and the prospect of some change in American policy. A factor of greater importance was certain internal developments in Hawaii. As has been noted, as early as 1894 Admiral Walker had called attention to the Japanese problem in the Islands. On January 5, 1895, Minister Willis noted the increasing importation of Japanese goods as well as growing immigration of Japanese labor as the result of the organization of several immigration companies in Japan.[35]

---

[32] Opinions cited in *New York Times,* January 24 and 25, 1895.
[33] *New York Times,* October 10, 1895.
[34] *Ibid.,* July 8. This report was also circulated in Honolulu. Such rumors were common in Hawaiian politics.
[35] Willis to Gresham, January 5, 1895, *Dispatches,* XXV.

Following the immigration convention of 1886 between Hawaii and Japan, which had been dictated by the need for greater supplies of cheap labor and the desire to offset Chinese predominance, the expansion of Japanese population had been rapid. At the time of the agreement, the Japanese in the Islands totalled a few hundred; by 1896 they numbered 24,407, or nearly one-fourth the population, and were increasing steadily. The Japanese Government was more and more sensitive to the suffrage and other rights of its nationals and demanded enfranchisement of Japanese in Hawaii as early as March, 1893. This situation was becoming a threatening one, causing alarm both in the Islands and in the United States. The need for Japanese labor in Hawaii was very great as the low price of sugar necessitated cheap labor from some source. Efforts were made to return to the use of Portuguese labor, while others toyed even with the idea of importing American negroes, Italians, British Indians, or even Armenians. The possibility of attracting American farmer immigrants was given consideration. In 1895 a Land Act was passed opening the public domain of Hawaii to homesteading, hoping thereby to attract farmers from the United States.

The year 1897 became a momentous one in the relations of the United States with Hawaii and a climax to the period of uncertainty which had existed more or less continuously since 1893. While business conditions had improved somewhat and political quiet reigned, the leaders of the Republic had not lost sight of their ultimate goal—annexation. The return of the Republican Party to power in Washington encouraged a definite resurgence in the agitation for annexation in Hawaii. It coincided with increased threats to the internal security of the Islands from the Japanese, as well as the ever present problem of possible revision of American tariff policy, with disastrous consequences for reciprocity.

The resulting insecurity encouraged increased dependence upon annexation as Hawaii's only salvation. The problems of labor, immigration, and land which had confronted the Republic were unsolved. Expressions of opinion favorable to annexation increased. The *Hawaiian Star* on January 11, 1897, declared, "It is either annexation or a feeble state that is anybody's meat. . . ." Thomas C. Hobson characterized the expansion of the Japanese as an "invasion" which threatened American interests. He wrote: "The people of the United States in view of the vast commercial interests, can ill afford to stand by and see this continue. For the safety of American capital and civilization, Hawaii must have closer political relations with the United States."[36]

---

[36] See article in Thrum, 1898; also William A. Russ, Jr., "Hawaiian Labor and Immigration Problems Before Annexation," *Journal of Modern History*, X.

The continued preponderance of American capital and enterprise in Hawaii must be rated as one of the vital factors in touching the nerve of national interest in the United States. On the eve of annexation American investors dominated the Hawaiian sugar industry and the general commercial and business life of the Islands. Out of the total capitalization of $36,841,690 for all sugar plantations, $21,700,689 was controlled by Americans and another $4,408,477 by Hawaiian-born Americans. Of forty sugar corporations with a capital stock of $28,224,300, four representing stock worth $13,800,000 were owned entirely by Californians. With other incidental holdings, it was estimated that Californians owned fifty-nine per cent of the stock of all the Hawaiian sugar companies. It was estimated that Americans also owned $2,250,907 of the $3,556,596 in trading goods in Honolulu.[37]

HAWAII FACES INTERNAL CRISIS

An Annexation Club had been organized at Honolulu by January, 1897, with monthly meetings to push the project. Early in February the State Department was informed of the "considerable activity" of the annexationists, and that A. S. Hartwell had left for Washington to promote the objective. Minister Hatch already was working assiduously to promote sentiment in Washington.[38]

Matters were brought to a head by the further sharp controversy with Japan. In March, 1897, the Hawaiian authorities refused admission to a group of Japanese immigrants. Tokyo officials, their ego inflamed by victory in the Sino-Japanese War, were irritated also by Hawaiian duties on Japanese *sake* designed to curb its use. Vigorous protests were lodged at Honolulu, and in May a Japanese naval vessel, the *Naniwa,* was dispatched to Hawaii with representatives of the government, the immigration companies, and the Japanese press on board. Rumors of war at Honolulu were as "thick as creditors around the Government building on pay day," according to a contemporary account. Stories were rife that the *Naniwa* had on board arms and a force of men who, in cooperation with Japanese residents who had seen military service in their homeland, would attack the Islands.

The new Minister for the McKinley administration was Harold M. Sewall, experienced in Pacific diplomacy. He was impelled to report upon the situation as having assumed "a serious aspect." Irritation and strong feeling has developed," he wrote. The tone of the Japanese

---

[37] Thrum, 1898.
[38] Mills to Olney, February 3 and 9, 1897, *Dispatches,* XXVIII. Minister Willis died early in January.

Minister in interviews was very strong. In a statement to the *Pacific Commercial Advertiser* the Minister emphasized that Japan demanded only "fairness and justice." "If she cannot get it—well, I do not know what will follow," he enigmatically declared. The possibility of arbitration was scouted as applicable in "small matters" but never "where the honor of a nation is at stake."[39] Some Hawaiian officials appear not to have been averse to continuing the controversy as a means of arousing American support for annexation.

THE ANNEXATION TREATY OF 1897

It was in the midst of this critical situation that a treaty for the annexation of Hawaii was completed. On April 5, 1897, Secretary Sherman had been informed by the Hawaiian Minister that the Hawaiian Government had the "most earnest desire that action might be taken by the Government of the United States in the matter of the annexation of Hawaii at the earliest moment." Attention was called to the fact that the Hawaiian Constitution specifically mandated such a procedure and that the Hawaiian Legislature on May 27, 1896, unanimously had adopted a resolution favoring the move. Furthermore, "in view of the momentous character of the questions likely to arise at any moment in Hawaii," there should be no delay.[40] This could refer, of course, only to the difficulty with Japan, a memorandum on which also was submitted to the State Department by Hatch five days later. At an earlier date an attempt appears to have been made to play on the old British menace theme.

The administration was not entirely unprepared for such a proposition because as early as March Senator Frye and former Secretary of State John W. Foster, as well as Minister Hatch and W. O. Smith, had all approached the President relative to annexation and found a much more friendly attitude prevalent in administration quarters than

---

[39] Sewall to Sherman, June 20, 1897, *Dispatches,* XXIX. See also enclosures from the *Pacific Commercial Advertiser.* Minister Buck from Tokyo informed the State Department of his belief that the Japanese Government desired to proceed cautiously despite considerable journalistic excitement and bombast. Naval vessels, he felt, had been sent to quiet clamor at home for vigorous action. Japan hesitated to push matters if for no other reason because it might foster annexation to the United States. See dispatch dated April 12, 1897, *Dispatches, Japan,* LXX. See *Literary Digest,* May 22, 1897, for citations from the Japanese press urging strong action. Same for June 26. "Japan has made her entry upon the world's stage in the Chinese war, and she may not shrink from asserting her rights," declared one Japanese paper, giving a clue to the influences behind her policy at this date.
[40] Hatch to Sherman, April 5, 1897, *Notes, Hawaii,* IV.

had been true under Cleveland.[41] Foster had visited Hawaii late in 1896, and returned fully devoted to annexation lest the Islands fall under British or Japanese control. Both President McKinley and his Secretary of State, John Sherman, appear to have shifted from at least a lukewarm attitude on annexation to one more favorable. There can be little doubt that from the American as well as from the Hawaiian standpoint, the threatening situation with relation to Japan was decisive in hastening action. Early in 1897 Hawaii had further enraged that power by returning numerous emigrants as illegal colonists.

Equally decisive, and apparently even more pressing as a factor hastening the submission of the annexation treaty, was the relation of the pending tariff to Hawaiian reciprocity. As early as May 31 it became evident that the continuance of the Reciprocity Treaty was a stumbling block to formulating the sugar schedule in the all important new tariff bill.[42] Efforts on June 10 to divorce extension of the treaty from the problem of framing the sugar schedules failed, and on the 12th the problem was tossed into the caucus of Senate Republicans. According to newspaper accounts, Senators Nelson of Minnesota and Thurston of Nebraska favored complete abrogation of the Hawaiian reciprocity agreement. Indefinite continuation of reciprocity and a remission of one-third the duty on Hawaiian sugar were other alternatives. So serious was the disagreement that it proved impossible to report a plan.[43] The Sugar Trust interests were reported to be definitely opposed to reciprocity, as were the beet sugar growers of the West and South.

Rumors of a possible solution through submission of an annexation treaty appeared in the press as early as June 12. Press accounts on June 16 reported that the sugar schedule had been completed but that the question of what to do about Hawaiian sugar had not been solved. It is interesting to note that while on June 15 the press reported definitely that no action on an annexation treaty was expected, President McKinley, absent from Washington on a brief trip, returned and following a Cabinet meeting rushed the annexation treaty, which had been drafted in May, to the Senate. According to the *New York Tribune* of June 17, and the explanation seems entirely adequate, "The desire of the President to relieve the tension both in Congress and in the

[41] See Pratt, 215ff., for valuable citations from Hawaiian archival sources. W. O. Smith had arrived in Washington early in March with a commission and instructions to negotiate an annexation treaty.

[42] *New York Tribune,* May 31, 1897. The *Tribune* is a very valuable source for this subject through its Washington correspondence. See also the *Independent.*

[43] *Ibid.,* June 13. *Independent,* June 17. The Minnesota and Nebraska Senators, of course, expressed the hostility of the rapidly growing American beet sugar industry to reciprocity.

islands themselves over the prospect of an exclusion of Hawaiian products from the American market, and that alone, was, in brief, the
controlling factor in to-day's sudden decision."[44]

Interestingly enough, it was John W. Foster who was entrusted
with drafting the treaty. Prepared earlier, evidently without thought
of immediate presentation, it was sent to the Senate on June 16 with
an accompanying message of support from both the President and
Secretary Sherman. The President reviewed the history of American
relations with Hawaii to justify the conclusion that annexation was a
logical and legitimate step rather than a new departure in foreign policy.
Stress was placed on the fact that the stability of the Republic based
on the people's will had been demonstrated since 1893.

The drafting of the treaty had offered no difficulties in view of the
fact that it differed in no major way from the ill-fated treaty of 1893,
other than the absence of any provision for the indemnification of the
former Queen. Reported favorably by the Committee on Foreign Relations July 14 with a resolution supporting ratification, no action was
possible in view of the conclusion of the session.[45] Opposition from beet
sugar Senators from the South and West was reported. Quick approval
apparently was not expected or even desired by the administration or
annexation supporters. "We are in no hurry; we can wait," was the
sentiment of friends of the treaty. "So without haste, without com-
pulsion, without pressure, we accept, but do not ask the annexation of
Hawaii. We accept the sons of our own noblest Christian patriots who
gave Hawaii its civilization and institutions," editorialized the *Independent* on June 24, 1897.

JAPAN AND THE ANNEXATION TREATY

Submission of the annexation treaty brought the Japanese difficulty
to a head in a short time. News of the treaty produced "general re-

---

[44] See also "Washington Letter" of Janet Jennings in the *Independent* for June
17 and 24. Janet Jennings was a pioneer in modern political gossip columning and
on the 17th reported that the beet sugar trust, in which Claus Spreckels was a
now dominant influence, was making a strong drive against reciprocity but that
Senate Republicans were fearful of the consequences. On June 24, she reported:
"But when the sugar schedule was reached and the tariff involved, in fact threatened, the abrogation of the Treaty between Hawaii and the United States, the
President at once came to the rescue and saved the Treaty of Reciprocity by the
Treaty of Annexation. Senators who are not especially in favor of annexation,
nevertheless withdrew all opposition to free sugar from Hawaii when assured of
the President's readiness to act promptly, and send in the Treaty of Annexation
even before any further progress on the Tariff." Hatch informed H. E. Cooper
on July 1. "Nothing however is more certain than this—that our sugars would
have been put on the dutiable list if the President had not come forward with
annexation."

[45] *Senate Executive Journal*, 55 Cong., 230. *Senate Report*, No. 681, 55 Cong.,
2 sess., has the text of the treaty, and the messages.

joicing" in Hawaii and was felt to have produced an amelioration of the tone of Japanese presentations.[46] On July 10 Secretary Sherman forwarded Minister Sewall instructions to watch the situation with the greatest care and, if any display of force was attempted by the Japanese, to consult with local authorities and the naval commander. If necessary, he was authorized to announce a provisional protectorate pending annexation. Sewall was informed, however, that this contingency was not expected and that he should use "discreet offices to promote resort to arbitration in every practicable and friendly way."[47]

In Washington, the Japanese Minister, uninformed of the proposed treaty negotiation, presented a vigorous protest as soon as he became aware of it. On June 28 Minister Buck at Tokyo transmitted a verbal note presented by Count Okuma on June 21 noting that Japan had "learned with surprise" of the treaty and viewed it with grave concern. This concern was based on three grounds—the fact that it disturbed radically the *status quo* in the Pacific, endangered Japanese treaty rights in Hawaii, and complicated settlement of existing difficulties with that government. The Count questioned as to whether "mischievous reports and rumors" as to Japanese desires had caused the hasty action of the United States. If so he wished "emphatically and categorically to deny that they have ever, at any time, entertained any designs whatever against the integrity or sovereignty of Hawaii." Buck indicated that the announcement of the treaty had "caused much surprise and considerable excitement" in the Japanese press. "The sentiment generally expressed is one of surprised regret rather than anger," he reported.[48]

Tension continued for some months and Buck reported in September from Tokyo that the Japanese press and people continued excited though government officials appeared desirous of amicable settlement of Hawaiian claims. In October, however, he noted growing impatience at the long delay and a desire for speedy arbitration of all claims. The Minister enclosed a statement from the English edition of *The Japan*

---

[46] Sewall to Sherman, June 24, 1897, *Dispatches*, XXIX.

[47] Sherman to Sewall, July 10, 1897, *Instructions*, III. Virtually identical instructions were given the Commander of the U. S. Naval force and the Commander of the *Oregon* was instructed to keep coaled and ready to proceed to Japan at short notice. See *Confidential Correspondence, July 12, 1894 to March 3, 1900,* Navy Department Archives. See also T. A. Bailey, "Japan's Protest Against the Annexation of Hawaii," *Journal of Modern History,* III.

[48] See dispatch dated June 28, 1897, *Dispatches, Japan,* LXX. Actual negotiation of the treaty was in the hands of Assistant Secretary Day. Secretary Sherman, when first queried by the Japanese Minister, had denied mistakenly that any treaty negotiations were under way. This heightened the Japanese irritation.

Times expressing surprise at "how assiduous and unscrupulous is a section of the American press to disseminate at Japan's expense, sensational information for the purpose of exciting sympathy for the cause of Hawaiian annexation."[49]

HAWAIIAN REACTIONS TO ANNEXATION

In Hawaii, the annexation treaty was hailed as the solution to all problems and unanimously ratified by the Senate with much more glorification on September 9. The *Hawaiian Star* rather significantly declared: "The annexation of Hawaii is for the benefit of the Hawaiian, the Latin, and the Anglo-Saxon races of these Islands. It is not and it does not pretend to be for the benefit of the Asiatics. It is meant as a bar to the Asiatics."[50] Negotiations with Japan were not apt to proceed satisfactorily in such an atmosphere and there is little doubt but that the treaty encouraged a stiffening of Hawaii's attitude. Tension, which was active in August, was eased in September with the departure of the *Naniwa,* dictated apparently by the feeling that its presence did more harm than good to Japanese relations. By December Japan withdrew its protest against annexation and ultimately settled its difficulties with the Republic in return for an indemnity of $75,000, after Washington had exerted pressure to end the disagreement prior to annexation.

The course of annexation was not smooth, despite the hasty assumption at Honolulu that the issue had been settled in 1897. As the prospect for early action on the treaty in the United States faded, Minister Sewall expressed increasing forebodings of difficulties to follow. In November, 1897, he reported that Hawaiian anti-annexationists were sending representatives to the United States to work against the treaty. He also warned that if it were not ratified "a serious situation will be created." The party in support of annexation, he pointed out, was made up of many discordant elements which would not well withstand a prolonged delay of the issue. The return to Hawaii of Princess Kaiulani, niece of the former Queen, aroused native enthusiasm for a restoration of the native monarchy.[51]

In January, 1898, Sewall renewed his warnings and indicated that failure of the treaty might encourage development of a party opposed to annexation and centering upon a scheme for national self-sufficiency for Hawaii. Reciprocity would be continued either with the United

[49] *Ibid.* See especially dispatches of September 2 and 3, and October 2.
[50] September 9. A native mass meeting demonstrated against the treaty.
[51] See Sewall to Sherman, November 20 and 28; December 9, 1897, *Dispatches,* XXX.

States or British possessions. Concessions could be obtained from Great Britain in return for the use of Necker Island as a cable station. Comments from the Hawaiian press were forwarded declaring that "annexation is dead as a door nail." Sewall reported further that President Dole was expected to visit Washington to aid the treaty and counteract anti-annexation sentiment.[52]

By February and March Sewall was even more concerned, and the usual rumors of a royalist insurrection began to appear. Attention was called to the activities of T. H. Davies, the wealthy English planter and patron of Hawaiian royalty, and "a bitter opponent of all American political influence here." Davies was taking the lead in urging abandonment both of the idea of a monarchy and that of annexation in favor of a policy of Hawaii for Hawaiians. The annexation party was reported disintegrating still more rapidly and British designs on Necker Island again were emphasized. The native population was reported as rather hostile to the American cause in the difficulties with Spain over Cuba.[53]

The planting interests were vitally concerned with the fate of reciprocity under Republican tariff policy and this produced the usual business uncertainty, though expansion and consolidation of the sugar industry continued. Annexation, thought a majority, would produce a more stable economy, though there were those who still feared the loss of cheap labor as a result of association with the United States. The growing fear of the Japanese overshadowed every other consideration, however, and more and more impelled even the most conservative to think in terms of annexation. The press of Hawaii was general in its support of the view that the ultimate problem was one of Asiatic conquest of the Islands or control by the United States. "The United States is our national guardian," asserted the *Hawaiian Star*.[54] With the Japanese population increasing by the thousands and Tokyo increasingly bellicose, this was an inevitable conclusion.

The final consummation of annexation was accomplished as a result of this background of disturbance in Hawaii, aided by the influence of the Spanish-American War upon the thinking of the United States. Some extremely careful students of the attendant circumstances are inclined to feel that had it not been for the Spanish War annexation

---

[52] See Sewall to Sherman, January 3 and 14, 1898, with enclosures.

[53] Sewall to Sherman, February 15 and March 15, 1898, *op. cit.* The American element in Hawaii, however, was most enthusiastic in its support of the American cause. Honolulu was "gay with patriotic displays and banners of welcome" for American forces stopping there during the war.

[54] Cited *Literary Digest,* June 26, 1898. See letter from Honolulu by Mary Gay Humphreys in *Harper's Weekly,* February 5, 1898, for a planter's view on the necessity for a "white man's government."

might never have become a reality.[55] This is doubtful assumption and ignores the acceleration of American thinking along imperial lines which was in itself a basic cause of war with Spain. It also fails to take into account the inevitable reliance of Hawaii upon the United States. The wishful thinking of those Hawaiians who believed in 1897-98 that some national self-sufficiency could be worked out was reminiscent of similar ideas in earlier periods of crisis. They always ended with a return to the conclusion that Hawaii's destiny was inevitably American. In the words of the *Hawaiian Star* for January 12, 1897, "It is annexation or it is disintegration." The needs of Hawaii and the desires of the United States were bound to meet at some time during that peculiar era of manifest destiny which closed one century and opened another in American history.

THE FAILURE OF THE ANNEXATION TREATY

On February 26, 1898, the *Literary Digest,* analyzing the opinion of the Hawaiian press, was forced to conclude, "From perfect confidence that the annexation of Hawaii will be an accomplished fact within a short time, the organs of the American element in Honolulu have changed to a doubtful, occasionally despondent tone." This state of mind was the result of the failure of the United States to ratify the treaty which Hawaii had accepted with such enthusiasm in 1897. In order to understand what happened to the treaty, however, it must be kept in mind, that it was drawn hastily and originally submitted primarily as a clever stratagem to prevent the sugar tariff from endangering the basic relationship of the Islands to the United States.[56] That such action indicated any objection to annexation, however, is not to be concluded. The McKinley administration was not inclined to act hastily on such matters and usually wished for time to develop and refine public opinion.

Contrary to popular views, it was not essentially an imperialistic administration but one rather forced into expansion. There is no doubt but that McKinley, while favorable to acquiring Hawaii, was desirous of having such a departure from tradition bulwarked by supporting public opinion. President McKinley appears to have assured such men as Carl Schurz and Senator Hoar of his basic objection to any forceful expansion of territory. To the former he declared that "there will be no

---

[55] See T. A. Bailey, "The United States and Hawaii During the Spanish-American War," *American Historical Review,* XXXVI.

[56] The *New York Tribune* correspondent had noted on June 17, 1897, that immediate action was not expected "nor is it greatly desired by the Republican leaders in the deliberative branch."

jingo nonsense under my administration." It is significant that in the election of 1896 McKinley did not indicate any real interest in foreign policy despite an expansionist plank in the Republican platform. It was to be an administration offering peace and quiet at home. The President told Carl Schurz on July 1, 1897, that he had sent the Hawaiian annexation treaty to the Senate to test public opinion.[57] The treaty, therefore, in part at least, was a trial balloon. McKinley, however, was not without advisors who urged expansion, and among the most influential was Whitelaw Reid of the *New York Tribune.* Reid wrote the President-elect on December 5, 1896, "Someday we will have Cuba, as well as the Sandwich Islands. . . . To get both, in your administration, would put it beside Jefferson's in the popular mind and ahead of it in history."[58]

Then too, the Cuban crisis and the Spanish War in the offing certainly did not incline the State Department to risk possible affront to those powers which might be interested in Hawaii. This was true especially regarding Japan and as late as July, 1898, when news of the final approval of annexation was transmitted by the State Department to Hawaii it was stressed, referring to Japanese indemnity claims, "It is of great importance that this be closed up before formal transfer of territory."[59] There is every evidence that the State Department did not wish to provoke trouble with Japan.

THE 1898 CRUSADE FOR ANNEXATION

All of these possible forebodings and reasons for temporizing were outweighed in 1898 by other factors. As indicated, leaders of annexation in Hawaii were fearful of the consequences of its defeat and therefore an aggressive and active lobby was maintained in the United States designed both to influence Congress and public opinion. While there is no single collection of papers revealing the nature of its operations, it is clear that such a campaign was waged, and the correspondence of Hawaiian leaders is full of references to it. As a part of it, President Dole visited the United States in February, and by his appearances and his dignified manner did much to impress the public with the truly American character of the Republic.

Lorrin Thurston prepared *A Handbook on the Annexation of Hawaii* in which he listed major reasons for annexation and provided detailed arguments on each. Cleverly enough, he listed as the first consideration the danger that if the Islands were not annexed they might become an "alien and possibly hostile stronghold in a position commanding the

[57] See C. M. Fuess, *Carl Schurz, Reformer, 1829-1906,* 349f.
[58] McKinley Papers.
[59] Day to Cooper, July 8, 1898, *Instructions,* III.

Pacific Coast and the commerce of the North Pacific." Another argument was that the United States must act at once or see the fruits of long years of its enterprise negated by growing Asiatic influence. Still another was an appeal to the business instinct with detailed tables showing how American trade would be benefited. A further reason for annexation was the ingenious one that it would remove Hawaii from international politics and preserve the peace and security of the Pacific. A perusal of newspaper editorials, magazine articles, and congressional speeches in favor of annexation is sufficient to indicate that the "propaganda line" laid down by Thurston was followed with little variation.[60]

Arguments that annexation was necessary to the strategic and commercial position of the United States in the Pacific fell upon ready ground in the nineties. At no time since the ardent forties had Americans turned their thoughts so much to that region. John R. Proctor echoed the sentiment of thousands when in the September, 1897, *Forum,* writing on "Hawaii and the Changing Front of the World," he declared that American expansion in the Pacific was to be one of the decisive developments of the century and denounced those whose craven fears would hold the nation from its great destiny.[61] The slowly developing consciousness of imperial destiny evident in the post-reconstruction years was ripening and even European observers noted a "rising spirit in American affairs" with "new enthusiasm kindling" which presaged sudden and overpowering changes.[62]

The appeal to the religious and civilizing influence which America had brought to bear upon Hawaii in past decades and which was now threatened by the Asiatic influx was another powerful lever with which Thurston and his cohorts were able to sway public sentiment. The Protestant churches of the United States were extremely alert to the Christianizing mission of the nation during this period. They appear especially to have been impressed with the opportunity in the Asiatic field with the so-called "awakening" of China and Japan. In the task of fulfilling "the manifest destiny of the Christian Republic," Hawaii

---

[60] See article by Senator John Morgan, "The Duty of Annexing Hawaii," *Forum,* March, 1898, for typical example. Several thousand copies of an address by John W. Foster before the National Geographic Society favoring annexation and extolling Hawaii's advantages were printed and distributed by the annexation supporters.

[61] Julius W. Pratt has provided a masterly analysis of the development of the imperial mind in America in this period in chapters six, seven, and eight of his *Expansionists of 1898.* See also Senator Lodge's article, "The American Policy of Territorial Expansion," *Independent,* January 13, 1898; also Rear Admiral George E. Belknap, "Hawaiian Annexation," *ibid.,* January 20.

[62] See "The Looker-on" in *Blackwood's Magazine,* April, 1898.

was of especial importance. In the words of John R. Mott, the Islands were "a veritable cross-roads of the nations" where the "Pacific is becoming increasingly the theatre of some of the largest activities of the world." Here God had "built up a strong Christian community" and "caused to be planted there a Christian nation which is at the same time a great lighthouse and a base of operations for the enterprise of universal evangelization."[63]

ANNEXATION IN CONGRESS

Playing upon these strings of national interest and Christian ardor was not enough, however, to carry the necessary sixty votes to ratify in the Senate the treaty negotiated in 1897. With the reassembling of Congress in January, 1898, debate was renewed in executive sessions. The small but powerful beet sugar lobby was on the alert and, according to Janet Jennings of the *Independent,* broadcasting pamphlets designed to emphasize the somewhat contradictory facts that the Islands were at one and the same time a danger to American sugar producers and that their productivity and importance as a place for investing American capital was overemphasized. Debate was opened by Senator Davis, chairman of the Committee on Foreign Relations, with stress upon the commercial and strategic importance of Hawaii. All but three or four of the sixty votes necessary for ratification were believed obtainable. Argument was especially vigorous during the weeks of January 27 and February 10 with the issue still in doubt. The de Lome incident and other developments in the Cuban situation created enough excitement in Congress to make it difficult to center attention on Hawaii. In March the strategy was suddenly shifted to the use of a joint resolution for annexation in order to by-pass the strangle hold which the beet sugar interests had obtained upon the votes necessary for ratification of a treaty.[64]

On March 16, 1898, a joint resolution on annexation was reported by the Senate Committee on Foreign Relations. In reporting it, the Committee placed great emphasis upon the dangers of Japanese influence in the Islands and the necessity for American acquisition of the "Key

---

[63] Cited in Pratt, 281f. See also editorial "Imperial America," *Independent,* June 9, 1898.

[64] It was the opinion of the Hawaiian Minister that the beet sugar interests led by Claus Spreckels were blocking action. This agrees with the analysis made by Janet Jennings for the *Independent.* There were enough confirmed anti-imperialists in the Senate to give the Senators from the beet sugar states a balance of power. The *Independent* through the period is a good source for the anlysis of debates and other developments as to annexation.

of the Pacific" in terms of naval importance and the "Crossroads of the Pacific," in its commercial significance.[65]

No immediate action on the Senate resolution was forthcoming and on May 4 a similar resolution was brought before the House and reported favorably by the Committee on Foreign Affairs thirteen days later with a vigorous minority dissent.[66] There the administration forces ran into the peculiar fact that Speaker Reed, a long and vigorous opponent of annexation and literally Czar of the House through his control over the Committee on Rules, refused to allow the proposition to be brought to a vote. Reed was too good a Republican to block the desires of his party permanently, however, and on June 10 it was agreed that the resolution would be brought to a vote on June 15. It passed by the overwhelming vote of 209-91, with Representative Dalzell of Pennsylvania presiding in the absence of Speaker Reed.

In the Senate, the issue was still debatable, though every possible administration pressure coming directly from the President himself was brought to bear for approval. The House-approved resolution, referred to the Senate Committee on Foreign Relations, was reported without change and debate began on June 20. Here the last great stand of the small number of Senators who had consistently fought what they regarded as the evil trend toward imperial expansion was made in some sixteen days of oratorical opposition. Like the Old Guard of Napoleon they might die outvoted but they would never surrender. The entire policy of colonial expansion was symbolized by Hawaiian annexation and attacked as such. Venerable Senator Morrill deserted his party and held forth with great sincerity upon the dangers of imperial expansion which annexation of Hawaii presaged. Democratic Senators who had stood with Cleveland in his stubborn resistance to imperialism once more rallied to the standard, but it was a lost cause and on July 6 the Senate by a vote of 42 to 21 approved the joint resolution for annexation of Hawaii.[67]

ANNEXATION ACCOMPLISHED

The news was greeted in Hawaii, according to Sewall, "with unbounded enthusiasm" and day and night celebration. The remnants even of the old royalist group appear to have accepted the inevitable. In the United States itself there was little public reaction and the event was

---

[65] *Senate Report* No. 681, 55 Cong., 2 sess., 30f.

[66] *House Report* No. 1355, 55 Cong., 2 sess. See William A. Robinson, *Thomas B. Reed, Parliamentarian*, 366f., for Reed's position.

[67] See *Cong. Rec.*, 55 Cong., 2 sess., 6022ff., for debate. Three Democrats, Morgan, long an expansionist, Gorman and Pettus voted with the Republicans for the resolution. Morrill was the principal Republican dissenter.

somewhat overshadowed by the national preoccupation with the Spanish War. The Democratic and independent press, long opposed to expansion, naturally was critical, but the opinions embodied a sense of futility. This was expressed aptly by the *New York Evening Post* in the comment, "All that could be said against the policy of annexation has been said, and it would be useless now to repeat it." *Harper's Weekly* characterized the action as "Seizure by Resolution," and warnings against further extension of the annexation craze were voiced by such papers as the *Springfield Republican,* the *Boston Transcript, Philadelphia Ledger,* and others.[68] Supporters of the administration accepted the passage of the joint resolution as the triumph of their demands voiced since 1893. Typical was the comment of the *New York Sun,* "It is the initial step in the orderly advance of American expansion and development on the lines marked out by destiny for the glorious future that is before this country." To Grover Cleveland, in retirement at Princeton, the whole business was "preposterous," and to the Associated Press he declared, "The mission of our nation is to build up and make a greater country out of what we have instead of annexing Islands."[69] Such was not the opinion, however, of a majority of the American people in the feverish days of 1898.

INTERNATIONAL REACTIONS TO ANNEXATION

Inevitably, in view of the interest of other powers in Hawaii, its actual annexation was an event of international significance. The situation in 1893 and again in 1897 already has been noted. Interestingly enough, shifts in policy had taken place within the short space of a year. The earlier vigorous Japanese objection to American control of Hawaii now was replaced by a much more complaisant view. In Washington the Japanese Minister gave "the most satisfactory assurances as to the disposition of his Government" though emphasizing the importance of an early adjustment of Hawaii's difficulties with his nation.[70] Japanese press comments were generally favorable to annexation. The Japanese press generally hailed the news of the joint resolution

[68] See *Literary Digest,* July 14, for comment.
[69] Statement to Associated Press in January.
[70] Moore to Hatch, June 29, 1898, *Notes, Hawaii,* I. See also Buck to Sherman, January 7 and 15; February 4; July 6, 1898, *Dispatches, Japan,* LXXI, for further information. Buck sent in January a copy of *The Japanese Times* of January 6, 1898, which indicated the government had assumed a stronger policy relative to Hawaii to please the public. In January, 1898, cabinet changes replaced Count Okuma as Foreign Minister with Baron Nissi. A more liberal party desirous of friendly relations with the United States and Great Britain and fearful of Russia and Germany came into control. This, of course, led ultimately to the Anglo-Japanese alliance to which the United States could have been a party.

without objection. "On the contrary, we would very much like to see Hawaii in the hands of the Americans," one paper declared. An independent Hawaii was apt to be a bone of contention in the Pacific. Dangers of possible Russian or German domination were cited.[71]

Potentially, the most likely opponent of American acquisition of Hawaii in 1898 was Germany, which had reversed its earlier attitude that the Islands virtually were an American protectorate. Germany was inclined to look with a jealous eye upon the possible expansion of the United States as a result of the Spanish War and sought to checkmate it. From London, energetic and Anglo-Saxon unity-minded John Hay urged upon the State Department early action on Hawaiian annexation on the basis of warnings from the British embassy at Berlin that Germany would demand "compensation" in the Pacific. These views appear to have been given considerable weight.[72] On July 12, 1898, the American Minister at Berlin was warned by "exceedingly influential persons" that, in view of prospective annexation of Hawaii and other islands by the United States, "Germany ought to have some assurances as to territory in the Pacific." He was also warned that Anglo-American cooperation carried too far "will certainly result in a continental coalition against the United States.[73] In a very real sense American annexation of Hawaii was promoted by the growing Anglo-American cordiality which was one of the distinctive developments of world diplomacy in this period. These friendly warnings were one of its significant expressions.

THE FRONTIER PROCESS COMPLETED

The long delay in achieving actual annexation should not lead to the hasty conclusion that it was made possible only by the Spanish American War and Dewey's victory at Manila. Such a view is a superficial one based only upon consideration of Hawaiian problems as they developed in relation to the nineties. It ignores the long history of American frontier enterprise in Hawaii. For over three-quarters of a century

---

[71] Enclosure in Buck to Sherman, *op. cit.* Japan also later favored American control of the Philippines. It is important to note, however, that this did not necessarily remove fear of the Japanese in Hawaii as an incentive for annexation, both for the Republic and the United States. The President gave this as one of the strongest reasons for early assertion of American control. See conversations with Senator Hoar, *Autobiography of Seventy Years,* II, 307f.

[72] See Stephen Gwynn (ed.), *The Letters and Friendship of Sir Cecil Spring-Rice,* I, 246f., for warnings to Hay. Also Tyler Dennett, *John Hay,* 279.

[73] See White to Day, July 12, 1898, *Dispatches, Germany,* LXVI. John Hay wrote the President on June 18, 1897, "I hear of no objections to annexation from any quarter." February 20, 1898, he again wrote glowingly "The greatest destiny the world ever knew is ours." McKinley Papers.

the Islands had been within the orbit of American activity and interest as had no other section beyond our continental limits. This interest had been both economic and religious. Its earliest expressions were provided by the necessary use of the Sandwich Islands, as they were then known, as a way station by the roving Yankee traders of the days of earliest American commerce in the Pacific. From this fleeting knowledge of the Islands and the conditions prevailing there had come the voyage of the *Thaddeus* and the heroic work of the American Board and its Hawaiian Mission.

The penetration and lodgment of American capital and commercial enterprise had gone on apace. The impact of the missionary and the trader set in motion forces which revolutionized the internal social and political structure of feudal Hawaii. By 1840 the Islands had become a potential prize for any one of several powers whose expanding Pacific interests led their naval commanders and foreign offices to cast an occasional ambitious glance toward Hawaii. What happened thereafter has been recited in some detail in preceding pages. The fact that the Islands by 1840 had been the seat of two decades of American New England missionary enterprise was certainly of decisive importance in producing the statement of American policy relating to Hawaii by President Tyler. The doctrine of paramount American interest, which was set forth late in 1842, went far beyond any other expression of American policy in the Pacific for that time or for many years thereafter.

Coming as they did, Tyler's assertions, aided by the inability of interested European powers, especially France and Great Britain, to cooperate in opposing American policy, preserved the independence of Hawaii at a most critical stage in its transformation from feudalism to a more modern economy and government. With the rise of American expansion in Mexican War days and the thrusting of the continental frontier to the Pacific itself, the interest and stake of the United States in Hawaii became national in scope. The strategic and commercial importance of the Islands in relation to the future development of the Pacific trade of the United States was second only to that of Cuba with regard to the Caribbean and the South Atlantic.

In every decade after 1840 some event or series of events combined to force upon the United States the realization that Hawaii must be an American possession, if it were to become anyone's possession. True, we desired an independent Hawaii, and one in which the open door was extended to all nations so far as investment and enterprise were concerned. But it is noticeable that the door was closed on every occasion where it appeared that any other nation might secure a predominant advantage. After 1880 we have seen that each secretary of state kept a watchful eye on every development which even indirectly threatened the independence of Hawaii.

The effects of reciprocity tightened the bonds of economic relations with the United States through the spectacular development of the Hawaiian sugar industry. At the same time, the rise of this industry created conditions within the Islands which operated to promote dependence upon the United States. The demand for cheap labor fastened Oriental immigration upon the Islands with its basic threat to white supremacy, as well as to the native Hawaiian race. The social forces generated by reciprocity produced the Revolution of 1893. A combination of racial and economic factors made it impossible for a native monarchy to satisfy any longer the desire of the white planters and merchants for a government more continuously responsible to their needs. Among these needs had been the easier acquisition of land, control over taxation and government finances, and supremacy of white property holders in at least office holding, if not the suffrage.

Annexation defeated in 1893, the Hawaiian Republic found itself faced with serious complications. Even though power was placed in the hands of the American element, it was evident that while the independence of Hawaii might be wished for it was little short of impossible to maintain. There is every evidence that probably a majority of the property holders, including the sugar planters, were not anxious for annexation. Independence would have been preferred if circumstances had permitted. The most overwhelming danger to the continued independent existence of the Republic was the threat of Oriental domination through immigration. The seriousness of the controversy with Japan over the immigration of its nationals to Hawaii and the inability to solve labor and economic problems demonstrated to the leaders of the Republic that independence was impossible and annexation inevitable.[74]

In the United States forces were working which meshed neatly with the current problems of Hawaii. For almost all of the period since 1842 there had been a steady strengthening of the influences which impelled the growth of a concept that Hawaii, of all areas in the Pacific, was within the fold of a continuous and binding sphere of special American influence. The force of this concept was well illustrated when Secretary Bayard, who certainly was not an ardent expansionist, admitted that

---

[74] See the very valuable article by William A. Russ, Jr., "The Role of Sugar in Hawaiian Annexation," *Pacific Historical Review*, XII.

the ultimate annexation of Hawaii was inevitable. The case of Hawaii in 1898 was entirely different from that of any of the Spanish colonies and cannot be considered in the light of the same circumstances. Hawaii had become an outpost in the Pacific which was the product of typical American frontier expansion generated during the era of agrarian imperialism. It was in much the same category as Texas, Oregon, and California where American pioneers had established a frontier. It was this basic difference in the status of Hawaii which made so ineffectual all the arguments of the anti-imperialists from 1893 to 1898.

The troubles of Americans in Hawaii were different from the difficulties of Cubans or Filipinos. These were the problems of the men and women of our own flesh and blood. A threat to Hawaii was scarcely less serious, in the minds of those who thought about the problem, than a threat to our Pacific coast itself. Hawaii, it can be assumed, would have been annexed in due time regardless of the difficulty with Spain. The dominance of American economic and cultural forces in the life of the Islands and the completely American character of the Republic meant that when faced with the Asiatic problem Hawaii must turn to the United States for protection. It is reasonably clear that President McKinley and a majority of the American people as early as 1897 were pledged to ultimate annexation.

Early in 1898 the time seemed ripe for harvesting this fruit of American frontier expansion. The international situation was favorable, with the exception of the Japanese difficulty. Public opinion at home had matured. In the words of the *Independent,* a majority of Americans had come to feel that "Hawaii is our contiguous right; not merely because she is contiguous, but because her people are Americans and desire the advantages of American citizenship."[75] The Spanish War provided then the stage for action, rather than the motive. When the formal cession of the Islands took place on August 12, 1898, the last step in the evolution of the old process of frontier expansion which had taken America from the Atlantic to the Pacific was completed. Long before its normal time the frontier had leaped far beyond the continental limits of the nation. As a result of the urge of the trader, the missionary, the merchant, and the planter, it had found root in the soil of a little group of Pacific islands. There it had matured and waited the fulfillment of its destiny in 1898. The story of Hawaii is a chapter, the last chapter, in the history of the spirit of manifest destiny and agrarian expansion which gave the United States Louisiana, the Floridas, Texas, California, and Oregon.

[75] June 23, 1898.

BIBLIOGRAPHY

MANUSCRIPT SOURCES

All of the manuscript archives of the State Department, now in the National Archives, which in any way relate to Hawaii have been consulted. These include *Dispatches, Hawaii* (the first volume is labelled *Sandwich Islands*) for the entire period from 1842 to 1898; *Instructions, Hawaii* for the same period; *Notes to Hawaii*, correspondence with the Hawaiian Legation; *Notes, Hawaii*, which contains correspondence from the Hawaiian Minister at Washington. In addition, pertinent volumes of *Dispatches, Germany; Dispatches, Great Britain; Dispatches, France; Dispatches, Japan* were consulted as well as *Instructions* for ministers to the same powers. *Miscellaneous Letters*, containing non-diplomatic correspondence, includes some Hawaiian material. *Memoranda of Conversations with the Secretary of State, 1893-1898* has several valuable items. The *Dispatches, Hawaii* frequently contain important newspaper clippings and sometimes entire copies of Hawaiian newspapers. Consular correspondence, including *Instructions, Notes* and *Dispatches,* contains a limited amount of material, especially on the commerce and economy of the Islands. The records of the American Legation at Honolulu from 1839 to 1900 also are available in Washington but not especially important as a source inasmuch as they are largely duplicated by material in the *Dispatches.*

Navy Department archives are valuable for movement of naval vessels and confidential instructions and reports. *Letters to Officers and Commandants,* No. 7; *Confidential Correspondence,* Vol. 2, and *Ciphers Sent,* Vol. 1, are significant.

Valuable notes on documents in the Archives of Hawaii from the *Foreign Office Letter Books, Treaty Documents,* and *Foreign Office and Executive File* covering especially the negotiation and renegotiation of the Reciprocity Treaty, 1873 to 1887, were furnished the author through the courtesy of Ralph S. Kuykendall of the University of Hawaii. Similar material in the form of photostats and transcripts for the later period are in the Spaulding Collection of the University of Michigan Library. The most significant portions of this material, however, have been used by Doctor Pratt in his *Expansionists of 1898,* and are, therefore, cited from this source.

A variety of collections of the papers of the presidents and secretaries of state have been consulted wherever available. These include the Marcy Papers, Hamilton Fish Papers, Gresham Papers, McKinley Papers, Olney Papers, Cleveland Papers, Hay Papers, John Sherman Papers, Blaine Papers, all in the Library of Congress, and Buchanan Papers in the Historical Society of Pennsylvania. Those mentioned are valuable for Hawaii, though many others were sifted without results. Information from the Harrison Papers was provided through the courtesy of Dr. Albert T. Volwiler of Ohio University.

The Elisha Allen Papers and Armstrong-Chapman Papers in the Library of Congress are extremely valuable. The former collection has important diplomatic material as well as information concerning Island politics and economy. The latter is important for the missionary viewpoint on Hawaiian affairs, information on internal political and economic history, and diplomatic influences of the missionary element in the forties and early fifties. Because of his leadership in the fight against imperialism, the Carl Schurz Papers in the Library of Congress are important. They contain much Gresham correspondence on Hawaii. The Justin Morrill Papers and John T. Morgan Papers in the Library of Congress contain a few items.

PRINTED SOURCE MATERIALS

A. GOVERNMENT DOCUMENTS

Important as printed sources are the various U. S. Government publications. *Papers Relating to the Foreign Relations of the United States,* better known as *Foreign Relations,* is, of course, indispensable and the volume for 1894, Appendix II (Washington, 1895) contains virtually all significant correspondence, messages, instructions, and treaties relating to Hawaii from the earliest diplomatic relations to that date. These are unusually complete due to the number of Congressional investigations and resolutions. Some have been slightly altered, however, and this fact plus omissions make it important to check with original State Department archives. Volumes for 1895 to 1898 contain material for those years. The *Journal of the Executive Proceedings of the Senate of the United States* (Washington, 1909), cited as *Senate Executive Journal,* contains a record of the action in executive sessions of the Senate. The *Congressional Globe* and the *Congressional Record* for the several congresses during which Hawaiian matters were under consideration are important for their record of debates, resolutions, and counter-resolutions. The reciprocity question was debated as was the policy of annexation in the nineties. Formal action on treaties in the Senate was usually in executive session and current newspaper accounts are the principal source for debates. *House Report,* No. 92, 28 Cong., 2 sess., has the report on the visit of Captain Jones to Hawaii. *House Report,* No. 3422, 51 Cong., 2 sess., contains a report on reciprocal trade with Hawaii; *House Report,* No. 1355, 55 Cong., 2 sess., has a report on the joint resolution on annexation. *House Executive Document,* No. 1, Part III, 52 Cong., 2 sess., has a report of the Secretary of the Navy on Hawaii in December, 1892; *House Document,* No. 3, 54 Cong., 1 sess., has a similar report for 1895. *Senate Report,* No. 227, 53 Cong., 2 sess., contains the famous report of the Senate Committee on Foreign Relations investigating the revolution of 1893; *Senate Report,* No. 681, 55 Cong., 2 sess., has the report on the joint resolution on annexation in March, 1898. *Senate Executive Document,* No. 16, 53 Cong., 3 sess., presents a report by Rear-Admiral Walker on conditions in Hawaii in 1894. James D. Richardson (ed.), *A Compilation of the Messages and Papers of the Presidents* (Washington, 1896-99), is, of course, the principal source for presidential statements of policy. W. M. Malloy, *Treaties, Conventions, International Acts, Protocols, and Agreements between the United States of America and Other Powers, 1776-1909* (Washington, 1910) is a source for treaties and agreements though the majority appear in *Foreign Relations, 1894, op. cit.* Hunter Miller (ed.), *Treaties and Other International Acts of the United States of America* (Washington, 1933) is another source. *Commercial Relations of the United States* contains information on Hawaii's economic development and especially its trade relations with the United States.

For Hawaii, the equivalent of *Foreign Relations* is the *Report of the Minister of Foreign Relations* (Honolulu, 1845-1893). The Appendix to the *Report* for 1851 and that for 1852 contains valuable materials on diplomatic development of that period. The *Report* for 1855 has information concerning the Haalilio-Richards mission. *Report of the Special Committee on Foreign Relations to the Hawaiian Assembly* (1878), *Report of the Proceedings of the Committee on Foreign Relations to the Legislature of 1890 in Regard to the Investigations of Treaty Matters* (1890), and *Minority Report, Committee on Foreign Relations* (1890), as well as the *Reply of Minister Austin to the Majority Report of Committee on Foreign Relations in the Legislative Assembly, June 13, 1890,* are of especial importance for negotiations with the United States. *The Report of the Historical Commission of the Territory of Hawaii* contains frequent reprints of documents from Hawaiian Archives. *The Annual Report of the Collector-General of Customs, Report of the President of the Bureau of Immigration,* and *Treaties and Conventions Concluded Between the Hawaiian Kingdom and Other Powers Since 1825* (Honolulu, 1887), are important. *The Hawaiian Islands Early Relations with England—Russia— France; Official Papers Read at the Captain Cook Sesquicentennial August 17, 1928* (Honolulu, 1930), contains important articles and documents on early diplomatic relations of Hawaii. See also *Official Correspondence between Anthony Ten Eyck, esquire, commissioner of the United States, and Robert Crichton Wyllie, His Hawaiian Majesty's minister of foreign relations, upon the subject of the mission to the governor of California of Theodore Shillaber, esquire* (Honolulu, 1848). *Report of the Proceedings and Evidence in the Arbitration between the King and Government of the Hawaiian Islands and Messrs. Ladd & Co.* (Honolulu, 1846) review this controversy.

B. Contemporary Publications, Articles, Reminiscences, Compilations

Alexander, William D., *A Brief History of the Hawaiian People,* New York, 1891.

Anderson, Rufus, *The Hawaiian Islands: their Progress and Condition under Missionary Labors,* Boston, 1864.

———, *History of the Missions of the American Board of Commissioners for Foreign Missions, Hawaiian Islands,* Boston, 1875.

Annual Report of the American Board of Commissioners for Foreign Missions, Boston, 1820-1864; see also *Letters to the American Board.*

Austin, Richard, *An American Congressman in the Orient* (undated pamphlet, probably 1898).

Baxley, Henry W., *What I Saw on the West Coast of South and North America and at the Sandwich Islands,* New York, 1865.

Belknap, Rear-Admiral George, "Hawaiian Annexation," *Independent,* January 20, 1898.

Bingham, Hiram, *A Residence of Twenty-one Years in the Sandwich Islands,* Hartford and New York, 1847.

Bishop, Isabella L., *The Hawaiian Archipelago,* London, 1876.

Bishop, Sereno E., "The Hawaiian Queen and her Kingdom," *Review of Reviews,* September, 1891; "The United States and Hawaii," *ibid.,* March, 1893.

Bliss, William R., *Paradise in the Pacific; a book of Travel, Adventure, and Facts on the Sandwich Islands,* New York, 1873.

Carpenter, Edmund J., *America in Hawaii, a History of the United States Influence in the Hawaiian Islands,* Boston, 1898.

Chambers, Henry E., *Constitutional History of Hawaii,* Baltimore, 1896.

Cheever, Henry T., *Life in the Sandwich Islands,* New York, 1851.

Cooley, T. M., "Grave Obstacles to Hawaiian Annexation," *Forum,* June, 1893.

Curtis, George Ticknor, "Is it Constitutional?" *North American Review,* March, 1893.

Davies, T. H., "The Hawaiian Situation," *North American Review,* June, 1893.

Dole, Sanford B., *Memoirs of the Hawaiian Revolution,* Andrew Farrell (ed.), Honolulu, 1936.

Dunn, A. W., *From Harrison to Harding,* 2 vols., New York, 1922.

Escott, Walter, "At the Court of the Kamehamehas; an American Diplomat in Hawaii During the Civil War," *Overland Monthly,* 1912.

Foster, John W., *Diplomatic Memoirs,* 2 vols., Boston and New York, 1909.

Harman, John A., Lt., U.S.N., "The Political Importance of Hawaii," *North American Review,* March, 1893.

Hawaiian Guide Book, San Francisco, 1888.

Hoar, George F., *Autobiography of Seventy Years,* 2 vols., New York, 1903.

Hopkins, Manley, *Hawaii; the Past, Present and Future of its Island Kingdom,* New York, 1860.

Humphreys, Mary Gay, "Hawaiian Annexation," *Harper's Weekly,* February 5, 1898.

Jarves, James J., "The Sandwich or Hawaiian Islands," *Hunt's Merchant's Magazine,* August, 1843.

———, *History of the Hawaiian Islands,* Honolulu, 1847.

Judd, Mrs. Laura F., Honolulu; *Sketches of Life, Social, Political and Religious in the Hawaiian Islands from 1828 to 1861,* New York, 1880.

Kohlsaat, H. H., *From McKinley to Harding,* New York, 1923.

Krout, Mary H., *Hawaii and a Revolution,* New York, 1893.

Liliuokalani, Queen, *Hawaii's Story by Hawaii's Queen,* Boston, 1898.

Lodge, Henry Cabot, *Selections from the Correspondence of Theodore Roosevelt and Henry Cabot Lodge,* 2 vols., New York, 1925.

———, "The American Policy of Territorial Expansion," *Independent,* January 13, 1898.

———, "Our Blundering Foreign Policy," *Forum,* March, 1895.

Madden, H. M. (ed.), "Letters of Sanford B. Dole and John W. Burgess," *Pacific Historical Review,* V, March, 1936.

Mahan, A. T., "Hawaii and our Future Seapower," *Forum,* March, 1893.

Marshall, J. F. B., "An Unpublished Chapter of Hawaiian History," *Harper's Magazine,* September, 1883.

Morgan, John T., "The Duty of Annexing Hawaii," *Forum,* March, 1898.

Nevins, Allan (ed.), *Letters of Grover Cleveland, 1850-1908,* Boston and New York, 1933.

Nordhoff, Charles, *Northern California, Oregon and the Sandwich Islands,* New York, 1874.

Palmer, Julius, A., Jr., *Memories of Hawaii and Hawaiian Correspondence,* Boston, 1894.

———, *Again in Hawaii,* Boston, 1895.

Parker, Samuel, *Journal of an Exploring Tour Beyond the Rocky Mountains, under the direction of the A. B. C. F. M., Performed in the years 1835, '36, and '37,* privately printed, Ithaca, New York, 1938.

Proctor, John R., "Hawaii and the Changing Front of the World," *Forum,* September, 1897.

Royal Hawaiian Agricultural Society, *Transactions,* Honolulu, 1850-56.

Schofield, J. M. and Alexander, "Report on Pearl Harbor, 1873," *American Historical Review,* XXX, April, 1925.

Schouler, James, "A Review of the Hawaiian Controversy," *Forum,* February, 1894.

Schurz, Carl, "Manifest Destiny," *Harper's Monthly,* October, 1893.

———, "Cold Facts and Hawaii," *Harper's Weekly,* February 8, 1894.

Simpson, Alexander, *The Life and Travels of Thomas Simpson, the Arctic Explorer,* London, 1845.

Smith, Theodore C., *The Life and Letters of James Abram Garfield,* 2 vols., New Haven, 1925.

Springer, William, "Our Present Duty," *North American Review,* December, 1893.

Stevens, John A., "A Plea for Annexation," *North American Review,* December, 1893.

"Symposium on Hawaii," *Independent,* February 8, 1894.

Teggart, Frederick J. (ed.), *Around the Horn to the Sandwich Islands and California, 1845-1850,* New Haven, 1924.

Thrum, T. G., *Hawaiian Almanac and Annual,* Honolulu, 1875-98.

Thurston, Lorrin A., *Handbook on the Annexation of Hawaii,* pamphlet, 1897.

———, *Memoirs of the Hawaiian Revolution,* Andrew Farrell (ed.), Honolulu, 1936.

———, "The Advantages of Annexation," *North American Review,* March, 1893.

Thurston, Lucy G., *The Life and Times of Lucy G. Thurston,* Honolulu, 1921.

Townsend, John K., *Narrative of a Journey across the Rocky Mountains to the Columbia River and a visit to the Sandwich Islands, Chile, etc.,* Philadelphia and Boston, 1839.

Tyler, Lyon G., *The Letters and Times of the Tylers,* 2 vols., Richmond, 1884.

Van Alstyne, Richard H. (ed.), "Documents on Anglo-American Relations, 1853-1857," *American Historical Review*, XXXVIII, April, 1937.

Volwiler, Albert T. (ed.), *The Correspondence Between Benjamin Harrison and James G. Blaine, 1882-1893*, Philadelphia, 1940.

Von Holst, H. E., *The Annexation of Hawaii*, pamphlet, Chicago, 1898.

Whitney, Henry M., *The Hawaiian Guidebook*, Honolulu, 1875.

Woolsey, T. S., *America's Foreign Policy*, New York, 1898.

——, "Concerning our Foreign Relations," *Yale Review*, August, 1892.

Young, Lucien, *The Boston at Hawaii*, Washington, 1898.

C. CONTEMPORARY PERIODICALS

(Dates indicate period of use)

Atlantic Monthly (Boston), 1850—.

Banker's Magazine and Statistical Review (New York), 1850-64.

Bradstreet's, A Journal of Trade, Finance and Public Economy (New York). 1881—.

Commercial and Financial Chronicle (New York), 1885—.

De Bow's Southern Review (New Orleans), 1846-60.

Edinburgh Review (American Edition), 1843—.

Forum (New York), 1886—.

Friend (Honolulu), 1843—.

Harper's New Monthly Magazine (New York), 1850—.

Harper's Weekly Magazine (New York), 1864—.

Independent (New York), 1879—.

Literary Digest (New York), 1894—.

Merchant's Magazine and Commercial Review (New York), 1839-65.

Missionary Herald (Boston), 1843—.

The Nation (New York), 1865—.

Nile's National Register, 1843—.

North American Review (Boston), 1870—.

Public Opinion (New York), 1886—.

Review of Reviews (London and New York), 1890—.

Scribners Magazine (New York), 1887—.

United States Magazine and Democratic Review (Washington), 1842-58.

B. CONTEMPORARY NEWSPAPERS

(Dates are of period of principal use as a check on development and opinion)

Amador Dispatch (Jackson, California), July, 1867-December, 1869

Anglo-Saxon (Boston), 1856-57.

Atlanta Constitution, 1868—.

Baltimore Sun, 1874—.

Boston Daily Globe, 1873-76.

Boston Evening Transcript, 1854-93.

Boston Herald, 1890—.
Charleston News and Courier, 1844—.
Chicago Daily News, 1876—.
Chicago Herald and Examiner, 1881—.
Chico Weekly Courant, November, 1867-April, 1869.
Daily Alta (San Francisco), 1850-1891.
Denver News, 1880—.
Detroit Free Press, 1884—.
Hawaiian Gazette (Honolulu) 1865—.
Hawaiian Star (Honolulu), 1893—.
Kennebec Journal, 1893—.
London Times, 1843—.
Morning Oregonian (Portland), 1862—.
New Orleans Picayune, 1866—.
New Orleans Times, 1867-77.
New Orleans Republican, 1867-78.
New York Evening Post, 1880—.
New York Herald, 1842—.
New York Times, 1851—.
New York Tribune, 1842—.
New York Sun, 1843—.
New York World, 1870—.
Pacific Commercial Advertiser (Honolulu), 1856—.
Philadelphia Inquirer, 1843—.
Philadelphia Press, 1857—.
Philadelphia Public Ledger, 1893—.
Philadelphia Record, 1872—.
Polynesian (Honolulu), 1842-1863.
Sandwich Islands News (Honolulu), 1846-48.
San Francisco Call, 1856—.
San Francisco Commercial Herald and Market Review, 1867—.
San Francisco Evening Bulletin, 1855—.
San Francisco Examiner, 1890—.
Springfield Republican, 1844—.
St. Louis Post-Dispatch, 1879—.
St. Louis Republic, 1871—.
Steamer Bulletin (San Francisco), 1859-60.
Washington Evening Star, 1852—.
Washington Post, 1888—.
Whalemen's Shipping List and Merchant's Transcript (New Bedford), 1844-81.

SECONDARY MATERIAL

Alexander, Mary C. (compiler), *William Patterson Alexander in Kentucky, the Marquesas, Hawaii* (Honolulu, 1934).
Bailey, Thomas A., "Japan's Protest Against the Annexation of Hawaii," *Journal of Modern History*, III, March, 1931.

———, "The United States and Hawaii during the Spanish-American War," *American Historical Review*, XXXVI, April, 1931.

Bancroft, H. H., *History of the Northwest Coast, San Francisco*, 1884.

———, *History of California*, San Francisco, 1885.

Bemis, Samuel F., *The American Secretaries of State and their Diplomacy*, 10 vols., New York, 1927-1929.

———, *A Diplomatic History of the United States*, New York, 1942.

——— and Grace Griffin (ed.), *Guide to the Diplomatic History of the United States, 1775-1921*, U. S. G. P. O., 1935.

Bishop, Sereno, *Reminiscences of Old Hawaii*, Honolulu, 1916.

Blue, George U., "The Project for a French Settlement in the Hawaiian Islands, 1824-1842," *Pacific Historical Review*, II.

Bradley, Harold W., *The American Frontier in Hawaii, the Pioneers, 1789-1843*, Stanford University Press, 1942.

———, "Hawaiian Islands and the Fur Trade, 1785-1813," *Pacific Northwest Quarterly*, XXX.

Brooks, Jean I., *International Rivalry in the Pacific Islands, 1800-1875*, Berkeley, 1941.

Caldwell, Robert G., *James A. Garfield, Party Chieftain*, New York, 1931.

Castle, William R. Jr., *Hawaii, Past and Present*, New York, 1917.

Chitwood, Oliver P., *John Tyler, Champion of the Old South*, New York and London, 1939.

Clark, R. C., *History of the Williamette Valley, Oregon*, Chicago, 1927.

Coman, Katherine, *The History of Contract Labor in the Hawaiian Islands*, New York, 1903.

Dennet, Tyler, *John Hay, from Poetry to Politics*, New York, 1933.

Dictionary of American Biography, 20 vols., New York, 1928.

Dictionary of American History, 5 vols., New York, 1942.

Dole, Sanford B., "The Evolution of Hawaiian Land Tenure," *Papers of the Hawaiian Historical Society*, No. 3.

Dozer, Donald M., "Opposition to Hawaiian Reciprocity, 1876-1888," *Pacific Historical Review*, XIV, 1945.

Dulebohn, George R., *Principles of Foreign Policy under Grover Cleveland*, University of Pennsylvania Press, 1940.

Dulles, Foster R., *America in the Pacific*, Boston and New York, 1942.

Emerson, Oliver P., *Pioneer Days in Hawaii*, New York, 1928.

Ettinger, A. A., "The Proposed Anglo-French-American Treaty of 1852 to Guarantee Cuba to Spain," *Transactions Royal Historical Society*, 4 series, XIII.

Fuess, Claude M., *Daniel Webster*, 2 vols., Boston, 1930.

———, *Carl Schurz, Reformer*, New York, 1932.

Golder, Frank A., "Russian-American Relations during the Crimean War," *American Historical Review*, XXXI, April, 1926.

Gresham, Matilda, *Life of Walter Quintin Gresham*, 2 vols., Chicago, 1919.

Gulick, Rev. and Mrs. Orramel, H., *The Pilgrims of Hawaii*, New York and Chicago, 1918.

Hawaiian Historical Society, *Annual Report,* Honolulu.

——, *Papers,* Honolulu.

Historical Commission of the Territory of Hawaii, *Reports,* Honolulu, 1922-1928.

Hohman, E. P., The *American Whaleman; A Study of Life and Labor in the Whaling Industry,* New York, 1928.

Holt, W. S., *Treaties Defeated by the Senate,* Baltimore, 1933.

Hooley, Osborne S., "Hawaiian Negotiations for Reciprocity, 1855-1857," *Pacific Historical Review,* VII, 1938.

Hyde, C. M., "The Educational Work of the American Mission for the Hawaiian People," Thrum, *Hawaiian Almanac and Annual,* 1892.

James, Henry, *Richard Olney and His Public Service,* Boston and New York, 1923.

Jarrett, Lorna H., *Hawaii and its People,* Honolulu, 1933.

Kuykendall, Ralph S., "American Interests and American Influence in Hawaii in 1842," *Annual Report of the Hawaiian Historical Society,* 1930.

——, "Constitutions of the Hawaiian Kingdom," *Papers of the Hawaiian Historical Society,* Number 21, Honolulu, 1940.

——, "The Earliest Japanese Labor Immigration to Hawaii," Honolulu, 1935.

——, "Early Hawaiian Commercial Development," *Pacific Historical Review,* III, December, 1934.

——, *The Hawaiian Kingdom, 1778-1854,* Honolulu, 1938.

——, "Negotiation of the Hawaiian Annexation Treaty of 1893," *Fifty-First Annual Report of the Hawaiian Historical Society for the Year 1942,* Honolulu, 1943.

Ladenson, Alex, "The Background of the Hawaiian-Japanese Labor Convention of 1886," *Pacific Historical Review,* X, December, 1940.

Lothrop, Thorton K., *William Henry Seward,* Boston and New York, 1896.

McElroy, Robert M., *Grover Cleveland, the Man and the Statesman,* 2 vols., New York.

McMaster, John Bach, *Daniel Webster,* New York, 1902.

Mesick, Mrs. Lillian S., *The Kingdom of Hawaii,* Honolulu, 1934.

Millis, Walter, *The Martial Spirit,* Boston, 1931.

Muzzey, David S., *James G. Blaine, a Political Idol of Other Days,* New York, 1934.

National Cyclopedia of American Biography, New York, 1898—.

Nevins, Aflan, *Grover Cleveland, a Study in Courage,* New York, 1932.

——, *Hamilton Fish; the Inner History of the Grant Administration,* New York, 1936.

Olcott, C. S., *The Life of William McKinley,* 2 vols., Boston and New York, 1916.

Patterson, John, "The United States and Hawaiian Reciprocity, 1867-1870," *Pacific Historical Review,* VII, March, 1938.

Pratt, Helen G., *In Hawaii, a Hundred Years,* New York, 1939.

Pratt, Julius W., *Expansionists of 1898, the Acquisition of Hawaii and the Spanish Islands,* Baltimore, 1936.

——, "The Hawaiian Revolution: A Reinterpretation," *Pacific Historical Review,* II, September, 1932.

Restarick, the Rt. Rev. Henry Bond, *Hawaii, 1778-1920, from the Viewpoint of a Bishop,* Honolulu, 1924.

Rhodes, James Ford, *The McKinley and Roosevelt Administration,* New York, 1922.

Robinson, William A., *Thomas Buchanan Reed, Parliamentarian,* New York, 1930.

Rowland, Donald, "The Establishment of the Republic of Hawaii, 1893-1894," *Pacific Historical Review,* V, September, 1935.

——, "Orientals and the Suffrage in Hawaii," *Pacific Historical Review,* XVII, March, 1943.

——, "The United States and the Contract Labor Question in Hawaii, 1862-1900," *Pacific Historical Review,* II, 1933.

Russ, William A., Jr., "Hawaiian Labor and Immigration Problems Before Annexation," *Journal of Modern History,* XV, September, 1943.

——, "The Role of Sugar in Hawaiian Annexation," *Pacific Historical Review,* XII, December, 1943.

Smith, T. C., "Expansion after the Civil War, 1865-1871," *Political Science Quarterly,* September, 1901.

Spaulding, T. M., *Cabinet Government in Hawaii, 1887-1893,* Honolulu, 1924.

Starbuck, A., *History of the American Whale Fishery from its Earliest Inception to the Year 1876,* Report U. S. Commission of Fish and Fisheries for 1875-76, IV.

Sullivan, Josephine, *A History of C. Brewer and Company, Limited; One Hundred Years in the Hawaiian Islands, 1826-1926,* Boston, 1926.

Tansill, Charles C., *The Foreign Policy of Thomas F. Bayard, 1885-1897,* New York, 1940.

——, "Diplomatic Relations Between the United States and Hawaii, 1885-1889," *Fordham University Studies,* 1940.

Thomas, Benjamin P., *Russo-American Relations, 1815-1867,* Baltimore, 1930.

Thrum, Thomas G., "Honolulu's Share in the Pacific Whaling Industry of By-Gone Days," *Hawaiian Almanac and Annual,* Honolulu, 1913.

Tyler, Alice F., *The Foreign Policy of James G. Blaine,* Minneapolis, 1928.

Van Alstyne, Richard W., "Great Britain, the United States and Hawaii," *Pacific Historical Review,* IV, March, 1935.

Weinberg, Albert K., *Manifest Destiny: A Study of Nationalist Expansionism in American History,* Baltimore, 1935.